Althochdeutsche Glossen: Nachträge
Old High German Glosses: A Supplement

Althochdeutsche Glossen: Nachträge
Old High German Glosses: A Supplement

HARTWIG MAYER

University of Toronto Press

© University of Toronto Press
Toronto and Buffalo
Printed in Canada
ISBN 0-8020-2116-6
LC 73-89849

Distributed in North America and the British Commonwealth
by University of Toronto Press and in the rest of the world
by Carl Winter Universitätsverlag

FÜR CHRISTINE

ERRATA

p.7, <u>add</u>: f.6v   iniuria, +vnera - PL 77,161C

p.10, f.228v, <u>read</u>: PL 22 (1854),533

p.14, <u>read</u>: F. Maassen, Bibliotheca

p.25, f.26v, <u>add</u>: lucifugis congesta cubilia blattis,
erphe grabevvarte - IV,243

p.102, <u>add</u>: f.193r   adrogat, +grimmit - 1302C

p.106, <u>read</u>: Clm 29005

p.116, f.11v, <u>read</u>: [Li] nsin.lens lendis niz

p.117, f.68v, <u>read</u>: Epodon
      f.69v, <u>read</u>: Epodon

p.119, f.4va, <u>read</u>: [<u>buterfligen</u>]

Contents/Inhalt

Introduction

Almost a century has elapsed since Elias von Stein-
meyer began publishing his <u>Old</u> <u>High</u> <u>German</u> <u>Glosses</u>, thereby providing us with the basic material for scholarly work
in this field. In the intervening decades a fair amount
of additional material has been published, most of it in
the form of articles;[1] and to these the present edition
now adds a total of some 1600 glosses culled from 148
manuscripts. It is based on data made available by Bernhard Bischoff, most of which have already been published
by Walter Stach.[2] The remaining items were passed on to
me by Bernhard Bischoff in person.

I am further indebted to Bernhard Bischoff for the dat-
ing of the glosses written by pen, and I have also followed him with regard to the origin, provenance and dat-
ing of the manuscripts in all cases where these details
are not contained in the secondary literature or where
there is some difference of opinion.

I have personally worked through every one of the 148
manuscripts, with the exception of the following:

BRESLAU (Biblioteka Uniwersytecka): III F 19.

DUBLIN (Trinity College Library): G.4.16.

KARLSRUHE (Badische Landesbibliothek): Fragment perg.20.

In the case of the Breslau and Dublin manuscripts I obtained microfilms or Xerox copies of the relevant pages.

---

[1] Taylor Starck und J.C.Wells, Althochdeutsches Glossenwörterbuch, 1.Lieferung (Heidelberg,1971), S.8ff.

[2] Walter Stach, Mitteilungen zur mittelalterlichen Glossographie in: Liber Floridus, Festschrift Paul Lehmann
(St.Ottilien,1950), S.11-18.

The Karlsruhe fragment perished during World War II, a loss which is, however, offset by Bernhard Bischoff's notes.

As for the order in which the manuscripts are dealt with, I have followed that of Rolf Bergmann's <u>Catalogue of Manuscripts Containing Old High German and Old Saxon Glosses</u>.[3] On the assumption that the serious student of Old High German glosses will be referring constantly to this work I have only included secondary literature not listed there. The addenda to Bergmann's catalogue are set out on the pages following this introduction.

A considerable number of glosses in my collection are scratched glosses which are for the most part exceedingly difficult to read. In fact, many of them are virtually indecipherable. On the other hand, the right kind of illumination can sometimes solve the problem, and there were frequent occasions when an ordinary flash light rendered the best service, largely because it allows the beam of light to be directed exactly as required.

I am left with the pleasant duty of recording my debt to all those who have contributed to this edition, and I must begin by mentioning the libraries where the various manuscripts are housed and by thanking them for the readiness with which they placed their resources at my disposal.

I am grateful to Rudolf Schützeichel for providing me with an opportunity of giving a brief report on my edit-

[3] Rolf Bergmann, Verzeichnis der althochdeutschen und altsächsischen Glossenhandschriften (Münster, 1973).

ion at a meeting of the Institute for Early Medieval Research of the University of Münster in the spring of 1970 and to Rolf Bergmann for his kindness in sending me a Xerox copy of the proofs of his catalogue.

I have also to thank John Wells for making the computer-concordance of the _Dictionary of Old High German Glosses_ available to me and for taking on the task of reading my manuscript.

Christine Eder sent me a copy of her dissertation on the Tegernsee manuscripts. She was also kind enough to answer many of my questions about the manuscripts in Munich.

I am further indebted to the Canada Council for a generous research grant towards the preparation of my edition.

Finally, I would like to express my thanks to the University of Toronto Press for according my edition a place in their publishing programme.

My debt to Bernhard Bischoff who first suggested this edition and subsequently accompanied its preparation with untiring guidance and encouragement will be evident to every attentive reader.

This book has been published with the help of a grant from the Humanities Research Council of Canada, using funds provided by the Canada Council.

Einleitung

Seitdem Elias von Steinmeyer seine <u>Althochdeutschen</u> <u>Glossen</u> veröffentlichte und damit die Grundlage zur Erforschung der althochdeutschen Glossen schuf, sind eine Reihe von Nachträgen - meist in der Form von Artikeln - erschienen,[1] denen diese Ausgabe noch einmal rund 1600 Glossen aus 148 Handschriften hinzufügt. Sie beruht auf Angaben Bernhard Bischoffs, die zum größten Teil 1950 von Walter Stach veröffentlicht wurden.[2] Den Rest teilte mir Bernhard Bischoff persönlich mit.

Ebenfalls von Bernhard Bischoff stammen die Datierungen der Federglossen, sowie Herkunft, Schriftheimat und Datierung der Handschriften, soweit sie nicht aus der Sekundärliteratur hervorgehen oder soweit sie von dieser abweichen.

Ich habe alle Handschriften selbst noch einmal durchgesehen mit den folgenden Ausnahmen:

BRESLAU (Biblioteka Uniwersytecka): III F 19.

DUBLIN (Trinity College Library): G.4.16.

KARLSRUHE (Badische Landesbibliothek): Fragment perg.20.
Von den beiden ersten besitze ich Mikrofilm- bzw. Xeroxaufnahmen der entsprechenden Seiten. Das Karlsruher Fragment ging im Krieg verloren. Ersatz dafür sind Bernhard Bischoffs Aufzeichnungen.

---

[1] Taylor Starck und J.C.Wells, Althochdeutsches Glossenwörterbuch, 1.Lieferung (Heidelberg,1971), S.8ff.

[2] Walter Stach, Mitteilungen zur mittelalterlichen Glossographie in: Liber Floridus, Festschrift Paul Lehmann (St.Ottilien,1950), S.11-18.

In der Anordnung der Handschriften folge ich dem <u>Verzeichnis der althochdeutschen und altsächsischen Glossenhandschriften</u> von Rolf Bergmann.[3] Da anzunehmen ist, daß in Zukunft jeder, der sich mit ahd. Glossen beschäftigt, dieses Verzeichnis zur Hand haben wird, gebe ich nur die Sekundärliteratur zu den Handschriften, die dort fehlt. Nachträge und Anmerkungen zu R. Bergmanns <u>Verzeichnis</u> führe ich im Anschluß an die Einleitung auf.

Ein großer Teil der von mir gesammelten Glossen sind Griffelglossen, die häufig nur unter großen Schwierigkeiten zu lesen sind, wenn überhaupt. Gute Beleuchtung kann allerdings die Aufgabe oft erleichtern, wobei sich eine einfache Taschenlampe, die es erlaubt, den Lichteinfall nach Belieben zu variieren, immer wieder als das beste Arbeitsgerät erwies.

Mir bleibt die angenehme Pflicht, allen zu danken, die zu dieser Ausgabe beigetragen haben, wobei zunächst die angeführten Bibliotheken zu nennen sind, die mir jegliche erbetene Hilfe zukommen ließen.

Rudolf Schützeichel gab mir die Gelegenheit, bei der Tagung des Instituts für Frühmittelalterforschung der Universität Münster im Frühjahr 1970 kurz über die Ausgabe zu berichten, während Rolf Bergmann mir freundlicherweise eine Xeroxkopie der Druckfahnen seines Glossenverzeichnisses schickte.

---

[3] Rolf Bergmann, Verzeichnis der althochdeutschen und altsächsischen Glossenhandschriften (Münster, 1973).

John Wells stellte mir die Computer-Konkordanz des ahd. Glossenwörterbuches zur Verfügung und nahm die Mühe auf sich, die Ausgabe im Manuskript zu lesen.

Christine Eder schickte mir ein Exemplar ihrer Dissertation über die Handschriften des Klosters Tegernsee. Sie half mir außerdem mit vielen Auskünften über die Handschriften in München.

Der Canada Council machte die Vorbereitung der Ausgabe durch ein großzügiges Forschungsstipendium möglich.

Der University of Toronto Press danke ich für die Aufnahme der Ausgabe in ihr Verlagsprogramm.

Wieviel die Ausgabe Bernhard Bischoff verdankt, der sie angeregt und ihre Vorbereitung mit unermüdlicher, geduldiger Hilfsbereitschaft begleitet hat, ist offensichtlich.

Diese Ausgabe wurde mit Hilfe eines Zuschusses des Humanities Research Council of Canada gedruckt.

Nachträge und Anmerkungen zu Rolf Bergmanns 'Verzeichnis der althochdeutschen und altsächsischen Glossenhandschriften'

NACHTRÄGE

Soweit die folgenden Glossenhandschriften nicht in R.Bergmanns <u>Verzeichnis</u> erscheinen, gebe ich ihnen die Nummer der vorhergehenden Handschrift plus a. Seitenverweise in eckigen Klammern beziehen sich auf meine Ausgabe.

16 AUGSBURG (Bischöfliche Ordinariatsbibliothek) Hs K 16: Die Handschrift enthält wesentlich mehr Glossen als von B.Kraft in seinem Katalog gedruckt wurden. Diese werden von Frau Dr. G.Müller in Leipzig bearbeitet.

65a BERN (Burgerbibliothek) Cod.334: Die Handschrift enthält auf f.352r offenbar ahd. Glossen von einer Hand der 2.Hälfte des 9.Jh. Diese sind gedruckt in H.Hagen, Scholia Bernensia ad Vergilii Bucolica atque Georgica (Leipzig,1867), S.22, Anm.5.

68a BOLOGNA (Biblioteca Universitaria) Hs. 1702 [vgl. S.17].

79a BRÜSSEL (Bibliothèque Royale) II - 1049: Die Handschrift enthält auf f.56r nach John Wells eine ahd. Glosse.

385a LENINGRAD (Saltykov-Ščedrin-Bibliothek) F.v.I.9:
Die Handschrift enthält nach Bernhard Bischoff auf
f.8v einige ahd. Interlinearglossen.

525 MÜNCHEN (Bayerische Staatsbibliothek) Clm 6308: Die
Handschrift enthält zusätzlich zu den von W.Stach
veröffentlichten Glossen 1 ahd. Interlinearglosse
[vgl. S.81f.].

558a   -   Clm 13024 [vgl. S.84].

695a   -   Clm 28911 [vgl. S.105].

696   -   Clm 29005: Diese Fragmente enthalten zusätzlich zu den von E.Steinmeyer bzw. B.Bischoff
veröffentlichten Glossen 1 ahd. Interlinearglosse
[vgl. S.106].

709a   -   Clm 29164 [vgl. S.107].

794a ROM (Biblioteca Apostolica Vaticana) Pal.lat.135
vgl.[S.114].

884a UTRECHT (Artbisschopelijke Museum) nr. 156 d: Die
Handschrift enthält nach Bernhard Bischoff auf f.
110r am oberen Rand eine ahd. Griffelglosse.

886a VERDUN (Bibliothèque Publique) Hs. 69: Die Handschrift enthält nach B.Bischoff einen ahd. Glosseneintrag.

999a WÜRZBURG (Universitätsbibliothek) M.p.misc.o.1.
[vgl. S.148].

Die folgende Liste enthält alle in meine Ausgabe nicht aufgenommenen Handschriften, die nach R.Bergmanns Verzeichnis (vgl. S.131) unveröffentlichte ahd. Glossen enthalten.

32   BASEL (Universitätsbibliothek) F.III.15e: Die Handschrift enthält keine unveröffentlichten ahd. Glossen.

88   CAMBRIDGE (Trinity College Library) B.14.3: Die Handschrift enthält keine ahd., sondern eine altenglische Glosse; vgl. N.R.Ker, Catalogue of Manuscripts Containing Anglo-Saxon (Oxford,1957), Nr.84, S.129.

123 EINSIEDELN (Stiftsbibliothek) cod.236 (491): Die von W.Stach erwähnten ahd. Glossen sind - soweit ich sehen kann - lateinisch.

145 ERLANGEN (Universitätsbibliothek) Erlangen-Nürnberg Ms. 396: Diese Handschrift habe ich nicht gesehen.

149 ESSEN (Münsterschatz) Evangeliar II: Die Handschrift enthält eine Reihe von ahd. Griffelglossen, die verhältnismäßig schwer zu lesen sind. Als ich die Handschrift sah, hatte ich nicht genügend Zeit, die Glossen zu sammeln.

165 FULDA (Hessische Landesbibliothek) Aa 20: Soweit ich sehen kann, enthält die Handschrift keine ahd. Glossen.

     -   Aa 31a: Die ahd. Glossen dieser Handschrift sind bereits veröffentlicht; vgl. J.Autenrieth, Die

Domschule von Konstanz zur Zeit des Investiturstreits
(Stuttgart,1956), S.92.

176 ST.GALLEN (Stiftsbibliothek) 44: Die Handschrift
enthält keine ahd. Glossen.

184 - 126: Die ahd. Glosse - von einer Hand des
9.Jh. - ist bereits veröffentlicht; vgl. CLA VII,
Nr.910.

245 - 868: Die ahd. Glosse ist bereits veröffentlicht; vgl. K.Grubmüller, AfdA 79 (1968), S.106.

318 KARLSRUHE (Universitätsbibliothek) Fragm. Aug.20:
Das von W.Stach erwähnte Fragment ist nicht identisch
mit Fragm. Aug.20 vgl. S.40f. .

343 KOBLENZ (Staatsarchiv) Abt.701, Nr.759: Die von W.
Stach als unveröffentlicht erwähnten Glossen sind
mit den von E.Steinmeyer gedruckten identisch.

357 KREMSMÜNSTER (Stiftsbibliothek) Hs.32: Die Handschrift enthält auf f.103r und f.117r einige Glossen, die jedoch mhd. sind.

369 LEIDEN (Universitätsbibliothek) Voss.lat.fol.88:
Die ahd. Glosse - von einer Hand der 1.Hälfte des
10.Jh. - ist bereits veröffentlicht; vgl. V.Rose
und H.Müller-Strübing, Vitruvii de architectura libri decem (Leipzig,1867), S.X.

370 - Voss.lat.q.5: Die ahd. Glosse - von einer
Hand des 8.-9.Jh. - ist bereits veröffentlicht; vgl.
MGH, Scriptores rerum Merovingicarum II (Hannover,
1888), S.76, Anm.h.

436 MERSEBURG (Domstiftsbibliothek) Ms.Nr.9: Soweit ich

sehen kann, enthält die Handschrift keine ahd. Glossen.

506 MÜNCHEN (Bayerische Staatsbibliothek) Clm 6233: Die Handschrift enthält einige ahd. Glossen, die ich jedoch nicht lesen konnte.

512 — Clm 6255: Die Handschrift enthält auf dem oberen Rand von f.59r einen und auf dem unteren Rand von f.159v zwei mhd. Ortsnamen.

529 — Clm 6325: Die Handschrift enthält keine unveröffentlichten ahd. Glossen.

552 — Clm 9638: Die Handschrift enthält eine vermutlich ahd. Griffelglosse, die ich nicht lesen konnte.

650 — Clm 18547b: Die Handschrift enthält keine unveröffentlichten ahd. Glossen.

691 — Clm 23796: Die Handschrift enthält keine unveröffentlichten ahd. Glossen.

748 PARIS (Bibliothèque Nationale) lat.7930: Die Handschrift enthält keine unveröffentlichten ahd. Glossen.

762 — lat.11219: Die Handschrift enthält keine unveröffentlichten ahd. Glossen.

767 — lat.13955: Die Handschrift enthält keine unveröffentlichten ahd. Glossen.

783 PRAG (Metropolitni Kapitula USV) Vita O83: Diese Handschrift habe ich nicht gesehen.

792 ROM (Biblioteca Apostolica Vaticana) Ottob.lat.3295:

Die Handschrift enthält mehrere hundert ahd. Griffelglossen, die ich erst im Sommer 1973 sammeln konnte und deshalb an anderer Stelle veröffentlichen
werde.

801   -   Pal.lat.430: Die Handschrift enthält auf
dem unteren Rand von f.51r dreieinhalb ausradierte
mhd. Zeilen, die mit Hilfe einer Ultraviolettlampe
teilweise gelesen werden können.

809   -   Pal.lat.1347: Soweit ich sehen kann, enthält die Handschrift keine ahd. Glossen.

845 SALZBURG (St.Peter) a XII 25: Die Handschrift enthält keine unveröffentlichten ahd. Glossen.

865 STUTTGART (Württembergische Landesbibliothek) H.B.
II.35: Die Handschrift enthält keine unveröffentlichten ahd. Glossen.

Althochdeutsche Glossen: Nachträge
Old High German Glosses: A Supplement

HANDSCHRIFTENBESCHREIBUNGEN

Die Kurzbeschreibungen der Handschriften umfassen - in dieser
Reihenfolge - Bibliotheksort, Signatur, kurze Inhaltsangabe,
Provenienz, Schriftheimat (diese steht nach der Provenienz
in runden Klammern; leere Klammer bedeutet Identität von Provenienz und Schriftheimat), Datierung, Blatt- oder Seiten-
zahl.

GLOSSEN

Interlinearglossen sind von ihrem Lemma durch ein Komma
getrennt, während Kontextglossen ohne Trennungszeichen
erscheinen und vor Marginalglossen das Lemma in runden
Klammern steht. Unsichere Buchstaben sind durch darunter
gesetzte Punkte gekennzeichnet. + bedeutet Griffelglosse,
während § anzeigt, daß die Glosse unter dem Lemma steht.
Kürzel in der Handschrift sind bei den Lemmata aufgelöst
und bei den ahd. Glossen beibehalten.

ABGEKÜRZTE BUCHTITEL

R.Bergmann = Rolf Bergmann, Verzeichnis der althochdeutschen
        und altsächsischen Glossenhandschriften (Mün-
        ster,1973).
J.-P.Migne, PL bzw. PG = Jean-Paul Migne, Patrologiae cursus
        completus, Series latina bzw. graeca
        (Paris,1844ff.).

2

Augsburg

AUGSBURG (Bischöfliche Ordinariatsbibliothek)

Hs.K 1: S.Benedictus, Regula.

Füssen, St.Mang (Benediktbeuren), 1.Hälfte des 9.Jh.,

84 Bl.

Lit.: R.Bergmann 12.

Glossen: 1 ahd. Marginalglosse von einer Hand des 9.Jh.

Text: J.-P.Migne, PL 66,215ff.

f.42v   (completorius), hirfullit [h am Rand halb
         weggeschnitten] - 460C

◩

Hs.K 4: Gregorius Magnus, Regula pastoralis.

Füssen, St.Mang, spätes 10.Jh., 74 Bl.

Lit.: R.Bergmann 14.

Glossen: Gegen hundert ahd. Marginal- und Interlinearglossen von mehreren Händen des späten 10.Jh. Ein Teil
der Marginalglossen sind verblichen und auch mit Hilfe
einer Ultraviolettlampe nicht mehr zu lesen. Die meisten
Glossen stammen von einer Hand (a), die marginal und interlinear lat. und ahd. glossiert; die ahd. Glossen sind
teilweise in bfk-Geheimschrift. Deutlich unterschieden
davon ist eine zweite Hand (b), die fast ausschließlich
ahd. Interlinearglossen schreibt.

Text: J.-P.Migne, PL 77,13ff.

3

Innen- deckel	propagetur, kiuuitpreitot uuerde (a) - 13B
f.1v	(confunditur), kihonit uuirdud (a) - 14B
	(queritur), stouot (a) - 14B
	(detestatur), leiditzoht (a) - 15A
	(exigente), kisculdendero (a) - 15A
f.2r	(limpidissimam aquam), lutirostiu uuazzer (a) - 15C
	peruertuntur, girrit uerdent (a) - 16A
f.2v	(destruit), girrit (a) - 16B
	(sub exteriori habitu), unt' leclihemo (a) -[<u>un-</u> <u>ter</u>] - 16B
f.2v	(utcumque), &tiuilo (a) [<u>ettiuilo</u>] - 16B
	breuiter, curcilic (b) - 16B
	(temerare), kiualgen (a) - 16C
f.3r	prohibet, peuert (b) - 16C
	(principari), herison (a) - 16C
	patibulum, galge (b) - 16D
	(probrose), scantliches (a) - 16D
	inquinant, peuelt (b) - 16D
	in elationem, in toleheit (a) - 17A
	usu, kiuuoneheite (a) - 17A
f.3v	(eneruiter), uueiho (a) - 17B
	fluxus, unstatiger (a) - 17B
	(obstaculo), uuiderstendo (a) - 17B
	(retractionis), uuidardanches (a) - 17B
	(deuerberat), ceuueibit (a) - 17B
	(inpar), ungaristiger (a) - 17C
	(insolentem), ungastoma (a) - 17C
	(solum modo), ...erhafto (a) - 17C
f.4r	(cellas), trisocha - 17D

4

facere, main (a) - 17D

(supetunt), kindigen (a) - 17D

(ore prophetico), ceihenliher (a) - 18A

f.4v   (erecti), antsaziga (a) - 18C

(priuata), so:ntkrkgb (a) [so:ntiriga] - 18C

f.4v   (sed supra candelabrum), sxntfrxpfdbsckfrcfstbl

(a) [sunter upe dasc kercestal] - 18D

f.5r   (cura pastoris), hirtintuom - (a) - 19A

uxorem, conun (b) - 19B

(cum dedecore), mit honido (a) - 19C

f.5v   (quietis), stkllk (a) [stilli] - 19C

secessum, fknptf (a) [einote] - 19C

(speculationis), dero hkmklk^{S}cun pescourigo (a)
[himiliscun] - 19C

de quo, uone dero (a) - 19C

(profuturus), pidirpin ^{S}culenter (a) - 19C

(inuitus), kinôtter (a) - 20A

f.6r   (cognoscere), xxkrdigen (a) [uuirdigen]- 20C

f.6v   (utrobique), ckkfxxfdf frea (a) [ciieuuedeerea]
- 20D

(metiendo), pidenchento (a) - 20D

(componat), kkrkte (a) [kirite] - 21B

f.7r   (expressione), urreckdo (a) - 21C

f.7v   (agitationum), illungo (a) - 22B

f.8r   (obstaculum), xxkdbri (a) [uuidari] - 22C

(pasiones), acuste (a) - 22D

(uulnus), uunten (a) - 22D

(inbecillitatem), uueihi (a) - 23A

f.8v   ...tur [metiatur], pkdfnche (a) [pidenche] - 23D

(damnabiliter), lasterbaro (a) - 23D

5

f.8v   torto, crūb (b) [crumb] - 24 A

            lippus, plehanouger (a) - 24A

            (pondorosus), holotter (a) - 24A

f.9r   porrigat, ruchi (b) - 24A

            (conticescent), firsuig... (c) [Ende des Wortes

            weggeschnitten] - 24A

            (desolata), lamiu (a) - 24B

f.9v   (crebro), ...icigo (c) [Beginn des Wortes weg-

            geschnitten] - 25A

            collirio, oucsa^{1}ben (a) - 25A

            (albuginem), heuisal (a) [h halb weggeschnitten]

            - 25B

            sinitur, glassin uuirt (b) - 25B

            arrogantia, romisali (b) - 25B

            ex eo, uone du (b) - 25B

            (petulantia), ketilosi (a) - 25C

f.10r   prosilit, uurspringit (b) - 25C

            perpeti, dultin (b) - 26A

            (uires), kimahtin (a) - 26B

f.10v   (lutum), uuascantiu (a) [das erste u halb weg-

            geschnitten] - 27A

            (sacraria), den himilscken (a) - 27B

            (propria), ..diginen (a) - 27B

f.11r   rationale, prustfano (b) - 27B

            uitbis, nestilon (b) - 27B

f.14r   (leuigatur), kismahit uuirdit (a) - 32A

f.17r   (feriant), ingeben (d) - 36C

f.35v   (recuperare), cipůzan (d) - 67C

f.36r   propositum, uuillen (b) - 68C

f.36v   (memoratur), kimanot uuar (e) - 69A

f.37v   (ita), sodoh (b) - 70C

f.38r   specie mentitur, pilidi (b) truginot (d) - 71A

f.45v   cocox, chohho (b) - 81C

f.47r   (largiuntur), kinerit vurdan (f) - 83C

f.66r   (gentibus), lebent... (g) [Ende des Wortes weg-
         geschnitten] - 11C

◘

Hs.K 10: Gregorius Magnus, Dialogi.

Füssen, St.Mang (Süddeutschland), Anfang des 9.Jh., 159
Bl.

Lit.: R.Bergmann 15.

Glossen: Die Handschrift enthält gegen 30 interlineare
ahd. Griffel- und Federglossen. 1 Federglosse stammt von
einer Hand des 9.Jh. (d), die übrigen von mehreren Händen des 10.Jh. Eine Hand (a) ersetzt die Vokale durch
Punkte.

Text: J.-P.Migne, PL 77,149ff.; PL 66,125ff.

f.3v   eximie, +...lihum - PL 77,156A

f.11v   cominus, +nah - PL 77,173B

f.43r   conticuit [Migne: tacuit], +kisuifteta - PL 66,
         158C

f.43v   conuiatorem, +kifert - PL 66,160A

f.79r   a leuibus, f::n:l::s:n (a) [foni losen] - PL 77,
         256C

         execrabilis, l::ds·ml:h (a) [leidsamlih] -
         PL 77,256C

f.80v   audacter, ...rstl::: (a) [...rstlio] - PL 77,260A

7

f.81r   remotiori, s∴ntr⋮C∷r⋮n (a) [<u>suntrocorin</u>] –
              PL 77,260D

f.89v   elangui, k⋮∴nm·ht:t· (a) [<u>kiunmahteta</u>] – PL 77,
              277C

f.89v   ferunt, s·lt:n (a) [<u>salten</u>] – PL 77,280A

f.90r   reperet, sl⋮h⋮ (a) [<u>slihi</u>] – PL 77,280A
              ad modernos, z⋮n·:n (a) [<u>zi naen</u>] – PL 77,280C

f.90v   non infero, ·n·n⋮pr⋮nC∷ (a) [<u>ana ni princo</u>] –
              PL 77,280C

f.97r   perfidiam, +unka... – PL 77,293B

f.98r   ad secedendum, ·nzikil⋮d·nn: (a) [<u>an zi kili-
              danne</u>] – PL 77,296C

f.98v   uentum est, k:m·n∴·s (a) [<u>koman uas</u>] – PL 77,

f.100r   defertur, ist ca altinót (d) – PL 77,300B

f.128v   uocauit, gladota (b) – PL 77,360A
              uisum est, geduhta (b) – PL 77,360A
              quid dixerat, uas er ersegta (b) – PL 77,360A

f.130r   praelibare, f∷r·m·rc∷n (a) [<u>foramarcon</u>] – PL 77,
              361B

f.139v   fistula duli (c) [beide Worte quer auf den Rand
              geschrieben] – zu PL 77,385A

f.153v   excubare, helfan (b) – PL 77,420A
              indagantes, arspurianti (b) – PL 77,420A

f.154v   euoluti, arkanana (b) – PL 77,421A

f.155r   et non mediocriter, enta nals mechafto (b) –
              PL 77,421C

f.155v   tandem post, az·ft·r∷s (a) [<u>azafteros</u>] – PL 77,
              424B
              nautam, f:r⋮∴n (a) [<u>feriun</u>] – PL 77,424C
              carabo, fl∷zsc⋮f (a) [<u>flozscif</u>] – PL 77,424C

f.156r   carine, p∷d∴m: (a) [<u>podume</u>] – PL 77,424D

8

Austin (Texas)

AUSTIN (Miriam Lutcher Stark Library)

Phill.816: Beda, De natura rerum; Chalcidius (Plato), Timaeus; Excerptum de astrologia Arati; Paulus Diaconus ex Festo; Berno, De initio adventus.
Niederaltaich (Tegernsee), 2.Viertel des 11.Jh., 102 Bl.

Lit.: R.Bergmann 18.
Christine Eder, Die Schule des Klosters Tegernsee im frühen Mittelalter im Spiegel der Tegernseer Handschriften (München,1972).

Glossen: Auf f.2r dieser Handschrift ist ein Blatt eingeklebt mit Besitzvermerk und Inhaltsangabe von Schwerzenbecks Hand. Dieses Blatt verdeckt teilweise ein Rezept mit 2 ahd. Interlinearglossen, d.h. eventuell befinden sich weitere ahd. Glossen in dem nicht sichtbaren Teil des Textes. Außerdem enthält die Handschrift 1 ahd. Marginalglosse zu einem Rezept, das sich an den Platotext anschließt, und eine lat.-ahd. Glosse am Rand zu Paulus Diaconus ex Festo. Alle Glossen sind nach Christine Eder von Händen der 2.Hälfte des 11.Jh.

Text: Glossaria latina IV, hrsg. von J.W.Pirie und W.M. Lindsay, (Paris,1930), S.71ff.

f.2r   axungia, midgern
          celidonie, scelli... [der Rest durch Klebstoff verdeckt]
f.25r   (argilla), leim
f.70v   manubrium, helza - zu S.255

9

Basel

BASEL (Universitätsbibliothek)

B.III.3: Augustinus, u.a. Tractatus in Evangelium Joannis (f.3rb-155va).
Basler Kartause (Westdeutschland), 2.Drittel des 9.Jh., 289 Bl.

Lit.: R.Bergmann 25.

Glossen: 1 ahd. Marginalglosse von einer Hand des 10.Jh.

Text: J.-P.Migne, PL 35,79ff.

f.10ra   (pituita), glinz - 1398

◨

B.VI.3: Paulus Diaconus, Homiliarum (f.2r-199r); Hieronymus, Epistola ad Nepotianum (f.223r-235r).
Basler Kartause (alemannisch), ca.Mitte des 9.Jh., 235 Bl.

Lit.: R.Bergmann 27.

Glossen: 1 ahd. Marginalglosse zur 71.Homilie Bedas und je eine ahd. Marginal- und Interlinearglosse zu Hieronymus. Die Glossen sind von einer Hand, etwa gleichzeitig mit der Handschrift.

Text: J.-P.Migne, PL 94,452ff.; PL 22 (1854),527ff.

f.197r   (profuturum), piderbi - PL 94,455A
f.228v   (stomachi), uuarh - PL (1854),533
         pulmonis, milizi - PL 22 (1854),533

Berlin

BERLIN (Deutsche Staatsbibliothek)

Phill.1810: Cicero, De inventione.
Jan Meerman (wohl nordöstliches Deutschland), 2.Hälfte
des 10.Jh., 39 Bl.

Lit.: R.Bergmann 41.

Glossen: 1 ahd. Marginalglosse in Geheimschrift von einer Hand des 11.Jh.

f.26v   (pactum), k:n:ng. [**kininga**] - II,22,68

◙

BERLIN (Staatsbibliothek Preußischer Kulturbesitz)

Ms.theol.lat.2° 480: Gregorius Magnus, Homiliae in
Ezechielem.
Amorbach (angelsächsisch) Anfang des 9.Jh., 124 Bl.

Lit.: R.Bergmann 56.
E.Lowe, English Uncial (Oxford,1960), S.25f.

Glossen: 1 ahd. Griffelglosse am unteren Rand von f.12v,
von der mir nicht klar ist, zu welchem Lemma sie gehört.

Text: J.-P.Migne, PL 76,785ff.

f.12v   +uualannu - zu 797C

◙

11

Ms.theol.lat.4° 139: Evangeliar.

Werden, St.Liudger (Werden), 1.-2.Viertel des 9.Jh.,
145 Bl.

Lit.: R.Bergmann 58.

Glossen: Eine ahd. Interlinearglosse von einer Hand
des 2.Viertels des 9.Jh. zum Prolog des Kommentars
des hl. Hieronymus zum Matthäusevangelium.

Text: J.-P.Migne, PL 26 (1884),15ff.

f.2r   disputat, thingat - 19C

◘

Ms.theol.lat.8° 159: Hilduinus, Vita S.Dionysii.
Colmar, 9.Jh., 53 Bl.

Lit.: R.Bergmann 59.

Glossen: Die Handschrift enthält einige ahd. Glossen in
einem spiegelbildlichen Leimabdruck auf der Innenseite
des Vorderdeckels, der offenbar ein Abdruck des "stark
zerfressenen und durch Feuchtigkeit beschäftigten Blattes
f.1v" der von E.Steinmeyer (IV,415) beschriebenen Handschrift Cheltenham (Phill.) 18908 ist. Die Glossen wurden von E.Steinmeyer (III,634,5ff.) gedruckt, während
die Handschrift selbst inzwischen verschollen ist. Ich
gebe die Glossen des Leimabdrucks, soweit und wie sie
von B.Bischoff und mir gelesen werden konnten.

    Sulula...

    ...Nada.a

12

...Segansa

Falcitula S

Z...

Propu...

Grafium Grefil

Scin.$\bar{e}$ Scin...

...Sp

Bern

BERN (Burgerbibliothek)

Cod.89: Gennadius, Liber de ecclesiasticis dogmatibus; Canones.

(wahrscheinlich Elsaß), 1.Viertel des 9.Jh., 172 Bl.

Lit.: R.Bergmann 61.

F.Massen, Biblioteca latina iuris canonici mss. VI, Sitzungsberichte der Wiener Akademie der Wissenschaften, phil.-hist. Klasse, LVI (1867), S.196ff.

Glossen: Neben den von E.Steinmeyer (II,87,1ff. und II,140, 11ff.) gedruckten Glossen rund 85 ahd. Griffelglossen, von denen ich gegen 70 lesen konnte.

Text: J.-P.Migne, PL 58,979ff.; PL 67,135ff.

f.9ra	(spatia), +uuitu - Genn.X; PL 58,983D
f.9va	fingit, +truginota - XIV; PL 58,984B
	per coitum, +kimahhida - XIV; PL 58,984B
f.10va	(commissus), +kimahot - XXI; PL 58,985B
	(admittente), kuntend - XXI; PL 58,985C
	pariter, +sama. - XXI; PL 58,985C
f.10vb	quod emendaret, +daz kipuazti - XXI; PL 58,985C
	manet, +uuisit - XXI; PL 58,985C
	inuitante, +ladonti - XXI; PL 58,985C
	(consequatur), +kual& [kualet] - XXI; PL 58,985C
	ut adquiescamus, +daz ki.engemes - XXI; PL 58,985D
f.10vb	ut adipiscamur, +daz kihadazki - XXI; PL 58,985D
	quod adquiescendo, +daz kihalon - XXI; PL 58,985D
	admonitioni, +manunga - XXI; PL 58,985D

14

f.11va   germina, +cunni - LII; PL 58,993D

          pestes, +suht - LII; PL 58,993D

          quamuis, +dohuuet - LIII; PL 58,994B

f.12vb   instigante, +anacentemo spuranti - LV; PL 58,995A

          incendas [Migne: compescendas], +cikistillenne -
          LV; PL 58,995A

          ne ingenuitatis, +noh infolihin hefti - LVI; PL 58,
          995A

          cogatur, +kipeitit... - LVI; PL 58,995B

f.13vb   pudicitiae, +kidikine - LXIV; PL 58,996B

          conparandas, +uuidarmezzonne - LXVII; PL 58,996C

f.14va   ambitionem, +.ziual - LXXII; PL 58,997B

          mancipata, +kieftit - LXXIII; PL 58,997B

f.15ra   conpacta, +kiuuagit - LXXVI; PL 58,998A

f.15va   qua [Migne: quo], +dhe - LXXVI; PL 58,998B

f.16rb   presumatur, +erpalde - LXXX; PL 58,998D

          indiciis, +cundidon - LXXXI; PL 58,999A

f.16vb   temperatis, +obemezhafter - LXXXV; PL 58,1000A

f.40ra   priuantur, +piskert - Conc.Nic.V; PL 67,148C

          (pusillanimitate), +uuehamote - V; PL 67,148C

          decentius, +giristlichor - V; PL 67,148C

f.40va   exommunicandi [Migne: excommunicati] -
          +caahtonti - V; PL 67,148D

f.41va   municipiis, +festida - VIII; PL 67,149B

          probentur, +picorot - VIII; PL 67,149C

          examine, +diu ursohhida - IX; PL 67,149C

f.42ra   ignorantium, +unuuis - X; PL 67,149D

          preuaricati sunt; +ubaruangana sint - XI; PL 67,
          149D

          ablationem, +arnomf - XI; PL 67,149D

          tyrannide, +uuotrihhi... - XI; PL 67,149D

15

f.43ra   cathecuminis, +gisego - XIV; PL 67,150C

f.43va   audacter, +citurstlihho - XVI; PL 67,150D

f.43vb   mutum [Migne: <u>mutuum</u>], +analehho - XVII; PL 67, 151A

f.48rb   adimere, +kineman - Conc.Ancyr.XXII; PL 67,151D

            sustinere, +tu... - XXIII; PL 67,151D

            trusi, +spilanti - XXIII; PL 67,151D

            uiolenter, +notliho - XXIII; PL 67,151D

            sacrificiis, +unmuazi - XXIII; PL 67,152C

f.48va   uelut, +sasama - XXIII; PL 67,152C

f.48vb   laetiores, +frauuara - XXIV; PL 67,152D

f.49rb   minis, +drauuuon - XXV; PL 67,153A

            paenitudinis, +prognissi - XXV; PL 67,153A

f.49va   occasione, +fristunga - XXV; PL 67,153B

            non negetur, +ni ercigan uuerde - XXV; PL 67,153B

f.50ra   acriori, +sarpfer - XXVIII; PL 67,153C

f.50va   uis inlata, +dher crefta - XXX; PL 67,154A

f.51rb   demum, +iungis - XXXV; PL 67,154D

f.67va   praefatio, +furisprahi - Conc.Neocaes.; [nicht bei Migne]

f.68ra   decreta, +urdeili - Conc.Gangr.LXIV; PL 67,157D

f.70rb   contumatiam, +uuidarbruhtig - LXXVI; PL 67,160A

f.73rb   conpetentem, +cilinpf... - Conc.Antioch.XXCVII; PL 67,161B

f.76vb   coerceatur, +piduuingan - C; PL 67,164A

Bologna

BOLOGNA (Biblioteca Universitaria)

Hs.1702: Venantius Fortunatus, Vita S.Germani (f.1r-34r);
Translatio S.Germani (f.34v-61v); Vita et miracula S.Germa-
ni (f.62r-74v); etc.
(eventuell Paris, S.Germanus; auf jeden Fall vom 10.-16.Jh.
in Deutschland), 4.Viertel des 9.Jh., 85 Bl.

Lit.: L.Frati, Indici dei codici latini conservati nella
Biblioteca Universitaria di Bologna (Florenz,1909), S.380.

Glossen: 8 ahd. Marginalglossen von einer Hand des 10.Jh.
in bfk-Geheimschrift.

Text: MGH, Auctores antiquissimi IV,2 (Berlin,1885), S.11ff.
MGH, Poetae latini IV (Berlin,1923), S.123ff.
Acta Sanctorum XIX, hrsg. von J.Bollandus und G.Henschenius,
(Paris und Rom,1866), S.778ff.

f.6r   (eulogiis), pxflekpn [oueleion] - Auct.ant., S.14,
         13
f.10r   (capistro), blbftrxn [alaftrun] - S.16,21
f.22r   (malagmate), xôsgf [uâsge] - S.22,12
f.29v   (pustulum), bₓllxn [bûllun] - S.25,35
f.31v   (ruga), zxchxngb [zuchunga] - S.26,27
f.56v   (coxam), dkpchscfnchkl [diochscenchil] - Acta SS,
         S.785, linke Spalte B
f.64r   (eulogiis), .i.pxflfkpn [oueleion] - Poet.lat.,
         S.126,41
f.67v   (patrini), fftdkrkn [fetdirin] - S.129,113

Breslau

BRESLAU (Biblioteka Uniwersytecka)

III F 19: Apuleius Platonicus, Herbarius.
(südaustrasisch, Metz?), Anfang des 9.Jh., 119 Bl.

Lit.: R.Bergmann 76.

Glossen: 4 ahd. Interlinear- und Marginalglossen von je
einer Hand des 10. (a) und 11. (b) Jh.

Text: Corpus medicorum latinorum IV, hrsg. von E.Howald
und H.E.Sigerist, (Leipzig und Berlin,1927), S.15ff.

f.64v   senecion, selueza (a) - S.137,1

f.77r   fungi id est boleti que nos rustice suuillis
           uocamus (b) - interlinear zu S.182,2

f.80v   buluinus rustice dicitur cussinus (b) - margi-
           nal zu S.198,3

f.111v   grillis, heimon (b) - S.277,3

Brügge

BRÜGGE (Stadsbibliotheek)

302: Petrus Damianus, Epistolae (f.1va-110va); Lanfran-
cus episcopus (f.110va-110vb); Petrus Damianus, Liber qui
appelatur Gratissimus (f.111ra-113rb).
2.Hälfte des 12.Jh., 113 Bl.

Lit.: R.Bergmann 78.

Glossen: 1 ahd. Glosse von einer Hand der 2.Hälfte des
12.Jh. auf dem unteren Rand von f.113r.

Text: J.-P.Migne, PL 145,99ff.

f.113r   (ornicem) [Migne: <u>perniciem</u>], teut worhenna
          [<u>teutonice</u>] - 126D

Cambridge

CAMBRIDGE (King's College)

Kings MS.52 (früher: Phill.16395): Juvenal.
Cheltenham (Nordostfrankreich), Ende des 9.Jh., 63 Bl.

Lit.: R.Bergmann 87.

Glossen: Ahd. Kontext- und Marginalglossen von einer Hand
vom Ende des 9.Jh. zu einem griech.-lat. Glossar auf der
ersten Seite, zu Juvenal und zu einer Scholie zu Juvenal.
Der Glossator ersetzt Vokale durch Punkte.

f.1r   crocos.i.krog: [krogo]

         resina.i.h:rz [harz]

f.46r   (lubricat), B·SL·D·T [bislidit] - XI,175

f.47r   (antemnas), s:g·lg:rden [segilgerden] - XII,19

f.48r   (cohortes), sc:r: [scara] - XII,109

f.48v   etsi, g·uis [giuis] - XII,119

         exaequet, g·h:p: [gihopo] - XII,130

f.50r   (cedit), g·u:ll:d [giualled] - Scholie zu XIII,
         104

f.50v   fletuomo.as.i.fl·:tm:n [flietmon] - unabhängig
         vom Text auf dem unteren Rand

Darmstadt

DARMSTADT (Hessische Landes- und Hochschulbibliothek)

739: Naturwissenschaftliche Sammelhandschrift aus mehreren, ursprünglich selbständigen Codices. Text 3: Eutyches, Ars de verbo (f.56r-61v).
Lüttich, St.Jakob (Text 3: Westdeutschland oder Lotharingien), Text 3: 2.Hälfte des 9.Jh., 252 Bl.

Lit.: R.Bergmann 94.

Glossen: Ahd. Interlinearglossen von einer Hand des 9.-10.Jh. zu Eutyches, Ars de verbo.

Text: H.Keil, Grammatici latini V (Leipzig,1868), S.447ff.

f.58v	fulcrum, hurd - S.455,3
f.59r	litura, plastar - S.456,18
f.59v	stilla, dropp - S.457,17
f.60r	armo, uafanu - S.458,8
	liber, fri - S.458,11
	contio, zerat - S.458,17
f.60v	agger, obe - S.458,21
	robur, sebbomi - S.458,23
	aries, ramma - S.458,26
	comitor, ieferdi - S.458,27
	os, mund - S.458,30
	ros, dau - S.458,30
	nex, dot - S.459,2
	uindex, durniri - S.459,2
	radix, cruo - S.459,3
	merx, copunoa - S.459,5

        gelu, uinter - S.459,8

        rabies, ụẹuuon - S.459,8

◨

895: Biblia latina.

Weingarten (Deutschland), 11.Jh., 111 Bl.

Lit.: R.Bergmann 95.

Glossen: Je eine ahd. Marginal- und Interlinearglosse von
einer Hand des 11.Jh.

f.73v   branciam, c^{h}eun - Tobias 6,4

         (exentera), scurfin - Tobias 6,5

Dublin

DUBLIN (Trinity College Library)

Ms.737 (früher: G.4.16): Die Handschrift besteht aus mehreren, ursprünglich selbständigen Codices. Text 1: u.a. Gregorius episcopus Turonensis, Liber de miraculis S.Andreae Apostoli.
Dublin, Trinity College (Bayern oder Hessen), Text 1: 1.Hälfte des 9.Jh., 126 Bl.

Lit.: R.Bergmann 101.

Glossen: 1 ahd. Interlinearglosse von einer Hand des 9.-10.Jh.

Text: MGH, Scriptores rerum Merovingicarum I (Hannover, 1885), S.821ff.

f.48r   scatens, chresanter - 844,31

Edinburgh

EDINBURGH (National Library of Scotland)

Adv.MS.18.5.10: Kommentare zu Juvenal, Lucanus, Persius, Sedulius, Horaz, Vergil und Prudentius.
1.Hälfte des 12.Jh., 39 Bl.

Lit.: R.Bergmann 107.

Glossen: Rund 60 ahd. Interlinear- und Kontextglossen der Texthand.

Text: -

f.3r   hippomanes.i.Rosvvrz qua equi commedentes in
          amentiam uertuntur ueneno - zu Juvenal VI,133

f.4r   olinthi.i.laster - XII,47

f.5v   rubiconis, rvvach - Lucanus, De bello civile I,
          185

          lemanno, podinise - I,396

          vogesi, vvasigv̄ [vvasigun] - I,397

          nemetius, spira - I,419

          sequana, nidirlenthi - I,425

          vagiones, vvormizze - I,431

          ararim, sauonna - I,434

          caicos.i.friesen - I,463

f.22v   (uiburna), summerlatv̄ [summerlatvn] - Vergil,
          Eclog.I,25

          frondator speth vel id est bfrosc [boumfrosc]
          vel qui frondes abcidit - I,57

          cithisum, pinesuge - I,78

          serpillum, chonela - II,11

ligustra, vvinda - II,18

uaccinnia, heidbere - II,18

aneti, tilli - II,48

f.23r   rubus, brama - III,89

sandix, vveit - IV,45

f.23v   ivniperi, vvechilta [vvechiltera] - VII,53

f.24r   licia, daht - VIII,74

tevi, bracco - VIII,107

ebuli, arehi - X,27

f.24v   lacune.i.fosse ubi aqua stant.i.vviger - Georg.
I,117

f.25r   visco, mistili - I,139

tribule, flegil - I,164

trahe, slite - I,164

bine aures, riester - I,172

stiua, rutte - I,174

fiscina, casibore - I,266

licia harlove - I,285

inspicat, findit.incidit - I,292

f.26v   stiria, hissilla - III,366

olentia, ancvveizze - III,564

alueariis vel himora, cresso - zu IV,39

melisphilla, beinvvalla - IV,63

cucumis, phedeme - IV,122

pruna, flumbŏm - IV,145

stelio, moltvv̄ [moltvvurm] - IV,243

fucus, treno - IV,244

f.27v   lignus proprie vvirstein, livthe [die Interlinearglosse über lignus] - zu Aen.I,726

vitte, tvnevvange - II,133

f.30r   coriti, pharetra vel bogevoter - X,169

           orichalco, rotcolt - XII,87

f.30v   maculum proprium dicitur masche - zu Cathemeri-

           non III,42

           surculus, scuzelinc - X,117

           cariosa, madevv̄ [madevvurm] - X,141

           catastas igneas.i.rostisen - Peristephanon I,56

           calagurris civitas vvascome - IV,31

           lictor vvizener - V,98

           fuligo, rŏz - V,198

           serra.i.erninehoz - zu V,217

           segmenta, segvnga - V,531

f.33v   pergamus, burchmure - zu Contra Symmachum I,194

           prima hasta draconis guntfano - II,711

           lanistris cleine nestelen - II,1094

EINSIEDELN (Stiftsbibliothek)

cod.18(576): Commentarius in psalmos I-LXX.
(Norditalien), Ende des 8.Jh., 342 S.

Lit.: R.Bergmann 110.

Glossen: 2 interlineare ahd. Griffelglossen.

Text: -

S.40   moliuntur, +maho - Kommentar zu Psalm X

S.41   commeare, +giuarana - Kommentar zu Psalm X

◘

cod.39(480): Smaragdus, Collectiones in Epistolas et Evangelia.
Reichenau (Westdeutschland), 2.Drittel des 9.Jh., 161 Bl.

Lit.: R.Bergmann 114.
A.Bruckner, Scriptoria V, S.24.
A.Holder, Die Reichenauer Handschriften III,2 (Leipzig,
1918), S.248.

Glossen: 2 ahd. Interlinearglossen von einer Hand des 9.-
10.Jh.

Text: J.-P.Migne, PL 102,9ff.

f.76r   mediator dicitur, medamari dicitur - 155B
          erat, uas - 155B

□

cod.319(645): Kalendarium etc.

Einsiedeln (), 10.-11.Jh., 300 S.

Lit.: R.Bergmann 130.

Glossen: Neben der von E.Steinmeyer (IV,425,Fußnote) angeführten ahd.Federglosse eine ahd Griffelglosse zu einer chronologischen Notiz.

S.274   nongentesimus nonagesimus sextus, +niunhund..
          niunzincsesiu

Frankfurt

FRANKFURT AM MAIN (Stadt- und Universitätsbibliothek)

Barth.50: Burchardus Wormatiensis, Liber decretorum.
Frankfurt, St.Bartholomäus (westdeutsch), 1.Hälfte des
11.Jh., 315 Bl.

Lit.: R.Bergmann 156.
(Der Katalog der Handschriften des Bartholomäusklosters
ist in Vorbereitung. Durch das Entgegenkommen der Bib-
liothek konnte ich die Druckfahnen einsehen).

Glossen: 1 ahd. Interlinearglosse von einer Hand der
1.Hälfte des 11.Jh. (vgl. Katalog).

Text: J.-P.Migne, PL 140,537ff.

f.255ra in ceruulo, .i. in dehsa - 965B

Fulda

FULDA (Hessische Landesbibliothek)

Aa 17: Augustinus, Commentarius in psalmos CXIX-CXXXII.
Konstanz, Dombibliothek (reichenauisch), 10.Jh., 151 Bl.

Lit.: R.Bergmann 164.

Glossen: 1 ahd. Marginalglosse zum Text von einer Hand
des 10.Jh. Außerdem auf der letzten Textseite von einer
zweiten Hand des 10.Jh. mehrere vom Text unabhängige lat.-
ahd. Glossen, die teilweise auf dem Rand und teilweise
zwischen den Textzeilen stehen. Bei den Glossen auf dem
Rand sind jeweils einige Buchstaben weggeschnitten.

Text: J.-P.Migne, PL 37,1596ff.

f.8r   (amphitheatri), spilehus - 1601
f.151r   et macerie depulse seregezune gestozene - margi-
         nal
         de ex...cione fona leidicinne - marginal
         uitupera... sleltug... lasteri - marginal
         ad radicem mambre ze nidenanti kemotale -
         interlinear
         incassum unkemeitun - interlinear
         dissimulante ufslahentemo - interlinear

St. Gallen

ST.GALLEN (Stiftsarchiv)

Pfävers X: Acta Sanctorum (f.1r-18r); Gregorius Magnus,
Excerpta (f.18v-19r); Gregorius Magnus, Dialogi (f.19v-
102r); Passio S.Eustasii (f.102v-107v).
Kloster Pfävers (wohl südliche Schweiz), 1.Hälfte des
9.Jh., 107 Bl.

Lit.: R.Bergmann 172.

Glossen: 1 ahd. Interlinearglosse von einer Hand des
9.-10.Jh. zu Gregors des Großen Moralia in Job.

Text: J.-P.Migne, PL 75,550ff.

f.19r   deprehenditur, ist caumun neminti - 552B

◘

ST.GALLEN (Stiftsbibliothek)

40: Die Handschrift besteht aus mehreren, ursprünglich
selbständigen Teilen. S.300-357: Gebete (S.301-303);
Explanatio super missam (S.304-322); Ambrosius, Augustinus etc., Excerpta (S.348-355).
St.Gallen (S.300-357: Schweiz), S.300-357: 1.-2.Vier-
tel des 9.Jh., 357 S.

Lit.: R.Bergmann 175.

Glossen: 2 lat.-ahd. Glossen von einer Hand aus der
Mitte des 9.Jh. auf dem freien Teil von S.303.

31

S.303   simio id est affo

           corcodrilla id est niechus

◨

49: Evangeliar.

St.Gallen (vielleicht St.Gallen), 2.Hälfte des 9.Jh., 314 S.

Lit.: R.Bergmann 177.

Glossen: Einige kaum lesbare interlineare Griffelglossen.

S.184a   curate infirmos, +taton creftigent - Lukas X,9
S.184b   paeniterent, +ruatin - X,13

          exaltata, +oroot.e - X,15

S.185a   subiciuntur [oder zu: non uiderunt?],

          +un.esaonso.n.ne - X,20 [oder X,24]

S.185b   non audierunt, +ungoordeans - X,24

◨

175: Augustinus, De Trinitate.

St.Gallen (), 9.Jh., 360 S.

Lit.: R.Bergmann 196.

Glossen: 1 ahd. Interlinearglosse von der Hand Ekkehards IV.

Text: J.-P.Migne, PL 42,819ff.

S.167   canorum, .i.nîumôn - 949

◨

196: Venantius Fortunatus, Carmina.
St.Gallen (), 2.Drittel des 9.Jh., 390 S.

Lit.: R.Bergmann 200.

Glossen: 6 ahd. Interlinearglossen von einer Hand der
2.Hälfte des 9.Jh.

Text: J.-P.Migne, PL 88,59ff.

S.3   atesim, .i.etisa - 62A

          drauum, .i.dra - 62A

          norico, .i.charanta - 62A

          oenum, .i.in - 62A

          sequanam, .i.sigina - 62A
S.71   siderei, s.sunthi - 126B

◙

276: Alcuinus; Augustinus, De perfectione (S.271-
279).
St.Gallen (gleiche süddeutsche Schule wie St.Gallen,
Stadtbibliothek Hs.336), 2.Viertel des 9.Jh., 280 S.

Lit.: R.Bergmann 215.

Glossen: 1 ahd. Interlinearglosse von einer Hand des
10.Jh.

Text: J.-P.Migne, PL 44,291ff.

S.275   caritas, minna - 295

◙

280: Florus Diaconus, Expositio in Epistolas S.Pauli.

St.Gallen (), 2.Hälfte des 9.Jh., 434 S.

Lit.: R.Bergmann 218.

Glossen: 1 ahd. Interlinearglosse von der Hand Ekkehards IV.

Text: J.-P.Migne, PL 119,279ff.

S.210   uentilator, .i.uuanare - PL 119,406B; (PL 37,1185)

Gent

GENT (Rijksuniversiteit, Centrale Bibliotheek)

301: Hieronymus, Expositio super Mattheum.
St.Maximin, Trier, 2.Hälfte des 9.Jh., 184 S.

Lit.: R.Bergmann 257.

Glossen: Auf S.56 ein längerer Glosseneintrag von einer
Hand des 10.Jh. Da mir der Sinn der zweiten Hälfte der
Glossen nicht klar ist, und die Einteilung in Worte aus
der Handschrift nicht hervorgeht, drucke ich den Text
nach uillata ohne Unterteilung.

S.56   herico ruomunt erindrut codrat checila elica
        cumit uillata auicnilissunsouillinhi

Gotha

GOTHA (Forschungsbibliothek)

M II 98: Martianus Capella, De nuptiis Philologiae et Mercurii.

Nürnberg, 11.Jh., 27 Bl.

Lit.: R.Bergmann 267.

C.Leonardi, I codici di Marziano Capella, Aevum 34 (1960), S.55.

Glossen: Einige ahd. Interlinearglossen, die auch mit Hilfe einer Ultraviolettlampe kaum zu lesen sind.

f.2r	inpotentia, unst.mi - I,7
f.3r	festinata, giltart - I,14
f.6r	ueris, teina - I,27
f.12r	illustris, vrmari - I,74
	geminorum, lichnis - I,75

GRAZ (Universitätsbibliothek)

412: Passiones et vitae Apostolorum et Sanctorum.
Benediktinerstift St.Lambrecht (oberitalienisch),
1.Hälfte des 9.Jh., 248 Bl.

Lit.: R.Bergmann 268.

Glossen: 1 ahd. Glosse von einer Hand des 10.Jh.
am oberen Rand von f.100r ohne Verbindung mit dem
Text.

f.100r   chnoph

Karlsruhe

KARLSRUHE (Badische Landesbibliothek)

Aug.XIV: Beda, Gregorius Magnus, Hieronymus etc., Homiliae.

Reichenau, 9.Jh., 110 Bl.

Lit.: R.Bergmann 290.

Glossen: 1 ahd. Interlinearglosse von einer Hand des
9.-10.Jh. auf einer Seite mit verschiedenen lat. Federproben.

f.109v   araneae, spinne uopes

◧

Aug.XV: Augustinus, Gregorius Magnus, Hieronymus etc.,
Homiliae.

Reichenau (westdeutsch), 1.Hälfte des 9.Jh., 163 Bl.

Lit.: R.Bergmann 291.

Glossen: 1 umgekehrt auf den Rand geschriebene ahd.
Glosse von einer Hand des späten 10.Jh.

f.151r   probacio deruaru

◧

Aug.XCIV: Hieronymus, Adversus Iouinianum; Medizini-
sche Rezepte (f.83v).

Reichenau (), Haupttext: Anfang des 9.Jh., Rezepte:
10.Jh., 83 Bl.

Lit.: R.Bergmann 295.

Glossen: 1 ahd. Interlinearglosse von einer Hand des
10.Jh. zu den Rezepten.

f.83v   stipteria, casselter

◨

Aug.CV: Hieronymus, Epistolae.
Reichenau (Lorsch), 8.-9.Jh., 234 Bl.

Lit.: R.Bergmann 297.

Glossen: 1 ahd. Marginalglosse von einer Hand des frühen
9.Jh. zur LX. Epistel des hl.Hieronymus.

Text: J.-P.Migne, PL 22 (1854),325ff.

f.83r   (antistat), furista^{a}t - 598

◨

Aug.CXLV: Gregorius Magnus, Homiliae in Evangelia.
Reichenau (alemannisch), Anfang des 9.Jh., 230 Bl.

Lit.: R.Bergmann 306.

Glossen: 1 ahd. Interlinearglosse von einer Hand der
1.Hälfte des 10.Jh. zur XL. Homilie.

Text: J.-P.Migne, PL 76,1075ff.

f.87r   preditum, gerihten - 1161D

◨

39

Aug.CCXL: Gregorius Magnus, Regula pastoralis.

Reichenau (Norditalien, vermutlich Verona), 7.-8.Jh.,
126 Bl.

Lit.: R.Bergmann 316.

Glossen: Zusätzlich zu den bei E.Steinmeyer (IV,330,8f.)
abgedruckten Glossen 4 mit roter Tinte sehr schwach geschriebene ahd. Interlinear- und Marginalglossen.

Text: J.-P.Migne, PL 77,13ff.

f.166r   (liquantes), sihine - 116D

        culicem, muccun - 116D

        anetum, tilli - 117A

        ciminum, cumin - 117A

◫

Fragm.perg.20: Aus Aug.XXXVII ausgelöstes Fragment einer
Pergamenturkunde.

1.Hälfte des 9.Jh., 57 mm breit, 56 mm hoch, einseitig be-
schrieben.

Ich drucke das Fragment in der Form, die mir Bernhard Bischoff mitteilte, der es 1934 abschrieb. Damals steckte
das Fragment mit anderen in einem mit "Fragm.perg.20" be-
zeichneten Kuvert, das inzwischen verloren ist.

Lit.: W.Stach, Mitteilungen zur mittelalterlichen Glossographie, in: Liber floridus, Mittellateinische Studien
Paul Lehmann gewidmet (St.Ottilien,1950), S.13.

..nueni Int tanharaduū[1]   [.<i>nueni inter tanharadum...]

..harado roncale In gi   [.<tan>harado roncale in gi...]

40

..fosͨra da tanharaḍ²   [..fos terra da tanharad<o>...]

..7 non credimus q̃ cõt   [..et non credimus quod cont..]

..ui comũtare uolueṛ³   [..ui commutare uoluer<it>...]

..ridii kl setembs an xẋ⁴[..<p>ridii kal. setembres anno xx..]

1) a von anderer Hand.
2) ᵀda' wahrscheinlich (räto)romanisch.
3) am Anfang <u>tui</u>?, <u>alicui</u>?.
4) unter 'setembs' noch eine Oberlänge zu erkennen.

" /ᵗ tanharad.......I...I/ " (Dorsualnotiz) und einige
Federproben auf der Rückseite. Teile des Formulars glaubt
B.Bischoff in rätischen Urkunden des St.Galler Urkunden-
buchs gefunden zu haben.

◙

Frag.Aug.183 (früher in: Aug.LXXI): Canonesglossar.
Reichenau, 1.Hälfte des 9.Jh.

Lit.: R.Bergmann 320.

Glossen: Einige ahd. Interlinear- und Kontextglossen der
Texthand.

> consultationi tua, dimu antfraga d...
>
> cassatum euacuat..., farmita...
>
> cohibent uue...
>
> confecta cat...
>
> ciangas hôsun

Köln

KÖLN (Historisches Archiv)

GB Kasten A Nr.12: Prudentiusfragmente.

Kloster Groß St.Martin, Köln, 9.-10.Jh.

Lit.: R.Bergmann 344.

Glossen: 1 ahd. Interlinearglosse von einer Hand derselben Zeit wie die Handschrift

    limat, figlot purgat - Hamartigenia 414

Kopenhagen

KOPENHAGEN (Det Kongelige Bibliotek)

Thott 167: Boetius, Isagoge Prophyrii (f.1r-16r); Boetius, Commentaria in Isagogen Porphyrii (f.16v-102v). Gallia (wohl westdeutsch), 2.Hälfte des 11.Jh., 102 Bl.

Lit.: R.Bergmann 356.

Glossen: 1 ahd. Interlinearglosse von einer Hand des 11.Jh.

Text: Porphyrii Isagoge et in Aristotelis categorias commentarium, Commentaria in Aristotelem graeca IV,1, hrsg. von Adolf Busse, (Berlin,1887), S.25ff.

f.1v   subsistunt, stentlic^he - S.25,10

Kremsmünster

KREMSMÜNSTER (Stiftsbibliothek)

Vergilfragment.

11.Jh.

Lit.: R.Bergmann 358.

Glossen: 1 ahd. Interlinearglosse.

    mergis, scarauon - Aen. V,128

Leiden

LEIDEN (Universitätsbibliothek)

Burm.q.3: Prudentius, Carmina.

Egmond (bei Paris), 1.Hälfte des 10.Jh., 181 Bl.

Lit.: R.Bergmann 363.

Glossen: 1 ahd. Marginalglosse von einer Hand der 1.Hälfte
des 10.Jh.

f.79r   (offas), stoz - Peristephanon X,808

◘

Lips.7: Plinius, Historia naturae.

Niederrhein (wahrscheinlich Murbach), 1.Hälfte des 9.Jh.,
378 Bl.

Lit.: R.Bergmann 364.

Glossen: Mehrere altniederländische Marginalglossen von
einer Hand des 10.Jh.

f.27r   (albis), elua - IV,14

          (uisurgis), vuisara - IV,14

          ostia rheni isla legka vual uehta rhin - am

          Rand zu IV,14

f.27v   spira vuormace - am Rand zu IV,17

          (colonae agrippinensis), colona - IV,17

f.69r   (scalperet), huoue - VII,37

          scalptura, heuan - am Rand zu VII,37

Leipzig

LEIPZIG (Universitätsbibliothek)

Rep.I.4: Sallust (f.1va-f.45vb); Horaz (f.46r-f.103v);
Lucanus (f.104r-163r); Martianus Capella (f.163v-184v).
Magdeburg, St.Johann (Deutschland), 11.Jh., 184 Bl.

Lit.: R.Bergmann 378.

C.Leonardi, I codici di Marziano Capella, Aevum 34
(1960), S.68f.

Glossen: 10 ahd. Interlinearglossen von einer Hand derselben Zeit wie die Handschrift.

f.8va	sentinam, puzian - Sallust, Catilina XXXVII,5
f.15ra	commeatus, .i.stipendia heritiuhc - LVIII,9
f.15va	propter aquilam, .i. uixta uonan - LIX,3
	aduersis, togivuendun - LXI,3
f.25vb	uades, gislas - Sallust, Iugurtha XXXV,9
f.31rb	tormentis, selfscotun - LVII,6
f.41rb	tormentis, selfscotun - XCIV,3
f.41va	seria, ernost - XCVI,3
f.145va	mittileneum, .i.lesboum - Lucanus, De bello civile VIII,109
	obside, .i.gisle - VIII,131

Melk

MELK (Stiftsbibliothek)

Nr.740 (früher 228; G.31): Boethius, Theologische Trak-
tate (f.1v-25v); Kommentar zu denselben Traktaten (f.26r-
38v).
Tegernsee (Froumund), spätes 10.Jh., 38 Bl.

Lit.: R.Bergmann 430.
Christine Eder, Die Schule des Klosters Tegernsee im frü-
hen Mittelalter im Spiegel der Tegernseer Handschriften
(München,1972), S.45ff.

Glossen: 1 ahd. Interlinearglosse von einer Hand derselben Zeit wie die Handschrift.

Text: E.K.Rand, Johannes Scottus (München,1906), S.30ff.

f.31r   seriis, ernosthaftlihen - S.50,27

47

München

MÜNCHEN (Bayerische Staatsbibliothek)

Clm 356: Defensor, Liber scintillarum.

H.Schedel (Salzburg?), 1.Hälfte des 9.Jh., 156 Bl.

Lit.: R.Bergmann 449.

Glossen: 2 ahd. Marginalglossen von einer Hand des
späten 9.Jh.

Text: J.-P.Migne, PL 88,597ff.

f.75v   (pila), stāph [stamph] - 652B
          (typsanas) Migne:[ptisanas] , mincliū
          [minclium] - 652B

◘

Clm 3747: Pseudo-Hieronymus, Breviarium in psalmos.
Augsburg, Dombibliothek (Regensburg, St.Emmeram), 1.Hälfte
des 9.Jh., 213 Bl.

Lit.: R.Bergmann 468.

Glossen: 2 interlineare ahd. Griffelglossen von einer Hand
des 9.Jh. zu Pseudo-Hieronymus und 1 lat.-ahd. Glosse am
oberen Rand von f.157r ohne Verbindung mit dem Text von
einer Hand des späten 10.Jh.

Text: J.-P.Migne, PL 26 (1884),849ff. Der Text der Handschrift unterscheidet sich bei beiden Glossen von dem Mig-
nes.

f.32v   gratis, +dancv [die Glosse über dem vorhergehen-
          den <u>nobis</u>] - 919A; zu Psalm XVII,2

f.109v   fortitudo, +trost - 1025D; zu Psalm XLVIII,15

f.157r   cumpost id est surgras

◨

Clm 4535: Ambrosius, Expositio in psalmum CXVIII.
Benediktbeuren (Deutschland), 10.-11.Jh., 200 Bl.

Lit.: R.Bergmann 475.

Paul Ruf, Kisyla von Kochel und ihre angeblichen Schen-
kungen, Studien und Mitteilungen zur Geschichte des Bene-
diktinerordens 47 (1929), S.467.

Glossen: 1 ahd. Interlinearglosse von einer Hand des frühen 11.Jh.

Text: J.-P.Migne, PL 15 (1887),1261ff.

f.92v   grintilin, repagulis - 1437A

◨

Clm 4541: Isidorus, Etymologiae.
Benediktbeuren (), 9.-10., 297 Bl.

Lit.: R.Bergmann 476.

Glossen: 12 ahd. Interlinearglossen von einer Hand des
10.Jh., die wohl von der Tegernseer Handschrift Clm 18192
(E.Steinmeyer V,29,9ff.) übernommen wurden (B.Bischoff).

Text: J.-P.Migne, PL 82,73ff.

f.62v   larbatio, slezt - 188A

f.139v   subcenturiati, halscara.i.subcenturia - 317A

f.156r   pelliciendo, spananto - 390C

f.185v   balenae, vvalera - 451B

          ocimi, morahes - 452B

f.186v   murenam, lantfrida - 455B

f.216   promunctorio, inseuvi - 514A

f.263v   asarum, hasalmusicha - 624B

f.265r   iosquianos, pilisa iusquiamus - 629A

f.292r   ianticulum, imbiz iantaculum - 707C

f.293v   pituita, greccun - 711B

f.294v   garum, sulza - 714A

◨

Clm 4542: Gregorius Magnus, Homiliae in Evangelia.
Benediktbeuren (), 8.-9.Jh., 256 Bl.

Lit.: R.Bergmann 477.

Glossen: Neben den von E.Steinmeyer (V,27,11ff.) gesammelten Federglossen enthält die Handschrift außer einigen
wenigen lat. Griffelglossen rund 650 meist interlineare
ahd. Griffelglossen, von denen ich etwas mehr als die
Hälfte lesen konnte. Von einem großen Teil dieser Glossen
ist jedoch nur eine abgekürzte Form gegeben. So finden wir
z.B. zu lat. nos neben unsih und uns die Formen un, sih,
s und h. Ich drucke die Abkürzungen in einer besonderen
Liste. Eine weitere Eigenart des Glossators ist, daß er
die meisten Glossen unter das Lemma schreibt, was ich mit
§ anzeige.

Text: J.-P.Migne, PL 76,1075ff.

50

f.17vb   impingimus, +anafarspurnames - 1088B

f.22ra   gratia, §+danc - 1096C

f.30ra   utcumque denuntiat, §+so uuenne so cundit - 1098B

f.33vb   quo, §+danna - 1101B

f.34ra   cui, +demo - 1102A

f.47ra   liceat, §+moz - 1112A

f.49vb   appetitum, +chiridu - 1113D

f.54va   combustione, +farprennidu - 1117C

f.57ra   doctrine, +dera lera - 1119B

f.57rb   intra, +inin - 1119C

f.58vb   archangeli, +cunnun - 1120D

          qui, +uueliha - 1120D

f.59ra   cui (reatu) suo, +deru () §+ira - 1120D

          qui, +uuelihiu - 1121A

f.60ra   irruerit, +anacafalit - 1121C

          ingruerit, +quimit - 1121C

f.60rb   generalis, +cameinlihiu - 1121D

f.61ra   nigerrimos, §+uuirsistun - 1122B

          se, +sinan - 1122C

f.61rb   grauiter, +drato - 1122C

          illius, +des - 1122C

f.64rb   uel, +ioh - 1125A

f.64va   transfixerunt, +stahun - 1125B

f.64vb   (primeuum), +erist - 1125B

          iuuentus, +iugent - 1125B

f.65rb   reuocat, +auarcaladot - 1125C

f.66rb   quantislibet, +so uue... - 1126C

f.68ra   commodis, §+caforun - 1128A

          eo, §+ine - 1128A

f.68rb   occasio, §+caforti - 1128A

f.71ra   perceptione, +antsegidu - 1130B

51

```
f.71vb    reuocet, +aruuentet - 1130C

          quelibet, §+eini..su - 1130C

f.73va    languente, +siuhhentemo - 1132A

f.75ra    suos, §+iro - 1133A

f.75va    liquorem, +nazzi - 1133C

          paleis, §+stroun - 1133C

f.75vb    pervia, +uueho - 1133C

f.76ra    quantum, §+so filu - 1134A

f.76va    fragrantia, +stanh - 1134B

f.76vb    quod, §+uuelihan - 1134B

f.80va    decalogi, §+zehanuorto - 1137B

f.88ra    sit, §+si - 1142B

          illa, §+siu - 1142B

f.89ra    summat, §+neme - 1143A

f.90ra    studiose, §+uuis - 1143C

f.90vb    cum, §+mit - 1144A

f.91vb    defuerit, §+prestit - 1144C

          est, +ist - 1144C

f.93rb    suis, §+iro - 1145C

f.93vb    aliud, +sumaz - 1146A

f.94va    se, +sin - 1146C

f.94vb    captamus, §+cafahames - 1146C

f.95ra    non distat, +ni ersch...t - 1147A

f.97rb    se, +sin - 1148B

f.100ra   non dedignatur, +caunuuirdota - 1150B

f.102vb   in personis, +in heitun - 1152A

f.103ra   intuito, §+casihti - 1152B

          ante, +er - 1152B

f.103rb   ergo, +ioh - 1152B

          ei, §+iru - 1152B

          obruere, +pifell... - 1152C
```

```
f.103va   ictibus, §+slegim - 1152C

f.104ra   reddat, §+far... - 1153A

f.107va   gerontas, +uralto = 1155B

f.107vb   appellant,+canemnant - 1155B

          prouectiores, +cadiganorun = 1155C

          adulescentia, §+chindischi - 1155C

f.122rb   nuper, +nunahun - 1158A

f.117ra   dilabitur, +sliffit - 1161C

f.126ra   eius, §+ira - 1167D

f.126vb   testimonium, +urchundi - 1168B

f.127vb   indixit, §+cazeleta - 1168D

f.133va   hoc, §+disiu - 1173B

f.137ra   suo, +iro - 1177A

f.137rb   sinu, §+scozziu - 1177B

f.143va   inlidit, +anapichnusit - 1184D

f.143rb   negotium, +ursuahhi... - 1184C

f.145ra   per trigonum, §+durh drifalt - 1186C

f.145vb   sternat, §+caca.uu.. - 1187B

f.146va   titulus, §+marha - 1188A

          eneruat, §+uueihit - 1188B

f.146vb   gressus, §+canc - 1188C

f.147va   sui, +sin - 1189C

          eius, §+iru - 1189C

f.149ra   usum, +sito - 1191A

f.150ra   tergum, §+uuanta - 1192B

f.150rb   cuius, +uues - 1192C

f.150va   proprium, +suntrie - 1192D

f.150vb   eo, §+diu - 1193A

f.151rb   sibi, +iru - 1193C

f.151vb   uiuicatoris, +des quiccones - 1194A

          succincte, §+scam.. - 1194B
```

53

```
                eodem, +demo - 1194B
f.152rb     sustilit, +canam - 1194C
                dum, §+denne - 1194C
                aculeus, §+...ort - 1194C
f.152va     appeteret, +cachoron - 1194D
                necaret, +erqueliti - 1195A
f.155va     presidens, §+forauu... - 1198D
f.156rb     ad quantum, §+za uu... - 1199D
f.156vb     uel, +ioh - 1200A
                gratia, +minnu - 1200B
f.157va     cuilibet, §+einiemo - 1201A
                per negationem, +dur lougan - 1201A
f.158rb     custos, +uuart - 1201D
                sperandarum, +cauuan.t... - 1202A
                substantia, §+cunni - 1202A
f.158vb     percurrit, +cafloz - 1202C
f.159vb     satagimus, +illames - 1203B
                insomnem, +unslafaner - 1203B
                uersaret, +analoti - 1203B
f.160va     odor, +stanh - 1204B
f.165rb     intermissis, +untarprohane - 1209B
f.166rb     (renititur), +uuidar... - 1210B
f.168va     quam, +uaz, §+uuho - 1213A
f.170vb     exorciomi, +pisoarani - 1215C
f.172ra     distinguitur, §+arscheidan - 1217A
                se, +sih - 1217B
f.172rb     (coitum), +hiuu - 1217B
f.173va     petiit, §+sota - 1219A
                ut ita, +soso - 1219A
f.175ra     respectum, +casit... - 1221A
f.175rb     adtestatione, §+cundidu - 1221B
54
```

f.179ra   formidinis, +ploodi - 1225B

f.180ra   adoptionem, +uuunsc̣ - 1226C

f.182rb   densatur, +ist cadicet - 1229B

f.185va   ueteri, +demo altiu - 1232C

          uetus, +der alto - 1232D

f.185va   se, +imo - 1233A

f.187ra   quod, §+daz - 1234C

f.188ra   desit, §+presta - 1235C

f.189ra   contra, §+ingagan - 1237A

          consolatoria, +ṭrostant - 1237A

f.191ra   cuius, §+uues - 1239C

f.192ra   contra se, §+ingagan imo - 1241A

f.192vb   ulterius non deriuetur, §+niueṛẹ cachereta - 1241D

f.194rb   suo,+ira - 1243B

          sui, §+ira - 1243B

f.195ra   uruntur, +prinnant - 1244A

f.197rb   sui, §+ira - 1246C

f.204vb   intimis, §+inuu... - 1254B

f.210rb   nos, +unsih - 1259C

f.210va   inequalitas, §+unepanlihi - 1260A

f.210vb   blandimenta, +lobun - 1260B

          serena, §+haitrun - 1260B

          subacta, +ca.ot - 1260B

f.213ra   retractione, §+uuid... - 1262C

f.216rb   (distare), +...scheidan - 1266A

f.219vb   aegiptius, +egiptisco - 1270A

f.220ra   praedam, +hunda - 1270A

f.220va   (frequentia),+menigi - 1270C

          numerositas, §+menigi - 1270C

f.221va   suis, §+ira - 1271C

f.221vb   adultera, §+farhaltan... - 1272A

55

f.222rb	inhiare, §+choron - 1272C	
f.223va	fragrantia, +dera sozzida - 1274B	
f.224ra	succumbere, +untarlican - 1274B	
f.224vb	incircumscriptum, +unupipifagenaz - 1275B	
f.225vb	in ea quam adgreditur, +in der ..inoga. ist - 1276B	
	multum, +filu - 1276C	
f.226va	faueant, §+helfen - 1277B	
f.226vb	necesarii, §+notdurfti - 1277C	
f.227ra	ad, +ze - 1277D	
f.228ra	placationis, §+huldi - 1278D	
	placat, +cahuldit - 1279A	
	absolutionem, +intsuntani - 1279A	
f.228va	quantum, +filu - 1279C	
f.229rb	liuore, §+uuarche - 1280B	
	sulcauerant, +furht... - 1280B	
f.229vb	suus, +iro - 1280D	
f.231ra	dissona, §+cal..an... - 1282B	
f.231va	liquido, +ofanlio - 1283A	
f.232va	ariditas, §+diur - 1284B	
f.233rb	cuius, +dera - 1285A	
f.235ra	angustatur, +uuas cadu...an - 1287A	
f.238vb	suas, +ira - 1291B	
f.239ra	animaduersione, +furistentidu - 1291C	
	usu, §+sitiu - 1291D	
f.239va	se, §+sin - 1292B	
f.239vb	discrepabat, §+missazufta - 1292C	
f.242vb	transfigitur, +durhs... - 1296B	
f.243va	suarum, §+ira - 1297A	
f.247vb	nitorem, §+scimo - 1302C	
f.249ra	adfuerint, §+sint - 1304A	
f.249va	nos, +unsih - 1304C	

56

f.251vb datum. §+tach - 1307C

f.252vb cognitio, §+hurcnat. - 1308C

f.253ra perpeti, +dolan - 1309A

   fuscat, §+salauuet - 1309A

f.253va inportunae, §+eroloso - 1310A

f.254ra illius, §+ira - 1309C

f.254rb custos, §+uuart - 1310C

Abgekürzte Glossen

(die Stellung der Glosse vor oder nach dem Bindestrich
zeigt, ob die Glosse am Anfang oder Ende des Lemmas steht)

f.34ra reuerentiae, §+ -ti - 1101B

   subdendo [oder manifestat], +to- - 1101B

f.47va cucurrit, §+pi.- - 1112A

f.53rb sagina, +diu- - 1116B

f.57rb hanc, + -iu - 1119C

f.58ra mos, §+un - 1120B

f.59ra que, +uu- - 1120D

f.61ra raperent, + -mun - 1122C

f.61rb perstrepens, +lir- - 1122C

   tetre, +deo-.. - 1122C

   imagines, + -itun - 1122C

f.64vb que, §+ -o - 1125B

f.66rb argenti, +si- - 1126C

f.71ra redeuntium [oder tristi], + -un - 1130A

f.71va priuamur, §+pi- - 1130C

f.71vb desiderat, §+ -te - 1130C

f.72ra peruentione, §+ -ni - 1130D

f.73vb immemoria, §+ -ti - 1132A

f.74vb aditum, +in- - 1133A

57

f.75ra   contraria, §+ -ru - 1133A

f.83ra   minus, + -un - 1139A

f.89vb   dicta, + -ti - 1143C

f.90ra   studiose, §+ -liho - 1143C

f.90va   deprehendunt, §+pi- - 1144A

f.93ra   humanos, §+ -chiu - 1145C

f.94ra   ualeamus, §+ -gun - 1146B

f.98vb   nos, §+ -h - 1149C

f.102rb   existent, + -n - 1151D

          aeterne, + -no - 1151D

f.103ra   remouit, §+ -ta - 1152B

          praeteriti, + -ra - 1152B

f.103va   obruere, +pi- - 1152C

f.104ra   humiliter, + -sen - 1152D

          perpendat, §+ -ot - 1153A

f.107vb   insinuent, + -n - 1155B

          pueritia, + -ti - 1155C

          iuuentute, §+ iu- - 1155C

f.108ra   caritatis, §+ua- - 1155C

f.109rb   uixerint, §+ -un - 1156C

f.119rb   animaduersio, + -zi - 1163B

f.120ra   caecidit, + -i - 1164A

f.120vb   existimus, + -run - 1164B

f.125ra   alta, + -hi - 1167B

          querant, §+ -em - 1177A

f.137ra   ipso, §+ -pun - 1177A

f.137rb   presumtibilis, §+ -lihio - 1177B

f.140va   quae, §+ -u - 1180D

f.143va   quod, §+ -u - 1184D

f.143vb   denegat, +far-ta - 1185A

```
          fatetur, §+ -t - 1185B

          situ, §+ -du - 1185B

f.144rb   dissensionibus, +uncazus- - 1185D

f.145ra   conprehendi, +pi- - 1186B

f.145rb   trium, + -o - 1186D

          inspicere, +ana- - 1186D

f.146ra   hoc, §+ -siu - 1187C

f.146va   cruciat, §+ca- - 1188B

f.146vb   consolatur, + -te - 1188C

          meum, + -ra - 1188C

          inperfectum, §+un- - 1188C

f.148va   infra, §+ -an - 1190C

          ipsum, + -mo - 1190C

f.149ra   usum oder incendium, + -nun - 1191A

          clarescit, + -tet - 1191A

f.149vb   toto, + -lu - 1192A

f.150rb   uirentia, + -te - 1192C

f.150va   commune, §+ -niu - 1192D

f.150vb   audit, §+ -ta - 1193A

f.151ra   tacita, §+ -ru - 1193B

f.151rb   credibile, + -lih - 1193C

          haec, + -sen - 1193C

          respondeat, §+ -t - 1193C

f.151vb   narrat, +s-ta - 1194A

f.155rb   deberet, §+ -ti - 1198C

          missio, §+ -tida - 1198C

f.156rb   demonice, + -s - 1199C

          putruit, + -ta - 1199C

f.156va   sortiuntur, + -ti - 1199D

f.156vb   damnet, + -lt - 1200A
```

inligandis, +inza- - 1200A

ipsa, + -pun - 1200B

f.157ra damnat, + -t - 1200B

quadriduani, +des- - 1200C

f.157vb alia, §+an-ru - 1201B

f.158vb absorbebit, §+ -tit - 1202B

influat, §+in- - 1202B

defluit, §+ -it - 1202B

f.159ra absorbuit, §+ -slant - 1202C

f.159vb usum, + -niu - 1203A

sollicita, + -..temo - 1203B

f.161va sponte, + -lih - 1205B

f.162ra ipse, §+ -pa - 1207A

f.163vb ipsi, §+ - piu - 1207D

f.164rb expediat, §+ -pit - 1208B

petitur, §+s- - 1208B

f.167ra rogatur, §+pi- - 1211B

f.168va sit, §+s- -1213A

adipisci, + -san - 1213A

f.169ra post pauca, §+diu iu- -1213D

f.170rb concupiscendas, §+ -nt - 1215A

est, §+ -u -1215A

f.173ra senitum, §+ -nis - 1218C

f.173va saliens, + -ton - 1219A

f.173vb manifestata, §+ -tiu - 1219B

f.174va sui, §+ -ro - 1220B

f.175rb operatur, §+ -it - 1221B

f.175va recedit, §+ -leit - 1221C

exorantes, + -nte - 1221D

f.176rb oculto, §+ -iu - 1222B

f.179vb aduersariis, §+ -tun - 1226B

```
f.181rb    est, + -u - 1228B

f.182ra    inspirata, §+in-niu - 1229A

f.182rb    occasionem, §+ -si - 1229B

f.182va    hoc, + -mo - 1229C

f.182vb    succumbit, §+u- - 1231A

f.184vb    corpus, §+ -mun - 1232A

f.185va    uite, §+pe - 1232C

           enutrite, §+ -mo - 1232C

f.188ra    increpat, §+ -sit - 1235C

f.188rb    tanta, §+ -riu - 1236A

f.189ra    gloriam, §+ -iu - 1237A

f.192rb    paradigma, §+ra- - 1241A

           interrogatur, §+u- - 1241A

           conuincitur, §+u- - 1241B

f.192vb    illud, §+ -un - 1241D

f.193rb    inclinemur, §+pi-.. - 1242B

f.193vb    torpescat, +un- - 1242D

f.194ra    nos, §+uns - 1243A

f.194rb    sponse, + -ti - 1243B

f.194vb    consumantur, §+un- - 1243C

f.198va    sua, §+si- - 1248A

f.199rb    quaelibet, §+ -iu - 1248C

f.200vb    quae, §+ -s - 1250A

f.203rb    inflammare, §+pi- - 1252C

f.204vb    superiora, §+ -rum - 1254B

f.209rb    inferior, §+ni- - 1258C

f.210ra    tardior, §+ -ra - 1259B

f.210vb    ultionis, §+ -ti - 1260B

           dileximus, §+ -tun - 1260B

f.211ra    confundunt, §+cahon- - 1260C

f.213rb    uictoris, + -nin - 1263A
```
61

```
f.213va   ueniens, §+ -tiu - 1263B

f.213vb   nos, +sih - 1263B

          nos, §+ -s - 1263B

f.215ra   exerceri, §+ -sa - 1264C

f.216va   extra, +uz- - 1266C

f.217ra   deuenerunt, §+p- - 1267A

f.217rb   extremo, + -gi - 1267B

f.217va   audiant, + -on - 1267C

f.217vb   largiri, + -pan - 1267D

f.218ra   excusantium, §+int- - 1268B

f.218va   sciens, §+ -tau - 1268C

          ignarus, §+ -ra - 1268C

f.220ra   sui, §+si- - 1270B

f.221ra   proponunt, +fu- - 1271B

          litora, §+ -dun - 1271B

f.221va   hoc, §+ -su - 1271C

f.221vb   nascatur, §+si- - 1272A

f.222rb   uoluerit, §+ -s - 1272C

f.222va   praeuentione, §+pi- - 1272D

f.224ra   fractione, §+ -u - 1274B

          mala, §+ -pile - 1274C

          animo, §+ -tot - 1274C

f.224va   comparata, §+uui- - 1275A

          aeterne uite, + -s -s - 1274B

          ipse, §+ -po - 1274B

f.226rb   hoc, §+ -sa -1277A

f.226vb   comparatio, §+ -mez - 1277C

          conputat, §+ -ut - 1277C

          aduersa, + -ri - 1277D

f.227ra   quod, §+ -iu - 1277D

f.227rb   comparatio, §+ -mez - 1278B
```
62

f.228ra   mactemus, §+sle- - 1278D

eius, + -mo - 1278D

hec, §+ -su - 1278A

f.228rb   reuogare, §+uui- - 1279B

f.228va   reuersus, §+uu- - 1279B

f.229ra   facta, §+ -naz - 1280A

f.229rb   testes, §+ur-di - 1280B

magne, §+ -ru - 1280B

f.229vb   oblata, +pru- - 1281A

f.230ra   uniri, + -chon - 1281A

f.230rb   cottidianae, §+ -u - 1281B

f.231ra   sibi, §+ -un - 1282B

f.233ra   grauius, §+ -mira - 1284D

respuant, §+ -t - 1284D

f.233rb   omne, §+ -u - 1285A

f.234va   acuminis, §+ -si - 1286D

f.234vb   mensuram, §+gi- - 1287A

f.235rb   fide, §+ -pu - 1287C

f.236ra   speciem, §+ -ni - 1288C

f.236rb   relinquat, +pi- - 1288D

inherens, §+ -tiu - 1288D

contemplationi, §+ -u - 1288D

f.236vb   aduersitatem, §+uui- - 1289A

haec, §+ -s - 1286B

f.237ra   non, §+n- - 1289C

f.237vb   malorum, + -ru - 1290B

f.238vb   hac, §+ -s - 1291C

f.239ra   intenderet, §+ -ta - 1291C

camelorum, §+ol-no - 1291D

uiuens, +l-§s - 1291D

f.239rb   putoris, + -ma - 1292A

63

f.239va   perterruit, §+ -ta - 1292B

f.239vb   est, §+ -u - 1292C

           cultus, §+pi- - 1292C

f.240ra   ininguine, §+ -si - 1292D

f.241va   qua, + -iu - 1294D

f.241vb   ipso, + -p - 1295A

f.245ra   praeualent, §+ -esun - 1298D

f.245va   iure, §+ -du - 1299C

f.247ra   exhalantibus, §+ -in - 1301B

f.247vb   figuraliter, §+pi- - 1302C

f.253ra   animum, + -te - 1309A

           pictura, + -lo - 1309A

f.253va   mandatis, + -ho - 1309C

Die Griffelglossen zu den folgenden lat. Worten konnte
ich nicht lesen:

f.20vb	uexatum		aditum
f.45vb	ab		uitalis
f.55ra	edomate	f.75rb	fasce
f.56ra	que	f.77ra	haec
f.58ra	aut	f.83ra	duos
	impinguet	f.85ra	alius
f.59ra	capere	f.88ra	stipendium
f.60ra	subsanabo	f.89ra	sumentes
	aduenerit	f.90ra	sordescat
f.66ra	timebatis		contendimus
f.66rb	urgent		que
f.67rb	pastor	f.90rb	labantur
f.69va	debeamus	f.90va	conponunt
f.74vb	inportunis		praeceptis

64

f.92rb	custodiri	f.146ra	euoluitur
	zelus		studio
f.93ra	priuantur		utcumque
f.93vb	uocamur	f.146rb	conuiuium
f.94ra	dum	f.146va	dissipant
f.94va	humiliter	f.146vb	ueridica
f.94vb	quelibet		transire
f.98va	estimatio	f.147ra	roborat
f.100ra	uirtute	f.147va	in re
f.101rb	minatur	f.149ra	speciem
f.102ra	reseruat	f.150rb	sui
f.107va	que	f.150rb	dicit
	centro sol	f.151ra	aeternitate
f.108ra	zelo		comprehenditur
f.113vb	susceptorem		illud
	toleramur	f.155rb	possit
f.120ra	conuenitur	f.155va	monstratur
f.122ra	susceptione	f.155vb	peruenire
f.124ra	nature		diligere
f.127va	misericordia	f.156ra	effusione
f.128ra	quam	f.156rb	gratia
	quantitas	f.156va	moderamina
f.140vb	studia		fiet
f.141vb	amabant	f.157va	ammouere
f.143rb	citius	f.158vb	liquore
	hoc		recurrit
f.143va	pensetur	f.159ra	uentrem
f.144rb	capiuntur	f.159rb	discordat
f.145rb	iteratur		festiua
f.145vb	refectionem		festis
			perducamur

f.159va	ergo	f.177rb	cognitationem
	perfruatur	f.179va	agitur
f.159vb	aduersario		quod
	sollicita		inlustrat
f.161va	adsequuntur		inmutat
f.163ra	ipse notitia	f.179vb	succumbebant
f.163vb	qui	f.180ra	uiuificantes
	summant	f.180rb	usum
f.167ra	ubi		sole
f.167rb	iussu	f.180vb	iuxta
f.168rb	ipso	f.182va	peruerso
f.168va	uideretur		potente
f.169rb	caelum	f.183ra	tangitur
	ascendat	f.183rb	quia
	corporaliter		senarius
f.169vb	increpata	f.187ra	nonnum
f.170va	ut	f.187va	ut
	inrigatio	f.188rb	professores
	cessabit		probationem
f.171ra	communia	f.189ra	uideant
f.171va	declamauit		subeunde
f.172ra	incrementa	f.189rb	praesumatur
	memoratus	f.189va	constatisset
	credentibus	f.190ra	illius
f.172rb	describit	f.190rb	neglegentes
f.173ra	ignorauit	f.191va	conterens
f.174va	sonitu	f.191vb	tenuiter
	permutauit	f.192ra	censura
f.175ra	ac	f.192va	incendit
f.176rb	ab imo	f.193va	superfluunt
f.176vb	ardet		utcumque

f.193vb	indigentia	f.219vb	delectuntur
f.194ra	ostendatur	f.220rb	dum
f.194rb	continuo	f.220vb	compelluntur
	per amorem	f.222va	respiciatur
f.195ra	temperate	f.222vb	reliquum
f.196rb	quanto	f.223vb	patebant
f.197rb	flagrat	f.224ra	illic
f.201ra	similius	f.224va	felicitati
f.203ra	deum		corruptionis
	flamma	f.224vb	hec
f.204rb	uos		audita
f.204va	deterius	f.225ra	dum
f.204vb	foras	f.225rb	nescianis
f.205ra	centena	f.226ra	affectibus
f.208vb	exploraret	f.226rb	gemunt
f.209ra	adiungens	f.228rb	captiuitate
f.209va	prebet	f.228va	oblate
f.210ra	aliud		consideratione
f.210va	perturbationis		omnipotenti domino
	tempestates	f.229rb	relaturus
f.211ra	praedicuntur	f.229vb	attigit
	conuersum	f.231ra	caene
f.213ra	exhibeant		memoratur
f.214vb	quando	f.233ra	caro
	ecclesiastica	f.233rb	mortiferum
f.215rb	proruat	f.234va	attestatur
f.216vb	inaediae	f.234vb	superius
f.217ra	excusare	f.235ra	seruantur
	conuiuium	f.236ra	uestibulum
f.219va	eligantur	f.237va	prociantur

67

f.238va	detrimenta	f.243vb	inexamine
f.238vb	res	f.245ra	ueniant
f.239ra	spes	f.247ra	infra
f.239rb	effectu	f.247vb	allegoricum
f.239va	existeret	f.249vb	illo
f.240ra	praemortuum		
	anhelebat		iuste
f.240va	habitus	f.252vb	supplicium
f.243ra	deceptoriis	f.253ra	aspectum
	fouent	f.253va	refectionis

◧

Clm 4557: Ambrosius, Expositio in Evangelium secundum Lucam.

Benediktbeuren (Deutschland), 12.Jh., 194 Bl.

Lit.: R.Bergmann 480.

Glossen: 1 ahd. Interlinearglosse von einer Hand des 12.Jh.

Text: J.-P.Migne, PL 15 (1887),1607ff.

f.135v   nocticorax, natprab - 1838A

◧

Clm: 4564: Alanus, Homiliarum, pars hiemalis.
Benediktbeuren (Umkreis von Benediktbeuren, Kochel?),
1.Drittel des 9.Jh., 247 Bl.

Lit.: R.Bergmann 482.

Glossen: 1 ahd. Interlinearglosse von einer Hand des

11. oder 12.Jh. zur XXVII. Predigt Leos des Großen.

Text: J.-P.Migne, PL 54,216ff.

f.43v   inseruit, inflaht - 218A

▣

Clm 4613: Heimo, Expositio super Cantica Canticorum (f.1r-
56v); Gregorius Magnus, Expositio super Cantica Canticorum (f.57r-121r).
Benediktbeuren (), 2.Hälfte des 11.Jh., 122 Bl.

Lit.: R.Bergmann 487.
Paul Ruf, Mittelalterliche Bibliothekskataloge Deutsch-
lands und der Schweiz III,1 (München,1932), S.64.

Glossen: 3 ahd. Interlinearglossen von einer Hand der
2.Hälfte des 11.Jh.

Text: J.-P.Migne, PL 117,295ff.; PL 79,471ff.

f.6r   tygna, wintpege [wintperege] - PL 117,301C
f.10r   putacionis, wintunon - PL 117,306B
f.82r   putacionis, wintunon - PL 79,498D

▣

Clm 5255: Paterius, Liber testimoniorum.
Chiemsee (Aachen), 8.-9. oder Anfang 9.Jh., 169 Bl.

Lit.: R.Bergmann 494.

Glossen: 1 ahd. Marginalglosse von einer Hand des 9.Jh.

Text: J.-P.Migne, PL 79,683ff.

69

f.55v   (fusiles), kagoz - 742B

□

Clm 6220: Libri regum.
Freising (), 9.Jh., 229 Bl.

Lit.: R.Bergmann 501.

Glossen: 1 interlineare ahd. Griffelglosse und 6 interlineare und marginale ahd. Federglossen, von denen eine
(a) sehr schwach geschrieben und deshalb nicht datiert
ist. Die anderen (b) stammen von einer Hand des 10.Jh.

f.20r   viri, man (a) - I,5,12
f.29v   contendam, +strit - I,12,7
f.116r   unde iratus dominus tradidit, pidiu arpolganer
         der trohtin salta (b) - Kapitelüberschrift
f.123v   cerethei, incneehta (b) - III,1,44
f.139r   (scutras), cu...hamâr (b) - III,7,45
         (in argillosam), in leimigero (b) - III,7,46
f.139v   (forcipes aureos), cu...canga (b) - III,7,49

□

Clm 6238: Sedulius Scotus, Collectanea in omnes B.Pauli
Epistolas.
Freising (süddeutsch), 10.Jh., 76 Bl.

Lit.: R.Bergmann 507.
H.Frede, Pelagius, Der irische Paulustext Sedulius Scotus (Freiburg,1961), S.99f.

Glossen: 1 ahd. Interlinearglosse der Texthand.

Text: J.-P.Migne, PL 103,9ff.

f.29v   contuli, redota - 183D

◻

Clm 6250: Isidorus, Etymologiae.

Freising (), 1.Hälfte des 9.Jh., 280 Bl.

Lit.: R.Bergmann 511.

Glossen: 4 ahd. Interlinearglossen von zwei Händen des
10.Jh.

Text: J.-P.Migne, PL 82,73ff.

f.163v   pelliciendo, spananto (a) - 390C
f.186r   glires, pilihmus (a) - 441A
f.191v   ocimi, .i.morhes (a) - 452B
f.218v   a qua, fonna dero (b) - 530A

◻

Clm 6260: Hrabanus Maurus, Commentarius in Genesim.

Freising (), 2.Hälfte des 9.Jh., 158 Bl.

Lit.: R.Bergmann 513.

Glossen: 1 ahd. Interlinearglosse von einer Hand des
9.Jh.

Text: J.-P.Migne, PL 107,439ff.

f.2v   (machina), giruste - 442C

◻

71

Clm 6263: Gregorius Magnus, Homiliae in Evangelia.
Freising (), 1.Hälfte des 9.Jh., 209 Bl.

Lit.: R.Bergmann 514.

Glossen: Interlineare und marginale ahd. Federglossen von einer Hand des 9.Jh. und interlineare ahd. Griffelglossen.

Text: J.-P.Migne, PL 76,1075ff.

f.2v   quam modo, +die nu - 1077C

f.3r   exhibitio, +ar.ugida - 1078C

f.8r   imitemur, +pnlidomen - 1084C

f.9r   cui (dux) suus, +demo sin - 1085D

f.10v · ne si quem, +das upi si ueliho - 1087C

f.13v   concessa, +glassanem - 1091B

f.14v   si quando, +upi uenne - 1092B

f.15r   minarum asperitatibus, +droono arendin - 1093A

f.18v   aspere inuectionis, +affu - 1097B

f.61r   praeceps, gahi - 1144C

          turbata, zornigiu - 1144C

f.99r   (euoluitur), erg& [erget] - 1187C

          (non retundit), neruuentot - 1187C

f.178v   (fete), melche - 1276C

f.191v   amitae meae, minero pasun [Glosse interlinear
          und marginal] - 1291B

◩

Clm 6276: Pseudo-Hieronymus, Breviarium in psalmos CI-CL.
Freising (südbayerisch), 8.-9.Jh., 211 Bl.

Lit.: R.Bergmann 517.

Glossen: 2 ahd. Interlinearglossen von einer Hand des
10.Jh.

Text: J.-P.Migne, PL 26 (1884),1194ff.

f.1r   domine, trotin - 1194C
f.143v   apud fratres, sam& den prudarun [samet] - 1298C

◘

Clm 6281: Grammatische Sammelhandschrift,u.a. Priscianus,
Instituto de nomine et pronomine et verbo (f.63r-71v).
Freising (), 9.Jh., 126 Bl.

Lit.: R.Bergmann 519.

Glossen:1 ahd. Interlinearglosse von einer Hand des 10.Jh.

Text: H.Keil, Grammatici latini III (Leipzig,1859), S.443ff.

f.64r   cognominatim, namalicho - S.444,30

◘

Clm 6283: Augustinus, Enchiridion de fide, spe et cari-
tate.
Freising (Fulda oder Mainz), 2.Viertel des 9.Jh., 45 Bl.

Lit.: R.Bergmann 520.

Glossen: 1 ahd. Interlinearglosse von einer Hand der
2.Hälfte des 9.Jh.

Text: J.-P.Migne, PL 40,231ff.

f.8v   quatinus, that - 239

Clm 6300: Gregorius Magnus, Moralia in Job, libri II-V.
Freising (Oberitalien?), 2.Hälfte des 8.Jh., 158 Bl.

Lit.: R.Bergmann 523.

Glossen: Die Handschrift enthält rund 200 interlineare
ahd. Griffelglossen, von denen ich gegen 150 lesen konnte.

Text: J.-P.Migne, PL 75,553ff.

f.2ra   inlicito, +unarlaupit - 591C
f.4va   ualidius, +starchor - 593C
             uastamur, +pirumahariot - 593C
             maturius, +riflihhor - 593C
f.7va   inlicitas, +unarlaupit - 595C
f.14vb   crimen, +suntha - 601C
f.17ra   fictile, +laiminum - 603C
f.18va   per exhibitam, +...den fargepanun - 604D
f.19ra   atque, +anti - 605B
f.19va   blandiens, +flehonti - 605C
f.19vb   pignorum, +dero chindo - 605D
f.22va   munimine, +mittero krafti - 608C
f.22vb   reticuit, +katagata - 608D
             studuit, +ilata - 608D
f.23ra   condicto, +den rat - 609A
f.34ra   inliciunt, +scuntent - 618C
f.34va   blandis, +lobanti - 619A
f.38rb   curiositatis, +dera piuuortnissa - 622B
f.38vb   foeditatem, +unsuparnissa - 622C
f.38vb   nitor, +scimo - 622D
f.39ra   exuritur, +inzunta - 623A

74

```
f.39va    hilarescit, +plidit - 623B

f.39vb    altercatione, +strit - 623C

          recte, +reht - 623D

f.41va    cum, +mittero - 625B

f.43vb    differt, +undarsceit - 626D

          scelestius, +unrehtira - 626D

f.44ra    incongrue, +unkalimflihemo - 627A

f.44rb    praepeditur, +zakamarren.e - 627B

          inopinatus, +unkauuanit - 627B

          retenendo, +habanto - 627B

f.46ra    rennuat, +furisakata - 628D

f.46vb    fastigia, +hohmoti - 629C

f.47vb    conficit, +kaqu..hitit - 630C

f.48va    censura, +diu stranka - 631A

f.48vb    munit, +festinot - 631B

f.52va    reatu, +fona deru sculdo - 635B

f.53rb    inhiant, +katunent - 635D

f.54ra    fecundata, +peranti - 636C

f.56vb    incongruum, +untaristic - 638B

f.57ra    emanauit, +arspar.. - 638C

f.59vb    solemus, +kauuonemes - 640A

f.60va    essentia, +eouuesanti - 640D

f.60vb    calamitatum, +dera armida - 641A

f.61va    fictis, +kalihet - 641C

f.61vb    ingenite, +unkaporan - 642A

f.64rb    mancipatur, +kahaftit - 644B

f.66ra    augere, +kaauh... - 645C

f.69ra    incassum, +inkameitun - 647D

f.69rb    arrogantes, +romanti - 648C

f.72vb    lamenta, +uuof - 651B
```

f.75vb	perstrepit, +sturmta - 654A	
	anxietas, +angust - 654A	
	salubriter, +heilantliho - 654A	
f.76ra	incorrectis, +unkaret - 654B	
f.76rb	reluctatur, +uuidarot - 654C	
f.76va	serene, +stilli - 654D	
f.77rb	adminicula, +folla... - 656C	
f.78va	reniti, +uuidoron - 657C	
	iure, +mit kauualti - 657C	
f.79ra	renitentes, +uuidoronti - 658B	
f.81ra	contemplandum, +scauuo... - 660B	
f.81va	inrogauit, +raihta - 660C	
f.82va	disiungitur, +arsceitan - 661C	
f.83va	adminiculis, +za helphon - 662C	
f.83vb	praecipitiis mersum sit, +mitte... pisantit - 662C	
f.85rb	intercipit, +untarfeng - 664A	
f.85va	ad audaciam, +diu katurst - 664B	
f.85vb	qua perfrui (quiete) potuisset, +desero pruhan scal - 664B	
f.88ra	remotioribus, +suntritem - 666B	
	intercessio mediatoris, +uuegon sonentes - 666B	
f.88va	reges, +karathi - 666D	
f.88vb	scemata, +kalihnissa - 667A	
f.89ra	dominio, +mittero kauualtidu - 667B	
f.89rb	iure, +mittero kauualtidu - 667B	
f.89vb	stipatus, +kaspriuzit - 668A	
f.90ra	fingit, +fotot - 668A	
	carere pertimescit, +anauuese furhtit - 668A	
f.90vb	perfruuntur, +pruhhant - 668C	
	tumultus, +unkareh - 668C	
	incompetens, +unkaristic - 668D	

76

f.91vb   comminatio, +drahunc - 668C

          terrificant, +furtent - 669C

f.93vb   primordio, +fona erist - 671C

f.94ra   caligantibus, +finstreta - 671D

f.94rb   clementer, +erhaftlicho, -672A

          edomuit, +kazamot - 672A

          fecundus, peranti - 672A

f.96ra   fessi, +modi - 674B

f.97va   marceat, +ardorret - 674B

f.97vb   non localis, +nalles statlih - 674C

f.98vb   refectionibus, +...azun - 675B

          adiumentum, +helph. - 675C

f.98vb   interimat, +arslahit - 675C

f.99rb   obligatione, +...nissa - 676A

          prepedimur, +kamarritet - 676A

          iure, +kauualtidu - 676A

f.100ra   decptionis, +...nissa - 676C

          contempnunt, +farmanent - 676D

          replicat, +arsaget - 676D

f.101rb   uenia, +fargepanissa - 678A

          ereptum, +kanaritan - 678B

f.101va   uenia, +dio fargepanissa - 678B

f.101vb   sine lesione, +ana scadun - 678C

f.102va   posterum, +aftero - 679B

f.103rb   liberior, +fri..ro - 679D

          clandistina, +pihalita - 680B

f.104va   extraneus, +framadi - 681B

f.105rb   uicissim, +untarhim - 682A

f.106rb   detrimenta, +uuopunga - 682C

          lucra, +kastraun - 682C

f.110ra   placari, +uueton - 685B

77

```
f.111ra   torpore, +...nissu - 686B

          uegitata, +kapareta - 686B

f.112ra   praepedita, +marrta - 687B

          retardatur, +ist kalazzit - 687B

f.112rb   uerebar, +ahteta - 687B

f.117va   erudiret, +piruhit - 691C

f.117vb   reprehenda sunt, +kalastrone sint - 691C

f.119ra   per triennium, +durh triu iar - 692D

f.121ra   delibetur, +ist gadiunet - 694B

f.122ra   dissidunt, +unkalihun - 695A

          grauitate, +kraftnissa - 695B

f.122va   origo, +anagin - 695C

f.130rb   saeuissimo, +grimmosto - 701C

f.131va   inprouisus, +ungauuar - 7L2C

          necat, +arslahit - 702C

f.131vb   praesumptione, +katurst - 702D

f.132ra   ereptus, +kanarit - 703B

f.132vb   susurii, +dera runizura - 703D

f.133ra   rimas, +rinnun - 704A

f.133vb   imago, +kalihnissi - 704D

          imaginaliter fingunt, +daz kamalet ist - 705A

f.134ra   didicissent, +kalirnetum - 705A

f.134va   specialiter arrogunt, +suntrigo kepont - 705C

f.136ra   per rimas, +durh deo rinnun - 707A

f.136va   emanat, +uuallet - 707B

f.138ra   innixum, +helfe - 708D

f.138vb   exercentur, +pika..assent - 709B

f.144va   deprehendi, +...rasgta - 714B

f.145rb   inopiam nostram immaniter, +unsero durftti.nissa
          drato - 715B

          lippientibus, +suraucun - 715B
```

78

f.147ra   obstaculo, +dera uuidarstantnissa - 716C

f.149va   detrimenta, +dera uuanunga - 719B

f.149vb   gemat, +amarot - 719B

f.150vb   adipisci, +gezzan - 720D

Die Griffelglossen zu den folgenden lat. Worten konnte
ich nicht lesen:

f.3ra	marcescit	f.82vb	utero
f.5rb	incolumitate	f.91va	incolatus
f.9ra	conpetenter		prolongatus
f.18ra	tamen		largitatem
f.19vb	damna	f.91vb	experimentum
f.21vb	atteritur	f.98vb	extenuatum
f.34va	censentur	f.105vb	indesinenter
	uero	f.110ra	fallantur
f.38ra	alligationibus		pestis
f.38va	saporis	f.115va	uenandi
	studiosus	f.119ra	dicenda
	decor	f.120ra	cassantur
f.38ra	concorditer	f.122va	propinatur
f.39va	experimentum	f.122vb	uacellanter
f.39vb	multa	f.124rb	adtestante
f.40ra	designatur		timore
f.45ra	turpiter	f.128rb	subiungit
f.53rb	spernat	f.129ra	colorem
f.55rb	praeeminent	f.129vb	pauore
f.59vb	liquido	f.130rb	inmanitate
f.62ra	restaurationem	f.134ra	titubant
f.66ra	blande	f.155va	palpitat

79

Clm 6305: Hieronymus, Expositio super Mattheum.
Freising (), 8.-9.Jh., 145 Bl.

Lit.: R.Bergmann 524.

Glossen: Gegen 50 ahd. Griffelglossen, von denen ich etwas
mehr als die Hälfte lesen konnte. Der Glossator ritzt neben
ahd. auch lat. Glossen.

Text: J.-P.Migne, PL 26 (1884),15ff.

f.2r   legationibus, +kapota - 19A
f.3r   spatio, +srini - 20C
         compensare, +kalan - 20C
f.6r   consequenter, +adalliho - 27A
f.7r   necem, +chuualm - 29A
f.8v   sine modo, +flazu essan - 31B
f.9r   deuteronomio, +kauuartaun - 32B
f.9v   iactantia, +hrumliho - 33B
f.10r   consequenter, +zump... - 34A
         paralyticos, +lamu - 34B
         redundarent, +meroen - 34B
         montana, +pirke - 34B
f.10v   simpliciorum, +hiura herzeno - 34C
f.53r   flaccidum, +ualuaz - 93B
f.54r   iecore, +lepero - 94C
f.66v   uerbi gratia, +...piludi des uuortes - 113A
f.84v   fortunam, +casuaft - 140C
f.98v   clauus, +zuecki - 160C
f.103v   stipendiaria, +cisitu - 168A

f.110v mente, +mizza - 178A

aneti, +tilli - 178A

f.117r municipatum, +frumu - 187B

f.137r sanctitum, +pifolhan - 216A

f.139v ferrugineas, +isarntuati - 220A

Die vermutlich ahd. Griffelglossen zu den folgenden lat.
Worten konnte ich nicht lesen:

f.17r	lasciuius	f.66r	perpetem
f.18r	murice		meatus
	iudicare	f.71v	in lecti
f.20r	iactans	f.72v	affectum
f.24r	tropologiam	f.83v	temperat
f.41v	inaediam	f.91v	oleastro
f.49r	deliramenta	f.96r	saeuientibus
f.49v	obscuris	f.97r	promissionem
f.52v	alterum	f.98v	factio
f.55r	dimissis	f.135r	apocryphum
f.64r	propter		

◘

Clm 6308: Paulus Orosius, Historia adversus paganos.
Freising (), Ende des 8.Jh., 149 Bl.

Lit.: R.Bergmann 525.

Glossen: Neben den von Walter Stach (Aus neuen Glossen-
funden 2, PBB 73, 1951, S.347f.) aufgeführten Glossen
1 ahd. Interlinearglosse von einer Hand der 2.Hälfte
des 10.Jh., die zwischen lat. Glossen derselben Hand
steht.

Text: J.-P.Migne, PL 31,665ff.

f.4v   meotidas (auget) paludes, merilihun môs - 673A

◙

Clm 6312: Pseudo-Augustinus, Quaestiones in Vetus et
Novum Testamentum.

Freising (), 9.Jh., 239 Bl.

Lit.: R.Bergmann 526.

Glossen: 3 marginale ahd. Griffelglossen.

Text: J.-P.Migne, PL 35,2215ff.

f.32r   (praestigium), +pitroc - 2233
f.81r   +foraquad [die Glosse steht am oberen Rand
          über diffidentia] - 2270
f.83r   (occasionem), +cafori - 2272

◙

Clm 6381: Eusebius, Historia ecclesiastica a Rufino trans-
lata.

Freising (Benediktbeuren), 9.Jh., 250 Bl.

Lit.: R.Bergmann 533.

Glossen: 1 sehr schwach mit Feder geschriebene ahd. Interlinearglosse.

Text: Eusebius, Werke II,1, hrsg. von E.Schwartz und Th.
Mommsen, (Leipzig,1903).

f.16r aeditui, custeres - S.49,17; Historia ecclesiastica I,6,3.

◘

Clm 6433: Sententiae variae patrum (f.24r-48r: Isidorus, Synonyma).

Freising (), 8.-9.Jh., 69 Bl.

Lit.: R.Bergmann 544.

Glossen: 3 interlineare ahd. Griffelglossen, von denen ich eine lesen konnte.

Text: J.-P.Migne, PL 83,825ff.

f.31r repentinum, +unforbuui - 852A

Die beiden Glossen zu f.30v praeuisio, inopinatum konnte ich nicht lesen.

◘

Clm 9673: Vitae patrum.

Oberaltaich (Bayern), Anfang des 12.Jh., 134 Bl.

Lit.: R.Bergmann 553.

Glossen: 1 ahd. Interlinearglosse von einer Hand des 12.Jh. (a) und 1 ahd. Interlinearglosse von einer Hand des 14.Jh. (b); beide zur Vita S.Hilarionis.

f.70v repagula, sloz (a) - 38C

f.78v myoparonibus, .i.scheidon (b) - 51C

□

Clm 13024: Augustinus, De civitate Dei.

Regensburg, Stadtbibliothek (Regensburg, St.Emmeram),

Anfang des 11.Jh., 255 Bl.

Lit.: -

Glossen: 1 ahd. Interlinearglosse von einer Hand des

11.Jh.

Text: J.-P.Migne, PL 41,13ff.

f.1v   succesent, vizzint - 16

□

Clm 13084: Alcuin, De rhetorica (f.1r-47v); Ars geo-

metrica (f.48r-69v); Hyginus, De astronomia (f.70rff.)

Regensburg, Stadtbibliothek (Freising), kurz nach der

Mitte des 9.Jh., 91 Bl.

Lit.: R.Bergmann 561.

Glossen: 1 ahd. Interlinearglosse von der Texthand zur

Ars geometrica.

Text: -

f.50v   auraturas, cospon

□

Clm 14018: Pentateuch, Libri Josuae, Judicum, Ruth.
Regensburg, St.Emmeram (), 2.Hälfte des 11.Jh., 199 Bl.

Lit.: R.Bergmann 564.
Albert Boeckler, Das Stuttgarter Passionale (Augsburg,
1923), S.30.

Glossen: 19 ahd. Interlinearglossen von einer Hand der
2.Hälfte des 11.Jh.

f.51vb   mutiet, vuuinsit - Exodus XI,7
f.62rb   interrasilem, vnterualota - XXV,25
f.62va   hastile, selpoum - XXV,31
          sperulas, scipun - XXV,31
          emunctoria, scarili - XXV,38
f.63ra   incastrature, tubilunga - XXVI,17
f.63rb   bysso retorta, kiziurnitemo - XXVI,31
f.65vb   laganum, platamuos - XXIX,23
f.83ra   sthrutionem, struz - Leviticus XI,16
          larum, mûsari - XI,16
          mergulum, tuchil - XI,17
          atachis, vuuibil - XI,22
f.83rb   migale, mardir - XI,30
          cameleon, harma - XI,30
          stelio, mol - XI,30
          talpa, scero - XI,30
f.84ra   pustula, anchuues.. [1 oder 2 Buchstaben am
          Ende ausradiert] - XIII,2
f.84vb   papularum, anchuueizza - XIV,56
f.111va   abortiuum, uruuerf - Numeri XII,12

◨

85

Clm 14066: Christianus Druthmarus, Expositio in Mattheum.
Regensburg, St.Emmeram (), frühes 11.Jh., 192 Bl.

Lit.: R.Bergmann 565.

B.Bischoff, Mittelalterliche Studien II (Stuttgart,1967),
S.110.

Glossen: 1 ahd. Interlinearglosse von einer Hand des frühen 11.Jh.

Text: J.-P.Migne, PL 106,1261ff.

f.88v   matertere, muama - 1578D

▣

Clm 14253: Clemens Romanus, Recognitiones.
Regensburg, St.Emmeram (), 4.Viertel des 9.Jh., 104 Bl.

Lit.: R.Bergmann 570.

Glossen: Neben den von Bernhard Bischoff und Paul Lehmann
(Nachträge zu den ahd. Glossen, PBB 52, 1928, S.159) aufgeführten Glossen 1 ahd. Interlinearglosse von einer Hand
aus dem 4.Viertel des 9.Jh. oder kurz danach.

Text: Bernhard Rehm, Die Pseudoklementinen II (Berlin,
1965).

f.7v   profligatis, uruuehanan - S.13

▣

Clm 14272: Lehrbücher der artes liberales (f.184ff.:
Priscianus, De constructione).
Regensburg, St.Emmeram (), 11.Jh., 192 Bl.

Lit.: R.Bergmann 571.

G.Swarzenski, Die Regensburger Buchmalerei des X. und
XI. Jahrhunderts (Stuttgart, ^{2}1969), S.56ff.

Glossen: 1 ahd. Interlinearglosse von einer Hand des
11.Jh.

Text: H.Keil, Grammatici latini III (Laipzig,1859),
S.107ff.

f.192r   glis gliris animal, .i.sisemus - im Anschluß
          an S.149,21

□

Clm 14349: Joannes Cassianus, De institutis coenobiorum.
Regensburg, St.Emmeram (), 11.Jh., 98 Bl.

Lit.: R.Bergmann 574.
B.Bischoff, Mittelalterliche Studien II (Stuttgart,1967),
S.109.

Glossen: 3 ahd. Interlinearglossen von einer Hand des
11.Jh.

Text: J.-P.Migne, PL 49,53ff.

f.29r   continentie, dera uuirtipurticheria - 207A
          idonea, ma..u. - 208A
          mansuetudo, mitauara - 208A

◨

Clm 14386: Augustinus, Beda, Gregorius Magnus, Hieronymus etc., Homiliae.
Regensburg, St.Emmeram (Umgebung von Regensburg), 9.Jh.,
247 Bl.

Lit.: R.Bergmann 577.

Glossen: 1 ahd. Marginalglosse von einer Hand des 9.Jh.
zum Sermo Petronii Episcopi Veronensis in natale Sancti
Zenonis.

Text: D.G.Morin, Deux petits discours d'un évêque Petro-
nius, du Ve siècle, Revue Benedictine 14 (1897), S.3ff.

f.32r   (pernicibus), enstritigun - S.4,26

◨

Clm 14388: Ursprünglich zwei selbständige Teile. Teil 2:
Physiologus (f.172r-183v); Glossaria latina (f.184r-f.238v).
Regensburg, St.Emmeram (Teil 2: nordwestdeutsch, Teil 2:
Mitte des 9.Jh., 238 Bl.

Lit.: R.Bergmann 578.

Glossen: 1 ahd. Interlinearglosse von einer Hand der Mitte
des 9.Jh.

Text: -

f.238v   ictus, slac

Clm 14425: Hieronymus, Commentarius in Jeremiam.
Regensburg, St.Emmeram (), 8.-9.Jh., 159 Bl.

Lit.: R.Bergmann 584.

Glossen: Rund 50 lat. und ahd. Griffelglossen. Soweit ich
sehen kann, sind 37 davon ahd., und von diesen konnte ich
27 lesen.

Text: J.-P.Migne, PL 24 (1845),679ff.

f.1v   stamina, +uurf - 679A
          subtemina [subtegmina], +her.. - 679A
          cilcia [licia], +fize - 679A
          disserendam, +sagantiu - 680A
f.2r   pultibus, +prium - 682A
f.4v   corticem, +helu - 685B
f.11r   surculo, +hadun - 693C
f.21r   nouale, +prahi - 709C
f.28r   sustentacula, +spru - 715D
f.32v   chartallum, +zeinun - 723B
f.38v   chrustis, +pretirum - 730A
f.42v   nemorosus, +dicke - 735A
f.51r   saltu, +uual - 747A
f.51v   purpura, +rotaz - 747C
f.78v   arceatur, +si piuert - 781C
f.85v   frustra, +teilpra - 792C
f.87r   iugulata, +quelit - 794D
          elingues, +urprei - 795A
f.90r   deliramenta, +topo - 799B

f.91r   testeum, +dohinat - 800A

nemus, +forst - 800B

tinniant, +taupent - 800C

f.92v   nomen est, +heiz - 802B

f.98v   siliam [silicem], +piloht - 810C

co^hartratam [coarctatam], +pilerit - 810C

f.101r   pingit, +male - 813D

f.103r   suggilat, +rochit - 816B

Die wahrscheinlich ahd. Glossen zu den folgenden lat.
Worten konnte ich nicht lesen:

f.1v	uulgo	f.33v	contestabor
	commentarios	f.64v	inbuatur
f.2r	potissimum	f.65r	digladientur
	stolidissimus	f.102v	inuassanda
f.31v	incrassatus		contignata

◪

Clm 14427: Hincmarus Remensi archiepiscopus, Epistola
ad Carolum Calvum de cavendis vitiis.
Regensburg, St.Emmeram (wohl St.Emmeram), 2.Hälfte des
11.Jh., 135 Bl.

Lit.: R.Bergmann 585.

Glossen: 1 ahd. Interlinearglosse von einer Hand der
2.Hälfte des 11.Jh.

Text: J.-P.Migne, PL 125,857ff.

f.21r   hystriones, spilmanna - 869D

■

Clm 14508: Sammelhandschrift, u.a. Expositiones symboli (f.67r-86v).

Regensburg, St.Emmeram (wohl nördliches Frankreich),
3.Viertel des 9.Jh., 148 Bl.

Lit.: R.Bergmann 595.
Ludwig Hödl, Die Geschichte der scholastischen Lite-
ratur und der Theologie der Schlüsselgewalt (Münster,
1960), S.290.

Glossen: 1 ahd. Interlinearglosse von einer Hand des
10.-11.Jh. zur Expositio symboli "Dum de symbolo con-
ferre."

Text: A.E.Burn, Zur Geschichte des Apostolischen Symbols, Zeitschrift für Kirchengeschichte 19 (1899),
S.186-190.

f.69v   mos est, situ ist - S.189

■

Clm 14614: Alcuinus, Candidus, Gregorius Magnus etc.,
Excerpta.

Regensburg, St.Emmeram, 9.Jh., 280 Bl.

Lit.: R.Bergmann 601.

Glossen: 2 ahd. Interlinearglossen von einer Hand des
10.Jh.

Text: J.-P.Migne, PL 75,687ff.

f.58r   peripsima, capassahi - Einschub in einer Be-
arbeitung von Auszügen aus Gregors des Großen
<u>Moralia</u> <u>in</u> <u>Job</u> (B.Bischoff)

f.60r   perstrepunt, cradamint - 690C

◘

Clm 14717: Priscianus, Excerpta.

Regensburg, St.Emmeram, Anfang des 13.Jh., 217 Bl.

Lit.: R.Bergmann 606.

Glossen: 20 ahd. Interlinearglossen von einer Hand derselben Zeit wie die Handschrift zu einigen der <u>Versus</u>
<u>de</u> <u>piscibus</u>, die auf dem unteren Teil von f.44 einge-
tragen sind.

f.44v   lucius, hecht

tincus, slige

capedo, alt

tricta, vorhe

timallus, asch

allec, hærinc

ballena, vvalir

esox, lahs

anguilla, æl

murena, lamprit

coracinus, rot

rombus, stur

allopida, rubt

scaurus, huse

92

echinus, salme

mullus, nase

smirua, phrise

cluma, pærbe

sarrahilis, gruntil

proca, charpf

◳

Clm 14727: Die Handschrift besteht aus drei ursprünglich selbständigen Codices. Text 3: Theodulfus Aureli-
anensis episcopus, Capitula ad presbyteros parochiae
suae (f.139r-170v).
Regensburg, St.Emmeram, Text 3: Anfang des 9.Jh.,
170 Bl.

Lit.: R.Bergmann 607.

Glossen: 5 interlineare ahd. Griffelglossen, von denen
ich drei lesen konnte.

Text: J.-P.Migne, PL 105,191ff.

f.141v   consecrationem, +...uuiht - 193A
f.144r   crebro, +uuola ofto - 194B
          negotia, +uuandelunga - 194B

Nicht lesen konnte ich die Glossen zu f.144r penitus
und uocabitur.

◳

◘

Clm 18475: Vitae patrum.

Tegernsee (), 3.Viertel des 11.Jh., 228 Bl.

Lit.: R.Bergmann 643.

Christine Eder, Die Schule des Klosters Tegernsee im frühen Mittelalter im Spiegel der Tegernseer Handschriften
(München,1972).

Glossen: 3 ahd. Interlinearglossen von einer Hand des späten 11.Jh.

Text: J.-P.Migne, PL 73,739ff.; PL 23 (1883),29ff.

f.66v   rafanaleonum, merratih - PL 73,871D

f.95r   cicer, arauueza - PL 73,906D

f.179r   myoparonibus, scedan - PL 23 (1883),51C

◘

Clm 18480: Boetius, Categoriae Aristotelis; Boetius, In
categorias Aristotelis; Boetius, De arithmetica; Boetius,
De musica.

Tegernsee (), 3.Fünftel des 11.Jh., 217 Bl.

Lit.: R.Bergmann 644.

Christine Eder, Die Schule des Klosters Tegernsee im frühen Mittelalter im Spiegel der Tegernseer Handschriften
(München,1972).

Glossen: Neben der von E.Steinmeyer gedruckten Federprobe
(IV,249,3) eine ahd. Interlinearglosse von einer Hand der
2.Hälfte des 11.Jh. zu Boethius, De musica.

95

Text: J.-P.Migne, PL 63,1167ff.

f.161r   turbonem, drindila - 1173D

□

Clm 18517b: Hieronymus, Epistolae.

Tegernsee (), 3.Viertel des 11.Jh., 174 Bl.

Lit.: R.Bergmann 645.

Christine Eder, Die Schule des Klosters Tegernsee im frühen Mittelalter im Spiegel der Tegernseer Handschriften
(München,1972), S.111.

Glossen: 5 ahd. Interlinear- und Marginalglossen von einer Hand des späten 11.Jh.

Text: J.-P.Migne, PL 22 (1854),325ff.

f.1r   forcipe, zanga - 370
f.1v   lammina, plech - 361
          funde, slinga - 362
f.23r   (donatiuum), lehan [Lemma am Rand wiederholt] -
          348
f.26r   scabra, rudoga - 354

□

Clm 18549a: Die Handschrift besteht aus zwei ursprünglich
selbständigen Teilen. Teil 1 (f.1-181): Joannes Cassianus,
Collationes, secunda pars; Isidorus, Synonyma; Hieronymus,
Epistolae; Augustinus, De doctrina christiana.

96

Tegernsee (), 2.Viertel des 11.Jh., 227 Bl.

Lit.: R.Bergmann 651.
Christine Eder, Die Schule des Klosters Tegernsee im frü-
hen Mittelalter im Spiegel der Tegernseer Handschriften
(München,1972), S.89.

Glossen: 1 ahd. Interlinearglosse von einer Hand des 11.Jh.
zur XIV. Epistel des hl. Hieronymus.

Text: J.-P.Migne, PL 22 (1854),347ff.

f.119v   donatiuum, lehan - 348

◨

Clm 18550a: Gregorius Magnus, Regula pastoralis.
Tegernsee (), spätes 8.Jh., 156 Bl.

Lit.: R.Bergmann 652.
Christine Eder, Die Schule des Klosters Tegernsee im frü-
hen Mittelalter im Spiegel der Tegernseer Handschriften
(München,1972), S.17.

Glossen: Zusätzlich zu den von E.Steinmeyer (II,218,5ff.)
gedruckten Glossen marginale Federglossen und marginale
und interlineare Griffelglossen neben einigen Korrekturen
zu E.Steinmeyer, die durch die Verwendung einer Ultraviolettlampe ermöglicht wurden.

Text: J.-P.Migne, PL 77,13ff.

f.4v   (accessus), cank - 13B
f.5v   (speciem), hluta... - 14B
f.6r   detestatur, +leidot - 15A
f.7r   (extenditur), preit... - 16A

f.8v   caruit, +firmisit - 17B

f.9r   (multa), .i.filo - 17C

f.10r   (saeueritate), hartnissidu [statt St.II,218,11
          uartnissidu] - 18C

f.11r   imponatur, +pifolan vuerda - 19B

f.12r   (prebuit), arpot [statt St.II,218,26 a..pot] -
          20B

f.12v   (utrobique), +za enga pedaru - 20D

f.14v   suppetit, +kihalot - 22B

f.17r   albuginem, +hovisalgise - 24A

f.19r   scabiem, +riupi - 25C

f.20v   (necesse est), pisit [statt St.II,218,42 risit]
          - 26D

f.29r   excedimus, +...gilidan - 33A

f.39r   aliquando, +sumanes - 41A

f.41v   (rigidae), starho - 43A
          (improbe), unpisu..o - 43B

f.61v   incestus, +unm..nt - 53C

f.72v   (intendat), +drouuidta - 66A

f.79r   (stagnum), cin 71A
          (ferrum), isarn - 71A
          (plumbum), pli - 71A
          stagnum, +cin - 71A

f.86r   protextu, +firterchineti - 76C

f.87v   resiliunt, +stalgepant - 77D

f.95r   contineri, +generit - 83C

f.140r   mentam, +minzun - 117A
          anetum, +tilli - 117A
          cyminum, +chumi - 117A

f.143r   dissipantis, +ziuerfentes - 118D

f.143v   fiduciam, +kara..a - 119B

Clm 18556a: Joannes Cassianus, Collationes, pars tertia.
Tegernsee (), um 1000, 213 Bl.

Lit.: R.Bergmann 653.
Christine Eder, Die Schule des Klosters Tegernsee im frü-
hen Mittelalter im Spiegel der Tegernseer Handschriften
(München,1972), S.29ff.

Glossen: Rund 350 lat. und ahd. Griffelglossen. Soweit ich
dies entscheiden konnte, sind gegen 145 der Glossen ahd.,
und von diesen konnte ich etwas mehr als 100 lesen.

Text: J.-P.Migne, PL 49,557ff.

f.11v	deterrimum, +fressuno	- 1102B
f.14v	conlabuntur, +pifa...	- 1106B
f.17v	incederet, +anamornot	- 1112A
f.19r	fulcitur, +holfun vuirdit	- 1113A
f.20r	pendula, +hagent..	- 1113C
f.21r	occasiones, +antsaga	- 1114B
f.26v	lineas, +spratvn	- 1117C
f.28v	secularium, +schaminv̄ [schaminvn]	- 1120A
f.31	uiuidum, +lepentes	- 1124A
f.34v	ferculum paulo susceptum, +dahtan scuzilla - 1127A	
f.36r	commendabat, +gilivpta	- nicht bei Migne
f.36v	iactantie, +upmuotes [upermuotes]	- 1129B
f.37r	coenodoxie, +uanede	- 1130A
f.45r	inmaturo, +vnzi	- 1141A
	impulerit, +anastoz	- 1141A

f.45v	eius ipsius, +dero selpvn - 1141A	
	tenuiter, +luzil - 1141B	
f.46r	(intempestiue), +vnzitliho - 1141B	
f.46v	(propacimente), +frazillihemo - 1141C	
f.47v	titillatione, +chizilongo - 1142B	
f.48r	argumenta, +pilidi - 1142C	
f.49r	instrumenta, +vuarnunga - 1143B	
f.50r	censor, +vrteilari - 1143C	
f.50v	apparatum, +giziv - 1144B	
f.58v	incuriosa, +ungivuaroliho - 1152B	
f.62r	defixo, +vuontin - 1157A	
f.66r	ignauia, +slafi - 1163B	
f.71v	circumspectione, +vuarnungo - 1169A	
	non magne proderit, +...mihiles ..rdes - 1170A	
f.75v	prouehitur, +gifurdrot vuare - 1171A	
	censuerit, +ahtoti - 1171A	
f.83r	definitione, +pimeinido - 1180A	
f.83v	(adscribendum), +pizellanno - 1180B	
f.85v	(tandem), +..tavuenni - 1181C	
f.86r	(ingeritur), +zuopraht vuirdit - 1182A	
f.86v	(definitionis), +sceitunga - 1182B	
	executionem, +fulatati - 1182B	
f.87v	(censuram), +gidvinc - 1183A	
f.92v	(fotum), +zuht - 1189C	
	(refectionem), +pisorgida - 1189C	
	(inconditus), +ungilimfliher - 1189C	
f.103v	tuemur, +piscirmen - nicht bei Migne	
f.104v	promulgata, +gimareiz - 1200B	
f.110v	(legali), +gisezido - 1209A	
f.111v	uim, +chraft - 1210A	
	(dicimus), +sagun - 1210A	

100

f.114v   (abiget), +...vuerti - 1213A

f.116v   (illa ipsa), +de. selpun - 1214C

f.118r   pertulisse, +insezit vuerden - 1215C

f.122r   (procrastinare), +leng..n - 1217B

f.122v   (obsceni), +unchiuskin - 1218B

f.123r   (inerti), +tragero - 1219A

f.125r   diriore, +grimmirin - 1221A

f.126v   conuenientes, +manonta - 1223B

f.130v   (medullitus), +invuertiges - 1222A

f.139v   collidetur, +nipichnussa... [Glosse auf dem
          unteren Rand] - 1239A

f.142r   stationis, +lenti - 1242B

f.144v   (aucupantes), +...enta - 1244A

f.146v   (abiectis), +fermanoten - 1246B

f.147r   conlatione, +...darmezzunga - 1246C

f.152r   numerositate, +mit manecfalti - 1251C
          transcenderat, +upsteic [upersteic] - 1251C
          diuelli, +gisceidan - 1252A

f.153r   potissimum, +pezisti - 1252C

f.153v   (uersutus), +hintscrenchiga [hintarscrenchiga] -
          1253B

f.155r   pendemus, +ginaemes - 1255A
          prosecutione, +sago - 1255A

f.155v   improbe, +vpiles - 1256A
          recessibus, +gisvasun - 1256A

f.158v   moliuntur, +mahont - 1259B
          basis, +stafal - 1259B

f.161r   arcet, +pivuerit - 1263A
          exceptione, +uzginomani - 1264A

f.162r   uersutus, +hintscrenichigo [hintarscrenichigo] -
          1266A

101

f.162v   ingenitam, +anapurtigemo - 1266A

f.163r   addictum, +pimaintun - 1267B

f.165r   opinio, +vvan, +ahtunga - 1270A

f.167r   (mediocribus), +niderorun - 1272A

f.173v   (denotat), +zeihnit - 1277B

f.175v   uentilata, +ars... - 1280A

f.178v   compendia, gifuori, commoda - 1283B

f.183r   acedia, +zurlusti - 1294A

f.183v   releuationem, +p.lihti - 1294B

          strenue, +frautliho - 1294B

f.184r   molitionem, +manungo - 1295A

f.189v   effebum, +iungeling [Glosse am unteren Rand] -
          nicht bei Migne

f.197v   perstruentes, +mahonta - 1308B

f.198r   norat, +vueiz - 1309A

          opinatus, +ahtont - 1309A

f.198v   coniecturam, +scvntvngo - 1309B

          opinatione, +vuane - 1309B

f.200v   inretitum, +zuoq̄mn [zuoquoman] - 1311A

          respirare, +zuogizispilen - 1311A

          trica +vualza [beide Worte am oberen Rand] -
          nicht bei Migne

          censura, +gidvinc - 1312A

f.201r   laxamentis, +vlazanin - 1312A

          ualetudinem, +vnmaht - 1312A

          retinere, +gilezan - nicht bei Migne

f.202r   lentescens, slafentes - 1315A

f.204r   adscribendum, +zapizellane - 1317A

f.204v   flagris, +villun - 1317B

f.205r   patrocinantibus, +folleistenten - 1317C

```
               auersio tua, +dana picherida - 1318A

f.208v    nacti, +pivindenta - 1322A

f.209r    centuplo, +zehunzicfalto - 1323A

f.210r    (expressam), +gioffanoten - 1324A

          (tantumden), samavilo - 1324A

f.212r    (dependerunt), +vuagvn - 1327A
```

Die wahrscheinlich ahd. Glossen zu den folgenden lat.
Worten konnte ich nicht lesen:

f.8r	excessu		aditum
	rudimentis		conterimus
f.9v	etiam	f.31r	ut
f.10v	cauernis	f.34v	sonitus
f.12v	sane	f.35r	praecipua
f.14v	inpreceps		instructio
f.15r	uidelicet		uinxisset
f.15v	deterius	f.36v	depromptum
f.17v	merito	f.37r	notam
f.24r	quodam	f.41v	suspensum
	concinnata	f.42v	qualibet
f.25v	durissimo	f.49r	suppetere
f.26r	merito	f.62r	obortum
	ipsius	f.106v	liuentis
	arrepticius		adtaminet
	decerpere	f.122r	infestationis
f.27r	hominis	f.125r	castri
	potuit	f.166v	necesse
f.28v	blasfemis		

◘

Clm 19415: Decreta.

Tegernsee (Freising oder Tegernsee), 9.Jh., 306 S.

Lit.: R.Bergmann 662.

Christine Eder, Die Schule des Klosters Tegernsee im frühen Mittelalter im Spiegel der Tegernseer Handschriften
(München,1972), S.90f.

Glossen: Neben den von E.Steinmeyer (II,353,1ff.) abgedruckten Glossen eine Federprobe von einer Hand des 9.Jh.
auf der leeren ersten Seite.

S.1   santa dir liubes

◘

Clm 23577: Sammelhandschrift, u.a. Alphabeta varia
(f.14rff.); Persius, Satirae (f.82rff.).
10.-11.Jh., 146 Bl.

Lit.: R.Bergmann 690.

Glossen: 3 ahd. Interlinearglossen von je einer Hand des
11. (a) und 12. (b) Jh.

f.15v   tesseres, vverfele (b) - zwischen zwei Alphabeten
f.83r   pulmo, lunga (a) - Sat.I,14
f.139v   obba, hanthaba (b) - Scholie zu Sat.V,148

◘

Clm 27152: Canones (f.1r-8v); Pasturalis liber (f.9r-15v);
Teile von: Gregorius Magnus, Regula pastoralis (f.16r-26v);
Gregorius Magnus, Homiliae (f.27rff.).
Tegernsee (Bayern), Anfang des 9.Jh., 88 Bl.

Lit.: R.Bergmann 693.
Christine Eder, Die Schule des Klosters Tegernsee im frü-
hen Mittelalter im Spiegel der Tegernseer Handschriften
(München,1972), S.21.

Glossen: Neben den von E.Steinmeyer (II,360,1 und II,242,
21ff.) gedruckten Glossen je 1 interlineare ahd. Griffelglosse zum Pasturalis liber und zur Regula pastoralis.

Text: Westenrieders Beyträge 1 (1788), S.22ff.
J.-P.Migne, PL 77,13ff.

f.11r   uerecundiam, +scama - Westenrieders Beyträge 1,
         S.25.
f.17r   otio, +slaf - PL 77,22C

◫

Clm 28911: Vita S.Antonii.
Leitzkau bei Magdeburg (Mitteldeutschland, vielleicht
Halberstadt), Mitte des 9.Jh., 65 Bl.

Lit.: -
Glossen: 1 ahd. Interlinearglosse von einer Hand vom
Ende des 9.Jh. auf der letzten, textfreien Seite.

f.65v   uagitus, scriunga

◻

Clm 29055: Vergilfragmente (Fragment Ia).
1.Hälfte des 11.Jh.

Lit.: R.Bergmann 696.

Glossen: 1 ahd. Interlinearglosse der Texthand.

proripit, buskit - Eclog.III,19

◻

Clm 29122: Glossarium latinum.
Tegernsee (Freising), Anfang des 9.Jh., 21 Bl.

Lit.: R.Bergmann 709.
B.Bischoff, Die südostdeutschen Schreibschulen und
Bibliotheken in der Karolingerzeit (Wiesbaden, [2]1960),
S.92ff.

Glossen: 2 ahd. Interlinearglossen von einer Hand des
10.Jh.

Text: G.Goetz, Corpus glossarium latinum IV (Leipzig,
1889), S.301ff.

urguet, k&izit [ketizit] - 403,11
stimulat, kartit - 403,11

Clm 29164: Sequenzen (Fragment aus Clm 7449).

Indersdorf, 9.-10.Jh.

(Ich sah das Fragment im Frühjahr 1971. Wie mir Christine
Eder brieflich mitteilte, ist es inzwischen verschwunden)

Glossen: 1 ahd. Marginalglosse.

    (dotalibus), vaidem gebon

Oxford

OXFORD (Bodleian Library)

Auct.T.1.26: Priscianus, Institutiones.

Im 18.Jh. im Jesuitenkolleg Clermont bei Paris (wohl Nordostfrankreich), 2.Hälfte des 9.Jh., 180 Bl.

Lit.: R.Bergmann 722.

Glossen: Neben der von E.Steinmeyer gedruckten Glosse (V,49) mehrere ahd. Interlinear- und Marginalglossen von einer Hand des 9.-10.Jh.

Text: H.Keil, Grammatici latini II (Leipzig,1855) und III (Leipzig,1859).

f.16r	cassis, galea pilleus.i.helm - II,50,20	
f.37r	arar, sigonna - II,149,14	
f.37v	asser, latta - II,151,16	
f.39r	cluniae, gofon - II,160,11	
	strigilis, skerra - II,161,15	
f.52r	obses, gisal - II,241,57	
f.65r	araris, fluuius sigonna - II,327,16	
f.124r	(ararim), araris fluuius occidentalis.i.sagonna - III,40,22	

Paris

PARIS (Bibliothèque Nationale)

lat.6400 G: Die Handschrift besteht aus mehreren, ursprünglich selbständigen Codices. Teil 1: Boetius (f.1r-111v).
Fleury, Teil 1: 2.Hälfte des 11.Jh., 193 Bl.

Lit.: R.Bergmann 743.

Glossen: Ahd. Interlinearglossen von einer Hand der 2.Hälfte des 11.Jh. zu einem zwischen De Syllogismo categorico und De Syllogismo hypothetico eingefügten Satz.

Text: -

f.109v   gratias refero domino omnipotenti, Gnada
          zele Goto alwal... [der Rest verwischt]

◘

lat.7537: Donatus.
Colbert (nordöstliches Frankreich?), 4.Viertel des 9.Jh.

Lit.: R.Bergmann 746.

Glossen: 1 ahd. Interlinearglosse zu einer lat. Glosse am oberen Rand von f.1v, die in keinem Zusammenhang mit dem Text steht. Lemma und Glosse stammen von einer Hand des 10.Jh.

f.1v   calamancus, dornhod

□

lat.8086: Prudentius.
(Reims oder seine Einflußsphäre), 2.Hälfte des 9.Jh.,
110 Bl.

Lit.: R.Bergmann 749.
M.P.Cunningham, The Older Manuscripts of Prudentius,
Sacris Erudiri 13 (1962), S.12.

Glossen: 1 lat.-ahd. Glosse von einer Hand derselben
Zeit wie die Handschrift am Ende eines kleinen lat.
Glossars auf einer freien Seite.

f.76v   hamus angul

□

lat.8670: Martianus Capella.
Claude Dupuy (Corbie), 9.Jh., 122 Bl.

Lit.: R.Bergmann 751.
C.Leonardi, I codici di Marziano Capella, Aevum 34 (1960),
S.437.
J.-P.Préaux, Deux manuscrits gantios de Martianus Capella,
Scriptorium 13 (1959), S.16, Anm.5.

Glossen: Auf der letzten textfreien Seite ein kleines Glossar von einer Hand des späten 9.Jh.

f.122v   texo uueuu
          scala lederi
          spola trama

...est appel

radiolum risle

liciatoria mittil

quid tunc uuatte ine

delfin merisuuin uel merikalf

nedredes thuneuuet

thorni spine

◻

lat.10444: Glossarium biblicum.
Lüttich (wohl westdeutsch), 1.Hälfte des 11.Jh.

Lit.: R.Bergmann 760.

Glossen: 1 ahd. Interlinearglosse von einer Hand derselben
Zeit wie die Handschrift.

f.8r   migale, hærmelo

◻

Nouv.acquis.lat.1297: Glossarium latinum.
Silos (wohl Nordspanien), 12.-13.Jh., 223 Bl.

Lit.: R.Bergmann 774.
F.Delisle, Mélange de Paléographie et de Bibliographie (Paris,1880), S.109.

Glossen: Eine Reihe von ahd. Kontextglossen als Teil des
Glossars. Die beiden mit Fragezeichen versehenen Glossen

111

sind offenbar weder lateinisch noch griechisch, aber sind
sie althochdeutsch?

Text: -

f.16r acrius furiosus uuotontes

f.18r beccatum reddoheo [?]

f.91v inprobitas ungauori

f.92r inculcetur karetan

f.118v nouitales zalihe

    nisi kiripan

    non ubidares procuratores actores uel comites uel

    gastaldi

f.142v pinus anifal [?]

f.160v plebeios psalmos seculares cantilenas aut ubileod

    portentuose ungahiuro

    proloxius longior sedicionem ungare

f.204v seuius criminor

    suffulcire gubernare uel adiuuare seu caspriuzan

Pommersfelden

POMMERSFELDEN (Graf von Schönbornsche Schloßbibliothek)

Hs.39 (2786): Boetius, De consolatione philosophiae.
Eventuell Erfurt, St.Peter (Deutschland), 11.Jh., 112 Bl.

Lit.: R.Bergmann 782.

Glossen: 2 ahd. Interlinearglossen von einer Hand des 11.Jh.

Text: J.-P.Migne, PL 63,579ff.

f.48v   ignobile, unmarazi - 755B

f.53r   fingi, componi arrâtan - 765A

Rom

ROM (Biblioteca Apostolica Vaticana)

Pal.lat.135: Glossarium latinum.

Lorsch (), 2.Hälfte des 9.Jh., 52 Bl.

Lit.: D. de Bruyne, Fragments d'anciennes versions latines
tirés d'un glossaire biblique, Archivum latinitatis medii
aevi 3 (1927), S.113ff.

Glossen: 1 ahd. Interlinearglosse als Teil eines Zusatzes
zum Bibelglossar hinter <u>larus</u> (Lev.11,16) und vor <u>bubo</u>
(Lev.11,17) von einer Hand derselben Zeit wie die Handschrift.

Text: -

---

f.2ra   pithonicus nicromanticus, hellirunari

▣

Pal.lat.261: Gregorius Magnus, Dialogi.
St.Laurentii in Capella = Heiligenkreuz unteres Kloster
(Rheinland), spätes 9.Jh., 116 Bl.

Lit.: R.Bergmann 796.
H.Stevenson jr., Codices Palatini latini Bibliothecae Va-
ticanae I (Rom,1886), S.67.

Glossen: Mehrere ahd. Marginalglossen von zwei Händen (a
und b) derselben Zeit wie die Handschrift. Die Glossen
sind teilweise am Rand abgeschnitten. Soweit mir die Zu-
ordnung zum lat. Text nicht klar ist, gebe ich die ganze
Zeile.

Text: J.-P.Migne, PL 66,125ff.; PL 77,149ff.

f.9v   (mansionarii), ...inari - 77,177C

f.9v   (lacessunt), zanont - 77,180A
         (pusillus), smah - 77,180B

f.27v   (eos quos), igilichemb - 66,154C
         (nisi in sago potuerunt quia lapsi saxa pari-
         etis eius non), ..lge - 66,156B

f.36v   (sublevari quo commoto atque sublevato dum
         quod excreverat), ..bori - 66,186C
         (ora dolii transiens pauimentum loci in quo
         incubu erant inunda), ..butin - 66,186C/D

f.43r   (citius per sua sit ut audita crederet et pro
         receptione), gispu... - 77,217B

f.47v   (cliuum), cū uáhalda (b) - 77,229B

◩

Pal.lat.829: Paulus Orosius, Historia adversus paganos.
Lorsch, 9.Jh., 115 Bl.

Lit.: R.Bergmann 803.

Glossen: 1 ahd. Interlinearglosse von einer Hand wohl
des 10.Jh.

Text: J.-P.Migne, PL 31,665ff.

f.86v   indicium, §inditium urcmaron - 1072A

◩

Pal.lat.1773: Glossarium latinum.

Lorsch (Lothringen), 1.Hälfte des 9.Jh., 349 Bl.

Lit.: R.Bergmann 817.

Glossen: Einige lat.-ahd. Glossen von einer Hand des 11.Jh. am unteren Rand von f.11v.

f.11v [Gl]is gliris ratta.Glis glissis niz

     [Gl]is Glittis letto.lens lentis letto

     [Li]nsin.lens lendis [die ersten beiden Buchsta-

     ben sind jeweils weggeschnitten]

◙

Reg.lat.1703: Horaz, Carmina.

Weißenburg (), 9.Jh., 145 Bl.

Lit.: R.Bergmann 828.

E.Chatelain, Paléographie de classiques latins I (Paris, 1884), Nr.87, S.26.

Glossen: 13 ahd. Interlinearglossen von einer Hand des 10.-11.Jh.

f.11r aegida, prústrohc - I,15,11

f.12r aratrum, heun aliter arietem - I,16,21

f.13r tympana, harf - I,18,14

     Parthum, unger - I,19,12

f.18v clauuos, cholben - I,35,18

     uncus, chrouuil - I,35,20

f.20v amicitior, holdera - II,1,25

f.23v malbathro, selbún - II,7,8

f.28r   murice, rihhun - II,16,36

f.29r   trahunt, heisint - II,18,8

f.32v   protinus, nuhehende - III,3,30

f.68v   mugientium, boum - Epedon II,11

f.69v   maluae, papelun - Epedon II,58

◘

Urb.lat.674: Priscianus, Periegesis (f.1r-f.22r); Incerti
(f.22v); Rufus Festus Avienus, Lemmata in Arati Phenomena
(f.23r); Auianus, Epistola ad Theodosium (f.23v).
(Frankreich), Mitte des 9.Jh., 23 Bl.

Lit.: R.Bergmann 832.

Glossen: 1 ahd. Interlinearglosse in bfk-Geheimschrift von
einer Hand des 11.Jh. zur Epistola ad Theodosium.

Text: E.Baehrens, Poetae latini minores V (Leipzig,1883),
S.33f.

f.23v   ridicula hpxga [houga] - S.34,9

◘

Vat.lat.625: Glossarium latinum (nach Isidorus, Etymologiae).
(vielleicht Schweiz), 12.-13.Jh., 73 Bl.

Lit.: R.Bergmann 833.

Glossen: Rund 260 spätahd. Interlinear- und Kontextglossen
der Texthand.

Vorsatz- blatt	carduus, distel
f.1ra	abilina nux uel arbor nucaria.i.hasel
	abiges genus arboris tanne
	abortivus frivorves
	abrumptus sterkchile
f.1rb	abhominacio vervvazūge [vervvazunge]
f.1va	acrifolium genus ligni, holend[y] [holender]
	acitula ampher herba
	actureda spinchvvrz
f.1vb	ador frumentum.i.spelte
f.3ra	alnus arbor, erle
f.3rb	lapa [eigentlich alapa, das erste a ausgelassen],
	orslach
	alx animal uel helde
	alitta verbum soůhe
	allebrox bano
	allec, herich
	alibrum haspel
	ablugo rus rost uel schimbel
f.3va	alliphanum saph
	allium clhovelůch
	alsa uel ascella ởhse
	amicus abhamo et catena caritatis
f.4ra	amarena vvihsel
	amphibolo mādel [mandel]
	amital ros
f.4rb	ancile, abukel
	anchora senechel
f.4va	andedia brātreite [brantreite]
	anetum herba.i.tille

118

anguis piscis .i.al

animula musca que dicitur but^{y}flige^{y}

[buterlfligen]

f.4vb   ansa hānthaba uel hasta

f.5ra   antica fꝸrbꝸge uel ferrum in scuto qui in manu
tenetur

f.5rb   apes mel portans peige

apium herba, epfich

aqua manilius pelius hantfaz

f.5vb   aranea vermis spine

ardea auis.i.raiger

f.6ra   argilla.i.mergil

ager richmos.i.numerus

f.6rb   arpago ferrum quo utitur cocus et est curuum
.i.fuscinula chrovvel

artocree meri panes chraphen

arula uel craticula uel patella, glꝸtphanne

arundo, ror

f.6va   ascella huhsen

ascolonium haslauch

ascia dechsel uel obliqua, uel maizel

aserum haselvvrz

aselle sceidun

f.6vb   aspiratilis phrillo

aspidiscos uncinus.i.chrapo

assis pondus quot potest in XII diuidi, medele

asser palus fustis uel lade

f.7ra   attacus hebera.i.humbel

f.7rb   auarium locus uel silua in qua aves manent,
vogelhꝸs

MISSIONS OF THE COLLEGE CURRICULUM

*A Contemporary Review
with Suggestions*

A COMMENTARY OF THE CARNEGIE
FOUNDATION FOR THE ADVANCEMENT
OF TEACHING

A Commentary of The Carnegie Foundation for the Advancement of Teaching

MISSIONS OF THE COLLEGE CURRICULUM

A Contemporary Review
with Suggestions

 Jossey-Bass Publishers
San Francisco • Washington • London • 1978

MISSIONS OF THE COLLEGE CURRICULUM
A Contemporary Review with Suggestions
The Carnegie Foundation for the Advancement of Teaching

*This report is issued by The Carnegie Foundation for the Advancement
of Teaching with headquarters at 437 Madison Avenue,
New York, New York 10022.*

*Copies are available from Jossey-Bass, San Francisco,
for the United States, Canada, and Possessions.
Copies for the rest of the world are available from
Jossey-Bass, London.*

Library of Congress Catalogue Card Number LC 77-84320

International Standard Book Number ISBN 0-87589-360-0

Manufactured in the United States of America

DESIGN BY WILLI BAUM

FIRST EDITION
First printing: December 1977
Second printing: February 1978

Code 7757

The Carnegie Council Series

The Federal Role in Postsecondary Education: Unfinished Business, 1975-1980
The Carnegie Council on Policy Studies in Higher Education

More than Survival: Prospects for Higher Education in a Period of Uncertainty
The Carnegie Foundation for the Advancement of Teaching

Making Affirmative Action Work in Higher Education: An Analysis of Institutional and Federal Policies with Recommendations
The Carnegie Council on Policy Studies in Higher Education

Presidents Confront Reality: From Edifice Complex to University Without Walls
Lyman A. Glenny, John R. Shea, Janet H. Ruyle, Kathryn H. Freschi

Progress and Problems in Medical and Dental Education: Federal Support Versus Federal Control
The Carnegie Council on Policy Studies in Higher Education

Faculty Bargaining in Public Higher Education: A Report and Two Essays
The Carnegie Council on Policy Studies in Higher Education, Joseph W. Garbarino, David E. Feller, Matthew W. Finkin

Low or No Tuition: The Feasibility of a National Policy for the First Two Years of College
The Carnegie Council on Policy Studies in Higher Education

Managing Multicampus Systems: Effective Administration in an Unsteady State
Eugene C. Lee, Frank M. Bowen

Challenges Past, Challenges Present: An Analysis of American Higher Education Since 1930
David D. Henry

The States and Higher Education: A Proud Past and a Vital Future
The Carnegie Foundation for the Advancement of Teaching

Educational Leaves for Employees: European Experience for American Consideration
Konrad von Moltke, Norbert Schneevoigt

Investment in Learning: The Individual and Social Value of American Higher Education
Howard R. Bowen with the collaboration of Peter Clecak, Jacqueline Powers Doud, Gordon K. Douglass

Selective Admissions in Higher
Education: Comment and
Recommendations and Two Reports
*The Carnegie Council on Policy
Studies in Higher Education,
Winton H. Manning, Warren W.
Willingham, Hunter M. Breland,
and Associates*

Curriculum: The American
Undergraduate Course of
Study Since 1636
Frederick Rudolph

Missions of the College Curriculum:
A Contemporary Review with
Suggestions
*The Carnegie Foundation for the
Advancement of Teaching*

*The following technical reports are available from the Carnegie Council on
Policy Studies in Higher Education, 2150 Shattuck Avenue, Berkeley, California 94704.*

The States and Higher Education:
A Proud Past and a Vital Future
SUPPLEMENT to a Commentary of
The Carnegie Foundation for the
Advancement of Teaching
*The Carnegie Foundation for
the Advancement of Teaching*

Changing Practices in
Undergraduate Education
*Robert Blackburn, Ellen
Armstrong, Clifton Conrad,
James Didham, Thomas McKune*

Aspects of American Higher
Education 1969-1975
Martin Trow

Contents

Contents

Preface

This commentary is concerned with the *undergraduate* curriculum. It seeks to do four things:

- Contribute to the slowly enlarging discussion on many campuses of curricular problems and possibilities
- Set forth some essential information that may help in understanding the existing curricular situation
- Present a view of the major issues of the current period and some suggested directions for change
- Indicate some of the more effective methods in obtaining desired curricular change

We seek to be of assistance in particular to those persons who are developing a concern for the curriculum for the first time: the new trustee, the faculty member appointed for the initial time to a committee on the curriculum, the new academic administrator, and the recently elected student leader. The individual with substantial experience with the curriculum, however, may also find in this report data that would not otherwise come to his or her attention.

We start from where we are in the United States today, and we seek to relate to the actual situation of this place and time. We begin with current practices, whatever their origins in American circumstances or aspirations may have been. We recognize that the curriculum can be, and sometimes is, approached from a more historical or more philosophical or more global point of view—reviewing historical developments, bringing to bear competing philosophical and psychological ap-

proaches, placing the curriculum within the larger context of intellectual and cultural evolution. We occasionally refer to the past in order to orient current trends and situations. We do not, however, attempt to discuss in any depth the relation between historical developments and current curricular practices nor to examine the connection between the curriculum of today and the contemporary cultural and intellectual climate.

We are more directed, in this report, to what is and what can be than to what has been or more ideally might be. We recognize the importance of the ideal as well as of the real and of consideration of major overall alternatives as well as of piecemeal adjustments to the changing status quo, but we concentrate here on activities and possibilities of the present situation as we see them.

Even this restricted assignment is a difficult one, seldom undertaken. There is such a diversity of institutions, of programs within institutions, of degrees, of faculty members, and of students that generalization is almost impossible and prescription most difficult and even hazardous.

We undertake this effort now especially for these reasons:

- Higher education has gone through a period of considerable change in its curricula over the past decade as a result, in particular, of the student revolts and the new labor market situation.
- Changes of substantial significance to curricular development are taking place today in the composition and the capacities of student bodies, and in the social concerns that animate students, faculty members, and the public alike.
- Prospectively ahead is a period of essentially no growth for higher education, but of fundamental social changes for society.

Consequently it appears to be a good time to review recent and current developments, and to explore the near future.

Curricular review is never easy. So many forces, external and internal, are at work on the curriculum, so many individuals have a concern with it, so many orientations compete as to the

purposes that it might serve, so few effective mechanisms exist at the campus level for an examination of the curriculum in its totality, and so few leverages are available for constructive change that any overall review is fraught with controversy and, in the end, with the risk of being ineffective in achieving results. Also there is, after the experiences of the late 1960s and early 1970s, much skepticism about the value of reputed reforms and much disenchantment with the process of change and innovation—it can lead to controversy and even disruption, it wearies and weakens the administrators, and it leaves behind it a trail of disappointed expectations. Consequently there have been few recent attempts at such overall review and even fewer achievements, both at the campus level and more broadly. We recognize all this, but we believe that the need for review outweighs the hazards of the effort.

As the result of our review, we have no panaceas but many suggestions, no unitary solution but several directions for movement along which improvements may lie, no vision of eternal perfection but some ideas about constructive changes here and now. The surrounding situation is marked by pluralism and dynamism, not by cultural unity and stasis, and we seek to speak in the mottled light of this pluralism and dynamism. We set forth no grand prophecy in Wagnerian tones, no solution good for all times and all places. We hope, rather, to be of some assistance to those who can affect or make practical decisions that will influence curricular development over the foreseeable future. We are more interested in action than in rhetoric. We recognize that not everything that is good is possible, and we concentrate on what we consider to be possible. We also recognize that choices must be made among many alternatives for action and so we concentrate our attention on seven areas as set forth at the end of Section One.

A note on our terminology is in order. We will speak of *undergraduate education* and *college education* interchangeably. The focus is on degree-credit curricula offered to students at the preassociate- or prebachelor-degree levels. When we speak of *colleges*, we will have in mind the undergraduate programs of both free-standing colleges and undergraduate colleges within

large universities. Our emphasis is on the *curriculum,* which we define as the body of courses that present the knowledge, principles, values, and skills that are the intended consequences of the formal education offered by a college. We also recognize the importance of the *extracurriculum,* which is composed of learning experiences provided informally through recreational, social, and cultural activities sponsored by colleges or by college-related organizations, and of what is often called the *hidden curriculum,* which consists of learning that is informally and sometimes inadvertently acquired by students in interactions with fellow students and faculty members and inferred from the rules and traditions of the institution.

The Carnegie Council has undertaken several studies related to this commentary, and the Carnegie Commission before it also published reports and studies that bear on this series of concerns (see Appendix A-1, A-2). The Trustees of The Carnegie Foundation for the Advancement of Teaching, who are issuing this commentary, have had the advice of a number of persons who have made many helpful suggestions. We express particular appreciation to members of special advisory groups and other individuals who reviewed drafts of the manuscript and gave us helpful information and suggestions (see Appendix A-3). Certain special studies of catalogs and of student and faculty opinion were undertaken (see Appendix A-4), and many site visits to campuses were conducted (see Appendix A-5).

The Trustees and the Council wish to express particular appreciation to Verne A. Stadtman for his contribution to the preparation of this commentary.

Robben Fleming
President
University of Michigan

*E. K. Fretwell, Jr.
President
State University of New York College at Buffalo

Donald N. Frey
Chairman of the Board
Bell & Howell Co.

Sheldon Hackney
President
Tulane University

John G. Kemeny
President
Dartmouth College

*Clark Kerr
Chairperson
Carnegie Council on Policy Studies in Higher Education

Sister Candida Lund
President
Rosary College

Richard W. Lyman
President
Stanford University

*Margaret L. A. MacVicar
Associate Professor of Physics
Massachusetts Institute of Technology

Malcolm C. Moos
President Emeritus
University of Minnesota

Barbara W. Newell
President
Wellesley College

*Also member of Carnegie Council on Policy Studies in Higher Education.

*James A. Perkins
Chairman of the Board
International Council for Educational Development

*Alan Pifer, *ex officio*
President
The Carnegie Foundation for the Advancement of Teaching

*Joseph B. Platt
President
Claremont University Center

Tomás Rivera
Vice President for Administration
University of Texas at San Antonio

George L. Shinn
Chairman of the Board
First Boston Corporation

*Stephen H. Spurr
Professor
LBJ School of Public Affairs
University of Texas at Austin

Pauline Tompkins
President
Cedar Crest College

Sidney J. Weinberg, Jr.
Partner
Goldman, Sachs & Co.

Clifton R. Wharton, Jr.
President
Michigan State University

O. Meredith Wilson
Director Emeritus
Center for Advanced Study in the Behavioral Sciences

*Also member of Carnegie Council on Policy Studies in Higher Education.

MISSIONS OF THE COLLEGE CURRICULUM

A Contemporary Review with Suggestions

A COMMENTARY OF THE CARNEGIE
FOUNDATION FOR THE ADVANCEMENT
OF TEACHING

All men by nature desire to know.

Aristotle

Education is the acquisition of the art of the utilization of knowledge.

A. N. Whitehead

Should the useful in life, or should virtue, or should the higher knowledge be the aim of our training?

Aristotle

The curriculum does not matter. If it did matter, we could not do anything about it. If we could do something about it, we would not know what to do.

Anon.

1

Orientation

---

1. *Origins.* Harvard, at first, had a clear purpose: "to advance learning and perpetuate it to posterity; dreading to leave an illiterate ministry to the churches, when our present ministers shall lie in the dust."[1] There were nine students in the first graduating class. All students took the same subjects (about ten) over a three-year period. These courses centered around classical languages and literature and the Bible. The president taught them all.

2. *New dimensions.* Today there are over 2 million classes taught by half a million faculty members to about 10 million students in about 3,000 institutions. The graduates enter hundreds of different professions and occupations. There are over 1,500 separate degrees.

3. *Many new endeavors, not just growth, separate 1640 and 1977.* The establishment of professional schools, of research universities, of comprehensive colleges and universities, of community colleges; the creation of departments and schools within institutions; the invention of majors and electives; and much else. Each has left its mark on the curriculum.

The curriculum always has been, and presumably always will be, in flux, but more at some times than at others. There are eternal points of tension: scholarship versus training; attention more to the past or to the present or to the future; integra-

---

[1] *New England's First Fruits* (London, 1643), as reproduced in Morison (1935), app. D.

tion versus fragmentation; socialization into the culture versus alienation from the culture; student choice versus institutional requirements; breadth versus depth; skills versus understanding versus personal interests; theory versus practice; ethical commitment versus ethical neutrality; among others. These conflicts are temporarily adjusted now one way and now another; but they never cease. There are no easy or permanent solutions.

4. *Historic changes.* Viewed broadly, there have been two periods of dramatic change in the recent history of American higher education.

The first of these was roughly from 1870 to 1910 which was characterized by the acceleration of specialization to reflect the new knowledge growing out of scientific study, the new occupations and professions introduced by rapid industrialization, and the new students drawn in by the land-grant movement. The department became the major vehicle of specialization. Specialization contributed greatly both to the pursuit of truth through research and to preparation for the new careers that modernization of the economy created. Specialization was a creative response, in particular, to the explosion of knowledge.

The second period cannot be easily assigned to certain years, because it came into existence more gradually, but it has been in pronounced ascendancy since about 1960. It is marked by greatly increased attention to consumer choice and to direct consumer influence. Students demanded, and often got, more electives and more "relevant" courses. New types of students, more of them part-time and more of them adults, came to campus to pick and choose what they wanted to take—and they rejected the "tie-in sales" of requirements. With the approach of a "steady state" marked by less enrollment growth in the 1970s, consumerism accelerated. Peripheral organizations such as proprietary schools, community centers, and free universities began to compete with colleges for their students. The community colleges, in particular, gave new attention to the consumer market, but many other institutions also became more market-oriented in their competition to attract students; and departments and schools within institutions began to compete more

actively with each other for enrollments as a means to keep or to get faculty positions.

It might be noted that these two great changes took place, first, when higher education enrollments were starting their historic expansion and second, when they began to approach a steady-state. Growth permitted, even encouraged, specialization; and the feared prospect of a steady-state encouraged a market orientation.

These two historic periods tend to divide the history of the college curriculum into three eras—the first two eras belonging to the past and present, the third belonging to an age we now seem to be entering. The first era, from 1636 to about 1870, was marked by a more or less standard curriculum that was "liberal" in the sense of its concentration on the cultural heritage of Western civilization. This liberal education, however, did serve vocational purposes because it was most helpful to students trying to enter the major professions of the time as clergymen, teachers, doctors, and lawyers. It reflected the "high culture" of the era, and passage through the curriculum helped to identify the members of the class of educated persons. The curriculum, with its central core, was largely controlled by the guild of college teachers, many of them also ministers. Even today, liberal education, now on a more secular and less religious basis, is an excellent preparation for advanced work in the ancient professions.

The second era, between 1870 and the 1960s, was marked more by attention to production both of new knowledge and of what later came to be called the "human capital" that would apply the new knowledge and new technology that sprang from it. The theme was investment for the sake of increase in the gross national product and in individual personal incomes. The curriculum came to be less oriented toward culture and more toward "knowledge for use" and productive employment. The new professional schools were in agriculture, engineering, and business, among others. The new subject matters were mostly in the sciences and the social sciences. New knowledge and new occupations came to influence the curriculum more, and ministers and the guild of teachers less. Requirements for the major

came to be the dominant theme in curricular development, and the most carefully considered and coherent parts of the curriculum. Manpower needs, expressed through the market and not by way of a plan, greatly influenced both enrollments and the curricula.

The curriculum of today strongly reflects these two earlier eras. It seems also now to be responding to a new consumerism. Greater consumer sovereignty results in more time allowed for electives, more courses presented in the arts, more courses created for nonmajors, more chances provided for students to stop in and stop out, more opportunities allowed to pick and choose individual courses by part-time students and by adults in extension courses. The "community service" courses in the community colleges, taking their place along with transfer and technical courses, are the epitome of this development—they are the fastest-growing part of the fastest-growing segment of higher education; they seek to respond to almost any request for instruction provided that some minimum number of persons join in the request. On some campuses students also are beginning to be better organized and situated to exercise direct power over curricular policy.

The curriculum is more strongly oriented than ever before toward the consumer and toward the provision of consumer "durable goods" to be enjoyed over a lifetime. Even the labor market pressures of the day have encouraged students to demand and quickly get more vocational courses.

The organized student movement of today, as never before, is oriented toward consumer protection, toward Naderism in the classroom—truth in advertising, responsibility for delivery of the promised product, and so forth; some students seem to want to have everything tested and graded and guaranteed except themselves. The student of today is less likely to be the youth who is a passive recipient of the offerings of the faculty expert and more likely to be the adult—sometimes one of many organized adults—shopping around.

Institutions have often gone along with this new consumerism both because they are competing more actively to get students and because they have, in their faculties and administra-

tors, fewer convictions than in earlier times about what is right and proper, about what they will and will not do. There are, of course, exceptions to this trend, including those universities and colleges strongly oriented toward scholarship and those colleges strongly concerned for the life and welfare of the "total student." The community colleges, the less highly selective liberal arts colleges, and the comprehensive colleges and universities are the most responsive to the new consumerism. "Social demand" is now a dominant influence on enrollments and on the curricula taken by many enrollees.

There is another, and not entirely unrelated theme, in this third era: the shift from elite to mass education and now to universal access to higher education. The students are more varied in their origins and in their destinations and, on the average, are less well prepared. This calls for more varied programs and options and for more compensatory education.

As a result of all of this, the United States, which once emulated British and German models, has run out of European antecedents for curricular adaptation and is now on its own.

As the first era has been grossly caricatured in the image of the "ivory tower" and the second of the "public service institution," so the third might be as the "academic shopping center." None of these designations really fit, although many roles have been played in the history of higher education—of preacher, of servant to power, of money changer. These caricatures are, of course, one-dimensional and distorted, but they do carry the message that major changes have taken place and that more than one function has been served.

Knowledge was once a passport for entry into the established professions and the company of cultivated persons; then the theme that "knowledge is power," as Bacon had asserted in the late sixteenth century ([1597] 1861) became more dominant as knowledge contributed increasingly to economic and political influence; and now knowledge is looked on more as an instrumental factor in individual lives—"education for choice" as Margaret Mead (1928) has phrased it, helping people to survey the alternatives and to learn how to make choices among them—college students are in a state of life where they are par-

ticularly concerned with searching for an identity, with making
life choices.

5. *Where do we stand today?* Undergraduates spread their
enrollments approximately as follows:

Area	Percent
Professional Schools	58
Social Sciences	8
Humanities	5
Sciences	15
Arts	6
Other or no major	8

Overall, the professional schools[2] have been growing as have the
biological sciences within the sciences.

The surprising figure is the 58 percent for professional
schools. It certainly reflects the job orientation of many students. It may also reflect the fact that these schools tend to provide more sense of community to their students (along with the
liberal arts colleges) and more coherence in their curricula. They
are goal oriented, which makes it easier both to develop an organized curriculum and to provide basic core courses for all students, and to give advice to students and to help place them in
jobs. Less limited by departmental lines, they treat in a more
rounded fashion with problems and solutions than do single
"disciplines" and draw more on insights from a series of disciplines. Additionally, some professional schools have changed
their orientation to make themselves more attractive to students; for example, the college of agriculture that becomes a
college of natural resources or the college of home economics
that becomes a college of human ecology or the school of architecture that provides the broadest synthesis of history and art
and social life that exists on its campus. For whatever reasons,

[2] For practical purposes, this category includes not only schools and departments training students for fields generally recognized as professions,
for example law, or business management, but also many occupational
fields and others not included in the social sciences, humanities, sciences,
or the arts.

the professional schools are now dominant over the departments in undergraduate enrollments.

Looked at in terms of the curriculum, students now divide their time almost equally as follows:

	Percent
on "general education"	33
on "major requirements"	34
on "electives"	33

"General education," which once constituted 100 percent of the classical curriculum, now claims one-third of student attention; the "majors" that came along with the specialization that marked the second historical period of concentration on production-oriented educational pursuits, now also claim one-third; and the "electives" that have grown so much recently (they accounted for one-fourth of time in 1967), also claim one-third. It is a great coincidence that the most representative aspect of each of these three historical periods should now draw one-third of student enrollments. It looks like a monumental standoff or truce among the central themes of the three historical periods, among three different philosophical approaches to the curriculum—what students should have to be cultured, what they need to be productive, and what they want here and now, among different interest groups—the educational administrators and the education policy-oriented faculty members who advocate general education, the disciplinary and professional faculty members who assert the interests of their discipline or profession, and the students who so often want to do as they please unencumbered by either general or major requirements, freed from the interests of both "breadth" or "depth," relying on their own judgments and choices.

6. *We offer at this point a few observations.* First, the curriculum is important but it is not the most important aspect of undergraduate education. The most important is the quality of the faculty: "that the teachers should . . . be alive with living thoughts" (Whitehead, 1929).

Second, no studies show that one undergraduate curricu-

lum is clearly better than another. Curricular preferences rest on judgments, not proof.

Third, the most marked characteristic of American higher education, and of its curriculum, is diversity.

Fourth, curricula are like huge beanbags that keep on being added to, bean by bean, as each new faculty member brings new courses with him or her, and these beanbags keep on reflecting, as they grow, the many impacts that come their way. Some of these impacts come largely from outside the undergraduate institutions themselves and most importantly in current times are new knowledge, new societal problems, and changed destinations of students in graduate schools and the labor market; but there are many others. Within undergraduate institutions, the greater impacts come (above all) from the departments and the professional schools that serve as departments, but also from the individual faculty members and from the students; but again there are other sources. Presidents and deans of letters and sciences are generally in relatively weak positions of influence, or, at least, act as though they were; but professional school deans tend to be in strong positions. Perhaps the most important impact of all is steady accretion, since little is ever subtracted. As a faculty position is added, it means some new courses, more in liberal arts colleges where the teaching loads are heavy and less in research universities where they are light. Generally, each new faculty position adds five courses (the range is eight to three). Thus the larger the faculty, the more courses and the greater the fractionalization of knowledge.[3] President Dunster in 1640 could teach ten subjects; the current Harvard faculty teaches more like 5,000. The size and composition of the faculty is a dominant explanation of the curriculum. The faculty in any institution reflects, of course, a myriad of historical and current forces, but a description of the faculty can serve as a good indication of what will be in the catalog. In the long run, the additive impact of the selection of

[3]This is not necessarily the case at community colleges, which hire many part-time instructors, some of whom may teach only one course.

individual faculty members largely determines the content of the catalog. Once the faculty is in place, the catalog has largely been written.

Fifth, it is customary to divide the curriculum into three components: general education, the major, and electives. We divide it into five. (A sixth division might be added and at some places, as at Princeton, independent study is added.) General education is "general" only in the sense that it is required of most or all students.[4] It has three quite separate components: (1) advanced learning skills courses, (2) "breadth" or "distribution" courses, and (3) integrative or "synoptic" courses (Phenix, 1964, pp. 233 ff.). They serve quite separate purposes and are divisible—"general education" in practice may include three or two or one of them. The first seek to impart language and mathematical skills of almost universal value in any advanced learning.[5] The second are concerned with giving the students some sampling of the major streams of human thought (the social sciences, the sciences, the humanities), both so that students can be assisted in selecting their major emphasis better after having been exposed to the principal alternatives and so that they will have some acquaintanceship with these different "ways of knowing" and these different approaches to the aspects of life the Greeks called the good, the true, and the beautiful. The third are concerned with giving the student a chance, at the most, to understand mankind's changing environment and the place of the individual within it, and, at the least, to think of some broad series of problems beyond the confines of the major or of individual elective courses. The purpose is

[4]It is necessary to distinguish between "general" and "liberal" education. We define liberal education as consisting of a curriculum more or less in its entirety organized around the cultural heritage of civilization and thus concentrating heavily on the humanities. (For a discussion of the many meanings that liberal education has had, see Sheldon Rothblatt, 1976.)

[5]We distinguish between advanced learning skills in college, some of which may be introductory in nature, and the basic skills that are taught in high school, but often inadequately, and that may be subject to remedial or compensatory efforts in college. The former are new to the student in college; the latter may be the subject of repetition.

"understanding," as Whitehead (1938) designated it.[6] General education can best be thought about by disaggregating it into its component parts as we seek to do.

7. *What is right about what we now have?* It represents the consensus of history about what should be offered and required —"What is is right." The observation that changing a curriculum is like trying to move a graveyard graphically reflects the prevailing academic attachment to this consensus. Both students and faculty members seem to be quite content with the status quo on their campuses generally (see Table 4-4). There must be few areas of American life where contentment now reigns so supreme. It is interesting to note that dissatisfaction is lowest and has fallen the most since 1969 in the selective liberal arts colleges (see Table 4-7).

Despite the consensus and the satisfaction, we see opportunities for improvements, and we now turn to a discussion of them.

8. *Lack of overall concern for the curriculum.* Faculty members pay attention to their individual courses, departments to their majors, and students to their choice of electives; but few persons, and sometimes none, pay attention to the other three components and to the overall enterprise. Yet a comprehensive view of the total curriculum is needed. The student is a total entity, not just a collection of separate parts, and society as a whole is more than just a series of disconnected sectors. If higher education is to react to the student as a whole and to advance the "arts of the citizen" as the Greeks thought of them, then the curriculum needs to be looked at in its entirety. Such efforts are now being undertaken at Harvard, the University of Pennsylvania, Long Beach State University, and other campuses.[7]

---

[6] "Civilized beings are those who survey the world with some large generality of understanding" (Whitehead, 1938, p. 5).

[7] Among other colleges and universities engaged in institutionwide reviews of undergraduate curricula during the past two years are Birmingham-Southern College, Brandeis University, Goddard College, Bennington College, Bethel College, Oberlin College, the University of Massachusetts at Boston, and Austin College.

Generally the current interest in curricula reform stems from three sources: from intellectual commitment, as, for example, at Harvard; from the need to survive by institutions in relatively humble circumstances; and from efforts to respond to the changing markets among and within campuses. Just as the origins of the efforts are different, so also are the contents of the discussions, the decision-making mechanisms, and the prospective outcomes. We expect the most interesting developments to arise on the periphery of the academic world as some threatened institutions seek to change their personalities, invent new curricular approaches, and identify themselves as unique enterprises. This will reverse history, since so many of the new endeavors have in the past come from the core, not the periphery. We expect the most searching intellectual reviews to take place in the great private research universities and some of the more distinctive liberal arts colleges. We expect pragmatic responses from the institutions competing most actively in their markets. The first two searches are more inner directed; the third is more outer directed.

We believe that one place to start curricular review is by considering the mission of the institution.

9. *Improvement of general education.* General education is now a disaster area. It has been on the defensive and losing ground for more than 100 years. It represents the accretions of history more than a thoughtful concern for specialized current needs.

There is a neglect of the advanced learning skills. Each institution should have a clear idea of what minimum level it will require in English language and mathematical skills. We note that statistical skills have become more important both in many occupations and for comprehension by the citizen of current developments, and that skill in using library sources is becoming more and more essential. Both these skills are frequently ignored. We note a widespread belief that a foreign language is becoming less important except as it is required for study in the major subject. (We call attention also to the possibility of interpreting "advanced learning skills" to include contact with different "means of learning"—by lectures, by independent study,

by seminars, by computers, and so forth—with each student given a chance to sample several means of learning.)[8] Learning how to learn is one of the best investments that can be made for an effective life.

Breadth or distribution requirements are too often either met by the introductory course intended for persons who plan to major in the field or have become so free and unlimited in their definition that they are, in effect, an expansion of electives. We suggest special courses for nonmajors (Chemistry 1A may not be the best way to introduce the nonmajor to the scientific method or the role of science in history) and specially designed courses along the lines of "modes of thought" or "ways of knowing" courses, and the addition to distribution requirements of contact with the arts as an addition to the standard list of the social sciences, sciences, and humanities.

Integrative courses or series of courses aimed at broad understanding are of exceptional importance, but they are also hard to teach. We have succumbed to what Bertrand Russell (1969) once called "the current trend toward fiercer specialisms." Specialisms have their place but they are better at description of specific facts than at full explanation of total situations; at partial theories than at coordinated understanding; at technical conclusions than at ethical judgments. Disciplines are better at analysis than synthesis; compartmentalization than bridge-building; dividing events, people, and knowledge, than integrating them. A rounded view of most important problems, as Piaget has noted (1973), requires moving across the lines of specialization; we live with specialized competences but with unspecialized consciences.[9] And this can be a source of trouble. The curriculum alone cannot bring wisdom, but it can help. We believe that programs should be available to students giving a

[8]Edwin F. Taylor speaks of "nine essential nutrients in a college education" that include the lecture and assigned classes, personalized system of instruction (PSI), concentrated study, student-as-teacher, small group seminars, apprenticeships, student initiated/student directed projects, scholarship/self-directed learning, and research.

[9]See the discussion in *The Democratic Prospect* (Frankel, 1962, pp. 148-151).

broad view of history and of thought. We agree with Bell (1968) on the central role of history; but we also call attention to philosophy and religion as areas that can make major contributions, and to the "Great Books" approach. We also call attention to what the Carnegie Commission called "broad learning experiences"[10] where a series of existing courses are put together in an additive way around some major theme such as "East Asian Civilization" or "Man and the Environment." We would now call this approach "integrative learning experiences."

The major gives the student experience with thinking in depth. Needed also is the experience in thinking in an integrative way about a broad range of facts and issues such as the "Greats" program has provided at Oxford.[11] Both experiences are important; in one, the mind moves vertically; in the other, more horizontally. Students could be given a series of alternatives to meet the requirements for programs that encourage integration of thought, that contribute to understanding of civilization generally. There is no exclusive way that best suits all students.

Fortunately, intellectual trends are now in the direction of integration, particularly in the areas of biochemistry, behavioral sciences, and in systems and operations analysis. We have been through a period when knowledge was fragmented but dreams of coherence survived. Throughout history, intellectuals, field by field and over many fields, have sought to recreate an intellectual whole after a period of fission. We seem to be entering a period of new attempts at synthesis. This is now coming more at the graduate than at the undergraduate level for a simple reason—the expanding edges of fields where new research mostly takes place are closer to each other than are the central

[10]The Carnegie Commission on Higher Education endorsed and elaborated on this concept in *Reform on Campus: Changing Students, Changing Academic Programs* (1972d).

[11]The integrative approach is not widespread in England, however. Joseph Ben-David (1977, p. 76) observes that "In spite of the idea that specialized education can also serve general educational purposes, specialization undertaken largely for a practical professional purpose has become overwhelmingly the end of university education in England."

cores of fields; but it may well follow at the undergraduate level as well.

The sequence of general education courses is important. Almost by definition, skill and distribution requirements should come early in the student's career, and the integrative courses should either be distributed throughout or be concentrated at the end. (The old "moral philosophy" course taught by the president, in the days of the classical curriculum, came in the senior year as a capstone effort.)

We note that, with the stabilization of the faculty labor market, there are more "home guard" faculty members now willing to devote attention to the three components of general education and to their articulation.

10. *The major.* The major is generally well handled by professional schools and departments. They have a clear interest in its effective management.

One of the central reasons for the dominant place of the department on campus is that it is the basic location for quality control over faculty and courses. Majors are not always narrow. Some are organized by "discipline" (economics), but some are organized by time (history), space (African studies), skill (mathematics), or field (religion). General education requirements, consequently, may be more needed for some majors than others.[12] We also note that some departments (particularly the sciences and the professional schools) tend to be very greedy for the time of their students, and some control may be

[12]Humanities majors generally confine themselves more to humanities courses than students in any other general area confine themselves to courses in their area of concentration, but since the humanities encompass within themselves great width of understanding, these majors can be the most specialized of all without loss of broad understanding of human affairs. So also with private liberal arts colleges. They tend to have the fewest general education requirements (see Table 6-1), but, being small in size and having small faculties, their courses are almost inevitably broader in their orientation—the whole campus is involved in general education. Some of them were also under intense student pressure in the late 1960s to relax requirements and had fewer bureaucratic defenses against the pressure than did larger institutions. They clearly reduced their general education requirements more than any other category of institutions, and electives have taken their place.

necessary over their imperialistic tendencies, so that they do not squeeze out general education.

11. *Electives.* We only call attention here to the fact that electives sometimes seem to be subject to aimless choices, that some individual or general guidance can be helpful to students in making their choices, and that electives may be subject to some reduction in favor of general education.

12. *Three directions for special effort.* We believe that there are three general directions in which effort should be made:

- *Basic skills.* They have clearly declined. We support more attention to assistance to the primary and secondary schools, and to effective compensatory programs on campus.
- *Connections with the world of work.* Just as English is the most vocationally useful of subjects, so understanding of and experience in the world of work can be one of the most humanizing. We make a number of suggestions on how the gap between thought and action can be bridged with benefit to both—so that the "adventure of thought" may meet the "adventure of action" (Whitehead, 1929, p. 25).
- *Moral values.* The campus can and should be an ethically stimulating environment. The ethical ideals of the academic community are high and can even be a model for the society at large. They need, however, to be made more explicit, to be refined, and, in some cases, more conscientiously observed. Respect for facts and for careful analysis, civility in argument, careful consideration of alternative points of view and of solutions to problems, and other academic attributes are clearly worthy of propagation on campus and off,[13] particularly as the campus becomes more and more the conscience

[13]As the Bressler Committee at Princeton noted, "It may well be that the most influential moral instruction is achieved through example and by introducing students into the thoughtways of scholarship. It is difficult to imagine a more bountiful ethical system than is implicit in the norms that sustain the process of inquiry" (The Commission on the Future of the College, 1973, p. 13). Shils (1975) cautions, however, that "the academic ethos is hard to grasp and resistant to systematic formulation."

of the nation. The more this conscience is brought to bear in full accord with the academic ethos, the more effective it will be.

13. *Being effective.* Curricular reform is charged with being seldom attempted and almost never successful when attempted. This charge cannot be substantiated. Curricular reform goes on all the time within the individual course, within the departmentmental and professional majors, and through the changing student choice of electives and majors. These are the areas where somebody is in charge. The one-third of the curriculum where reform is neglected is the one-third where nobody is in charge— general education. Our comments will relate to reform in this area.

The first main point is that somebody should be in charge whether the president or a dean of the college (as at Princeton) or a dean of liberal education (as at Utah) or a provost for academic affairs (as at Simmons); although we acknowledge that administrative leadership is very much in demand until it is exercised.[14] Trustees may need to give a nudge. The second point is that it is generally better to proceed constantly and quietly than all at once in a publicized effort, to disaggregate any reform program.[15] The third point is that curricular reform

[14]Aside from the question of authority and the willingness to exercise it, there is also the issue of the capacity and interest of administrators in this period of history to undertake curricular reform, as Steven Muller (1974, pp. 148-158) notes: "What are the prospects for university administrators providing constructive leadership in the restoration of general knowledge? Again, the answer must be that such prospects are dim. The principal reason is . . . that its role has become predominantly managerial." University administrators currently, also, frequently concentrate on a low-profile approach to all of their assignments. Additionally, more influence over the curriculum is now located off campus and power on campus is more fractionated.

[15]Curricular reform of significance requires (1) overall thought but (2) piecemeal action. Overall thought tends to lead to attempts at overall action, but overall action tends to lead to overall resistance. Piecemeal action tends to follow piecemeal thought. The difficult task is to get overall thought and then to have the patience and the persistence to carry out its conclusions one at a time; and this takes more time than is usually now available to administrators. Big changes, historically, have come only under

cannot be separated from the making of the budget and attention to the politics of the campus—it will not go far without persuasion and at least passive consent. Curricular change has almost as many economic and political as academic aspects; in fact, where there are formulas, the curriculum too slavishly follows the budget, and the budget follows full-time equivalent (FTE) enrollments. The fourth point is that we should liberate progressive forces by giving them a chance, whether as individuals or members of small groups, to experiment in advance of review rather than by giving review committees the chance to condemn in advance. The fifth point is that one should expect resistance: "The surest way to guarantee a long, disputatious, unsettled, and unsettling faculty meeting is to bring to the floor almost *any* proposal for a change in the nature or content of the requirements governing the undergraduate program" (W. Bowen, 1977, p. 11); but resistance should be minimized by not making the curriculum an issue that comes to the floor unless absolutely necessary. Academicians have a well-proven capacity to raise self-interest to the level of a fundamental principle in a public debate. The sixth point is that we should structure decision making within reasonably small and more cohesive units within a big institution, such as "cluster colleges" or divisions within a college of letters and sciences, or delegate responsibility to a committee.

14. *It is not possible, even if it were desirable, to recapture the past, particularly, the distant past.* It may be possible, however, through careful thought and attention, to capture for constructive action some aspects of the future. It is clearly possible to improve on current performance, at least in the following areas:

---

both special circumstances and with outstanding leadership; but most big attempts have failed. More generally, the revolutions that have succeeded have been those that have been barely noticed and those for which little credit is taken at the time. President Lowell at Harvard, who pioneered the "breadth and depth" approach to the curriculum, had as one of his operating principles: never cackle like a hen that laid an egg (Lowell, 1938, p. 21). It is difficult to "make no little plans" but then to proceed tactically as though "one step enough for me."

- Formulating more clearly the necessary advanced learning skills and better training in them
- Giving more attention to and greater ingenuity in improving distribution requirements included in a college's curriculum
- Making integrative courses on basic understanding of where we are in history, on how we got here, and on what the various alternatives are for the future a more central feature of intellectual activity; concentrating on broad structures of thought as well as on areas for more specific analysis
- Aiding the primary and secondary schools in teaching basic skills and providing compensatory training in them when necessary at the campus level
- Bridging the gap between thought and action by creating more opportunities for students to understand the world of work, the part it plays in human lives, and the lessons it holds for the practical attainment of desired goals
- Clarifying and applying more precisely the essential moral principles of academic life for the sake of the integrity of campus life and for the contribution that can be made to the skills of citizenship more generally
- Asserting the corporate interest of the academic community in the quality of the curriculum in its totality as well as in its component parts

The curriculum is the major statement any institution makes about itself, about what it can contribute to the intellectual development of students, about what it thinks is important in its teaching service to society. It deserves more attention and merits less neglect than has been accorded it by most institutions of higher education in recent years. For at least a decade now, higher education has been more intent on responding to internal and external pressures on the curriculum—and they have been severe—than in developing coherent educational policies. We believe that attention to these policies is by now a high priority, that the curriculum of the future should be less the result of pressures and more the consequences of sustained thought, and that higher education should demonstrate that it can think about what is needed as well as respond to what is demanded.

2

The Movement
Toward Diversity

Undergraduate colleges in America continually evolve. They began modestly, but over the years they became more numerous, grew in average size, added functions, served ever-increasing proportions of the expanding population, enriched and enlarged their knowledge inventories, and adopted new techniques and formats for fulfilling their educational missions. Today, the new coexists to a considerable extent with the old, for there has been little pruning and much grafting.

Changing Social Perspectives

Oscar and Mary Handlin (1970, p. 10) observe that when John Adams went to Harvard he did not go there for professional reasons. To learn how to practice law, he served as an apprentice in a lawyer's office. "For young men like Adams," the Handlins explain, "the value of a higher education lay not in professional training but elsewhere. It derived from the belief that the course of learning endowed those who completed it with cultural attributes that were signs of superior status." That is not to say that a Harvard education was not useful preparation for a career. It was well suited as training for the ministry, for example, and had been designed, in part, with that use in mind. It was equally suited, although not as specifically, to be the foundation of any other occupation for which the cultural attributes and superior status the Handlins speak of were assets. But relatively few

young men attended college in colonial times. In 1770, out of
an estimated population of perhaps 3,000,000, the total living
alumni of all American colleges numbered fewer than 3,000
(Handlin and Handlin, 1970). In a country that was new and
undeveloped, opportunities for young men to make their way,
even without much formal schooling, were abundant.

Accomplishment, not inherited wealth or privilege or
social and family origins, soon came to be regarded as the true
measure of personal merit. In the same spirit, advanced learning,
which was available only at considerable expense to students or
their families, came to be regarded by many Americans as elit-
ist, perhaps even pretentious. Efforts to raise the minimum level
of the education available to all citizens encountered resistance
for many years. As late as 1890, the number of pupils in public
secondary schools was 200,000 and constituted only 1 out of
15 persons 14 to 17 years old (Raubinger, Rowe, Piper, and
West, 1969, p. 97).

Public resistance to educational efforts gradually eroded as
colleges introduced "practical" subjects, such as agriculture and
engineering, into their curricula; as public colleges became more
numerous and brought lower-cost education within reach of
more prospective students; as high school attendance became
more nearly universal and the floor of minimal learning for all
citizens was raised; as opportunities for boys and girls to engage
in productive, remunerative activities dwindled under pressure
of urbanization and the unionization of labor; as the industrial
revolution created demands for specialists and managers with
higher-level training than could be obtained in high school or on
the job; and as the rewards for having attended college—whether
they were in the form of more interesting lives and opportunities
or higher-than-average salaries—became more widely recognized.

By 1975 participation in higher education had reached a
point where 7.3 million persons were enrolled in undergraduate
degree-credit programs in American colleges and universities.
Among all members of the population over 25 years old, 30.8
million (26 percent) had spent at least one year in college (National Center for Education Statistics, 1976b, p. 102; U.S. Bureau
of the Census, 1975, p. 17).

Changing Students

American students are no longer dominantly the white Protestant sons of well-to-do fathers they once were. Of the fathers of 235 Harvard students listed in a survey of parents from 1677 to 1703, the largest groups were ministers (79—one out of three); "merchants, shopkeepers, and master mariners" (45); magistrates and lawyers (34); and "wealthy farmers, military officers, etc." (28) (Brubacher and Rudy, 1976, p. 39).[1] Colleges now serve not only the nation's sons but also its daughters, who, in 1975, made up 45 percent of the undergraduate enrollment (National Center for Education Statistics, 1976b, tables 1 and 2). And in 1976, the fathers of American students represented a broad range of the occupational spectrum. The highest percentage of them (20) were skilled wage earners; followed by professionals, including teachers and professors (18 percent); executives and managers in business and industry (15 percent); owners of small businesses (12 percent); and semiskilled and unskilled wage workers and farm laborers (11 percent). (See Table 1.

In 1960, members of racial minorities comprised 6.5 percent of the total enrollment; by 1970, this figure had risen to 11 percent; and by 1974, it had risen to 12 percent (The Carnegie Foundation for the Advancement of Teaching, 1975, p. 30; U.S. Bureau of the Census, 1975; and U.S. Department of Health, Education, and Welfare, 1976). In 1976, 45 percent of the nation's undergraduates were Protestant, 25 percent were Roman Catholic, 3 percent were Jewish, 5 percent were of other religions, and 21 percent stated that they had no religion (Carnegie Council Surveys, 1975-1976).

[1]Eleven were "ordinary farmers" and 7 were physicians and schoolmasters. The occupational status of 65 fathers "could not be determined." At the time of this survey, there were only three colleges in the United States —Harvard, William and Mary, and Yale (which was only two years old). Historians leave the impression that at this stage of American college development differences among the backgrounds of students from college to college were probably minor.

Table 1. Occupations of fathers of undergraduates in colleges
and universities in the United States in 1976

Occupation	Percent
College or university teaching	2
Elementary or secondary school teaching or administration	3
Other professional	13
Owner of large business	2
Executive or managerial in business or industry	15
Other managerial or administrative	6
Technical and semiprofessional	7
Owner, small business	12
Other white-collar, clerical, retail sales	6
Skilled wage worker	20
Semiskilled and unskilled wage worker, farm laborer	11
Armed forces	3

Note: Farmers are probably included under the categories "owner of large business" or "owner, small business." The most recent comparable data available are for 1969, when 9 percent of the fathers of undergraduates had "farmer, rancher, or other agricultural" as their occupation.

Source: Carnegie Council Surveys, 1975-1976.

Students also are older than they were in the first century of American higher education. Of the 28 students who entered Harvard in 1756, one was 12 and the oldest was 19; the average age was 15 years and 5 months (Thwing, 1906, p. 86). Of the 2,557,000 freshmen entering American colleges in 1974, not even 0.5 percent were less than 16 years old (U.S. Bureau of the Census, 1975, pp. 48, 49). In what many expect to be an increasing trend, more than 30 percent of all undergraduates in 1975 were over 21 years old (U.S. Bureau of the Census, 1975, pp. 48, 49).[2]

[2] Actually, the percentage of older students is understated by this figure, because only degree-credit enrollment is included in the Bureau of Census figures. If nondegree credit were reported, the percentages would have been much higher.

Many students in the 1970s have off-campus responsibilities and do not give college their full-time attention. In 1976, 83 percent of the nation's undergraduates were enrolled full-time for credit; 16 percent were enrolled part-time for credit; and 1 percent were enrolled in noncredit programs. More than half were employed half time or more, and four out of five had some classes at night (Carnegie Council Surveys, 1975-1976).

To serve this large, diversified clientele, the nation's colleges have developed extensive, varied, and, in some cases, flexible curricula.

Changing Colleges

Americans have always been college builders. Between 1636 and 1861, more than 700 colleges were started within the nation's boundaries (Rudolph, 1962, p. 47; Tewksbury, 1969, p. 16). Of that number, about 250 survived to the time of the Civil War. Now, 2,896 colleges and universities in the United States offer undergraduate education.[3]

Most colleges are larger. By 1770, Yale had 328 students and Harvard had 413 (Brubacher and Rudy, 1976, p. 22) and they were among only 10 colleges that had more than 150 undergraduates in 1836 (Hofstadter and Metzger, 1955). In contrast, in 1977, the ten largest campuses in the United States have undergraduate enrollments in excess of 25,000. But there are still more than 140 colleges, largely seminaries and specialized schools, that have less than 150 undergraduates.

America's early colleges were basically four-year institutions that emphasized liberal arts instruction, and, for nearly two centuries after the founding of Harvard, they enrolled only men. Institutions of higher education in the 1970s are of many kinds. Some offer only two years of college-level instruction; some offer only liberal arts; some offer liberal arts and many other subjects as well; and universities and some colleges sup-

---

[3]Carnegie Council staff estimates prepared for a forthcoming revised version of *A Classification of Institutions of Higher Education* (Carnegie Commission, 1973a). The figure used here excludes medical schools and centers, other separate health professional schools, schools of law, and other specialized institutions.

port research and offer graduate and professional instruction to the Ph.D. level. Some institutions are privately supported; some are supported by local and state governments. Of those that are private, 786 are associated with one of the many religious denominations that actively support higher education. Higher education for women began to be available with the opening of the Troy Female Seminary in Troy, New York in 1821. Although most institutions of all types are now coeducational and "single-sex" colleges appeared for a time to be an endangered species, there are still 29 colleges attended only by women, 119 attended only by men, and 12 institutions with separate colleges for students of each sex (National Center for Education Statistics, 1976a, p. xxix). Efforts to establish institutions of higher learning for blacks began early in the nineteenth century but were, for the most part, frustrated until the founding in 1837 of what became Cheyney State College. Lincoln University was founded in 1854 and Wilberforce in 1856 (Bowles and DeCosta, 1971, pp. 288, 294). There are now at least 112 colleges that were either founded for blacks or are now predominantly attended by them (Blake, Lambert, and Martin, 1974). There are also colleges for other racial and ethnic groups.

Changing Curricula

American colleges have never claimed to teach everything that could be known. The early colleges sought only to provide the tools of learning—logic, mathematical skills, languages that cultivated a facility in communication and disciplined thought and reason; and a familiarity with the elementary facts, major ideas, and basic principles that could be drawn from what was known about man and nature. The need to master a subject for its own sake was not recognized, except in professional schools, until well into the nineteenth century.

Until the late 1700s, American college students received substantially, if not totally, prescribed instruction in an amount that could not exceed what one man could teach in four years. R. Freeman Butts (1971, p. 28) has put the Harvard curriculum of 1642 into modern terminology and into comparative units of time devoted to class hours. His analysis indicates that in studies

for the bachelor of arts degree: "Eighteen percent of the time was spent on Greek, 18 percent on Hebrew and other eastern tongues, 18 percent on rhetoric, 9 percent on logic, and 9 percent on divinity. Now if these are [put] together into what we would call humanities, they amount to a total of 72 percent of the curriculum. In contrast, 15 percent was devoted to mathematics and science—12 percent to arithmetic, geometry, and astronomy, and 3 percent to physics (largely Aristotelian); and .5 of 1 percent to botany, which was offered on Saturday afternoons in the summers. What we might call the social sciences or the social studies included 12 percent of the student's time that was devoted to ethics and politics (Aristotle) and .5 of 1 percent to history on Saturday afternoons in the winter."

At all colleges today, the curricula are much broader, but there is an enormous range. There are colleges with fewer than 200 courses and large research institutions with as many as 9,000. Along with the vestiges of the classical trivium (grammar, rhetoric, and logic) and quadrivium (arithmetic, music, geometry, and astronomy) that are still imbedded in the curricula, one now finds varying amounts of the physical sciences that were first introduced into American colleges in the eighteenth century; modern languages, which were introduced in the nineteenth century; the social and behavioral sciences, which emerged from the moral philosophy and metaphysics courses of the early American colleges but flowered only in the present century; the arts, which are only now beginning to get a foothold in higher education (Morrison, 1973); and certain new professions (Cheit, 1975) including architecture, forestry, business, and agriculture, many of which have been represented in the college and university curricula for little more than 100 years. There are also such atypical bachelor's degree programs as automotive technology, equestrian science, and building construction, some of which were once found only in academies and vocational schools.

As the curricula have expanded, degrees and degree programs have become more numerous and less standardized. Master's degrees, although they were available in colonial colleges, did not acquire status as earned degrees until 1858 (Spurr,

1970, p. 64); doctorates did not become available in American colleges until after 1861 (p. 117); and the associate's degree did not appear until the 1890s (p. 44).

There are now almost 200 associate's degrees and more than 650 bachelor's degrees for which "common abbreviations" are listed by the American Council on Education (Furniss, 1973, pp. 1760-1765). But such designations do not begin to describe the actual variety. When transcripts of 50 recent history graduates of different institutions were studied by Jonathan Warren of the Educational Testing Service, those showing similar course patterns could be grouped into clusters that identified three or four types of programs in each field. For example, Warren (1975, p. 142) reports:

> In history . . . the geographic area studied was one basis for a broad grouping; in other words, some transcripts showed that 15 to 20 percent of the history courses were devoted to Asian history, whereas others showed little or no Asian history. Almost all the history transcripts showed substantial amounts of American and European history, but the relative proportions differed, providing another basis for clustering. One cluster showed twice as much American as European history; another showed slightly more European than American. One type of transcript differed from others by indicating a heavier emphasis on historiography and the philosophy of historical study. Another cluster, identified by much less depth and scope of historical study than others, showed a heavy concentration of courses in education in the out-of-field courses.

Such findings probably could be replicated in almost every discipline. The fact that subtle and profound differences lie so deep within the curriculum is well hidden by the common terms with which its parts are described—*courses, majors, minors, credits,* and the like, capped, of course, by *bachelor's degree.* Such terms seem to bestow on the undergraduate curriculum a

commonality it does not really possess. Employers, government agencies, and others who routinely evaluate college-educated men and women under the assumption that the bachelor's degree conforms to a single standard should bear in mind the admonition of Stephen Spurr, who reminds us that the degrees of American colleges are not based on "the attainment of a certain level of intellectual competence or upon the mastery of any common body of knowledge. The degree simply records the successful completion of a number of requirements, the general nature of which are common to most institutions but which vary greatly in specific detail as to their intellectual content, subject matter, rigor, and difficulty" (Spurr, 1976, p. 13). Clearly then, it is wrong to assume that everyone who has a bachelor's degree has had the same kind and level of education. Such an assumption is unwarranted not only for people whose degrees are earned from different institutions, but even for people who earn degrees in the same institution but in different academic divisions or departments.

During the past 341 years, colleges have extended their reach to include increasing numbers of students and to cover a rapidly expanding knowledge base. There has also been experimentation with new structures and procedures to accommodate new functions and the new interests, goals, and abilities of students. Not all of these efforts are compatible with one another, and there has been no attempt to integrate them into any single type of undergraduate curriculum. Instead, a diverse effort has emerged that involves many kinds of institutions and many programs within institutions.

This diversity has advantages. It enables many colleges to accommodate heterogeneous student bodies and serve a broader, more diversified portion of society. It enables colleges and universities to pursue self-determined missions and to conduct themselves in accordance with self-determined philosophies.

But such diversity also has shortcomings. It obscures the question of whether or not there should be some common characteristics of the education all colleges offer to their students. It also leaves colleges without generally recognized reference points in the quest for quality. Under such conditions, the

undergraduate curriculum becomes governed mostly by market forces. What is offered is what is desired—or can be sold.

*   *   *

For further information on subjects discussed in this section, see the chapters on "History of Undergraduate Education" —specifically "Introduction and Capsule Overview" and "A Chronological History of Undergraduate Education: The American Experience"—in the Carnegie Council on Policy Studies in Higher Education, *Handbook on Undergraduate Curriculum.*

3

External Forces
That Shape the Curriculum

Colleges have enormous potential for altering people's lives and
contributing to changes in our society, so they are the concerns
of many externally based public and private interests (Figure 1).
Some of these interests are more obvious and important than

Figure 1. External influences on the undergraduate curriculum

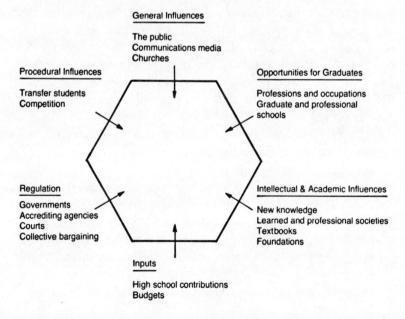

General Influences

The public
Communications media
Churches

Procedural Influences

Transfer students
Competition

Opportunities for Graduates

Professions and occupations
Graduate and professional
schools

Regulation

Governments
Accrediting agencies
Courts
Collective bargaining

Intellectual & Academic Influences

New knowledge
Learned and professional societies
Textbooks
Foundations

Inputs

High school contributions
Budgets

others, but most of them can make a difference in the scope
and kind of education that college students receive.

General Influences

To a remarkable degree, the curricula of American colleges reflect the concerns of the general society and of the institutions
that shape public opinion.

The public. The concerns of the general public often emerge un-
expectedly, and sometimes they are short-lived. In 1957, the
Russians launched *Sputnik,* an achievement that aroused the
American public's interest in curricula geared to both better
science instruction and better preparation of teachers. With the
help of federal and state financing, colleges made impressive
strides in such programs within the ensuing decade. In the
1950s, Americans also became increasingly aware of the decline
of their cities; today, 27 percent of all four-year colleges and 12
percent of all two-year colleges offer urban studies programs
(Catalog Study, 1976).[1] Throughout the 1960s, civil rights, including those that involved opportunities for members of
minorities to participate equitably in education and to understand the role and tradition of their own ethnic groups within
the general society, rose to prominence in the public consciousness. Today, 26 percent of America's four-year colleges and 23
percent of its two-year colleges have ethnic studies programs.
Fears of unchecked population growth and the deterioration of
the natural environment that were prevalent in the 1960s are
now reflected in special environmental studies programs at 28
percent of America's four-year colleges and 18 percent of its
two-year colleges (Catalog Study, 1976). Within the past
decade, there have been new demands for equality in the rights,
recognition, rewards, and opportunities accorded to women,
and, today, there are women's studies programs in 20 percent of
the country's four-year institutions and 6 percent of its two-
year colleges (Catalog Study, 1976). The formal programs instituted in response to current public interest are often supple-

[1] See Appendix A-4 for description of Catalog Studies.

mented by informal colloquia, lectures, seminars, and other programs that are prominently announced in student newspapers and oncampus bulletin boards. Moreover, much of the subject matter of these special programs frequently finds its way into the general college curricula—where it is a part of the mainstream instruction and no longer "special."

Communication media. There is a sense in which newspapers, magazines, and television broadcasting compete with educational institutions as sources of information and explanation about the world we live in. Whether they are the distractions from formal learning some critics claim they are; whether they are cultivating visual and emotional ways of learning at the expense of verbal and rational ways, as other critics claim; or whether they supplement and enrich the learning offered in the classrooms, as many observers and defenders argue, they are unmistakably a learning resource of considerable power. That both public and commercial television stations and networks are aware of the educational potentials of the medium is shown by their development of cultural and historical programming, of which "The Adams Chronicles," "Civilization," the highly popular "Roots," and the early-morning televised classroom broadcasts offered in some parts of the country are well-known examples. Many of the educational programs found on public and commercial television channels have been taped for subsequent presentation in college classrooms as part of the formal curriculum. Some urban colleges offer televised instruction for credit.

The print media are also becoming more consciously involved in educational activities. In 1976-77, in a program supported by the National Endowment for the Humanities, more than 500 newspapers offered 16-week courses on "Oceans: Our Continuing Frontier" and "Moral Choices in Contemporary Society" that were recognized for credit by more than 300 colleges and universities. They were built around a series of short, printed lectures, and an estimated 20 million readers sampled at least one lecture in each course.

As impressive as these education activities are, the major

influence of the media on the college curriculum derives from
the way they present the cultural, civic, and moral interests of
the country to the American people. Coverage of scientific
breakthroughs, whether in nuclear science, medicine, space,
meteorology, or energy, arouses public interest. The current demands of the public and many educators for more value-
oriented education are, at least in part, a response to Watergate
and other national scandals reported to the American people by
a persistent press. Media attention to the campus disturbances
of the 1960s, to the difficulties college graduates experienced in
finding jobs in the 1970s, and to the decline in student achievement and the rise of grade inflation similarly generated public
pressures felt by schools and colleges throughout the country.

In American society, the communications media often act
as diagnosticians. Educational institutions are expected, often
unrealistically, to produce cures.

Churches. Just as the quest for religious freedom inspired European colonizers to settle in America in the seventeenth century,
the desire to preserve and extend the influence of religion in
American life was instrumental in the creation and spread of the
nation's colleges. The earliest colleges had as one of their basic
missions the education of an American ministry. The emphasis
on classical languages in the early curricula was considered useful, in part, because these languages were used for scholarship
on the Bible. As the American frontier moved westward, college
building accompanied it, with the encouragement and financial
support of missionary societies and denominations. More than
one college was created in the newly opened territories because
there were some settlers who felt that it would be unfortunate
if the only well-educated neighbors they had were products of
colleges supported by denominations other than their own. Although Protestant denominations were the first to become
involved in college building, the Roman Catholics founded
Georgetown in 1789, and by 1976-77 there were 242 Catholic
colleges and universities. In the same year, there were 504 Protestant institutions, 24 Jewish colleges or universities, and 15
colleges supported by other religions (National Center for Education Statistics, 1977).

American Protestant colleges were active contributors to the spiritual awakening in the United States in the early part of the nineteenth century. C. Robert Pace (1972, p. 11) reported that Timothy Dwight, who became president of Yale in 1795, exhorted the students to embrace Christianity, and "in 1802, a third of the students made professions of faith. Amherst, Dartmouth, Princeton, Williams, and other colleges reported student conversions. Dynamic Christian leaders became college presidents and professors. Campus prayer days became common. Collegiate awakenings and evangelical religion supplied the principal impetus for the creation of many new colleges." Since that time, other periods of religious revivalism have had influences on the campuses and have resulted in the establishment of new colleges.

But there has also been a trend toward secularization. The most notable cause was the development of public institutions of higher education that spread rapidly after the Civil War and that now claim the majority of college enrollments. These institutions, from the beginning, have observed a strict neutrality in religious matters, and other colleges have followed their lead. Even many colleges that were founded by religious denominations are no longer tied closely to their original sponsors. Many of them have become more secular out of practical necessity—to obtain a broader base for enrollments, to qualify for foundation and other support denied to church-related institutions, or to acquire faculty in sufficient numbers to accommodate more students and expanding curricula. As a consequence, church-related schools fall within a spectrum that includes, at one end, institutions with very strong ties to their sponsoring denominations (in matters of admissions, faculty hiring, composition of governing boards, sources of support, and observance of religious practices on campus) and, at the other end, some with denominational ties so loose that they are virtually indistinguishable from totally secular institutions.

The trend toward secularization has not, however, eliminated the influence of churches completely. Seventeen percent of all general education programs still require students to take courses in religion, and another 19 percent accept religion courses as satisfying breadth requirements (Catalog Study,

1976). A few colleges still require all students to attend chapel. Many church-related colleges give their religiously oriented missions prominence in their catalogs. In describing its "educational perspectives," for example, Seattle Pacific announces that it is "thoroughly committed to evangelical Christian doctrine and standards of conduct. Accepting the fundamentals of the Christian faith, it stands unequivocally for (1) the inspiration of the Old and New Testaments, (2) the deity of Christ, (3) the need and efficacy of the atonement, (4) the new birth as a divine work wrought in the repentent heart by the Holy Spirit, (5) the need and glorious possibility of the born-again Christian being so cleansed from sin and filled with the love of God by the Holy Spirit that he can and should live a life of victory over sin, and (6) the personal return of the Lord Jesus Christ" (*Seattle Pacific College Bulletin 1974-76,* 1974, p. 5). Muhlenberg College makes a somewhat more oblique reference: "The College does not believe in religious indoctrination; neither does it believe that there is a special religious version of the arts and sciences. The College does believe, however, that its religious traditions enhance the kind of community within which the search for truth, beauty and the good life may flourish" (*Muhlenberg College Catalog, 1975/1976,* 1975, p. 5).

There is, in fact, a difference in the education offered by church-related institutions. Studies show that alumni of Protestant colleges consistently are more inclined than alumni of colleges and universities generally to count among the benefits of their education such outcomes as: "Appreciation of religion—moral and ethical standards; citizenship—understanding and interest in the style and quality of civic and political life; tolerance of other people and their values; social development—experience and skill in relating to other people; broadened literary acquaintance and appreciation; [and] awareness of different philosophies, cultures, and ways of life" (Pace, 1972, pp. 49-53).

In a similar study of Catholic colleges, Andrew Greeley (1969, p. 103) found that more Catholic college alumni than alumni generally said that their colleges "developed my abilities to think and to express myself; gave me a broad knowledge of

the arts and sciences; expanded my tolerance for people and ideas; helped me to form valuable and lasting friendships; helped me formulate the values and goals of my life; [and] helped prepare me for marriage and family life."

One might note that these outcomes could reasonably be anticipated from an educational experience at any liberal arts college. On the other hand, it is only fair to point out that it is in precisely these kinds of institutions that the influence of the churches is most strongly felt.

Prospects for Graduates

Although many of them may not realize such goals, one-third of the community college undergraduates and about two-thirds of the undergraduates at liberal arts colleges are now planning to extend their formal education beyond the bachelor's level. For such students, the stakes of the undergraduate "game" are high, because what happens there can affect their chances of pursuing still higher goals.

Steven Muller, president of Johns Hopkins University, describes the situation this way: "Most undergraduates in effect write off their undergraduate years in terms of intrinsic values. They are not 'real' years; they are only 'pre-' years. Their value is seen to lie mostly in what follows them, not in what they themselves contain. Stated simply, they are not regarded as years of learning but as years of effort to qualify for something else; and learning and trying to qualify can be two entirely different things" (in Byrom, 1977, p. 9).

The areas of postgraduate endeavor that have the greatest influence on undergraduate education are professions and occupations and graduate study. Both areas influence students' choices of courses to study and their desire to compile strong records of academic achievement.

Professions and occupations. During the current decade, the American people have assigned particularly high priority to career preparation as a function of higher education. Their concern is generated in large part by the disappointment of many young men and women whose college educations failed in

recent years to give them entry to the level of jobs that might have been readily open to them a decade ago. This situation followed two decades marked by expansion in national research and development activities, including the rapid development of the computer and aerospace industries, and progression through the school of the children born during the post-World War II "baby boom." These two factors accounted for an exceptional increase in demand for college graduates in the 1950s and 1960s. Since the late 1960s, however, research and development activity has declined, the last of the postwar babies have been finishing school, and, to make employment prospects worse, the country began to feel the effects of a recession in 1970 and 1971 (Gordon, 1976, p. 3).

In the past few years, job prospects in engineering, business administration, the sciences, mathematics, public health, and statistics have been relatively consistent with the number of graduates in those fields. Women with degrees in business administration, accounting, data processing, and engineering have been sought out by industry, and blacks have been doing well in managerial positions. But, partly because of declining needs for teachers, more graduates in the social sciences and humanities than in the past have had to accept jobs of a routine character that were unrelated to their fields of training.

The effect has not been one of severe unemployment for college graduates. It has been one in which they have been forced to accept jobs that are lower on the occupational ladder than they expected (Gordon, 1976, p. 7). There appear to be two consequent trends. One is for occupations to be upgraded by requiring persons who enter them, as a condition of employment, to have higher educational attainments without specific regard for occupational performance. The trend may be particularly noticeable in occupations and professions in which those who are already working control job entry by determining licensing requirements and other regulations governing access to such jobs as may be available. The other is for occupations to be upgraded through educational programs that improve the technical performance of those who enter them—as is the case in relatively new occupations found in allied health care, the mental health fields, and daycare programs.

Students respond to such shifts in manpower demand by seeking out courses that specifically prepare them for the new situations that develop. They also respond by maximizing opportunities to compile impressive achievement records and minimizing academic risks. Their concerns have contributed significantly to the "grade inflation" that was first identified as a national problem by David Riesman in 1971 and documented statistically by Arvo E. Juola at Michigan State University in 1974 (Jacobson, 1976, p. 1).[2]

The Carnegie survey of undergraduates confirms the inflation. The percentage of undergraduates who reported cumulative averages at grades A+ through C— and below in 1969 and 1976 are as follows:

Grades	1969		1976	
A, A+	2	} 7	8	} 19
A—	5		11	
B+	11	} 28	18	} 40
B	17		22	
B—	19		15	
C+	23		15	
C	18		10	
C— and less	7		3	

Note: Totals are more than 100 because of rounding.

Source: Carnegie Surveys, 1969-70, 1975-76.

In 1975, the year before the Carnegie Council's survey of undergraduates was made, average grades dropped slightly, breaking a pattern of successive increases that had lasted at least 10 years. The increase between 1974 and 1975 was 1.74 (on a 4.0 scale) as compared to 1.71 between 1973 and 1974 (Jacobson, 1976, p. 1).

Graduate and professional schools. While maintaining unspoiled academic records may give job seekers an advantage, it is abso-

[2] See Appendix D for technical notes on grade inflation.

lutely crucial for approximately one-half of all undergraduates who expect their college curriculum to lead them to studies at the postbaccalaureate level. Competition for entry into professional and graduate school is keen, and failure to win admission on any grounds often means that a student must abandon his or her preferred professional plans forever.

One way for students to increase their chances for admission to graduate schools is to avoid venturing into difficult courses that are unrelated to their graduate study plans. Only when such risks are reduced by nonpunitive options such as pass-no record grading are they likely to be considered safe. On the other hand, some faculty members and their departments may feel restrained from using such grading practices for fear that the options themselves will not be approved or accepted by graduate school admissions officers. These fears are not entirely unfounded. Some graduate and professional schools are, in fact, critical of nontraditional grading and curricula and make it difficult for the graduates of such colleges that use them to pursue more advanced learning.

At colleges and universities where the proportions of students who plan to attend graduate school are particularly high—at selective liberal arts colleges and doctoral degree-granting and research universities, for example—academic departments may design their own major programs as introductions to specialization at the graduate and professional level, rather than as concentrations appropriate for students who plan to terminate their education after receiving the bachelor's degree. While this practice may be helpful in some fields, it could backfire. Some graduate schools actually prefer to have students who have not yet specialized in their discipline or subject field. Such policies reflect a preference for graduate students who are prepared to pursue highly specialized studies based on broad education foundations.

Although there are inevitable linkages between undergraduate and graduate studies in many fields, our basic contention in this commentary is that an undergraduate curriculum should have a complete and coherent character of its own and that its function of preparing students for graduate schools should not be overstressed.

Intellectual and Academic Influences

New knowledge. Totally beyond the control of the colleges is the growth of knowledge itself. American higher education began almost simultaneously with the beginning of the scientific revolution and the "age of reason." Galileo's dialogues on the two-world system were published only four years before the founding of Harvard and his work on mechanics appeared in 1637. Newton's law of gravitation was published in 1687, and John Locke's essay on human understanding was published in 1690, three years before the founding of America's second college, William and Mary. It is not necessary for us to trace here all of the philosophical and scientific achievements of this historic period. It is enough to note that in the seventeenth and eighteenth centuries, when our colleges were beginning, both the presumed limits of human understanding and the methods of acquiring knowledge of humans and their world were being redefined. The time was over when informed men could believe that anything it was possible to know was already revealed and available through the work of recognized authorities.

America's colleges began to make room for the individual sciences in 1711 when William and Mary established a professorship of natural philosophy and mathematics (Rudolph, 1977), and, as the sciences matured, each won representation someplace within a college or university. The real breakthrough, however, involved the reorganization of some American colleges in ways that promoted the conduct of research. At first tentatively, through associations with scientific and technical institutions, and eventually in a more integrated way, with the creation of graduate divisions and research facilities in the institutions themselves, American universities began to participate in the systematic studies of man, nature, and society that the techniques of science encouraged and facilitated. New ideas and findings generated further study, and scholarly practice and thought were cultivated in ways that created new academic disciplines. Powerful tools were developed to improve our vision, our memories, our communication, and our abilities to process information rapidly. The result has been a spiraling rate of knowledge growth.

Toffler (1971, pp. 30, 31) measures that growth in terms

of published books, observing that by the mid-1960s, the world output of books in a single day matched Europe's production of books in a whole year prior to 1500. Dressel (1971, p. 7) reported that the number of distinct specializations in the natural sciences alone increased from about 50 in 1950 to nearly 1,000 in 1970. Such indicators are crude and perhaps document the obvious, but they all point to the same unsettling conclusion. Measured against all that is now collectively known by human beings, the ignorance of even the wisest and most educated person grows every day. So does the stock of knowledge to be sampled, and the challenge to colleges to convey it to their students effectively.

The most obvious consequence of the growth of knowledge for the curriculum is that in any four-year period, the proportion of the world's total knowledge a college can offer to its students inevitably will be less than that of the period that immediately preceded it. Moreover, it is becoming harder for colleges to insist that any specific amount and kind of knowledge is adequately representative of everything that there is to know. To get a substantial sampling of the world of knowledge, people must now spend more time on formal education than they once did, either all at once or in several stages throughout life. And most of us still have to settle for a much smaller share of the knowledge that is available than colleges were once able to offer —even though what we get is vastly more substantial than was available to our ancestors.

For the colleges, the growth of knowledge presents difficult administrative and planning problems. The capacity of faculty members to keep up with developments is severely taxed, and there are limits to any college's ability to maintain a faculty that is even superficially representative of all of the important academic disciplines and subfields. In the final analysis, such practical considerations may determine the most important dimension of the curriculum—its scope at any college.

Learned and professional societies. Because their members are drawn so heavily from the college and university faculties, learned societies might be expected to have a significant influ-

ence on the college curriculum. To test this assumption, in 1974 and 1975, the Carnegie Council on Policy Studies in Higher Education conducted an informal survey of 38 learned societies. These organizations were asked to provide information on their current programs related to undergraduate education, to report on any ongoing or recently completed studies of undergraduate education they had conducted, and to comment on the roles they considered appropriate for their societies in the development of undergraduate curricula.

Eight of the organizations did not reply. Of those that did reply, 21 said that they either could not provide any of the information requested or that they had not recently completed a study on the curriculum. But nine said that they had completed such studies and provided information about them. Of the 21 associations that indicated that they could not provide studies for the Council, several did have within their organizational structure a committee or section on undergraduate education.[3]

In general, the societies that take an interest in the curriculum concentrate on professional and graduate school training. Moreover, most of the societies that have sections on undergraduate education do not, as a matter of policy, discuss which courses ought to be taught or why. Instead, they are concerned with *how* their discipline is taught. Most refrain from issuing policy statements on the curriculum, justifying their actions by such statements as "Diversity and the accompanying freedom to innovate, experiment, and do one's own thing, like any form of liberty, are always possible only in conditions where freedom is allowed. The potential influence of APA [American Psychological Association] was seen as a threat to this freedom, and it was concluded that the Association should not be engaged in the specification of curricula nor in the development of texts or

[3]*Change* Magazine reports that in June 1976, 17 representatives of 13 disciplines "ranging from philosophy and religion to biology and economics" met "to examine what, if anything, was happening in the disciplines to foster improvement in undergraduate teaching" (McNamara, 1976, p. 22). A few of the disciplines represented were not among those that responded to the Council's inquiries.

other teaching materials." And the American Political Science Association made the following statement "Members of the Steering Committee agreed that the (education) Program's mission to improve undergraduate education would be served best by taking, as our frame of reference, the discipline's substantive theoretical and methodological pluralism."

In sharp contrast to these positions is that of the Mathematical Association of America, which details precisely what courses should be offered, the sequence of courses, and the topics that should be covered in each course.

On other fronts, the American Association of Physics Teachers has conducted a survey of introductory physics courses for use in preparing instructional modules (independent units of instruction with clearly defined objectives), and both the American Institute of Biological Sciences and the American Geological Institute have sponsored development of teaching materials and special reports related to undergraduate education. The American Psychological Association and the American Geological Institute have also disseminated major studies of undergraduate education to their members, and the American Psychological Society's *Directory of Teaching Innovations in Psychology* (1973) has been singled out for special praise by representatives of other disciplines that are actively concerned with undergraduate education (McNamara, 1976). The Modern Language Association has recently published *Options for Teaching of English: The Undergraduate Curriculum (1975)*, based on a survey of 23 departments and which offers ideas for curriculum improvements.

The American Political Science Association and the American Sociological Association are among those that have special sections that generate studies and discussion of instructional techniques and procedures and encourage development of experimental learning materials for use at the undergraduate level.

Although some of the efforts of these societies to improve undergraduate education have been supported by such federal agencies as the National Science Foundation and the Fund for the Improvement of Postsecondary Education, the organizations continue to feel the restraint of inadequate funding, par-

ticularly for field projects (McNamara, 1976). Such activities are so important, however, that where external funding is not available from philanthropic foundations or the federal government, we would hope that the societies themselves might reallocate some of their resources so that at least some programs related to undergraduate education will be possible.

Textbook authors and publishers. So far, no one has devised anything as inexpensive and portable as a book for presenting the basic principles and information that underlie a course of instruction. Textbooks, therefore, promise to be prominent fixtures on college campuses for many years to come.

The publishers of textbooks disclaim any intention of shaping the structure of the curriculum or even, for that matter, a course of instruction, but they work hard to anticipate the need for new textbooks and to produce works that have sufficient impact to remain useful for a long time. One frequently cited example is Paul Samuelson's introduction to economics, which was first issued in 1948 and, in its various editions, has sold more than 3 million copies.

One publisher told us that textbooks are the product of a three-way relationship between what the teachers say they need, what the author can write, and what the publisher can produce and sell. Ideally, the author himself might be a master teacher.

Occasionally, publishers have an opportunity to share in the development of a new discipline. Such was the case more than 50 years ago when 15 prominent chemical engineers met in New York to plan the development of a literature for their embryonic profession. The result of their labors was a series of texts and references published by McGraw-Hill Book Company.

Profound changes in a discipline can also be anticipated by individual authors. Linus Pauling overturned years of tradition in the teaching of chemistry when he wrote a book that, instead of being simply descriptive, was built on basic principles. Today, almost all chemistry textbooks use his approach. In 1974, Frank Press and Raymond Siever helped to introduce profound changes in the teaching of geology by writing a text-

book in which plate tectonics, usually consigned to a single chapter, became the guiding principle. Undoubtedly many other such examples could be drawn from lists of textbooks in print, but these few should make our point.

A relatively new approach to textbook publishing draws on the tools of market and systems analysis. The process begins with a survey of faculty members in a discipline to determine what kinds of books they need, what the shortcomings of existing texts are, and what the characteristics of prospective users are. The publishers then prepare detailed specifications on content, topics, and sequence of subject development and invite experts on each topic to prepare a draft in accord with the specifications. The chapters are later rewritten and published by the book's editor. "Managed texts" as these books are sometimes called, may make up in versatility whatever they lack in spontaneity and virtuosity, but there is some danger that they may also cater to the lowest common denominators of student interest and ability.

Publishers are giving increasing attention to the "readability" of textbooks, with the result that in some cases texts are being prepared for college students whose reading skills are those of eighth- or ninth-graders. According to publishers interviewed by *The Chronicle of Higher Education,* the market for "rigorous materials"—defined as those written at or above the twelfth-grade level has been dwindling (Scully, 1974, p. 11).

As long as there are professors who "teach the text," it is hard to discount the influence of the textbook on the college tradition. If anything, that influence is being reasserted after a few years during which the traditional textbooks were being abandoned in favor of reading lists made up of "relevant" paperbacks. The combination of increasing paperback prices, the need to use several such books to cover the basic subject matter in a course, and the difficulty many students encounter in dealing with unstructured readings has renewed faculty interest in the basic guides to principles and applications the conventional textbooks have become.

Foundations. One of the more profound influences on the curricula of America's high schools and colleges was the invention

of the "unit" by a committee of the National Education Association in 1899 and its use by The Carnegie Foundation for the Advancement of Teaching in 1906 to define colleges in terms of units required for admission. That definition, in turn, was used to designate institutions whose faculty members were eligible for participation in pension programs set up by the Foundation (Carnegie Commission, 1973b, p. 14). The unit system is now very widely used throughout American education, and its utilization affects not only the time devoted to certain subjects but also the sequence in which subjects are offered. But, as pervasive as this innovation has become, it does not begin to suggest the full range of influences foundations have had on college curricula.

One of the major functions of private foundations in the United States is to make possible new ventures and programs for which adequate support is not available from other sources. And many foundations have performed that function with special attention to educational activities. It is not necessary to belabor this fact, and it would be impossible and inappropriate to attempt to list here all of the influences on the curricula of colleges and universities that foundation support has made possible. By way of example, they have contributed to the creation of Metropolitan State University, a unique upper-division college serving the Minneapolis-St. Paul area; have encouraged development of three-year bachelor's degree programs; have provided the kind of general assistance to colleges and universities that made possible the creation of the University of Alabama's experimental and influential New College; and have provided support for the development of new competency-based curricula that, ironically, tend to break away from the "Carnegie unit" tradition.

In assessing the influence of foundations on the curriculum, it may be worth noting that, for the most part, the only "external" part of their influence is the funding they provide. The ideas and programs they help to realize usually originate with the institutions themselves.

Inputs

Both the quality and the character of the college curriculum are determined significantly by the investment of talent and financial resources that society is willing to invest in it.

High school contributions. From the very beginning, public schools in the United States have had, as a major function, the preparation of young persons for attending college. By the end of the nineteenth century, the character of that preparation was fairly well defined as consisting of two years of a foreign language, two years of mathematics, two years of English, one year of history, and one year of science (Carnegie Commission, 1973b, p. 14). Those elements are still regarded as basic to preparation for entry to many colleges. But because of changes in both high schools and colleges, the likelihood has been reduced of a close match between the preparation that is provided and a college's admissions requirements.

The changes began in about 1910 when high schools became less institutions for college-bound students and became more schools for everyone. Their functions were expanded to include general preparation for adult responsibilities and training for an occupation. During this period, college enrollments grew slowly, while school enrollments, as a proportion of America's 14- to 17-year-olds, increased very rapidly—reaching 75 percent in 1940 and 93.6 percent in 1975 (Carnegie Commission, 1973b, p. 17; U.S. Bureau of Census, 1976b, p. 8). After 1940, the enrollments of colleges increased, and the colleges themselves began to serve more diversified student bodies. Community colleges (first called "junior colleges") were and are, in many cases, open to all high school graduates. At state colleges and universities, admission also may be open to all high school graduates but frequently is restricted to students who are in some specified top percentage of their high school graduating classes. Some selective state universities limit admission to persons within the top 10 to 15 percent. Private institutions include both highly selective and relatively low-selective colleges.

High schools continue to be feeder institutions for all colleges and universities, and the achievement and ability levels of their graduates determine the threshold level of the undergraduate curriculum.

Our basic position on the relationship of the high schools to the college curriculum may be stated in the following propositions:

1. High schools are the highest-level institutions of learning attended by nearly all people in the United States. Consequently, any instruction that any state considers essential for preparing all youth for responsible adulthood and citizenship properly should be given in these schools, not in colleges and universities that are attended by only a portion of the people.

2. Because of near-universal attendance in them, high schools have a responsibility for providing all of their students with instruction designed to familiarize them with the major divisions of knowledge and with some of the ways such divisions relate to one another. General education is appropriate to all levels of schooling.

3. All Americans, whether they attend college or not, need to acquire skills in reading, writing, and oral communication in English and in basic mathematics. Although education is cumulative and high schools do not alone bear the responsibility for deficiencies in such skills, they should persist, with the cooperation and assistance of colleges and elementary schools, in efforts to reduce the deficiencies in such skills among high school graduates.

4. High schools share a responsibility with colleges to make certain that no student is impeded in his or her progress toward completion of secondary and higher education goals. Students with the ability and desire to do so should be assisted in efforts to accelerate their educational progress through early high school graduation and admission to college, completion of college-level instruction for college credit while still enrolled in high school, or by any other appropriate means.

Budgets. Financial stringency has four effects on the college curriculum. First, it forces colleges to review the curriculum itself to look for places to reduce expenses. Fifty percent of the nation's colleges reported that between 1968 and 1974 they had resorted to "extensive" or "some" elimination or consolidation of courses in order to reallocate resources (Glenny, Shea, Ruyle, and Freschi, 1976, p. 29). Seventy-five percent indicated that they expect to make such changes between 1974 and 1980 (Glenny et al., 1976, p. 29).

A second effect is to increase the influence of a college's central administration in curricular decisions. In hard times, presidents and academic deans are especially likely to ask departments to justify average class size and teaching loads of faculty members and to encourage use of teaching methods and media that promise savings.

The third effect of budgetary restraint is to diminish incentive for trying out unfamiliar curricular ideas. Unusual courses or programs may be hard to fund when the emphasis is on standardization and "essentials." Only innovations that promise early fiscal savings, increased enrollment, favorable public reaction, or philanthropic support will be championed and instituted with relative ease.

A fourth effect is to intensify efforts to offer courses that reflect popular interests and attract enrollments. Early this year, the *Christian Science Monitor* reported on the following new courses that had been created at colleges "to foster enrollment." Among those cited were "Why the Sky is Blue and Things Like That" at Ithaca College; "Dreams," "Clowns," "Alka-Seltzer, Salad Oil, and Salt on Wintry Roads," at Hampshire College; and "The God Question," at Boston College (Karp, 1977). Without carefully studying the descriptions and objectives of such courses, it is unfair to assume that they are frivolous or superficial, but the labeling does illustrate our basic point. Colleges that experiment with novel teaching methods and curriculum arrangements usually do so for educationally sound reasons. But some of them may also hope such practices will attract students. Other institutions tried to build enrollments by making curricula more open and attractive to adults, part-time students, and students with lower academic ability and achievements. Because they expand educational opportunity and challenge the historic tradition that college is exclusively for the young and exceptionally able, these efforts to build enrollments have extended the mission and objectives of the colleges and have benefited society. However, they are accompanied by expensive obligations, including those of providing increasing amounts of compensatory or remedial education for more of their students and meeting the costs of converting old systems to new ones.

Regulation

Historically, colleges and universities have been accorded substantial amounts of independence and freedom, particularly in matters related to the curriculum. Some of that independence has been lost to state governments and voluntary accrediting agencies in recent years, and there is a potential danger that more of it will be lost in the future to the courts and to collective bargaining.

Governments. In the judgment of Paul J. Olscamp, president of Western Washington State College, the "battle of the century, and perhaps longer" for most American colleges "will be over the question of whether our programs should be determined by quantitative data such as student demand, job placement rate, cost per semester hour, and average lifetime wage, or whether the final determinant shall rest upon considerations such as the value to our civilization of a population tolerant of ambiguity, who find challenge and pleasure in diversity, who can compare their own culture as well as commerce to that of other nation-states, and who have lives with which they are more satisfied because of the range of choices made available to them through their education" (Olscamp, 1976, p. 10). The principal contenders in the battle will be the colleges versus the governmental agencies that endeavor to regulate them.

As the battle wages, a great and growing concern of college presidents and academic leaders is what appears to them to be the insatiable demands of state and federal agencies for information. The rationale for these requests is that the government owes the taxpayers an accounting of the use of public funding for education. Government agencies are also interested in creating data bases that enable them to develop objective formulas for the determination of levels of support for universities and colleges. In the process, they tend to identify "averages" and "optimum" levels of funding and expenditures that become targets and, in some cases, limits for institutional effort. The fear expressed by many presidents is that the institutions that desire to do more than the statistical average or to budget curricular development in patterns that are not anticipated by "average" practices may not be able to do so. Ideally, each college strives

to design a curriculum that is consistent with an institutionally designed mission (see Section Seven). That mission takes into account not only the amount of financial support available to the college but also the character and interests of the faculty members and many other, often unmeasurable qualities associated with location, size, age, facilities, climate (natural and intellectual), and, perhaps most important of all, tradition. Accountability data that may be comparable for all colleges and universities cannot allow for such factors. Moreover, evaluations of colleges that rely wholly on comparable data could ultimately restrict the freedom of teachers to teach and students to learn by limiting their educational options to those that fit governmentally imposed formulas.

If college officials seem wary of the subtle but potentially important influences of increased governmental data collection, it may be because they are aware that, particularly in public institutions, considerable governmental inroads have already been made in their power to control the curricula of their institutions. In a study of members of the American Association of State Colleges and Universities conducted in 1975, it was found that although 70 percent of the institutions have final authority to make changes in specific courses, their academic programs are affected or finally approved by a statewide coordinating body. In one out of twelve cases, both the program and specific courses must be approved by a statewide coordinating body (Harcleroad, 1975, p. 12). In Florida, the 1975-76 legislative appropriations act required that the state university system develop uniform course numbering for all institutions in the system. The California Community College Board of Governors reviews the academic master plans for each district and requires that community college academic deans obtain its approval for any courses added to their curricula outside of approved programs. Since 1976, the board has been required by law to review and monitor approved programs periodically. In Colorado, the board of education divided the state into major occupational planning areas so that the occupational curricula of community colleges could be allocated on the basis of a statewide scheme (Cohen, 1974, p. 45).

Governments can also influence curricular policy by giving special support to certain types of programs, for example, career preparation. In the years after *Sputnik*, the federal government exerted such influence by offering financial assistance in forms that favored students in the sciences and those who planned to become teachers. Although government incentives of this kind are often necessary to accelerate educational responses to state and national needs, they can unintentionally load the scales of student choice in ways that set the stage for long-term changes in the number and quality of faculty and facilities available in lower-priority subject areas.

Curricular planners at two-year and four-year colleges that prepare persons for entry into certain occupations are inevitably concerned with the regulations and policies of state occupational licensing boards. Such boards often use tests to certify persons for employment or practice in the occupations under their jurisdiction, and colleges must be sure that their instruction gives students the skills and knowledge the tests might cover. In some cases, licensing may be even more directly related to the curriculum in that it specifies units and times of the formal education that candidates must attain. Colleges that expect their graduates to be employed in fields with such requirements are under strong pressures to make sure that the curricula they offer meet licensing criteria.

State legislatures can have an expansive effect on curricula by making special appropriations to colleges and universities for teaching and research in subjects of current interest either to an entire state or to some locality or group within the state. They can also have a regulatory effect, not only by reducing general state support for higher learning but also by prescribing the minimum number of hours that faculty must spend teaching, as was done by the legislature in the state of Washington. Such actions inevitably have an effect on the college's options in the utilization of resources and faculty members and reduce curricular flexibility in the process.

Accrediting agencies. Most of America's colleges and universities submit to periodic evaluation by one of six regional accrediting

agencies and, for their specific programs, some of the 59 professional accrediting agencies in the country ("A Moral Crusade," 1976, pp. 223-228). All of the regional agencies and 53 of the professional ones are officially recognized by the U.S. Office of Education, and their accrediting decisions can affect the eligibility of colleges for participation in federal financing and assistance to students and institutions. Accreditation is taken into account by the states in establishing education requirements for persons who receive licenses to practice certain occupations or professions. It is also a consideration in the evaluation of the transcripts of students who are transferring from one institution to another or who are applying for graduate school admission. Without it, colleges can count on little cooperation from high schools when they are recruiting students (Dickey and Miller, 1972, p. 28) and may find that prospective donors will not be attentive to their appeals for financial support.

Many students and their parents assume that accreditation indicates a quality ranking among colleges. That assumption is totally unwarranted. Relatively few colleges are not accredited. What accrediting agencies actually do is encourage colleges and universities to subject themselves and some of their programs to periodic self-examination and to evaluate their success in terms of their own purposes and characteristics. By publishing guidelines for the self-evaluation process; by sending accrediting teams to make on-site visits to colleges undergoing review; and, finally, by deciding whether or not to grant or renew accreditation, however, they do exert an external judgment on an institution's resources and performance. Such judgment may be particularly crucial when a college seeks accreditation for the first time or when it is for one reason or another having financial, structural, or operational difficulties. Institutions that are clearly in secure positions may be given the option in some regions of foregoing an institution-wide study and devoting the usual review period to concentrated consideration of special problems. They must still present some basic data for review, but the bulk of their efforts involve study of the special topics they themselves select for emphasis. Such topics might include the broadening of financial support, the development of core courses or programs, or the improvement of general education.

The basic data required for self-evaluation in the accrediting process includes information on the qualifications of staff members; admission policies and practices; the availability of laboratories, libraries, and instructional facilities; and student-faculty ratios. Some agencies are concerned with the process of curriculum development—with how new courses are proposed, considered, and adopted. There is also considerable emphasis on the balance of the components of the undergraduate curriculum and the fairness with which the curriculum is described to the general public.

Some of the standards reveal concerns for very specific policies and practices. For example, the Western Association of Schools and Colleges (1975, p. 38) asks, "Are units of credit limited to approximately one semester unit or its equivalent for a week of full-time study?" And the Commission on Institutions of Higher Education for the New England Association of Schools and Colleges (1974, p. 2) stipulates that "terminal programs and curricula in technical, specialized or professional fields are expected to show an appropriate regard to the three major areas of knowledge, i.e., the humanities, the natural sciences, and the social sciences, by insuring that at least a quarter of the typical student's program consists of general education courses from among these three areas."

Professional accrediting agencies, which are often related to learned societies or groups of professional institutions, are likely to have an even more detailed interest in the curriculum than regional associations have. Their concern is for the quality both of the institution's work and of the professional or pre-professional graduates the institutions produce. In some instances, such agencies not only accredit colleges and universities but also prepare examinations that qualify candidates for entrance into the professions they represent (Orlans, 1975, p. 11).

The American Chemical Society[4] issued "Objectives and

[4]In 1974, the American Chemical Society lost its recognition by the U.S. Office of Education for "deficiencies" in compliance with criteria specified in 1969. The deficiencies involved the society's review procedures and compliance with certain organizational requirements. The U.S. Office of Education also decided that the society's accreditation is not necessary for institutions to receive federal funds or for chemistry graduates to receive professional licensure ("U.S.O.E. Drops the Chemical Society," 1974, p.

Guidelines for Undergraduate Programs in Chemistry" in 1972 and included in the document a "sample recommended curriculum." It stipulated that the first two years of a curriculum in chemistry will often need to include basic physical chemical principles, a generous amount of descriptive chemistry of the elements, a substantial amount of organic and biochemistry, important basic features of the determination and interpretation of molecular structure and reaction rates, and laboratory work that employs modern techniques and instruments useful to students in other disciplines. It describes the core material to be presented for majors and nonmajors in chemistry; advanced work and interdisciplinary programs; laboratory work; and procedures needed to protect the institutional resources and faculty time invested in independent study and research. The Society is quite specific about the way an undergraduate planning to be a professional chemist should spend his or her time—at least 500 hours of laboratory work in chemistry and the equivalent of 400 hours of traditional classroom work—about 40 percent of a student's total course load for a bachelor's degree measured in semester hours. Some colleges find these requirements excessive for students who are not planning to become professional chemists and offer less demanding majors in the subject for students who plan to terminate their higher education at the bachelor's degree level.

Both the regional and professional accrediting agencies influence college and university curricula, although they officially declare a disinterest in restricting programs of individual institutions. Regional agencies are more successful in this regard than the professional agencies, because regional agencies are organized by and for the institutions they evaluate and consider the institution in its totality. Professional associations, on the other hand, are more likely to emphasize the interests of the members of professions, including the individual faculty members in the departments and schools they evaluate, rather than colleges and universities.

---

7). The society has decided not to take action to have its recognition restored.

Efforts are being made by several regional associations to develop appropriate procedures for evaluating nontraditional programs. The Southern Association of Colleges and Schools is now particularly active in this field, and the Middle States Association of Colleges and Secondary Schools emphasizes outcomes of the college education in its evaluation procedures. It asks such questions as "How successful are the college's graduates?" "Does the college program work?" and "Does the college achieve what it claims to do?"

But the forces that define and defend the status quo in the curricula of colleges and universities are hard to resist. In developing standards, it is often easier to argue for the dominant and traditional program than it is to promote experimental and nontraditional ones.

The courts. The courts have been reluctant to exert authority in matters involving the curriculum, holding that educators are the most reliable experts in such matters. Increasingly, however, they have been called on to decide issues involving the provision of access to colleges and universities, use of due process in suspension or dismissal of students or faculty members, and protecting individual rights of members of the campus community.

The attitude of the courts is indicated by some of their opinions. In denying a mother's request that the court direct a college and high school to reevaluate her son's academic record in a special high school course for the purpose of making an adjustment of seven-tenths of a percent on his scholastic average and thus qualifying him for admission to the college, an appeal court said, "Courts may not interfere with the administrative discretion exercised by agencies which are vested with the administration and control of educational institutions, unless the circumstances disclosed by the record leave no scope for the use of that discretion in the matter under scrutiny. . . . The judicial task ends when it is found that the applicant has received from college authorities uniform treatment under reasonable regulations fairly administered" (239 N.Y.S. 2nd 776, 1963, cited in Brubacher, 1971).

More directly related to the curriculum are a series of

court cases based on the assumption that a college's catalog and promotional materials constitute a legally binding offer or contract. The assumption itself has not yet been legally tested, but several cases have been heard in which students have claimed that the education they received was not what was advertised. One of the best known of these involved a student at Columbia University who refused to pay a promissory note for his tuition on the grounds that the university had not taught him "wisdom" as he contended its catalogs and brochures led him to believe it would. The court decided the case by explicitly endorsing the affidavit of the Columbia College dean, who said: "All that any college can do through its teachers, libraries, laboratories, and other facilities is to endeavor to teach the student the known facts, acquaint him with the nature of those matters which are unknown, and thereby assist him in developing mentally, morally, and physically. Wisdom is a hoped-for end product of education, experience, and ability which many seek and many fail to attain" (148 A. 2nd 63, 1959, in Brubacher, 1971, p. 104). A group of students at St. Cloud State College based a suit on the fact that the college catalog announced an academic year of 172 days, yet permitted a "Time Out for Today" program to take place. During that day, the regular classes were suspended, and activities were organized around speakers and films on such topics as "war, sex, the politics of protest, and so on." The court refused to intervene, indicating that control of the curriculum was at the discretion of the college president and that the "plaintiffs have no more right to choose the contents and formats of their classes than they would have to hire or fire faculty or select the textbooks for their classmates" (Brubacher, 1971, p. 106).

In a more recent case, a student at the University of Bridgeport filed a claim to recover $150 in tuition plus the cost of her books and legal fees on the grounds that a course in "Methods and Materials in Teaching Basic Business Subjects" was not what the catalog led her to believe it would be. She claimed that all she learned was how to operate an overhead projector and that the only requirement for her course was to turn in a book report. All students in the course received A's

("Student Sues University," March 10, 1975, p. 2). The case was decided in favor of the college.

Another type of case concerns the exercise of discretionary authority by college officials. A student at Columbia University sought a court order to compel the university to reinstate him as a certified candidate for the doctor of philosophy degree after the faculty committee had rejected his original dissertation and he had refused to submit a revised version (O'Hara and Hill, 1972, pp. 40, 41). The college was sustained by the court. In reporting this, and similar cases, W. T. O'Hara and J. G. Hill conclude (p. 41), "When issues involving grades, course credit, and graduation arise, the courts will be hesitant to interfere with institutional decisions unless it can be clearly shown that the decision was arbitrary, capricious, or made in bad faith."

Faculty collective bargaining. About 25 percent of the nation's full-time college faculty members are now included in some form of collective bargaining organization on about 30 percent of the nation's campuses (Carnegie Council, Garbarino, J., Feller, D. and Finkin, M., 1977, p. 2), and faculty sentiment favoring collective action is growing. The scope of bargaining in institutions of higher education usually is limited by statute to wages, hours, and terms and conditions of employment, but the line between such issues and those that have to do with the curriculum is not easily drawn. Collective bargaining could have increasing impacts on undergraduate education in the years ahead.

Pointing out that the curriculum, teaching, and research are "at the heart of the academic enterprise," the Carnegie Council has urged that state legislation governing public employees' rights to bargain collectively specifically exempt:

- The selection and conduct of research by individual faculty members
- The content of courses and methods of teaching by individual faculty, or the development of programs of study
- The selection and promotion to tenure of individual faculty members

- The determination of individual student grades and the awarding of individual degrees
- The selection of individual academic leadership

College Interaction

Colleges do not exist in isolation. They base their curricula on knowledge that is equally available to all institutions of higher learning, and their students can move easily from one college to another. Despite their great diversity, therefore, they frequently interact.

Transfer students. By 1976, about one-third of the college students in the United States had attended at least one college other than the one in which they were currently enrolled (Carnegie Council Surveys, 1975-1976). In some institutions, the proportion of transfers is considerably higher. At the University of California at Berkeley, for example, in a random sample of seniors graduating in 1975, only 41 percent of the men and 29 percent of the women had come to the campus directly from high school. Half of the men and 54 percent of the women entered the University at Berkeley with either junior or senior status (Frank, 1976, p. 4). This general picture probably is duplicated at many other institutions.

Community colleges have provided only the first two years of a baccalaureate education since their junior college days and are acutely sensitive to the insistence of admissions officers at four-year institutions that there be as much conformity as possible in the first years of the academic curriculum for all institutions. The community colleges are also increasingly confronted with a new transfer phenomenon—the four-year college student who transfers to a community college, sometimes after receiving a baccalaureate degree, in order to obtain the specialized training needed for entry into an occupation. In 1970, 9 percent of the community college students nationwide were "reverse transfer students," and in 1974 two-year colleges were receiving as many transfers from four-year colleges as they were sending to them (Lee, 1976). De Anza College in California has more students transferring in from the University of California than are transferring out to the university.

By keeping their doors open to students at all stages of their academic careers, American colleges have given millions of Americans a "second chance" to acquire the kind of education they want and need.

There are consequences to this openness that are not altogether good, however, and their impacts on the curriculum should be borne in mind throughout this commentary. They are:

1. A national dependence on the academic accounting system that translates the undergraduate experience into the units and grade points that are accepted (despite wide variations in the content and quality of instruction at different institutions) as common tender across the desks of college admission officers.

2. Perpetuation of the "course" as measured in quarter, semester, or year lengths as the basic unit of the curriculum, although there is no inherent relationship between the objectives of instruction offered in a program and the time allotted for its completion. Some instruction that is now packaged in semester lengths might be more efficiently taught in either less or more time if the structure of the curriculum permitted use of such modules.

3. Discontinuities in the completion of institutionally prescribed instruction. Transfer students may leave one institution before completing its basic requirements and may arrive too late to take the full sequence of institutionally prescribed courses at a new college. Where, in such circumstances, is the compromise to be made? In the extension of the student's schedule to pick up what was missed? In the standards and character of the instruction an institution proposes to offer?

The choices that may have to be made if this situation is to be improved are difficult. They may entail restricting the opportunities of students to transfer from one institution to another. That choice would be repugnant to us on the grounds that it limits student options for procedural rather than educational reasons. The choice might also entail standardizing the undergraduate curriculum. It discourages experimentation and

encourages development of a monolithic undergraduate curriculum subject to centralized manipulation that can affect the offerings of many institutions simultaneously.

The long-term solution, one that has been adopted by several colleges for at least part of their curriculum, is to shift undergraduate education from an emphasis on programs and experiences that enable students to achieve predetermined objectives or competencies on a variable time schedule. This option will be discussed in greater detail in Section Five.

Competition. Between 1953 and 1975, the number of colleges and universities in the United States increased from 1,845 to 2,765—an increase of about 49 percent (National Center for Education Statistics, 1977, pp. 107, 108).[5] While this increase has given students more opportunities and more options for higher learning, it has also intensified competition among institutions for both enrollments and financial support.

Competition may be encountered on several levels:

1. *Price competition as reflected in tuition.* Public colleges enjoy a distinctive price advantage over private colleges. The Carnegie Commission on Higher Education (1974, p. 3) reported that public tuition was estimated to be about 24 percent of educational costs and private tuition was estimated to be about 62 percent of educational costs. In areas where there are few public institutions, the effects of this differential may not be severe. The effects are also less acute in areas that favor development of private colleges by maintaining relatively high tuitions in public institutions. But the absence of these mitigating factors will very likely generate competition on the programmatic level.

2. *Curricular competition.* Colleges that find themselves at a pricing disadvantage or that are located in geographical areas where there are few prospective students to draw from may compete in terms of curriculum content. The object of such

---

[5] If all campuses within institutions are counted, the total number is 3,026 for 1975. Comparable data is not available for 1953.

competition is for an institution to become a sole source, if possible, of certain kinds of instruction. The strategy may be to introduce a greater variety of disciplines and courses than other colleges or to introduce courses that appeal to the special concerns of students in target geographical areas or interest groups. Private liberal arts colleges are often disadvantaged in such competition because they lack financial and other resources needed to expand their curricula. (This "disadvantage" may also work in their favor, however, because some students regard comprehensive curricula as bewildering and consider more restricted curricula to be qualitatively superior.) Regardless of source of support, institutions may compete for students by striving to be the first to offer instruction in new, popular fields, or in subjects related to preparation of students for new kinds of jobs. The danger of such competition is that it sometimes leads institutions into programs and levels of instruction for which their available financial and faculty resources are inadequate. Occasionally it also duplicates unnecessarily offerings that may already be available in a geographical area.

3. *Procedural competition.* Another form of competition involves introducing policies and practices that prospective students may find opportune, convenient, interesting, or in some other way attractive. Such competition has less to do with the content of the curriculum than it has with the way it is structured and packaged. Education may be offered to previously unserved students, for example, by changing admissions policies and procedures and offering instruction in high-demand subjects at hours that are convenient for older, working students. It may be offered in small classes or may be individualized by employing special instructional methods and technology. It may be offered in modules that require a short time to complete. Or it may include travel abroad, work experience, or other activities as a part of the total program. It may also be made attractive by using grading systems that students consider nonthreatening.

Competition provides a powerful incentive for curricular

and instructional experimentation and change and explains to a
considerable degree why the institutions that tend to be most
competitive—private liberal arts colleges with relatively low
selectivity and student admissions policies—tend also to be the
ones that are heavily engaged in nontraditional and experimental programs.

Cooperation. Many colleges expand their curricula and student
services by joining forces with other institutions that share similar interests, needs, and circumstances. By 1973, there were at
least 80 such alliances, characterized by a voluntary formal
organization, three or more member institutions, multiacademic
programs, at least one full-time professional administrator, and
a required annual contribution or other indication of a long-
term commitment of member institutions (Patterson, 1974, pp.
2, 3). Pioneered by the Claremont colleges in California and the
Atlanta University System in Georgia, such cooperation may
entail sharing library resources, allowing students to cross register for instruction, sharing faculty members, and jointly offering graduate programs. Some consortia of colleges are organized
specifically for special purposes, such as sharing expensive facilities (computer centers, libraries, or special research laboratories,
for example) or offering adult education. The obvious impact of
such arrangements on the curriculum is to give it breadth and
depth that few participating colleges could provide on their
own.

Summary

The undergraduate curriculum is often thought of as being insu-
lated from influences outside the college, and it is true that
overt manipulation by the general public or external agencies is
strongly resisted by administrators, faculty members, and students alike. The curriculum is nevertheless responsive to the
public interest and to changes in a college's relationship to professional and occupational groups, to the quality and level of
preparation given to college students by high schools, to the
levels of financial support available, to regulation and monitor-
ing by governmental and accrediting agencies, and to the laws of

survival and competition that govern the colleges' coexistence with other institutions of higher learning. The curriculum is particularly responsive to the growth of knowledge and to the rise and fall of subject fields in public interest.

Most of these external influences have been felt by the curriculum for a long time, although two of them—the courts and academic collective bargaining—are as yet more potentially an influence than they are in practice. Most of the influences are, on the whole, benign or even advantageous—although, like many good things, harmful in excess. Whether they are good or bad, they cannot be ignored. In many ways, they set the horizons of feasible curricular policy.

*   *   *

For further information on subjects discussed in this section, see the chapter on "Characteristics of Curriculum Change," in the Carnegie Council on Policy Studies in Higher Education, *Handbook on Undergraduate Curriculum.*

4

Internal Influences on the Curriculum

Although many external factors influence the undergraduate curriculum, it continues to be shaped in its specifics mostly by internal forces. The general concerns of outsiders must be taken into consideration, but the basic responsibility for deciding what particular subjects will be taught, what instructional format will be used, how long the instruction in a subject will take, and whether it will be offered at an introductory or advanced level belongs to faculty members, students, and others on the campuses who have professional interests in the intellectual and personal development of undergraduates.

A truly comprehensive accounting of everyone at a college who has influence on the curriculum would include the admissions officers who select the students enrolled and who, in doing so, help determine the level of instruction to each freshman class; the registrars who schedule times and places for instruction and keep the accounts of students' academic achievement; deans of students who may administer counseling programs, students' personal adjustments, and the extracurriculum; and librarians who make available the information re sources that support and supplement classroom instruction. In this commentary, we cannot do justice to all such influences, however, so we will concentrate on six that we consider to be central (see Figure 2):

Figure 2. Internal influences on the undergraduate curriculum

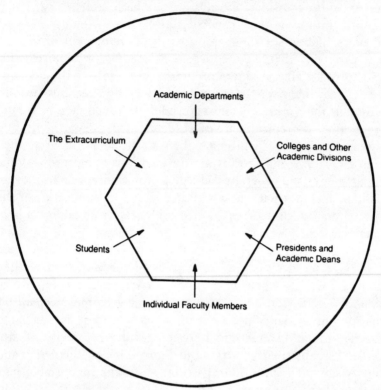

- Academic departments
- The college or other academic division
- The president and academic deans
- Individual faculty members
- The students
- The extracurriculum

Departmental Roles

Martin Trow (March, 1976, p. 11; and in McHenry, 1977, p. 13) describes the academic department as the "central link between the university and the disciplines ... between an organized body of learning—a body of knowledge and characteristic ways of extending knowledge—and the institution in which teaching

and learning are carried on." In most institutions, the departments and professional schools are the basic units of curricular administration and give particular attention to the design of sequences of courses for majors, to the development of courses and programs that meet college-wide graduation requirements, and to organizing graduate programs. In these activities, departments may be given considerable leeway by their institutions, although they must take into consideration such factors as budget trends, the enrollment of students in the department, and the availability of faculty members to teach the courses they plan to offer. Administratively, the decisions of nonprofessional departments are generally subject to review by a college dean, perhaps by a curriculum or educational policy committee of the entire faculty, and often by a president (whose approval is in many cases pro forma).

The academic departments of American universities are greatly admired by educators in parts of the world where they do not exist. They provide a means of decentralizing administration of instruction and research and can become mechanisms that permit academic decisions to be made as close as possible to the day-to-day interactions between faculty members and students. Perhaps their greatest contribution lies in the design and supervision of instruction of majors—now the most stable part of the college curriculum.

Internally, departments acquire characteristics that are an aggregate of the influences of the men and women who are their members. As a result, they offer opportunities for undergraduates to study with men and women who represent many interests and points of view. But few departments have either budgets or enrollments to justify hiring specialists in all subfields, philosophical orientations, and tradition of scholarship in a discipline. Any one department, therefore, may be heavily oriented toward a subspecialty rather than toward a discipline as a whole.

By overemphasizing specialization, departments create weaknesses in the remainder of the curriculum. Dean McHenry (1977, p. 212) points out that while they "may prove efficient for teaching their particular subject matter," they are "less than

effective for helping students learning about overarching cross-disciplinary relationships" and "neglect the major issues of human life, none of which lies in one discipline." To overcome such problems, McHenry recommends that institutions break down departmental insularity by developing coordinating units for groups of departments or programs with similar intellectual interests. For new institutions, he suggests further experimentation with academic structures that are not narrowly organized around individual disciplines but rather are organized around broad problem areas, subject fields (the general subjects, such as the social sciences, physical sciences, and humanities, within which most specific disciplines are now grouped), and other interdisciplinary units.

Colleges also should periodically review and evaluate the scope and quality of departmental undergraduate programs in the context of both their own institutional missions and the departments' educational objectives. On the basis of such reviews, colleges should provide rewards, in the form of staff augmentation or other assistance, for departments that make extraordinary efforts in undergraduate education.

To administer such programs fairly, the college must, in advance, develop and announce the criteria to be utilized. Adequate use of resources may be measured, for example, by such indicators as instructional costs per student, enrollments and student retention, and the extent to which departmental programs contribute to the outcomes implicit in the institution's mission and the departments' own objectives. Extraordinary effort might be indicated by participation in faculty development programs, efforts to provide effective general education and broad learning experiences, offering seminars on teaching for graduate students, and the design of instruction that makes appropriate use of instructional technology and, where appropriate, nontraditional teaching and learning methods. On the basis of periodic review, colleges should also reduce the resources of any department that are intended for undergraduate education but are inadequately utilized or misdirected to other purposes (such as graduate instruction or research). The object of such policies should be to make sure that an institution's

resources for undergraduate education are made available to departments that use them most effectively for that purpose.

Colleges and Other Internal Academic Divisions

Depending on the size of an institution and the structure of its academic government, there may be one or more layers of authority above that of the department that have responsibilities related to the undergraduate curriculum. At very large universities, there are likely to be professional schools and (under any of several designations) colleges of arts and sciences that function in relationship to departments in much the same manner as do most free-standing colleges.

A college or university might also have institution-wide faculty committees on the budget, on educational policy, and on the curriculum. Such committees may be responsible to some institution-wide faculty council or senate or to a college's governing board. They can develop their own review and evaluation procedures and, in some cases, make the final decisions, subject to a vote of the entire faculty, on whether new courses of instruction are to be offered and new educational programs funded.

Role of Presidents and Academic Deans

The college president can occupy a pivotal position in the planning and development of undergraduate education. He or she is frequently called on to articulate the institution's educational mission to the general public and to prospective students and benefactors. Internally, the president often has the task of interpreting the goals of the academic departments and divisions to boards of trustees. Theoretically, the president is also responsible for communicating the interests of the governing board, particularly its conception of the institution's educational mission, to the college's top academic officers and, through them, to the planners of undergraduate curricula at the departmental level.

The extent to which a president actually becomes involved in all of these activities will depend on the size of his or her institution and the extent to which its administrative structure

tends to separate the external and financial responsibilities of the presidency from academic concerns. Where such separation is sharp, much of the administrative influence upon the curriculum will come from a vice-president or dean of academic affairs. In the case of a large university that includes professional schools and colleges of arts and sciences, administrative authority may also be shared with the deans of such divisions.

Of all the responsibilities held by the president, the most important, in terms of the educational strength of the college, is that of evaluating and approving faculty appointments and promotions. In the exercise of that responsibility, the president can determine to a considerable extent whether or not an institution will have quality teaching as well as quality research; whether it will have faculty members who are interested in instructional experimentation; and whether it will have departments that are sufficiently broad in their subject matter orientation to make effective contributions at the undergraduate level. None of these actions necessarily requires new funding. They require only the effective use of funds that become available through normal staff attrition and close supervision of resource use for academic purposes.

In recent years, presidents have sometimes played a role in initiating special instruction that responds to demands of the times. We have been told by several presidents that the introduction of ethnic studies, women's studies, and environmental programs on their campuses would not have been possible through normal departmental procedures. Administrative intervention was necessary to get them started. The prestige and authority of presidents have also been used to encourage and sustain instructional innovations and the effective use of instructional technology.

In its report on *The More Effective Use of Resources,* the Carnegie Commission on Higher Education (1972c, p. 105) recommended that "colleges and universities develop a 'self-renewal' fund of 1 to 3 percent each year taken from existing allocations." For private institutions, that practice apparently has not proved feasible, because of inflation and their limited financial resources. Even so, the idea has merit. If it cannot be

financed through reallocation of existing funds, perhaps what one college president prefers to call a "hot idea fund" can be provided through special fund-raising efforts. At public institutions, presidents might urge on their state coordinating agencies and state legislatures a policy much like the one adopted in Florida, which guarantees all colleges an allocation of 2 percent of the previous year's budget for staff and program development. We still prefer, however, that to the extent possible, such funds be created through a process of careful review of existing programs with an eye toward curtailing ineffective, marginal, or overfunded activities and toward identifying needs and new ideas that deserve special attention. One of the surest ways to impose quality control on a college curriculum is to make clear to everyone that no instructional program is so "safe" that it will be exempt from thorough review when budgets are prepared and approved at the institution-wide level.

Faculty Role

Faculty members play multiple roles in the development of the curriculum. As members of curriculum or educational policy committees at the college-wide level, they may participate in decisions on such broad, basic questions as whether a new department should be added, whether an existing department should be split up to recognize the emergence and promise of new subfields, or whether new interdisciplinary courses should be introduced. In a department, they may be held responsible for maintaining expertise in one or more subfields and for generally contributing to the department's capacity to satisfy a broad range of teaching and research needs. As they advance through the ranks, they assume increasing responsibility for the review and evaluation of prospective and continuing colleagues for employment and promotion.

Academic personnel policies almost always have consequences for the curriculum. Proposals to improve the faculty-student ratio, for example, are well intentioned, but sometimes fail to consider the probability that any new professors that are hired to achieve such goals will not only teach courses that are essential or basic to the curriculum but also will be permitted to

teach courses of their own devising that draw on their specialized scholarship and expertise. When faculty members in excess of enrollment-generated need become "tenured in," a similar situation is created.

We have found that, on the average, there are four to five courses in the curriculum for every member of the faculty (counted on a full-time basis) (Table 2). While courses that enter the catalog as a result of faculty hiring enrich the curricula, they may also inflate it. The point of this observation is not that adding faculty or improving faculty-student ratios should be prohibited, but that in hiring, promoting, and retiring faculty members, the considerations that should be given greatest weight are educational. Such actions should not be decided by generalized personnel policies alone.

Once a course is approved, faculty members typically have wide latitude in its development and presentation. In fact, they view interference, even to the extent of uninvited attendance of colleagues and department chairmen in their classes, as an abridgment of fundamental academic privilege—or even their academic freedom. On their own, they plan the sequence and content of their lectures and demonstrations, choose the general instructional methods and technologies to be used, and decide how student performance and achievement are to be evaluated.

Faculty development. The independence of an individual faculty member is rationalized on the basis of his or her command of a subject and not necessarily on prior training for teaching. Relatively few future college teachers are exposed to courses in learning theory, course design, and practical teaching, for example. Consequently, professors develop their instructional skills mainly with reference to whatever succeeded or failed in their own education. They may pattern themselves after their own favorite teachers, and many utilize the instructional methods that they found useful as students and are suspicious of technology and procedures with which they are unfamiliar. Early in their careers, college professors may spend several years perfecting instructional strategies that they consider effective for their own students and consistent with their own personal style.

Table 2. Relationship between number of faculty and courses in colleges and universities, by Carnegie Commission classification

	Full-time equivalent faculty	Number of courses offered			Course/faculty ratio		
		Undergraduate	Graduate	Total	Undergraduate	Graduate	Total
Research universities I	1,605	2,385	2,132	4,517	1.5	1.3	2.8
Research universities II	992	2,285	1,754	4,039	2.3	1.8	4.1
Doctoral degree-granting universities I	678	1,835	1,043	2,878	2.7	1.5	4.2
Doctoral degree-granting universities II	623	1,767	916	2,683	2.8	1.5	4.3
Comprehensive universities and colleges I	297	1,226	298	1,524	4.1	1.0	5.1
Comprehensive universities and colleges II	236	874	108	982	3.7	.4	4.1
Liberal arts colleges I	76	579	12	591	7.6	.2	7.8
Liberal arts colleges II	64	501	3	504	7.8	.1	7.9
Two-year colleges	141	463	0	463	3.3	0	3.3
Average	432	1,160	536	1,699	4.0	.7	4.7

Source: Catalog Study, 1977.

Note: The Carnegie Commission on Higher Education classifies the institutions with which we are concerned in this report as follows: *Research universities I* are the 50 leading universities in terms of federal support of academic science between 1968 and 1971; *Research universities II* were among the top 100 universities in terms of federal support for two of the same three years and awarded at least 50 Ph.D. degrees in 1969-70 or were among the top 50 institutions in terms of granting Ph.D. degrees from 1960 to 1970; *Doctorate-granting universities I* awarded 40 or more Ph.D.'s in 1969-70 or received at least $3 million in either 1969-70 or 1971. *Doctorate-granting universities II* awarded at least 10 Ph.D.'s in 1969-70. *Comprehensive universities and colleges I* included all institutions that offered a liberal arts program as well as several other programs, such as engineering and business administration. *Comprehensive universities and colleges II* offered liberal arts programs and at least one professional or occupational program, such as teacher training, or nursing. *Liberal arts colleges I* were institutions ranking high on a national index of student selectivity or were among 200 leading baccalaureate-granting institutions in terms of the numbers of their graduates receiving Ph.D.'s at leading doctoral-granting institutions; *Liberal arts colleges II* included all liberal arts colleges that did not meet the criteria for inclusion in the first group. *Two-year colleges and institutions are referred to in this commentary as community colleges.*

Once they reach that point, they are reluctant to consider changing.

Many colleges and universities are beginning to help faculty members improve their teaching through special programs. Of about 2,600 colleges and universities of all types surveyed by the Educational Testing Service in November 1975, 60 percent (1,044) "had an organized program or set of practices for faculty development and improving instruction" (Centra, 1976, p. 100). In a further study of a subsample of 756 institutions that had faculty development programs, investigators in this study found that the most effective practices for faculty development were summer grants for projects to improve instruction, sabbatical leaves, and travel funds to attend professional conferences (Table 3). Least effective were two activities that are fairly common on college campuses—annual awards for teaching excellence and a newsletter on faculty development.

In *The Academic Revolution,* Christopher Jencks and David Riesman (1968, p. 534) proposed what might be called a "content" approach to faculty development, involving the organization of the faculty and teaching assistants of large undergraduate courses into seminars that meet weekly "to discuss books they were reading with undergraduates, preparing seminar papers that would also be delivered as course lectures, and discussing individual lectures given in the course in both substantive and pedagogic terms."

Although the Jencks and Riesman proposal is intended for adoption by institutions with graduate departments, it can be adapted on a smaller scale for liberal arts institutions that offer large, interdisciplinary core courses. At Coe College, for example, members of the teaching team for "Introduction to the Liberal Arts," a course required for all freshmen, meet weekly to discuss readings, lectures, and other matters related to the instruction. In general, team teaching that involves faculty interaction in course planning and requires observation of and by colleagues in teaching situations is itself useful for faculty development.

Several institutions use an approach to faculty development that concentrates on the instruction that is given. Among those approaches are the 13 listed in Table 3. In addition, there

Table 3. Use and estimated effectiveness of institution-wide policies or practices in development

	Percentage of institutions at which the practice existed				Percentage indicating practice was effective or very effective[a]				Unused practices considered essential (percentage responding)[b]
	All (N = 756)	2-year (326)	4-year (315)	University (93)	All	2-year	4-year	University	
1. Annual awards to faculty for excellence in teaching	38	20	44	79	28	37	24	27	6
2. Circulation of newsletter, articles, etc. that are pertinent to teaching improvement or faculty development	68	71	65	67	27	32	22	25	3
3. A specific calendar period is set aside for professional development	44	62	33	14	52	52	55	38	5
4. There is a periodic review of the performance of all faculty members, whether tenured or not	78	87	71	77	59	63	56	49	4
5. Sabbatical leaves with at least half salary	67	60	72	82	66	60	73	61	5
6. A policy of unpaid leaves that covers educational or development purposes	72	70	73	80	51	47	55	49	1
7. Lighter than normal teaching load for first year faculty	21	15	23	25	53	64	51	45	6
8. Temporary teaching load reductions to work on a new course, major course revision, or research area	61	58	59	81	64	68	63	59	8
9. Travel grants to refresh or update knowledge in a particular field	52	46	56	61	64	67	64	57	4

10. Travel funds available to attend professional conferences	93	95	92	95	62	69	59	51	1
11. Visiting scholars program that brings people to the campus for short or long periods	55	37	65	86	57	60	57	54	3
12. Summer grants for projects to improve instruction or courses	58	61	56	62	70	72	66	74	5
13. There is a campus committee on faculty development	61	63	60	62	50	55	48	46	5

[a]Percentages based only on institutions at which practice existed.

[b]Percentages are based on all institutions ($N = 756$).

Source: Centra, 1976, p. 12.

are programs variously designated as faculty colleges, development centers, or institutes that offer noncredit courses for faculty members who wish to learn about new developments in their academic fields, new teaching techniques, and new instructional technologies or who wish to participate in other activities for improving teaching effectiveness. Such centers are to be found, among other places, at the University of Wisconsin-Oshkosh; the University of Texas, Arlington; and the University of Cincinnati.

Faculty contributions to instructional innovation. Some faculty members become dissatisfied with dominant practices and strike out in new directions or become advocates of certain educational approaches. In the 1960s, Fred S. Keller, who had gained a reputation as an educational innovator at Columbia University, and J. G. Sherman, who had been a graduate student there, developed, first at the University of Brazilia and subsequently at Arizona State University, courses that relied heavily on textbooks and written study guides covering short, independent units of instruction with clearly defined objectives that required students to master a unit of instruction before proceeding to a more advanced one, and introduced the use of undergraduates as teachers and proctors in the day-to-day instruction and testing required by the system. By 1972 there were 877 courses based on this model in psychology alone throughout the United States, and there has been great growth since that time (Cross, 1976, p. 93). In 1975, 37.1 percent of the nation's undergraduates had used "self-paced instruction with programmed texts or study guides" (Carnegie Council Surveys, 1975-1976).

In the 1960s, Samuel N. Postlethwait, a professor of biology at Purdue, developed a system of instruction that involved specially equipped student carrels in which students could examine specimens and other instructional materials provided for their use, watch short movie or slide demonstrations, and conduct experiments under the guidance of tape-recorded instruction. The independent studies in the laboratory are supplemented by lectures, films, and other presentations. In the prototypical version of the system, students participate in sections

during which each student is expected to instruct a small group of fellow students in some part of the material covered during the week. Most students who have experience with it like the audio-tutorial approach and learn at least as well using the system as they do in conventional classes (Cross, 1976, p. 89). By 1976, almost one-fourth (24.5 percent) of all undergraduate students had received instruction using audio-tutorial methods (Carnegie Council Surveys, 1975-1976).

Similar faculty initiatives have been responsible for the introduction of gaming and simulation, the utilization of television for instruction, and the continuing development of computer-assisted instruction that takes the form not only of computer-controlled drill and programmed learning but also of complex simulation and that provides a vastly expanded opportunity for students to work with large data bases in their studies of many subjects.

Less well known are the efforts of Ralph W. Lewis at Michigan State University's University College to promote the formal use of a "hypothetico-deductive" system, which he describes as the "pattern of organization and thought similar to that found in Euclidean geometry" as a central feature in the teaching of all fundamental disciplines.

Faculty members also initiate most experimental college programs and curricula, as did Joseph Tussman and Charles Muscatine with their experimental subcolleges at the University of California at Berkeley in the 1960s and 1970s, and James Cass and Harry Carman, who designed the "peace issues" course that was eventually converted into Columbia's "Contemporary Civilization" course.

There is a dilemma to be reckoned with, however. On the one hand, change and experimentation in the curriculum and undergraduate instruction are impossible without the participation of at least some members of a college's faculty. On the other hand, many faculty members already have heavy workloads and participation in new projects can be time-consuming. At its best, undergraduate teaching is demanding, even in its conventional forms, because undergraduates are less sophisticated learners than postgraduates and are more dependent on

their professors and teaching assistants. Nontraditional instruction may demand even more from an instructor. Participation in
an interdisciplinary program may require that a professor not
only reorganize his own teaching on a subject but also that he
review or learn anew the significant points of view of other disciplines as well. Participation in such instruction frequently
involves regular seminars and planning meetings of the participating faculty members. Much time and energy that could go
into teaching are diverted to advocating or defending procedure
and policy. Converting conventional instruction into some of
the newer forms may involve breaking down a course of instruction originally organized around broad topics into small, discrete units with clear-cut objectives, assembling exhibits, taping
presentations, supervising instructional assistants and proctors,
and giving individual counsel to students who encounter difficulties. Faculty members who overcommit themselves to such
activities risk suffering from early "burn-out" that jeopardizes
their teaching effectiveness and enthusiasm and weakens their
capacity for vigorous scholarship.

Because it is more demanding and, for many faculty members, less satisfying than graduate education, a case might well
be developed for limiting participation in undergraduate education to the best teachers in a faculty and paying premium salaries to those chosen for such work. Even if colleges go that far,
however, they will still have to do more than most do now to
reward faculty for participating in particularly demanding
teaching programs and for developing new instructional formats
and uses for new instructional technology. To do this, colleges
should temporarily lighten course loads to free a faculty member's time for such activities and should take such activities into
account when a faculty member is considered for promotion.

Faculty contributions to student satisfaction. In the final analysis, a student's satisfaction or dissatisfaction, success or failure,
in a college's curriculum, may depend more on the quality and
interest of individual faculty members than on any other factor.

In Figure 3, we have plotted the relationship between student satisfaction with teaching and certain characteristics of fac-

ulty members at different types of institutions. The two most important correlations involve the percentage of faculty members whose teaching responsibilities are entirely at the undergraduate level and who spend at least nine hours per week teaching undergraduates. The highest percentages, in both instances, occur in liberal arts and community colleges—which also have the highest levels of undergraduate satisfaction.

Before pursuing that observation farther, we should point out that no faculty member's workload can be measured only in terms of hours spent in the classroom. We share with many professors and college administrators the frustration generated by some legislators and college critics who fail to understand that a faculty member's job involves much more than the hours spent in front of a class. For each hour spent in this way, most faculty members spend many more hours preparing instruction, evaluating student work, conferring with students and colleagues, engaging in research, and participating in other activities that serve the colleges and their students.

The time spent by faculty members in undergraduate classrooms is, however, a significant index of their general involvement and commitment to the matters that are of special concern to us in this commentary. We use nine hours of instruction per week as a reference point because it is clearly above the range of seven to eight hours below which half of the faculty participating in the Carnegie Council Surveys in 1975 say that they devote to formal classroom instruction in undergraduate courses—that is, it is just above the median for all faculty members (Table 4).

There appears to be an inverse relationship between the extent to which faculty members are involved in teaching undergraduates and both the highest degree offered by an institution and the proportion of faculty members at an institution that hold doctoral-level degrees. The greatest faculty involvement with undergraduate teaching occurs, as one would expect, in the community colleges, where all students are undergraduates, only 10 percent of the faculty have Ph.D. degrees, and 78 percent of the faculty spend more than nine hours per week "in formal classroom instruction in undergraduate courses" (Table 4 and Figure 3). At the other end of the scale are the faculty

Figure 3. Relationship of student satisfaction with teaching to selected
faculty characteristics of five types of institutions of higher education

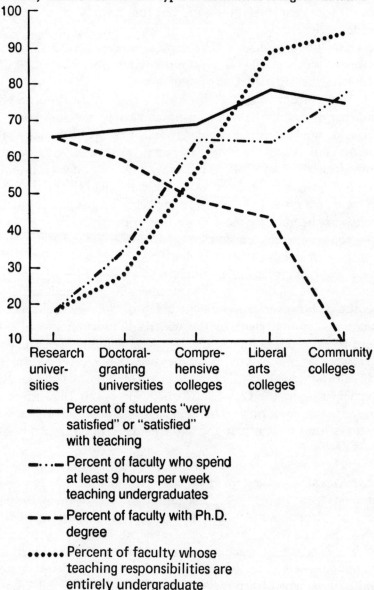

Source: Carnegie Council Surveys, 1975-1976.

Table 4. Percentages of faculty members engaged in formal classroom instruction in undergraduate courses, for average numbers of hours per week, by Carnegie Commission classification, 1975

Hours	0	1-2	3-4	5-6	7-8	9-10	11-12	13-16	17-20	21+
Community colleges	2	1	8	8	3	6	13	31	16	12
Liberal arts colleges I	3	1	10	11	13	26	18	12	4	3
Liberal arts colleges II	3	1	10	8	9	16	22	20	7	5
Comprehensive colleges I	6	2	11	13	7	17	21	14	6	4
Comprehensive colleges II	4	1	7	12	6	18	28	15	5	4
Doctoral colleges I	10	4	21	18	12	16	9	6	3	2
Doctoral colleges II	9	3	19	18	11	15	11	6	5	4
Research universities I	26	7	26	16	8	7	4	4	2	1
Research universities II	19	5	21	18	9	11	7	4	3	2

Source: Carnegie Council Surveys, 1975-1976.

members of research universities 65 percent of whom have doctoral-level degrees, although only 17 percent spend more than nine hours per week in formal classroom instruction in undergraduate courses. In fact, about one-fourth of the faculty in the more heavily research-oriented universities spend *no* time in classes in which undergraduate instruction is given (Table 4).

The liberal arts colleges merit special attention in this connection. These institutions are often at a disadvantage in competing for faculty members in the academic marketplace, because some of them have very limited financial resources. All of them have only undergraduate programs and offer few, if any, opportunities for faculty members to engage in research or in teaching at the graduate level. In these colleges, 44 percent of the faculty have Ph.D.'s, and 64 percent of the faculty members spend more than nine hours per week in formal classroom instruction in undergraduate courses (Table 5).

These relationships between research interests and competence, as indicated by the degrees faculty members hold and the time faculty members spend in teaching undergraduates, may account in some measure for the fact that 79 percent of the undergraduates at liberal arts colleges and 76 percent of the

Table 5. Percentages of students satisfied with aspects of college
and faculty characteristics at five types of higher education institutions

	Research univer- sities	Doctorate- granting univer- sities	Compre- hensive colleges and uni- versities	Liberal arts colleges	Com- munity colleges
Student Satisfaction[a]					
With college overall	69	71	68	72	71
With teaching	65	67	69	79	76
With evaluation and grading	46	52	53	62	62
Faculty Satisfaction					
Percentage who say their college is "very good" or "fairly good" for them	93	91	91	91	93
Percentage who "strongly agree" or "agree with reser- vations" that undergradu- ates at their colleges are basically satisfied with their education	61	63	65	70	75
Faculty Degrees					
Percentage with Ph.D.	65	60	47	44	10
Percentage with Ph.D., D.A., Ed.D., or "other doctorate"	72	71	61	53	16
Faculty teaching					
Percentage teaching under- graduates more than nine hours a week	17	34	65	64	77
Percentage who prefer courses focused on limited specialties	49	47	46	39	45
Percentage teaching entirely undergraduates in 1975	17	28	55	88	93
Percentage teaching under- graduates and graduates in 1975	55	58	38	7	2

[a]Percentage of undergraduates responding "very satisfied" or "satisfied."

Source: Carnegie Council Surveys, 1975-1976.

**Figure 4. Undergraduate and faculty satisfaction in five types of
institutions of higher education**

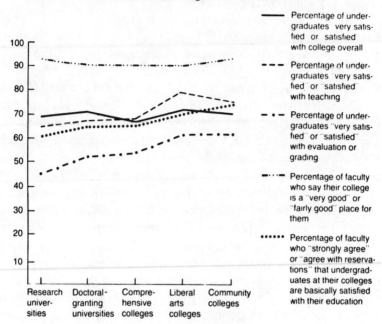

Percentage of under-
graduates very satis-
fied or satisfied
with college overall

Percentage of under-
graduates very satis-
fied or "satisfied"
with teaching

Percentage of under-
graduates "very satis-
fied" or "satisfied"
with evaluation or
grading

Percentage of faculty
who say their college
is a "very good" or
"fairly good" place for
them

Percentage of faculty
who "strongly agree"
or "agree with reserva-
tions" that undergrad-
uates at their colleges
are basically satisfied
with their education

Source: Carnegie Council Surveys, 1975-1976.

undergraduates at community colleges say they are either "very satisfied" or "satisfied" with the teaching they receive, while at research universities the percentage drops to 65 percent (Table 5). As a general rule, undergraduate satisfaction with the quality of teaching rises with a declining percentage of Ph.D.'s on the faculty (Figure 3).

These findings may, among other things, suggest the need for alternatives to the research-oriented Ph.D. as the degree for college teachers. Whether the alternative is a doctor of arts degree of the type recommended by the Carnegie Commission on Higher Education or some other degree granted for the same purpose, it should be more widely available. Students should be encouraged to seek it; it should be given equal status with the Ph.D. in the evaluation of faculty by accrediting agencies; and more colleges with substantial undergraduate enrollments

should give favorable consideration to holders of such degrees
who apply for faculty positions.

In 1975, faculty members participating in the Carnegie
Council survey were asked, "In general, how do you feel about
this institution?" In all types of colleges and universities, more
than 90 percent of the faculty members responded either "It is
a very good place for me" or "It is fairly good for me" (Carnegie Council Survey, 1975-1976; Figure 4). If one takes into consideration the great variety of colleges and universities in the
United States, both the high level and consistency of this faculty satisfaction are remarkable.

Asked to rate the satisfaction of students, faculty members
at all types of institutions tended to underestimate (at least in
comparison with the satisfaction students claimed for themselves) the positive attitudes of undergraduates. In comprehensive colleges, liberal arts colleges, and community colleges,
faculty members could get some encouragement from the fact
that students were slightly more satisfied with the teaching they
received than they were with their colleges overall. At all institutions, however, students' satisfaction with evaluation and
grading practices was significantly lower than their satisfaction
both with teaching and with college overall. Faculty members
might be expected to be particularly sensitive to this dissatisfaction, and it is a frequent reason for students and faculty members to meet on an individual, face-to-face basis. It could, therefore, lead faculty members to hold a somewhat less positive
attitude toward student satisfaction generally than might be
justified.

The faculty as role models. Although faculty members on most
campuses are no longer held responsible for the supervision of
student conduct, they continue to exercise an influence on students outside the classrooms as advisors and role models. As advisors, even in informal situations, faculty members owe their
students reliability. There is little excuse, for example, for any
faculty member not knowing a college's basic requirements for
graduation or the requirements for a major in his or her own
department or subject field. And, when questions arise that a

Table 6. Degrees held by faculty members, by Carnegie Commission classification, 1975 (in percentages)

	Less than bachelor's (A.A., etc.)	Undergraduate bachelor's	First professional law degree	First professional medical degree (e.g., M.D., D.D.S.)	Other first professional beyond undergraduate bachelor's	Master's (except first professional)	Doctor of arts or equivalent degree for doctorate without dissertation	Ph.D.	Ed.D.	Other doctorate (except first professional)	None
Community colleges	16	77	1	1	13	69	2	10	3	1	2
Liberal arts colleges I	7	88	1	2	10	70	3	57	4	1	7
Liberal arts colleges II	9	87	1	2	15	78	2	39	6	3	1
Comprehensive colleges I	11	87	2	1	11	79	3	48	9	3	1
Comprehensive colleges II	8	87	2	1	13	79	3	45	9	3	1
Doctoral colleges I	8	87	3	2	8	75	2	64	5	3	1
Doctoral colleges II	10	88	3	1	12	76	2	57	8	3	1
Research universities I	8	86	3	11	10	62	1	66	2	4	1
Research universities II	7	86	3	8	10	68	1	63	4	2	1

Source: Carnegie Council Surveys, 1975-1976.

professor cannot answer, a conscientious attempt should be made to find the information needed or to refer the student to someone who is sure to have it.

In another section of this commentary, we will talk about the values that are inherent in the academic tradition—such as recognizing the importance of information as a basis for judgments, tolerance for ideas of others, and fair use of ideas and information that are not one's own. If such values are communicated to undergraduates at all, they are transmitted by the men and women who teach. Colleges should be entitled, therefore, to take a faculty member's performance in such matters into consideration in making evaluations for promotions.

Faculty members are also able to convey to students some of the meaning of individual differences among people. Students should be reminded as frequently as possible that women and members of racial and other minorities can and do participate equally with men and members of the majority in all fields of learning. The best reminder is a diversified faculty in which qualified professors who are women or members of minorities breach stereotypes by teaching in subject fields that have, in the past, been considered the domain of white males. More than that, an appropriately diversified faculty exposes students to what may be unfamiliar and enriching points of view. Colleges that fail to make a conscious effort to include on their faculties men and women with a variety of cultural and social backgrounds deprive their students of valuable and interesting lessons of a sort that the formal curriculum can never provide.

Role of the Students

Until the 1960s, it was widely assumed that students play a passive role in determining the shape of the curriculum. Many college officials and faculty members asserted that undergraduate education was "for" rather than "by" the students, and nearly all students accepted that proposition.

Usually overlooked in this assumption is the enormous influence students exert simply by exercising their options. There is no such thing as compulsory college attendance. Students may choose not to go at all. When they do go, they have

many institutions to consider. If their first choices do not offer the courses, the conveniences, or the atmosphere they want, they can go elsewhere. Once enrolled, they exercise similar options about the courses they study, the majors they select, and, to some extent, the professors who teach them. They "vote with their feet." And their votes count, because when they leave they also take a certain amount of financial support with them. During the campus unrest that began in the middle of the last decade, students demonstrated by mass actions a power they had held individually always—to cease participating in classroom activities and, if they were willing to risk the consequences of doing so, to disrupt them.

Two demands often asserted by students during this period were that they be given a direct voice in curricular matters and that colleges recognize the legitimacy of courses designed and offered on student initiative. The most ambitious effort toward such ends was undertaken at Brown University where student interest in the curriculum began in a spirit of protest. After a year of reading and discussions on the subject, which were encouraged by the college itself, the students submitted proposals for major changes, most of which were adopted.

Students also asserted during this period that their own evaluations of their teachers should be taken into consideration in the faculty promotion process, and students on some campuses published course and faculty evaluations as "supplements" to their colleges' catalogs. Many of these are still issued. Intended as consumer's guides to the curriculum, these publications are sometimes sanctioned by the colleges whose offerings are reviewed. In most cases, they rely on polls of students who have already taken the courses that are described. Bad reviews can embarrass professors and their departments and can drive students from negatively assessed courses to competing ones taught by other instructors. In this way, student guides to the curriculum call into play the most powerful of all student influences on undergraduate education—the student's option to be present in a class or stay away.

Colleges now give the impacts of that option serious attention. They no longer consider it bad form to advertise their

offerings. In a recent educational supplement to the *New York Times* (Nov. 14, 1976), Dowling College advertised a "Tradition of small classes and close contact between student and faculty and programs offering Bachelor of Science Degrees in Aeronautics, Business and Accounting, Marine Science, and Teacher Education"; Antioch College called attention to its "Academic Rigor, Work as Education, Freedom with Responsibility, Participatory Governance, Education Abroad"; and Louisburg College, a two-year institution in North Carolina, described itself as "halfway between New York and Florida, and halfway between the mountains and the sea, but all the way in Liberal Arts, Business, and Preprofessional Curricula!"

As colleges become more forward in their efforts to attract students, the students and national student organizations become more aware not only of student influence on higher education but also of student vulnerability to misleading claims and promises. Indicative of national interest in this matter was a study on "Improving the Consumer Protection Function in Postsecondary Education," conducted by The American Institutes for Research for the U.S. Office of Education in 1976. The study identified 14 "abuse categories," ranging from misleading recruiting and admissions practices to inadequate programs, unqualified instructional staff, and misrepresentation or misuse of chartered, approved, or accredited status. It also yielded a student guide entitled "Safeguarding Your Education: A Student's Consumer Guide to College and Occupational Education" (American Institutes for Research, 1977, p. 8) and made 11 suggestions to institutions of postsecondary education, states, federal government agencies, and other concerned groups. The suggestions are aimed at collecting better information on "abusive institutional conditions," involving accrediting agencies and the federal government in invoking sanctions against institutions that fail adequately to protect students' interests as consumers, and disseminating information about potentially abusive situations and practices. Such activities could have significant national impacts on educational policies.

On the campuses themselves, meanwhile, an increasingly favorable climate exists for student participation in matters re-

lated to their instruction. Students and faculty members substantially agree, for instance, that undergraduates should at least be consulted on such matters as bachelor's degree requirements and provision and content of courses—although the percentages of students favoring such participation have declined slightly since 1969 (Table 7).[1] There is also growing approval of the stu-

Table 7. Percentages of students and faculty who prefer selected roles for undergraduates in determining bachelor's degree requirements and provision and content of courses

Question: What role do you believe undergraduates should play in decisions on:	Students		Faculty	
	1969	*1976*	*1969*	*1975*
a. Bachelor's degree requirements				
Control	2	3	—	—
Voting power on committees	25	22	13	13
Formal consultation	35 {83}	31 {79}	29 {67}	28 {71}
Information consultation	21	24	25	30
Little or no role	17	21	33	29
b. Provision and content of courses				
Control	4	4	—	—
Voting power on committees	38	28	15	16
Formal consultation	34 {93}	35 {90}	32 {87}	37 {85}
Information consultation	17	23	40	32
Little or no role	7	10	13	14

Sources: Carnegie Surveys, 1969-70; Carnegie Council Surveys, 1975-1976.

[1] It is probably safe to speculate that one reason for the decline is that students in 1976 were less protest-prone and that their urge to exercise "student power"—always a side issue (although a real one) in the student unrest of the 1960s—was not as strong as it was in 1969 and in the spring of 1977. Faculty members had less reason in 1975 to feel conciliatory. Moreover, anecdotal reports on experience with formal student participation in such matters suggest that the reaction of both students and faculty members has been, at best, mixed.

dent role in evaluating faculty members for promotion. In 1969, 50 percent of the students and 57 percent of the faculty agreed "strongly" or "with reservations" that faculty promotions should be based on student evaluations. In 1975-76, the percentages for students and faculty were 53 and 77 percent respectively (Carnegie Surveys, 1969-70; Carnegie Council Surveys, 1975-1976).

Even at the peak of student dissent, students who were either "satisfied" or "very satisfied" with their colleges was high (66 percent). Since that time, the level of satisfaction has remained high and has even increased slightly. In 1976, 72 percent of the nation's undergraduates reported that they were either "satisfied" or "very satisfied" with their colleges. Generally speaking, the increased satisfaction appears to reflect a relaxation of campus tensions and recent efforts of many colleges, perhaps because of competition for enrollments, to relax requirements and introduce programs and methods that appeal to undergraduates.

But the increase in satisfaction varies for different kinds of institutions. Table 8 shows the percentage of students in each of nine types of institutions that is either "satisfied" or "very satisfied" with their colleges. The highest percentage of students who are satisfied with their colleges overall is found among students of selective liberal arts colleges. The lowest (68 percent) is found among the least comprehensive of the comprehensive colleges and among doctorate-granting universities awarding relatively few Ph.D.'s.

There are many possible ways to explain why students at the more selective liberal arts colleges are more likely to be satisfied than students of other types of colleges, but some of them are difficult to document. From analysis of the Carnegie Council Surveys of 1975-1976 and studies of the educational programs described in institutional catalogs, we have come to a few conclusions about the differences that deserve attention. One of these is that at institutions where students are satisfied with their teaching they are also satisfied with their institutions overall. When students were asked, in 1976, to indicate satisfaction or dissatisfaction with teaching available at their colleges,

Table 8. Percentages of undergraduates satisfied with their colleges,
by Carnegie Commission classification, 1969 and 1976

	Very satisfied with my college	*"Satisfied" or "very satisfied" with my college*	*On the fence*	*"Dissatisfied" or "very dissatisfied" with my college*	*Very dissatisfied with my college*
Community colleges					
1969	18	64	23	13	4
1976	20	73	20	7	1
Liberal arts colleges I					
1969	29	72	18	11	3
1976	37	80	14	6	1
Liberal arts colleges II					
1969	19	62	23	15	4
1976	23	70	21	10	2
Comprehensive colleges I					
1969	16	64	23	12	3
1976	17	70	22	9	2
Comprehensive colleges II					
1969	14	65	23	13	4
1976	15	68	22	10	2
Doctoral colleges I					
1969	21	67	21	13	3
1976	25	77	15	8	1
Doctoral colleges II					
1969	17	60	22	17	6
1976	15	68	23	9	2

(continued on next page)

Table 8 *(continued)*

	Very satisfied with my college	"Satisfied" or "very satisfied" with my college	On the fence	"Dissatisfied" or "very dissatisfied" with my college	Very dissatisfied with my college
Research universities I					
1969	30	77	15	7	2
1976	21	71	20	9	1
Research universities II					
1969	23	70	19	11	3
1976	18	70	21	9	1
Total					
1969	19	66	22	13	4
1976	20	72	20	8	1

Note: The question asked was "What is your overall evaluation of your college?" See footnote to Table 2, page 72 for definitions of classifications.

Source: Carnegie Council Surveys, 1975-1976; Carnegie Surveys, 1969-70.

the highest percentage (85 percent) claiming satisfaction was again found among students of selective liberal arts colleges. The next largest percentages were at other liberal arts colleges and at community colleges.

In search for other correlates of a satisfying college experience, we found that there was relatively little relationship between the size of classes and student satisfaction. We also found that there are about as many students at selective liberal arts colleges who say that they are lonely (34 percent) as there are at universities heavily engaged in research (33 percent). What does make a difference, apparently, is the students' perception of their colleges' attitudes toward them. Only 9 percent of students at selective liberal arts colleges, for example, feel that they are treated like "numbers in a book," as compared to 60 to 65 percent of the students who feel that way at research universities. And the percentages of liberal arts college students

who say that they have had faculty members take an interest in their academic or personal progress are very high, compared to the percentages of students who had the same experience at other institutions. More students at liberal arts colleges than at other institutions are also likely to say that the counseling provided by the college on academic, financial, and personal matters is either "adequate" or "highly adequate" (Carnegie Council Surveys, 1975-1976).

Finally, there is the matter of the freedom of choice available in the curriculum. Here, the liberal arts colleges have far outstripped other types of institutions, allocating 50 percent of the undergraduate curriculum to free electives (Catalog Study, 1976). At these colleges, only 9 percent of the undergraduates, the lowest percentage of students in any of the institutional classifications, say that they are not interested in most of their courses.

In absolute terms, the percentage of students at research or doctorate-granting universities who are "satisfied" or "very satisfied" is quite high—71 and 70 percent for the two classifications of research universities and 77 and 68 percent for the two classifications of doctorate-granting universities. But, as is seen in Table 8, for students at universities that are most heavily involved in research a moderate decrease in percentage of students who are satisfied took place between 1969 and 1976. This suggests that whatever the explanations of the relative dissatisfaction of students at these institutions may be, they may be recent and thus perhaps reversible.

There is no denying that the high levels of student satisfaction indicated in the Carnegie Council Surveys should be viewed as caution signals to those who would propose revolutionary changes in undergraduate education in the 1970s and 1980s. We should point out, however, that the Carnegie Council Surveys are unable to tell us anything about the attitudes of persons who are *not* in college because they are dissatisfied with what such institutions now offer. For such information, we must turn to Alexander Astin's study of students who entered college with the class of 1968. He discovered that almost one out of every four of them dropped out before earning their bachelor's de-

grees and that what might be considered dissatisfaction with instruction and the curriculum was a factor in many of their decisions. Thirty-two percent of them were bored with their courses; 22 percent had poor grades; 22 percent were dissatisfied with requirements or regulations; and 11 percent said they had been unable to take desired courses or programs (Astin, 1975, pp. 10, 14). Nevertheless, the fact that students are either satisfied or dissatisfied should not alone decide curricular policy. There are many other educational purposes and interests at stake, and providing students with satisfying educational experiences may have more to do with creating favorable conditions for learning than it has with the ends and forms of the learning itself.

The extracurriculum. When American colleges began to devote more official attention to academic programs and less to the behavior and personal development of students, it was the students themselves who filled the breach by organizing debating clubs, societies, sports activities, fraternities and sororities, and eventually scores of other activities that honored certain campus traditions, provided peer heroes, and supported the intellectual, emotional, and social development of students.

The easy tendency to dismiss all of these activities as frilly and frivolous overlooks the fact that, while many extracurricular activities might deserve such characterizations, a substantial number of them were actually extensions of the educational enterprise. They made provision for learning activities that could not (or at least were not) provided by the colleges themselves. The first college libraries in which students were welcome were those collected and organized by student societies for the use of their members. Senior members of such organizations often provided individual counseling and tutoring to younger members, and in some societies papers written as classroom assignments were routinely read and corrected by senior members before they were submitted for final reading and grading. Debates organized by students gave them opportunities to apply their education to issues of current interest and to learn

how to view subjects from more than one perspective. It was also in the student societies and clubs that students were first encouraged to experiment with the creative arts as an alternative way to express their developing understanding and appreciation of the world about them.

Some of the out-of-classroom concerns of students, including English literature, American history, fine arts, and music, eventually found their way into the formal curriculum (Rudolph, 1977). And some of the modern vocabulary of nontraditional educators renames practices devised by students for their own uses and needs years ago. Peer teaching, subject integration, relevance, group learning, individualized instruction, and personal development, all have crude but identifiable prototypes in the more serious side of the extracurriculum throughout the history of the American college.

Attempts have been made in the past to link the curriculum and extracurriculum formally. When Bennington was started, it was hoped that the extracurriculum there would be the place where students would practice what they learned in the formal curriculum and that such activities would eventually be translated into formal courses. At colleges such as Harvard and Yale, residential programs make possible a partial combination of the curriculum and extracurriculum.

But most institutions maintain a sharp distinction between the two realms. At Swarthmore, the extracurriculum has been used, in part, as the place to offer instruction in the applied arts and other subjects inappropriate to the formal curriculum. The prevailing practice at most colleges, however, is simply to leave the faculty and students to their separate curricular domains and to protect both from incursions on their respective authority.

An ineffective undergraduate curriculum certainly can be devised without attempting to accommodate the extracurriculum within it. The formal curriculum might be made better, however, if it were planned with full cognizance of the learning that students organize for themselves. Complementary instruction could then be offered where it seems needed and appro-

priate, and pressures to offer types of learning experiences already made available outside the curriculum could be more effectively resisted.

Internal Dynamics

The formal curriculum of a college or university is the one that is described in the course catalog. It includes hundreds (at large institutions, thousands) of courses and is partly the product of the size of the faculty. As we noted earlier in this section, there appear to be four to five courses in the curriculum for every faculty member, with the greatest number per faculty member offered at the liberal arts colleges (eight courses per faculty member) and the fewest at the most research-oriented universities (between one and two courses per faculty member) (Catalog Study, 1976). There is a relatively low course-faculty ratio at community colleges (3.3), which is probably explained by the fact that many faculty members at these institutions are part-time instructors and teach only one or two courses. In other words, in these institutions both the number of courses and the number of faculty at any given time may reflect consumer demand. In liberal arts colleges, on the other hand, the number of courses may expand to meet student needs and demands while the number of faculty remains more or less constant. In any case, it appears that in liberal arts colleges faculty members may be more generalistic in their orientations, even within their own subject fields, than faculty members at research universities who teach only two or three courses. This may explain why faculty members in liberal arts colleges may find it somewhat easier than those in research universities to engage in interdisciplinary instruction. Students who choose to attend research universities, on the other hand, may not have professors whose interests are as broad as those at liberal arts colleges but are likely to have professors who are highly expert in their own specialties. Moreover, because of the sheer numbers of faculty at universities, students who attend them are likely to have between three and four times as many courses to choose from as their counterparts at smaller colleges.

But such generalizations are fairly crude, and one must still

make allowances for the exceptional individual faculty members at all kinds of institutions who may be more broadly interested or more intensely specialized than the data suggest and for the fact that because all courses listed in catalogs are not actually given in every term there may be some exaggeration in our data of both the number of courses taught by faculty members at the liberal arts colleges and the number of courses actually available at universities. At research universities, about 45 percent of the courses included in the catalogs are at the graduate level (Table 2), and many of them are not open to undergraduates. At most colleges, some courses are included in the catalogs that are not actually offered on a regular basis.

The "real" curricula are not found in college catalogs. Instead, they take shape in the students' transcripts, where, from the hundreds of courses listed in the formal curriculum, the 32 to 40 that make up a student's four-year program are recorded. In an analysis of student transcripts recently undertaken by the dean of instruction and curriculum planning at the University of Pennsylvania, it was discovered that arts and sciences students who graduated in May 1976 had selected a core of 29 courses. Among them, Music 21, taken by 7 percent of the graduates; Chemistry II, taken by 9 percent; and Psychology 160, taken by 10 percent; were those chosen by the fewest students. Psychology I, taken by 52 percent; and Mathematics 140 and 150 (combined to get a picture of the number of students completing first-year calculus), taken by 47 percent; were on the transcripts of the largest numbers of students. Disciplines represented in the full list included biology, chemistry, economics, English, French, mathematics, music, physics, psychology, sociology, and Spanish. But even this de facto core was not studied by all students, and many of the thousands of courses in the catalog that were not included in the core list were found on individual student transcripts. As a result, the "real" curricula of no two students is likely to be exactly alike, and the number of course combinations that actually occur is astronomical. In general, the University of Pennsylvania experience probably would be encountered on most other campuses of the country.

The shape of both the formal and "real" curriculum on a campus is the product of tensions among academic departments, faculty members who have their individual professional priorities, students who have their personal preferences and goals, and the administrators who develop the procedures, services, and facilities that support the total educational enterprise.

For faculty members, the strongest interest is in their specialty, then in their department, then in their college or academic division, and, if the institution is very large, last in the institution itself. In practice, this usually means that each faculty member feels an obligation to teach one course that is considered essential to the instructional objectives of a department and one or two others that are, in effect, his or her own. The ultimate justification for continuing a course is likely to be the number of students who are enrolled in it. For that reason, faculty members can form coalitions to seek recognition of certain courses as requirements for the major or for graduation, or to relax requirements in certain subject fields—such as the humanities or the physical sciences—to free student time to take courses they support or want retained. Departments can compete for students by seeking recognition of their courses as graduation requirements; by offering courses on popular subjects, particularly for nonmajors; and by adopting liberal grading practices. Students prove to be bright and interested consumers of education, but they have little experience with academic concerns and may not see the overall, long-term objectives of departments or colleges. Their efforts are usually directed at acquiring freedom from curricular requirements and at group action to achieve representation in curricular policy making.

In summarizing the consequences of these pressures and relationships within colleges, we note in particular that:

• Faculty members make a strong contribution to the curriculum in the development of courses close to their own personal interests and specialties but are weak in their contribution to general education.
• Departments have been generally successful in developing full and open majors. Spurred by the need to maintain course enrollments, they have also been reasonably successful in devel-

oping courses for nonmajors. They share with individual faculty members, however, a record of generally weak contributions to general education.

- Colleges and other academic divisions have been the principal sources of stability for general education. But they have not been too effective in overcoming faculty and departmental resistance to curricular change.
- Vice-presidents of undergraduate education, deans of instruction and the curriculum, or other comparable officers, where they exist, can counterbalance curricular demands of graduate divisions. They can also create broad learning options, involve students in the curriculum-planning process and in the evaluation of teaching, and establish cluster and theme colleges or divisions.
- Presidents do not always play a strong role in curriculum planning or policy making, but they are in a position to do much more. They can, for example, arouse interest in the curriculum throughout the institution, encourage departmental participation in programs designed to improve general education and impart skills to nonmajors; and offset pressures on the curriculum from organized faculty, students, and departments seeking special advantages.
- Governing boards typically regard curriculum matters as a domain that belongs to professional educators. They are slow to initiate curriculum changes on their own. Their reticence is appropriate, but they should maintain an interest in the curriculum at all times and should be prepared to support presidents and other principal academic officers in any initiative designed to overcome deficiencies that are not adequately dealt with in the routine channels of academic administration and policy making.

* * *

For further information on subjects discussed in this section, see the chapters on "Characteristics of Curriculum Change," "The Major or Concentration," and "Methods of Instruction," in the Carnegie Council on Policy Studies in Higher Education, *Handbook on Undergraduate Curriculum.*

5

Components
of the Curriculum

The college curriculum has three main dimensions that are constantly interacting with one another. The first dimension is determined by the range of subject matter that is taught and by the way that an institution is structured to accommodate different realms of knowledge. The second dimension is determined by the uses of knowledge for various purposes—to acquire learning in depth about one subject, to acquire breadth of understanding through an acquaintance with several subjects, or to acquire certain skills. The third dimension is determined by the size, character, and mission of different types of institutions. In this section of our commentary, we explore the first two dimensions. The third will be discussed in Section Six.

Subject Fields

In discussing the realms of knowledge, we use the term *discipline* to mean a discrete subject and its characteristic regimen of investigation and analysis—geography, political science, psychology, and English are examples. In most American colleges and universities, such realms are structurally accommodated in departments, which administer the teaching and research in the individual disciplines. For various purposes, colleges also aggregate several disciplines into groups that utilize similar techniques of study to explore a common, broadly defined subject

matter. These aggregations are structurally accommodated by the establishment of *divisions* or subcolleges to coordinate, and, in some instances, administer instruction and research in all of their disciplinary components. Frequently these aggregations are also called *disciplines*, but in this commentary it will be necessary to maintain a distinction between the more discrete realms of knowledge and the aggregates to which the various colleges have consigned them. For that reason, we will refer throughout the commentary to the aggregates as *subject fields.* They usually are designated as the humanities, social sciences, physical sciences, biological sciences, the arts, and the professions but are defined differently for different purposes and by different institutions. There are also some disciplines—history, for example—with branches that are comfortably at home in more than one subject field and others that may not be completely at home in any of them. Therefore, generalizations about subject fields can be made only with considerable difficulty.

The humanities. Historically, the humanities have had as their concern "thinking and creative man, that is, man at the acme of his power, at his most civilized and civilizing" (Cannon, 1973, pp. 173-174). Alexander Meiklejohn (1920, pp. 27-28), remembering Alexander Pope's observation, expressed similar sentiments when he said: "We have not yet forgotten that fundamentally the proper study of mankind is man." Later, Roger Shattuck (1973, p. 10) said that "the humanities stand not for an autonomous tradition of knowledge for knowledge's sake but for its ultimate usefulness to what is most human in us, to the individual as the accountable agent of his actions and as the potential seat of human greatness."

Once the core and spirit of the American college curriculum, the humanities are now encountering difficulties. Part of their problem is that their realm has been trimmed down over the years. In fact, Shattuck (1973, p. 96) suggests that one definition of the humanities is "what is left of the knowledge pie after the sciences, natural and social, have taken their generous slices." The analogy is apt, because the root of the humanities is

the ancient trivium of grammar, rhetoric, and logic that became
what we now know as languages and literature (including history) and philosophy (which was once the campground of all
sorts of new disciplines—psychology and economics, for example—until they found permanent homes in the curriculum). On
a few campuses, the humanities once were also the home of the
arts and physical education. In fact, "arts and humanities" is
still encountered as a rubric in the curricula of many colleges,
and the "arts" part of such labels as "arts and sciences" is generally understood to include the humanities. Increasingly, however, the visual and performing arts are considered a subject
field unto themselves. Languages and literature remain intact,
although the emphasis has shifted from classical to modern languages and particularly to English language and literature. Much
of the once all-embracing philosophy included in the humanities
has been carved away by disciplines that eventually became a
part of the physical and natural sciences. History is, in a sense,
now divided, with some historians observing the literary tradition while others pursue a more analytical style that is characteristic of the social sciences. Another split discipline is that of
journalism, which is often taught within English departments
but which on many campuses claims independent status as one
of the newer professions.

Many colleges report a decline in enrollments in the humanities. The most acutely affected disciplines are the foreign
languages that were once routinely designated as subjects that
had to be studied to meet graduation requirements but that decreasingly have such status. Lyman Glenny and his associates at
the University of California report a decrease in foreign-
language enrollment between 1968 and 1974 at no fewer than
48 percent of the colleges in any of the institutional classifications studied. Decreases in foreign-language enrollment were
particularly large in the private sector—reported in 76 percent
of the comprehensive colleges and in 75 percent of both the liberal arts and community colleges (Glenny et al., 1976, table 4).
Decreases in the other humanities were more modest, but also
may have been related to the removal of certain subjects from
those required for graduation.

Enrollments in humanities majors dropped sharply from 9 to 5 percent of all undergraduates between 1969 and 1976 (Figure 5). Although the U.S. Bureau of Census indicates that there was an increase of almost 8 percent in majors in English, journalism and "other humanities" between 1966 and 1974 ("Business," March 5, 1976), these figures apparently include the arts. For our

Figure 5. Percentages of undergraduate enrollments and teaching faculty in subject fields, 1969 and 1975-1976

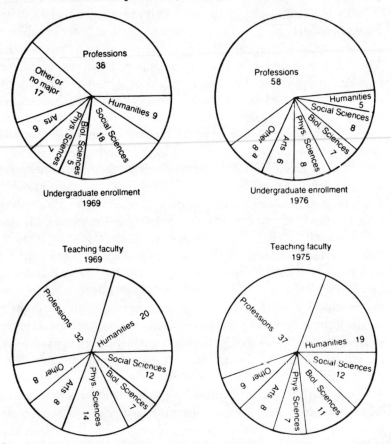

[a]Includes "no major" and such subjects as ethnic studies, women's studies, and environmental studies, all of which have very low enrollments.

Note: Numbers may not add to 100 owing to rounding.

Source: Carnegie Surveys, 1969-1970, 1975-1976.

comparisons, journalism is considered a profession and not one of the humanities and only the first-mentioned subjects in double majors are counted. But there is much variation in increases and decreases among types of institutions. There are fewer humanities majors than there were in 1969 at community colleges and at the more extensive doctoral degree-granting universities; enrollments are up in the liberal arts colleges and unchanged in all other institutions (Carnegie Surveys, 1969-70; Carnegie Council Surveys, 1975-1976).

In 1969, 20 percent of the faculty members in the United States were teaching in the humanities, although these subjects claimed only 9 percent of the undergraduates as majors. By 1976, the proportion of faculty members teaching in the humanities dropped to 19 percent (Figure 5), but relative to enrollments this level is still high. Instruction in the humanities appears to be expensive for colleges, particularly in comparison to the professions, which have 58 percent of the majors and 37 percent of the faculty. Instruction in the humanities has always been "labor intensive." One reason is that these disciplines have always been the providers of service courses for majors in other disciplines and of stable components of general education—they provide much of the core of the undergraduate education. Another reason is that they cover a large domain—the history, thought, and literature of the past and present in many cultures and many lands. And, finally, although enrollments have declined (with the dropping of language and literature graduation requirements by some colleges), the number of faculty members in the humanities may not have dropped proportionately because of tenure and other personnel considerations. By contrast, the professional school enrollments are rising and the number of faculty has not caught up.

One difficulty confronted by the humanities is that, precisely at a time when career outcomes are widely cited as significant measures of an education's ultimate worth, the humanities lack an easily identifiable professional or occupational constituency. Their graduates are widely distributed as teachers in high schools and colleges and among members of a large number of other occupational and professional fields that are not

obviously related to a humanities major. Of all the subject fields, the humanities are very likely to be the most thoroughly integrated into the life and practice of America's educated men and women, yet the least visible.

To regain visibility and standing, humanists have been urged to be more aggressive in proclaiming their own worth and in demonstrating their importance to other fields. Humanists at community colleges, for example, have been advised that if the allied health fields can insist that "people need health" and if occupational educators can call attention to the fact that "people need work" perhaps humanists can make a stronger case than they now do that "people need to live as humans" (Cohen, 1977). They have also been urged to develop very brief learning modules on humanities disciplines that are relevant to technical fields. For example, a unit on business ethics might be prepared to use in courses in auto mechanics, and a unit on Greek and Latin roots of medical terms might be offered to medical technology students (Cohen, 1977). Beyond such measures, we believe that a strong case can be made for the use of the humanities, particularly literature, to improve our general understanding of the recurrent central themes addressed by social and political policy. What, for example, does the literature of different periods and countries tell us about such central concepts as equality, authority, the limits of regulation of human lives, and the ethical and moral systems of various parts of society at different points in time? Such questions do not distract from the humanists' traditional preoccupation with the individual but rather enlarge the context in which the individual is viewed. Moreover, although such interest might lead more humanists into cognitive domains of thought and learning and more analytic activities, it need not and should not reduce the importance of sensibility (intuition and imagination) that Shattuck identifies as the domain humanists often regard as requiring their special support and protection. A blending of both domains is hardly inhuman and justifies the particular attention of the humanists, because their traditions will enable them to bridge the widening gap between rational analysis and other ways of coming to know.

Social sciences. Whereas the humanities are concerned with human beings as individuals, the social sciences are concerned with human beings in general and in their relationships to one another. They are comparatively young disciplines, although, as we have mentioned earlier, they have origins in subjects, particularly philosophy, that have been a concern of higher education virtually from the beginning of medieval universities. Within the subject field, social science disciplines are differentiated by their concentration on certain contexts of social behavior— economical, political, social, or behavioral. To the extent that their subject matters permit, the social sciences also are characterized by efforts to develop a theoretical foundation for their disciplines and for their use of controlled experimentation or systematically acquired observational and statistical data as a means of acquiring empirical knowledge (Smelser, 1973, pp. 124-126).

The social science majors enrolled 8 percent of all undergraduates in 1976 and no longer have the largest share of the enrollment of any subject field other than the combined professions (Figure 5). They share with the humanities the lack of an immediately identifiable employment market for graduates at the bachelor's level. Possibly as a consequence of that fact, the percentage of undergraduates enrolled in social science majors has decreased by more than half between 1969 and 1976 (Carnegie Surveys, 1969-70; Carnegie Council Surveys, 1975-1976). The decrease occurred in all types of institutions but was particularly acute at research universities and some of the doctoral degree-granting institutions where, compared to most other institutions, the 1969 levels were quite high.

The percentage of faculty members teaching in the social sciences was the same in 1976 as it was in 1969—12 percent (Figure 5).

Today all of the social science disciplines are becoming more technical and more specialized, and it is becoming harder for students and faculty to move from one discipline—or even subdiscipline—to another. Neil Smelser (1973, p. 141) also finds that much of the curriculum traditionally offered at the undergraduate level has now been introduced to students in second-

ary school or is acquired in the students' general readings or from other sources before they reach college. At universities, Smelser also reports that the social sciences have become increasingly involved in "big research," with the result that some faculty members withdraw from undergraduate instruction and others become so specialized in their orientation that they may not be able to teach at levels appropriate to undergraduate interest and concern.

Nathan Glazer (1975, pp. 4-5) has expressed related concern, namely that, unlike the natural sciences, most of the social sciences do not have what he describes as "a sequence or hierarchy of secure, if changing, principles—laws, theories, concepts." The result is that there is no logical place for students to begin their studies of the social sciences. In fact, many of the courses in the social sciences are so independent of the structure of the discipline that they may be taken by almost anyone at any time.

But Glazer was speaking basically to the question of how the social sciences could be made a part of the common learning of everyone. The enormous variety of courses available in the whole subject field is not likely to pose problems for students who intend to major in only one of the social science disciplines. Smelser suggests (1973, p. 149) that a social science major could commence with two years of required instruction "in the general principles but not the specialized knowledge and detailed techniques of the discipline." At the junior and senior level, he would urge departments to present courses that deal with general ideas and problems—for example (in sociology), "The Implications of Bureaucracy for Human Freedom," or "The Costs and Benefits of Social Inequality." Detailed consideration of technical subdivisions of the major discipline would be postponed until graduate school. For the more highly structured disciplines, such as economics, this plan might unduly delay a student's progress toward advanced education. And those who plan the major might have to augment it or offer an alternative for students who will terminate their education after earning the bachelor's degree in a social science discipline. But for many students such a plan has at least the advantage of

assuring that they will become familiar with basic principles of the discipline and have several opportunities to see how those principles relate to the perennial questions that confront humanity.

The sciences. The physical and biological sciences were suspect when they first entered the curriculum, because they looked beyond the authority of the written word to experimentation and observation as a source for truth, because they emphasized reason and mistrusted the intuition and imagination that are regarded by humanists as equally reliable sources of knowledge, and because some of them entered the college from the outside, rather than as subjects emerging from within. Eventually, however, the position of the sciences in the curriculum grew stronger, reaching a peak, perhaps during and immediately after World War II. Since that time, there has been a change.

If the biological sciences are excluded from consideration, the percentage of undergraduates enrolled in the sciences may now be lower than it has been in more than 50 years. Paul Doty and Dorothy Zinberg (1973, p. 163) reported that "if agricultural sciences and mathematics are included and engineering excluded, we find that about 20 percent of the graduates from 1900 to the late 1920s were science or mathematics majors. Then the number decreased, largely because of the contraction in agricultural sciences, and remained at about 13 percent until the early 1950s. Later, with the onset of more reliable data, and excluding agricultural and health sciences, the percentage of science and mathematics majors dropped to 9 percent in 1955, then rose to 12.5 percent in 1964, and fell off to 11.5 percent in the late 1960s." In 1976, 8 percent of the undergraduates responding to the Carnegie Council Surveys were majors in the physical sciences, a modest percentage-point increase over the enrollment in 1969 (Figure 5; Carnegie Surveys, 1969-70; Carnegie Council Surveys, 1975-1976). In a similar but even stronger pattern, majors in the biological sciences attracted 5 percent of the undergraduates in 1969 and 7 percent in 1976 (Carnegie Surveys, 1969-70; Carnegie Council Surveys, 1975-1976). The net result of these shifts is that if the physical and biological

sciences are combined, the percentage of undergraduates majoring in these two branches of the sciences (outside the professions) increased by about 25 percent between 1969 and 1976. This increase might have been even greater if the historic expansion of the physical sciences during the postwar and post-*Sputnik* eras of defensive buildup and nuclear and space exploration had not largely run its course by 1970. Federal support for scientific research and development plant and equipment dropped from $126 million in 1965 to $29 million in 1974 and then rose to $44 million in 1975 (Greenberg, 1977, pp. 1, 12), and these decreased levels adversely affect prospects for the academic employment of mathematicians, chemists, and physicists (Cartter, 1976, p. 233). In fact, the percentage of teaching faculty in the physical sciences decreased from 15 to 7 between 1969 and 1975 (Figure 5). Meanwhile, there has been an expansion of interest in the environment, ecology, nutrition, and in paraprofessional activities in the health sciences. These developments create favorable prospects not only for majors in the basic medical sciences, such as anatomy and physiology, but also for majors in botany and biology. Moreover, there are somewhat greater opportunities for holders of bachelor's degrees to find employment in such fields than has been the case in the physical sciences, where advanced degrees are more frequently required for job entry. There is also an improved academic employment situation, as the percentage of faculty members teaching in biological sciences increased from 7 percent to 11 percent between 1969 and 1976 (Figure 5).

If the social sciences suffer from lack of a commonly accepted sequence and structure, the physical and biological sciences may suffer from an inflexibility that results from the opposite condition. The importance of sequencing and structure makes science curricula slow to change, and they are more likely than the curricula of other disciplines to have similarity from institution to institution.

Doty and Zinberg (1973, pp. 180-181) describe the typical science curriculum as follows: "Sixty to 70 percent of the first three years is committed to basic science and mathematics and intermediate science courses in the field of the major, together

with required courses in English composition and foreign language. The senior year allows electives within the major field and senior research. The fact that courses and not curriculums have become the vehicle of change is not accidental. Curricular design cannot change the irreducible core of material which makes up the discipline and which must be learned in sequence. Calculus is a prerequisite for essential parts of physics; organic chemistry presupposes some competence in general chemistry; genetics presupposes a grasp of elementary biology." They go on to explain that relatively standardized courses are also necessary in order to accommodate students who transfer from one college to another. "To allow these students to maintain a science major with its sequential requirements forces the use of standardized courses as a kind of currency" (Doty and Zinberg, 1973, pp. 180-181).

Despite their structural coherence, the sciences may not be much better off than the social sciences in devising foundation instruction for nonmajors. They share with the social sciences, for example, the problem of having many subdisciplines and of the development of a variety of technical procedures and special languages that do not easily translate into a basic, common level of expertise. Yet it is generally believed by both scientists and nonscientists that all educated persons need to have some fundamental scientific literacy. Doty and Zinberg suggest that the answer may be partly provided by further strengthening the science programs offered in secondary schools, at least to the extent that college-bound high school students acquire physics, chemistry, and biology, and perhaps calculus and computer science as well. They advocate offering such courses in the freshman year of college for students who miss them in high school. In addition, they suggest that freshmen in college should be required to take a one-semester or one-year course of "the sciences for the nonscientist" type in both the physical and biological areas. Finally, they suggest that the physical and biological sciences each could offer several alternative courses, since the basic substantive material in the three major scientific fields will have been mastered in high school.

The arts. The arts have entered the undergraduate curriculum through the humanities, through extracurricular pursuits of students, and through programs that have been introduced since the mid-nineteenth century as "practical" education, or education that prepares men and women for "the several pursuits and professions in life" (Ackerman, 1973, p. 230). Now, "after 300 years of waiting in the wings to get into the act" (Morrison, 1973, p. 6), they are beginning to be taken seriously as a part of higher education on increasing numbers of campuses.

But the penetration is uneven. The Arts, Education, and Americans Panel (1977, p. 122) recently reported that only 705 postsecondary schools—23.7 percent of those in the nation—offer music majors; only 1,134 schools, or 37.1 percent, offer a major in art, and 1,214 teach only a single course in art; only 233 higher colleges and universities confer the bachelor of fine arts degree; and just 130 offer master of fine arts degrees. But such figures understate the penetration in terms of students affected. For example, in 1976 there were more students majoring in the arts than in the physical sciences in all categories of institutions except research universities. Attracting 6 percent of all undergraduates, majors in the fine arts outdrew competition from the humanities (5 percent) and were not far behind the biological sciences (7 percent) (Figure 5 and Carnegie Council Surveys, 1975-1976). The arts majors' share of the total enrollment between 1969 and 1976 remained unchanged at 6 percent, but Lyman Glenny and his associates anticipated a continued strong net increase in fine arts enrollments between 1974 and 1980 (Glenny et al., 1976, table 41).

The proportion of faculty members teaching in arts departments has also remained stable between 1969 at 8 percent (Figure 5). One would expect the ratio of faculty to enrollment in majors in the arts to be relatively high because of the individual instruction required in this subject field.

The justification for including the arts in the college curriculum is made on many grounds—on their contributions to the esthetics of the educational environment, on their recreational use by students and graduates, and as a creative experience. In

an essay written for the Carnegie Commission, James Ackerman takes exception to such justifications and urges that more serious attention be given to the arts as ways of knowing. He says, "I am speaking of the arts here as alternatives to the symbolic modes of words and figures and to the ways of knowing and feeling that they can convey. Throughout history, significant content has been expressed through images in two and three dimensions, construction in sound, and the movement of the body; today the college and university are better equipped than other institutions to further through teaching the heritage of these modes" (Ackerman, 1973, p. 222). Later he says, "The first aim of an arts education, then, should not be to produce the tiny number of distinguished artists in each generation but rather to introduce interested students to a range of disciplines that offer, apart from professional skills, ways of perceiving the physical and human environment and ways of expressing their perceptions that are quite different from those which may be gained by reading books, doing experiments, solving problems, or writing essays and theses" (Ackerman, 1973, p. 223).

To improve education in the arts, colleges have been urged to make arts courses rigorous and disciplined and to discourage amateurism within the formal curriculum. Ackerman has urged that colleges devise liberal arts courses in the arts "which are distinguished from professional courses not by being less demanding but by being less technical and more involved with principles and more linked with the liberal arts curriculum" (Ackerman, 1973, p. 263). He has also stressed the importance of arranging academic schedules that permit arts students to spend the time "required for serious involvement in their art without exceptional sacrifice" (1973, p. 263). Jack Morrison (1973, p. 163) has urged faculty members in the arts to become more sophisticated about the organization and budgeting procedures of their colleges so that they can be more effective in strengthening their departments. His advice reflects one of the basic problems of this subject field. Its faculty often do not (and it is doubtful that they need to) have high academic degrees and often lack both experience and clout in the internal politics of a campus. They are particularly vulnerable when they

are organizationally placed within another discipline instead of in independent departments.

Undergraduate Education in the Professions

For centuries, there has been a strong link between the status accorded to members of professions and the advanced level of their education (Ben-David, 1977). That linkage is particularly clear in Abraham Flexner's assertion in 1915 (in McGrath, 1959, p. 26) that "professions involve essentially intellectual operations with large individual responsibility; they derive their raw material from science and learning; this material they work up to a practical and definite end; they possess an educationally communicable technique; they tend to self-organization; they are becoming increasingly altruistic in motivation." Much of that assessment continues to be accepted today, although more recent definitions include such concepts as influence over the lives of many people, adherence to a code of ethics, and self-policing to remove incompetents and malefactors from membership.

The educational element remains strong, however—strong enough that inclusion in a college curriculum of the skills and knowledge essential to an endeavor is virtually prerequisite to its recognition as having professional status. But on college and university campuses there is a more pragmatic view of the situation. As Earl McGrath pointed out in 1959 (p. 27), it is common in American higher education to refer to any divisions of the curricula outside the liberal arts as professional schools and colleges. It is in this simplified but useful context that professional schools are discussed in this section.

The first schools for the professions of law and medicine were the offices of practicing attorneys and physicians where young men studied as apprentices. Later, proprietary schools were established for students in law and medicine, but most of them were undistinguished, and some were disreputable. In the next stage of their development, professional schools in these fields were affiliated with colleges or universities, at first loosely, but with gradually strengthening ties based on the needs of their students for the basic instruction provided in regular

undergraduate departments. Eventually, these older professions required that their students complete undergraduate general education before beginning professional studies, and, as a result, medical schools, some schools of theology, and schools for several other professions are now almost all graduate schools that accept only persons with bachelor's degrees as students (McGrath, 1959, pp. 28-33). Law schools typically require only three years of undergraduate college work, but most of their students complete the baccalaureate program before taking up their professional studies (Packer and Ehrlich, 1972, p. 77).

Of the new professions that have developed over the past 100 years or so, some were practiced by men and women who, like lawyers and doctors, trained in apprenticeships and proprietary schools and, later, in schools associated with colleges. But education for some of the newer professions was introduced directly into the undergraduate programs of colleges and universities, and a score or more of them are represented in the undergraduate programs of colleges and universities today. In the 270 institutions whose catalogs were studied by the staff of the Carnegie Council in 1976, 16 professions were identified as being represented by separate schools within undergraduate colleges. Among them are architecture, agriculture, business administration, engineering, journalism, and social work. They are most concentrated in community colleges (although the education offered there may be more occupational than professional). They are least concentrated in liberal arts colleges (Figure 6).

In 1976, 58 percent of all undergraduates reported that they were currently majoring in the professional studies these schools offer (Figure 6)—although at many colleges the majors are offered by departments rather than schools (Carnegie Council Surveys, 1975-1976).

Typically, undergraduate professional schools have an administratively autonomous position in colleges and universities (Walters, 1970, vol. 2, p. 189) and have considerable control of their own curricula, students, and faculty. Some deans of professional schools report directly to the central administration of their colleges or universities. But their autonomy is not absolute —they depend on funding provided by the college or university,

Figure 6. Percentages of undergraduates majoring in professional programs
by type of institution, 1976

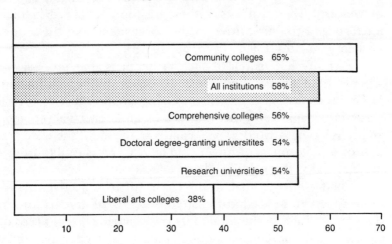

Source: Carnegie Council Surveys, 1975-1976.

most of them are regularly reviewed by professional accrediting associations, and their graduates often must qualify for state or local licensing or certification before they can practice—a requirement that directly affects the curriculum.

Within a college or university, undergraduate professional schools tend to offer their students only specialized education, relying on other undergraduate units in the institution to provide general education. But they expect their students to spend a substantial part of their undergraduate education in the professional major—the median amount is between 61 and 70 percent of all courses that must be taken to get a bachelor's or associate's degree. Moreover, in these schools the traditional single subject major is required in more than 60 percent of the institutions. Only in schools of education is the interdisciplinary major an option available at more than half of the professional schools (Catalog Study, 1976).

Within the past decade, the professional schools on the nation's campuses have acquired more stature and influence. Their enrollments have grown, partially in response to national preoccupation with vocationalism during these years, partly in

response to the emergence of new professional subfields. But because of their new prominence they also have become objects of concern. Their critics say they are too specialized in their interests and too insensitive to the consequences of the actions of their graduates (Cheit, 1975, pp. 14-15).

Part of the answer to such criticism is that professional schools have always had more to offer than specialization. McGrath argued in 1959 that training in the skills of logical reasoning, making an orderly attack on an intellectual problem, and developing attitudes, personality traits, and "the excogitation of a philosophy of life" could be reached as easily through professional as through liberal arts education.

Cheit contends that in the clarity of its objectives, its responsiveness to new educational approaches, its foundations in the practical and useful, and in its relevance to current needs of students and the general public, professional education may provide a new model for liberal education. He cites H. Bradley Sagen's assertion that liberal arts colleges could draw from the experience of the professions by "(1) clarifying the role which knowledge plays in the lives of most persons; (2) delineating the competencies necessary in a fast changing and increasingly complex world; (3) establishing vocational choice and career development as legitimate dimensions of personal growth and development; (4) developing an appropriate sense of responsibility to the rest of society" (cited in Cheit, 1975, p. 139). Some of these activities parallel suggestions we make in this commentary for strengthening the total undergraduate curriculum.

Undergraduates have a rather mixed reaction to professional education. For example, 58 percent of all students who say that they are either "satisfied" or "very satisfied" with their college overall are in professional schools or departments, but 50 percent of the undergraduates who say they are "dissatisfied" or "very dissatisfied" are also in these schools and departments.

Compared to all undergraduates in 1976, the undergraduates in professional schools appear to be somewhat less satisfied with the teaching and grading at their colleges; less satisfied with most of their advising (except for academic advising); and less trustful that their faculty is looking out for students' inter-

ests (Table 9). On the other hand, they seem somewhat more inclined to say that they would rather be going to college now

Table 9. Comparison of satisfaction of professional school undergraduates and all undergraduates on selected indicators, 1976 (in percentages)

	Professional school under-graduates	All under-graduates
I am "satisfied" or "very satisfied" with college	71	72
I am "satisfied" or "very satisfied" with teaching at my college	69	74
I am "satisfied" or "very satisfied" with grading at my college	53	57
Vocational advising is "highly adequate" or "adequate"	28	31
Academic advising is "highly adequate" or "adequate"	60	57
Financial advising is "highly adequate" or "adequate"	31	32
Personal advising is "highly adequate" or "adequate"	22	24
I trust the faculty here to look out for the students' interests[a]	73	77
I would rather be going to college now than doing anything else[a]	72	69
I find myself bored in class[a]	42	40
Undergraduate education would be improved if more course work were more relevant to contemporary life and problems[a]	80	81
Undergraduate education would be improved if more attention were paid to the emotional development of students[a]	76	74
My college is much like high school[a]	18	27
I am often lonely[a]	31	29
Most students are treated like numbers in a book[a]	48	41

[a]"Strongly agree" or "agree with reservations."

Source: Carnegie Council Survey, 1975-1976.

than doing anything else, and less likely to feel that their college is like high school (Table 9). But they are more likely to be lonely than students generally and to think that "most students are treated like numbers in a book" (Table 9).

Professional education may now be at a turning point. If it follows the precedent set by education for law and medicine, it will move increasingly into the graduate level, leaving to undergraduate colleges the basic task of providing general education and preprofessional training. There is already some movement in that direction. Many of the professional schools that offer undergraduate education also have graduate programs. The increasing importance of the master's degree in business administration may be leading in the historic direction. Several professional fields, such as library sciences, social welfare, and public health now consist mainly of master's degree programs built on four years of baccalaureate preparation.

One potential alternative to this development would be to develop somewhat more compressed general education and preprofessional options within the undergraduate curriculum that can be combined with professional school programs to make possible bachelor's degrees in four or five years or master's degrees in a professional field within a total of five or six years.

But there is also evidence that professional schools may evolve in ways that make them strong contenders for important roles as alternative providers of liberal education. In other countries, law is regarded as a useful part of education at the undergraduate level, because the legal profession touches many human endeavors and is fundamentally concerned with the balance of freedom and authority in the general society. Herbert Packer and Thomas Ehrlich (1972) advocate the study of law as "art and artifact" and as "methods of thought":

> The study of law as fact and artifact focuses the student's attention on the conception of a legal system: who operates in it, how they function, what impact they have, how the system changes, the impact the system has on other elements of our society, and vice versa. Here the effort is to give the student an idea of

law as a social process, the functions it performs, the institutions involved, and how changes take place. It gives at least an introductory idea of the structures and processes involved in society's efforts to shape and organize individual and group behavior—a view of law as an ordering process.

The study of law as methods of thought focuses on several complex rational processes. Involved are the abilities to analyze the significance attributed to verbal signals and messages; to employ communication as a planning and control mechanism; to capture the consequences of courses of action; and to digest and synthesize as well as break a problem into components and reassemble it. Studying law with this focus gives students exposure to a method of thought involving values and value choices tied directly to the making of decisions that result in action, and it is in this respect different from those focuses generally used in the social and natural sciences.

Architecture, which can bring together such varied disciplines as art, engineering, history, and the new environmental studies, and social work, which can draw on psychology, sociology, political science, certain of the health fields, economics, and other subjects, can also offer what are unquestionably broad learning experiences of a practical and significant kind. But a question needs to be asked: Must one plan to become a professional in order to acquire a good undergraduate education?

The answer depends on one's faith in the traditional concept of general education as a useful core of nonprofessional undergraduate education. If one's faith is weak, the alternative of a professional core is difficult to resist.

The Uses of Learning

Academic planners no longer attempt to answer questions about the curriculum in terms of how much of the world's knowledge students should try to obtain. Such questions are simply unanswerable. As Wayne C. Booth (1967, p. 4) explains, "Every-

one lives on the assumption that a great deal of knowledge is not worth bothering about; though we all know what looks trivial in one man's hands may turn out to be earthshaking in another's, we simply cannot know very much, compared with what might be known, and we must therefore choose." The structure of the modern curriculum, therefore, is not (at all but a very few places) one that prescribes the same knowledge for everyone. Instead, it presumes that much of what is studied will be a matter of student choice, that foundations must be laid for making informed choices possible, and that alternatives must be provided for students who change their minds. It also presumes, however, that there are some things students should be able to study in order to achieve their life goals and that should be taught if the colleges are to serve not only individuals but also the general society.

Since it is impossible for any college or university to expose its students to all available knowledge, perhaps the basic objectives of the curriculum will be to provide students with skills for lifelong learning. These will include the ability to analyze written and spoken ideas and exposition, to use computational tools properly, to integrate information gathered from more than one source to produce new conclusions or observations, to test the validity of conclusions, and to use knowledge to solve problems.

In addition, and among other objectives not defined here, colleges may seek to provide:

- Certain learning experiences that all students in a college have in common
- Opportunities for a student to become familiar with at least one subject in depth
- Programs that make students aware of the concerns, methods, and history of several broad fields of learning
- Instruction and experiences that develop students' awareness of their own physical and mental capacities, convictions, values, and beliefs
- Programs and environments that help students cultivate tolerance for ideas that are different from their own

It is from such concepts as these, rather than from attempts to package and disseminate the world's available knowledge, that academic planners must now receive guidance in determining the components of the curriculum.

Basic Components of the Curriculum

Most of the colleges in the United States have degree requirements that consist of five main components:

- Advanced learning skills
- "General understanding" components of general education
- Breadth components of general education
- The major (or concentration)
- Electives

For purposes of this commentary, these components are defined as follows.

Advanced Learning Skills

Advanced learning skills are those that students need in order to embark on college-level education. Subjects in this component may include English composition, a year of a foreign language, mathematics through geometry and two years of algebra, and (less frequently now than in years past) physical education. These subjects are offered by high schools, but colleges may include some of them in their own curricula in order to offer students a chance to review basic subjects, to practice and develop skills acquired in prior education, to study elementary subjects they missed or did not complete satisfactorily in high school, or to meet prerequisites for advanced study in certain fields (for example, comparative literature or statistics).

General Understanding Components of General Education

"General understanding" components of general education are intended to give students a common, basic undergraduate learning experience. They may provide a broad perspective—as is the case with the "Introduction to the Liberal Arts" course required of all students enrolled in Coe College and the "Western

Civilization" courses that have developed at several institutions on the model introduced at Columbia University after World War II. They may also include courses that comply with laws of those states that require that all graduates of public colleges receive instruction in American and state governments and constitutions, or they may honor the religious orientation of a college by including instruction in the Bible or theology.

Breadth Components of General Education

Breadth components of general education introduce students to the concerns and methods of several broad subject fields—typically the social sciences, the humanities, the physical sciences, the biological sciences, and, occasionally, the fine arts. This component of general education is often referred to as *distribution.*

The Major (or Concentration)

The major (or concentration) is that part of the curriculum in which a student concentrates on one subject or a group of subjects. Its content is usually defined by one academic department, but it can also be defined jointly by two or more departments and, in special cases (and with faculty advice and approval) by individual students. Departments can, and fre ⋅ quently do, require their majors to take certain courses (major *cognates*) in other departments. At some colleges, students may be required (or have the option) to pursue, in addition to the major a less intense concentration, or *minor,* in a subject other than the one chosen for a major.

Electives

Electives are subjects students study of their own free choice. The only basic requirement is that students must take enough elective units, in addition to those earned in the major and in required general education, to meet the minimum number of units the college requires each student to take in order to graduate or earn a degree. From the perspective of an individual student, electives are often that part of the curriculum that is left after institutional and major requirements are satisfied. These "free" electives do not necessarily represent the full range of

student choice, however. The number of courses required for the major or for general education may be greater than the number of courses specifically identified as meeting those requirements. Students are permitted to fill out the difference with undesignated courses available in their major departments or broad subject field. In general education, particularly in the case of distribution requirements, there may be an opportunity for students to choose at least some and perhaps all of their courses as long as they take enough courses in each subject field to satisfy the overall requirement.

Components' Shares of the Curriculum

In a study of the curriculum conducted by Robert Blackburn and his associates at the University of Michigan, the components we have identified as "advanced learning skills," "general understanding components of general education," and "breadth components of general education" were not disaggregated from what the investigators called *general education.* As a result, that study was concerned with only three components general education, the major, and electives. The shares of the curriculum occupied by these three components in 1967 and 1974 are shown in Figure 7. The overall change involves a dramatic reduction in general education and a corresponding increase in electives, with the result that by 1974 the three major components came to have essentially equal shares of the curriculum (Figure 7).

The major, general education courses, and electives are found in the curricula of the overwhelming majority of colleges in the United States, but they are not universal. Some institutions do not require majors, some have virtually no required general education courses, and some offer no free electives. These variations suggest that the question of the balance, content, and perhaps even the validity of the various curriculum components is by no means settled for all time.

The Competency-Based Curriculum

The components of the curriculum described thus far in this section are subject or course based and consist of time-measured blocks of knowledge or experience. Some colleges are now

Figure 7. Percentages of curriculum devoted to major requirements, general education requirements, and free electives in four-year institutions of higher education, 1967 and 1974

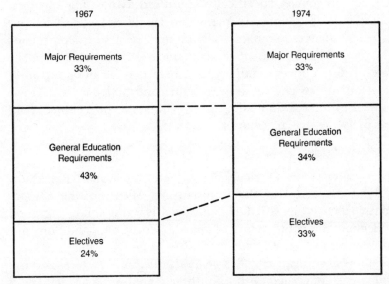

Source: Adapted from Blackburn, Armstrong, Conrad, Didham, and McKune, 1976, pp. 10-17.

departing from this formulation of the curriculum by emphasizing the outcomes for which the education is intended. The idea is not really new, because it has been applied to the teaching of technical skills and the fine arts for a long time (Knott, 1975, p. 26), but it spread into other parts of the curriculum in the 1960s as colleges sought alternatives to traditional curricular patterns.

The curricula that emerged from these particular efforts are called *competency based* because the outcomes sought are expressed in terms of competences, or abilities to perform in an observable and verifiable way. At Alverno College, for example, eight competences must be achieved if "a person is to be able to manage his or her life, make decisions, develop initiative, and be responsible and confident." The eight competences, as reported by Trivett (1975, pp. 34, 35), are to:

1. Develop effective communication skill.
2. Sharpen analytical capabilities.
3. Develop workable problem-solving skill.
4. Develop facility in making independent value judgments and independent decisions.
5. Develop facility for social interaction.
6. Achieve understanding of the relationship of the individual and the environment.
7. Develop awareness and understanding of the world in which the individual lives.
8. Develop knowledge, understanding, and responsiveness to the arts and humanities.

Some other liberal arts colleges that have adopted the competency-based approach are Mars Hill College in North Carolina, and Sterling College in Kansas (Trivett, 1975, p. 32). Competency-based programs are also found in subunits of institutions, as is the case with a program in nursing at Mount Hood Community College in Oregon and one in biotechnology in Central Washington State College in Washington (Trivett, 1975, p. 32). In 1975, Harold Hodgkinson reported that more than 200 institutions were then using or seriously considering adopting some form of competency-based education. The following year, 9 percent of the undergraduates participating in the Carnegie surveys (possibly 800,000 students nationally) had had competency-based instruction.

Competency-based curricula are different from subject-based curricula in the following respects:

1. They are directed toward the achievement of outcomes that are explicitly defined and made known to students in advance.
2. They recognize competences wherever they are achieved—in class, in class at another institution, through work experience, or through some other learning activity.
3. There is (theoretically) no time schedule for the completion of the program.

4. They are sometimes developed in ways that assess the margin of competence specifically added by the college experience and are thus adapted to each individual. In such cases, a diagnostic assessment is made when the student begins the program, and a summational assessment is made when he or she completes it.
5. They endeavor to assess not only the student's cognitive development, as evidenced by what they know, but also their affective development, as evidenced by the manner in which they perform.

Students at competency-based colleges often choose traditional courses as vehicles for acquiring and demonstrating competence. They also may have majors that are offered in subject-based formats. To that extent, studying at competency-based institutions may not appear to be much different from studying at traditional colleges. But both in theory and in practice their curricula are sufficiently distinctive as to make attempts to describe them in terms of the usual curricular components virtually meaningless.

In General

Although it is easy to identify the main components of the undergraduate curriculum, it is nearly impossible to generalize about their use in institutions of higher education. Different institutions give different weight to each component.

To correct this situation, we suggest that consideration be given to the development of an analytical transcript that classifies courses taken by students in terms of their type and purpose. For example, courses could be listed under the following headings:

• Advanced-level skills
• Courses in the major subject(s)
• Courses in the minor
• Courses that meet breadth requirements
• Broad learning experiences and courses that meet general understanding requirements

A useful refinement would be to designate with an asterisk or some other clear device courses that were specifically required.

The advantage of such a transcript would be that it would give a better indication than most transcripts now do of the true range of options open to students in different programs, of the direction of students' own interests and inclinations as opposed to those of the college, and of the tendency of students to take risks, be imaginative, or play it safe in the development of their programs. As a totality, American higher education makes available an exceedingly rich curriculum for its undergraduates. Somewhere within all of our colleges and universities, there is something for almost everyone. There is also provision for access to the curriculum at several levels suited to a national student body whose individual members come to college unevenly prepared academically and with different personal educational objectives.

Two choices seem open to us. One is to follow the direction of current trends and restructure American higher education as a totally open system with a common beginning, many places to stop in or out, but with almost no provision for either learning experiences common to all students in the college or for institutional goals short of whatever ultimate aim each person draws as an individual. The other choice is to reassert the value of undergraduate education not only as preparation for the student embarking on a career or advanced education but also as something that makes a positive, intended difference in the lives of those who are exposed to it and through them, in society as well.

*   *   *

For further information on subjects discussed in this chapter, see the following chapters in the Carnegie Council on Policy Studies in Higher Education, *Handbook on Undergraduate Curriculum*: "General Education," "Basic Skills and Knowledge," "Major or Concentration," "Tests and Grades," "Advising," "Education and Work," "Credits and Degrees," and "The Structure of Academic Time."

6

Institutional Contours

If there were such a thing as a contour map of the curricula of American colleges, it would depict very uneven terrain. There is great diversity. Among the significant differences are the variety of programs and level of degrees offered and the ability and educational aspirations of students.

Community Colleges

The two-year community colleges are easily the most diverse of all colleges in the country. Not only are they distinctive as compared to one another, but they also pride themselves in encouraging diversity of programs within each college. The result is a spectrum of institutions in which colleges with narrowly defined technical or vocational programs are at one end and multi-unit community colleges are at the other. In between are colleges with a basic transfer curriculum and variations of structure and offerings that move in both directions along the spectrum. In addition, there are two-year branch campuses of colleges and universities, proprietary institutions that have similar missions, and other specialized institutions, such as the Community College of the Air Force.

The curricula of these colleges are basically related to their training functions and the degrees and certificates they award, but an increasing focus of comprehensive two-year colleges on community services and human-development activities has produced programs that often go far beyond those defined by their degree and certificate programs.

The degrees offered by community colleges include the *associate of arts* degree, which is designed primarily as a transfer degree and includes courses that parallel the offerings of four-year institutions at the sophomore level. Work for the degree normally includes studies in major and minor fields and general education electives. The concentrations required in the associate of arts program are often linked to the majors·students intend to pursue after transferring. At private two-year colleges, the curriculum may be entirely devoted to such instruction.[1]

Community colleges may also offer an *associate of science* degree, which is usually intended to prepare one for immediate employment in a specialized field but which is sometimes used as a transfer degree in the sciences. The *associate of applied science* degree offered by community colleges certifies both competence in a technical and occupational field enough to merit entry into employment and academic achievement that can be transferred to a four-year college. About 50 percent of all community college students are in such programs. Increasingly, four-year colleges and universities are designing baccalaureate-level degrees that allow the development of "upside-down" programs that permit students to concentrate on occupational preparation at the beginning rather than at the end of the undergraduate career. Other colleges, such as the Capitol Campus of Penn State University and the Upper Division College of SUNY at Utica/Rome, New York, are structuring their programs to accommodate students who want to transfer out of career programs.

Certificates are awarded by two-year colleges for a range of offerings with special purposes. They may be awarded for completion of vocational training requirements linked closely with

[1]The studies of the curriculum made by Blackburn and his associates provide the data for Table 10, which shows the shares of curricular components found in different types of institutions. It shows no major requirements at two-year colleges, because the analysis assumed that in transfer programs (that is, associate of arts programs) at the community college level, no majors would be required. The Catalog Study indicates that in degree programs that terminate at the associate of arts level many two-year colleges do require their students to have a concentration or major—and often a minor as well.

Table 10. Proportions of undergraduate education spent in general education, the major, and electives, by Carnegie Commission classification (in percentages)

	General education (mean)		Major requirements (median)[a]		Available electives (median)[a]	
	1967	1974	1967	1974	1967	1974
Research universities I—public	42	41	33	31	26	28
Research universities I—private	42	33	30	33	29	35
Research universities II—public	41	35	34	33	25	33
Research universities II—private	44	33	34	35	22	33
Doctoral-granting universities I—public	40	36	35	35	25	28
Doctoral-granting universities I—private	45	37	34	34	22	29
Doctoral-granting universities II—public	40	30	36	37	24	34
Doctoral-granting universities II—private	44	37	33	34	23	29
Comprehensive colleges and universities I—public	43	36	37	36	21	28
Comprehensive colleges and universities I—private	49	35	34	24	18	32
Comprehensive colleges and universities II—public	43	38	39	38	23	25
Comprehensive colleges and universities II—private	38	35	31	31	31	35
Liberal arts colleges I—private	43	23	28	28	29	50
Liberal arts colleges II—public	46	27	36	34	21	34
Liberal arts colleges II—private	45	31	31	30	29	44
Community colleges—public	53	53			47	47
Community colleges—private	68	55			32	45

[a]Estimated.

Source: Adapted from Blackburn et al., 1976, table 6, p. 33.

apprenticeship training, or with the training needs of governmental and social service agencies. Certificate programs often involve concentration on one field of study with no additional general education or distribution requirements. Some may be of short duration, lasting from 9 to 20 weeks.

Except for the requirements for those degrees and certificates graduates may need to obtain licensing for employment in certain fields, the degree and certificate requirements of community colleges do not necessarily govern a student's educational choices. If students intend from the beginning to transfer to a four-year institution, the degree requirements of their community college may have less influence on their course of studies than the entrance requirements of the college to which they plan to transfer. The curricula of two-year colleges are open-ended, and the students who attend them may have more free choice than published degree requirements would suggest.

Community colleges do not typically have professional schools or separate colleges of arts and sciences. They do have departments that represent such fields, however. For example, 93 percent have departments of business, 69 percent have departments of education, 55 percent have departments of engineering, and 63 percent have departments of health sciences (Catalog Study, 1976). Undergraduate enrollments in majors in the various subfields and disciplines are highest in business, commerce, management, engineering, and health sciences (Figure 8).

Of the approximately 1,000 community colleges in the United States, all but 231 are public institutions (National Center for Education Statistics, 1976). These public institutions enroll 97 percent of all two-year college students (National Center for Education Statistics, 1976a). These public institutions accept all high school graduates and all persons over 18 years old for admission. About 30 percent of their new students arrive with high school grade-point averages of C or lower and 17 percent come with averages of A or A— (Table 11). Far fewer community college students than the average at all institutions have had geometry, second-year algebra, English com-

Figure 8. Percentages of undergraduates majoring in professional programs and other subject fields in community colleges in 1976

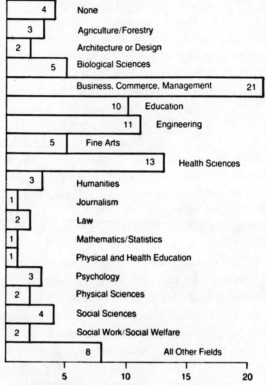

Note: Percentages do not add to 100 because of rounding.

Source: Carnegie Council Surveys, 1975-1976.

position, a foreign language, or a year of a specific science (such as chemistry or biology) before coming to college (Table 12). Community colleges also accommodate a large number of students who come to college before they have mastered college-level learning skills. To help such students, 78 percent of the two-year institutions included in the Carnegie Council Catalog Study in 1976 offered compensatory education for credit, and 53 percent offered such instruction without credit.

Most community college students are clearly career ori-

Table 11. Overall high school grade-point averages of undergraduates in institutions of higher education, by Carnegie Commission classification, 1976 (in percentages)

	A or A−	B+, B, or B−	C or less
Community colleges	17	52	31
Liberal arts colleges I	44	51	7
Liberal arts colleges II	30	51	19
Comprehensive colleges and universities I	27	54	19
Comprehensive colleges and universities II	26	58	18
Doctoral degree-granting universities I	35	50	15
Doctoral degree-granting universities II	33	54	13
Research universities I	48	43	9
Research universities II	42	44	11

Source: Carnegie Council Surveys, 1975-1976.

ented. Fewer students of these colleges than of any others say they consider themselves to be intellectuals (although the proportion that does—60 percent—is substantial) (Table 13). A higher proportion of community college students than students at all colleges believe it is essential to get a detailed grasp of a special field from their college experience, and 73 percent, the highest proportion of students in any type of institution, say it is essential to get training and skills for an occupation. They are also more likely to say that if they could get a job now or the same job after finishing school they would take the job now or that if they thought that attending college was not helping their job chances they would drop out (Table 13). Although 21 percent of these students intend to end their educational career with associate's degrees, 32 percent (approximately the same

Table 12. Courses taken by college undergraduates while they were
in high school, by Carnegie Commission classification, 1976
(in percentages)

	Geometry	Second year algebra	English composition in junior or senior year	One year foreign language	One year specific science
Community colleges	63	48	67	58	70
Liberal arts colleges I	94	85	74	95	90
Liberal arts colleges II	79	64	74	73	84
Comprehensive colleges and universities I	85	69	74	73	84
Comprehensive colleges and universities II	85	77	69	84	84
Doctoral degree-granting universities I	90	73	78	79	87
Doctoral degree-granting universities II	91	79	76	82	87
Universities I	94	83	82	89	84
Universities II	90	85	82	81	89

Source: Carnegie Council Surveys, 1975-1976.

percentage as students in all colleges) say that they plan to obtain the bachelor's degree, and 35 percent plan to seek advanced degrees (Table 15).

Liberal Arts Colleges

The tone for undergraduate education in the United States may well be set by our liberal arts colleges. In function and curriculum, they remain most like those colleges that provided higher education to American from colonial times into the 1860s, and the colleges and universities that have developed since that time are, to a great extent, adaptations. The statements of missions for these colleges refer to providing education for the whole person, freeing individuals to realize their fullest potentials, and

Table 13. Selected attitudes of undergraduates at different types
of institutions, by Carnegie Commission classification, 1976

	Perccentage that agree strongly or with reservations		
	I consider myself an intellectual	*If I could get a job now or the same job after finishing school I would take the job now*	*If I thought attending college wasn't helping my job chances, I would drop out*
Community colleges	60	47	51
Liberal arts colleges I	71	19	24
Liberal arts colleges II	66	31	43
Comprehensive colleges and universities I	63	37	47
Comprehensive colleges and universities II	64	37	45
Doctoral degree-granting universities I	64	32	41
Doctoral degree-granting universities II	68	31	42
Research universities I	68	27	37
Research universities II	64	29	44

Source: Carnegie Council Surveys, 1975-1976.

helping people to understand themselves and the world they live in. They offer their students opportunities to sample knowledge from the major fields of learning, to acquire the skills people need for lifelong self-instruction and to cultivate special interests in at least one subject.

The degrees that they offer are the *bachelor of arts*, particularly in the humanities, social sciences, and fine arts, but also in the sciences; and the *bachelor of science*, which may be a degree in a scientific subject or, in some institutions, a degree representing completion of all courses for the bachelor of arts except those in foreign languages (Spurr, 1970, pp. 56, 57). There may be still other variations in the use of the B.S. degree.

Table 14. Percentages of undergraduates rating five objectives of attending colleges essential, fairly important, or not important

Question: Please indicate how important it is to get each of the following out of college	Community colleges	Liberal arts		Comprehensive		Doctoral universities		Research universities		All institutions
		I	II	I	II	I	II	I	II	
A detailed grasp of a special field										
Essential	69	53	70	71	70	64	69	62	66	68
Fairly important	27	40	27	26	28	33	28	33	30	28
Not important	4	8	3	2	3	3	3	5	4	4
A well-rounded general education										
Essential	56	71	62	56	59	58	55	58	55	57
Fairly important	41	27	37	41	38	38	40	39	42	40
Not important	3	2	2	3	3	3	6	4	3	3
Training and skills for an occupation										
Essential	73	36	65	70	67	62	68	55	65	67
Fairly important	24	42	30	26	27	33	27	36	29	27
Not important	4	22	5	4	6	4	5	9	6	5
Learning to get along with people										
Essential	61	72	74	70	68	70	70	64	69	66
Fairly important	33	23	23	27	28	26	26	31	29	30
Not important	5	5	3	3	4	4	4	5	3	4
Formulating the values and goals of my life										
Essential	60	67	70	63	64	62	61	58	60	62
Fairly important	31	28	26	30	29	33	32	34	35	31
Not important	9	5	4	7	7	5	7	9	5	7

Source: Carnegie Council Surveys, 1975-1976.

Table 15. Highest degrees undergraduates intend to obtain by types of institutions in which they are currently enrolled, 1976 (in percentages)

	None	Associate	Bachelor's	Law degree	M.D. D.D.S. or D.V.M.	Other professional	Master's degree	Ed.D.	Ph.D.	Other
Community colleges	8	21	32	2	2	3	20	1	4	3
Liberal arts colleges I	2	0	23	9	8	6	32	–	17	1
Liberal arts colleges II	2	2	36	3	5	5	32	1	11	2
Comprehensive colleges and universities I	2	5	37	4	4	6	32	1	9	1
Comprehensive colleges and universities II	2	2	33	5	4	5	39	1	8	1
Doctoral degree-granting universities I	1	2	35	6	5	7	31	1	10	1
Doctoral degree-granting universities II	1	1	37	6	3	6	31	1	10	1
Research universities I	1	1	27	9	10	8	30	1	13	1
Research universities II	1	2	34	6	8	6	32	1	10	1
All institutions (average)	2	4	33	4	4	5	25	1	8	2

Source: Carnegie Council Surveys, 1975-1976.

It frequently involves more required studies—more advanced courses, fewer electives, a minor, a thesis or other senior project, or special general education requirements. The B.A. degree, on the other hand, is likely to require more general education than the B.S.—but there is enormous variety, and some colleges offer students a choice of either the B.S. or B.A. with no distinction between them. Colleges may also offer specialized bachelor's degrees, such as bachelor of music, bachelor of fine arts, bachelor of business administration, and at one institution in the Carnegie Council's 1976 Catalog Study, bachelor of ceramics. These colleges have relatively few major offerings— averaging between 25 and 30 (Catalog Study, 1976).

The curricula of liberal arts colleges have a bimodal character, because some of these institutions are highly selective in their admissions policies (the Carnegie Commission designates these as Liberal Arts Colleges I), and some are not. Forty-four percent of the students in highly selective colleges had A or A— averages in high school, while 30 percent of the students at other liberal arts colleges had grades at that level. Even more significantly, at the less selective liberal arts colleges in 1976, 19 percent of the students (a somewhat higher percentage than at community colleges) had grade-point averages of C or less, while only 6 percent of the students at selective liberal arts colleges had grades in that range (Table 11).

The undergraduates at the two types of liberal arts colleges do not, apparently, share the same educational goals. The highest proportion (71 percent) of students in any of the institutional classifications who consider themselves intellectuals is found in the selective liberal arts colleges (Table 13). And only about one-third of students in these institutions (36 percent), compared to 65 percent in the other liberal arts colleges, consider it essential that their college give them training and skills for an occupation (Table 14). But very substantial percentages (within a range of 62 to 74 percent) of students in both types of institution consider it essential for their college to give them a well-rounded general education, to help them learn to get along with people, and to help them in formulating the values and goals of their lives (Carnegie Council Surveys, 1975-1976).

The educational aspirations of undergraduates at the two types of liberal arts colleges are also different, with 73 percent of the students in highly selective liberal arts colleges planning to pursue postgraduate education and 56 percent of the students in other liberal arts colleges anticipating such studies after receiving their bachelors' degrees (Table 15). In this regard, it is worth noting that about as many of the students in selective liberal arts colleges as in many research universities plan to study for an M.D., D.D.S., or D.V.M. This fact may also explain why higher proportions of students in highly selective liberal arts colleges than in any other type of institution major in the biological sciences as undergraduates.

The significance of these differences in student achievement levels, interests, and aspirations is readily seen in the pattern of choice in selecting majors in liberal arts institutions. In the more selective liberal arts colleges, somewhat higher percentages than in any other type of institution chose to major in the humanities, fine arts, social sciences, biological sciences, and psychology. In the other liberal arts colleges, the proportions enrolling in the humanities (15 percent) were not as high as they were in the selective colleges (20 percent) but were still higher than other types of institutions (Figure 9). In virtually every other field, the proportion of students at less selective liberal arts colleges choosing a listed major was not significantly different from the average proportion of students from all types of colleges in those fields. But the proportion of students in less selective liberal arts colleges majoring in business and education exceeded that of students in the selective colleges by significant margins (Carnegie Council Survey, 1975-1976).

One of the distinguishing features of most liberal arts colleges is that they tend to be relatively small. The average size of the more selective colleges in this category is 1,400 and that of the less selective private colleges is 900. For this reason, they can afford to provide more intensive counseling for their students and to give them more personal attention generally. These institutions also tend to be privately controlled (only 4 percent of the liberal arts colleges listed in the Carnegie Commission's *Classification of Institutions of Higher Education,* 1973a, were

Figure 9. Percentages of undergraduates majoring in professional programs and other subject fields in liberal arts colleges in 1976

Field	Percentage
None	1
Agriculture/Forestry	1
Biological Sciences	10
Business, Commerce, Management	11
Education	15
Engineering	1
Fine Arts	9
Health Sciences	7
Home Economics	1
Humanities	16
Journalism	1
Law	1
Mathematics/Statistics	3
Physical and Health Education	2
Physical Sciences	2
Psychology	5
Social Sciences	9
Social Work/Social Welfare	2
All Other Fields	3

Source: Carnegie Council Surveys, 1975-1976.

public). This situation makes some of these institutions particularly sensitive to student interests and preferences.

These factors help to explain the dramatic shift away from general education requirements to electives in these institutions since 1967 (Table 10). Another reason is that the smaller liberal arts colleges offer relatively few courses, and all of those listed in the catalog therefore become to some extent breadth courses. These colleges also have better advising than larger institutions and are less dependent on requirements to make sure that students obtain a balanced education. In the selective liberal arts colleges, the proportion of the curriculum devoted to general

education dropped by 20 percentage points, while the proportion devoted to electives increased by 21 percentage points. In other private liberal arts colleges, the proportion of general education decreased by 14 percentage points, while the proportion devoted to electives increased by 15.

Comprehensive Colleges and Universities

Comprehensive colleges and universities offer not only a liberal arts curriculum but also at least one professional and specialized program, such as engineering or business administration. Seventeen percent of their students major in education, and precisely the same percentage major in business, commerce, and management (Figure 10). About 10 percent major in the health sciences, 8 percent in the fine arts, and 7 percent in the biological sciences (Carnegie Council Surveys, 1975-1976). The difference between the two categories within this classification has nothing to do with admissions requirements. Instead, it is related to the size of the institutions' educational programs and to the size of their enrollments.

The larger comprehensive institutions had enrollments in excess of 4,000 in 1970. And their programs are sometimes quite extensive. In addition to a letters and sciences or arts and sciences unit, 60 percent of these colleges had schools of business and schools of education, about one-third had engineering schools, one-fifth had schools for health sciences and nursing, and about one-sixth had schools of fine arts and music, and trade and vocational schools (Catalog Study, 1976). Some of them also had agriculture schools, architecture schools, journalism schools, dental schools, divinity schools, schools of forestry, schools of library science, and schools of social welfare, to provide only a partial listing. Either in place of separate schools or in addition to them, more than 30 percent of the colleges had departments of business, education, and health sciences, and a few had departments of engineering and trade and technology within their colleges of arts and sciences (Catalog Study, 1976).

The larger comprehensive colleges offered both the B.A. and B.S. degree. A few of them also offered a *bachelor of general studies,* which emphasizes general education and requires

Figure 10. Percentages of undergraduates majoring in professional
programs and other subject fields in comprehensive colleges
and universities in 1976

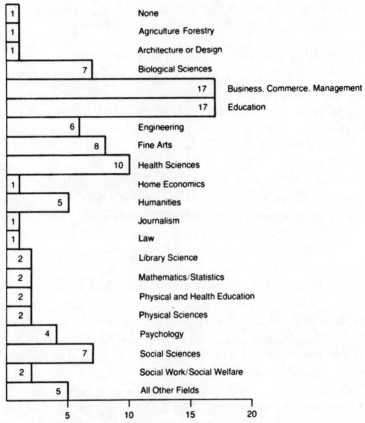

Note: Percentages do not add to 100 because of rounding.

Source: Carnegie Council Surveys, 1975-1976.

no concentration and generally represents an accumulation of
course credits in subjects chosen entirely by the students themselves. At least a dozen specialized bachelor's degrees—for example, the bachelor of music or bachelor of business administration—were given by at least one of the 69 colleges of this type
in the Council's staff study; some were offered by 30 percent of
the colleges (Catalog Study, 1976). The associate of arts degree

was offered by 60 percent of the colleges, and the associate of science degree was offered by 20 percent. A very small number offered the associate in applied science degree.

The smaller comprehensive colleges had very few schools in addition to their colleges of arts and sciences, but high percentages had departments of business (79 percent) and departments of education (88 percent) (Catalog Study, 1976). Departments of engineering, health sciences, and trade and technology are also listed in catalogs of a few of these colleges. Virtually all of them offer the bachelor of arts and bachelor of science degrees, and a few offer a bachelor of general science degree. Compared to the larger comprehensive colleges, fewer of these institutions offered associate degree programs.

With respect to the allocation of shares of the curriculum to general education, majors, and electives, the comprehensive colleges divide more along public and private lines than along lines of their relative comprehensiveness. The private institutions, about one-third of the total number, compete for students with liberal arts colleges, and in their distribution of the components—particularly in their generous provision of electives —they are quite similar to those institutions. The public comprehensive colleges and universities, on the other hand, have resisted the idea of permitting students to exercise so much choice in their studies (Table 10).

Because of the preponderance of public institutions in this classification, the colleges are less likely than liberal arts colleges to have selective admissions requirements and are more likely to provide access to students who need at least some remedial instruction. More than one-fourth (26 percent) of the students in both categories of comprehensive colleges had high school grade-point averages of A— or better, and about one-fifth had high school grade-point averages below a B— (Table 11). The proportions of the students in these colleges who had taken geometry, second-year algebra, junior- or senior-year English composition, a year of foreign language, and a year of a specialized science in high school were at about the average for all institutional types (Table 12). But more than half of the comprehensive colleges and universities offer compensatory pro-

grams (Catalog Study, 1976). Fifty-eight percent of the more comprehensive of these institutions offer compensatory education for credit, and 29 percent offer it without credit. In the less comprehensive colleges of this type, 35 percent offer compensatory education for credit, and 67 percent provide it without credit.

Students at comprehensive colleges and universities share with students at community colleges and with the less selective liberal arts colleges a strong orientation toward a specialization and career preparation (Tables 13, 14). Sixty-three percent of the students at larger comprehensive colleges and 65 percent of students at the smaller ones consider themselves intellectuals, but at these institutions much higher proportions of undergraduates than the average for all types of colleges are in occupation-related majors—business, education, and health-related sciences. The proportions of students in the smaller comprehensive institutions that are majoring in social sciences, however, are exceeded only by those of students in the highly selective liberal arts colleges (Carnegie Council Surveys, 1975-1976). Between 50 and 60 percent of the students in comprehensive colleges plan to pursue study beyond the bachelor's degree (Table 15).

Doctoral Degree-Granting Universities

The distinguishing feature of these institutions is that their programs include study leading to doctoral degrees. Ironically, however, the proportion of the undergraduates in these institutions that intend to study for degrees at that level is actually lower than that of undergraduates in the liberal arts colleges and the smaller comprehensive colleges (Table 15).

At the undergraduate level, all doctoral degree-granting institutions offer the bachelor of arts and bachelor of science degree, and a few offer the bachelor of general studies. Very few offer associate's degrees (Catalog Study, 1976).

In the allocation of shares of the curriculum to general education, the major, and electives, doctoral degree-granting universities exhibit some of the same conservatism that is found in comprehensive colleges (Table 10).

From the point of view of undergraduates, the main distinction of doctoral degree-granting institutions is likely to be the richness of their programs. That is not to say that the programs they offer may not be found at other types of institutions, but the proportions of these institutions that have a particular program may be greater. For example, schools of business and commerce, which are found in 60 percent of the comprehensive colleges and in 68 percent of the less heavily research oriented of the research universities, are found in 86 percent of the larger doctoral degree-granting universities and in 90 percent of the smaller institutions in this category. Many of these universities are former normal schools, and more of them than any other type of institution have schools of education. Many are also land-grant institutions, and this group of universities has more schools of agriculture than any type of institution except the research universities (Catalog Study, 1976).

The entering students at the doctoral degree-granting institutions are relatively well prepared. About one-third arrive after compiling A or A– averages in high school and 12 percent have averages of less than a B– (Table 11). The proportions of their students who have completed geometry, second-year algebra, junior- or senior-English composition, a year of foreign language, and a year of special science either match or exceed that of the average for all institutions (Table 12). Nevertheless, it is in these institutions, which offer the broadest range of doctoral programs, that we find the largest proportions of universities and colleges (80 percent or more offer it without credit; 70 percent offer it with credit) with compensatory education programs.

About two-thirds of the undergraduates in these institutions consider themselves intellectuals (Table 13). About the same proportion say it is essential to get a detailed grasp of a special field and to get training and skill for an occupation, 70 percent believe it is essential to learn to get along with people, a little less than one-third believe it is essential to get help in formulating the values and goals of their lives, and between 55 and 58 percent say that it is essential to get a well-rounded education (Table 14).

In their choice of majors, the undergraduates at doctoral degree-granting universities are very similar to those at comprehensive colleges. The most obvious exception is that more undergraduates in these institutions than in comprehensive colleges major in engineering, agriculture and forestry, architecture and design, and home economics (Figure 11).

Figure 11. Percentages of undergraduates majoring in professional programs and other subject fields in doctoral degree-granting universities in 1976

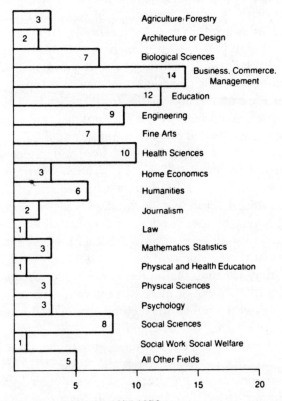

Source: Carnegie Council Surveys, 1975-1976.

Research Universities

In terms of the undergraduate curriculum, there is very little difference between research universities and doctoral degree-

granting universities. They offer the same degrees in virtually the same subjects. In a few fields that must be supported with expensive equipment and physical facilities—for example, medicine and engineering—research universities are somewhat more likely than doctoral degree-granting institutions to offer undergraduate programs. There are also many land-grant institutions in this category, so it is not uncommon for some of them to offer agricultural programs (Catalog Study, 1976).

In allocating shares of the curriculum to general education, the major, and electives, the public research universities appear to be moving less slowly than the private research universities, particularly in the shift of emphasis from general education to electives. But the shift has taken place (Table 10).

The high school preparation of students at research institutions is very good. Almost half of the students at the most heavily research-oriented universities have A or A– averages in high school, and 40 percent of the undergraduates in the other research universities had such records (Table 11). A substantial number of these institutions have compensatory education programs, however. Compensatory courses for credit are to be found in 52 percent of the most research-oriented universities and in 48 percent of the other universities. Compensatory education without credit is offered by 81 percent of the more research-oriented universities and 55 percent of the others (Catalog Study, 1976).

Two-thirds of the students at these institutions consider themselves intellectuals (Table 13), and they score relatively low, compared to undergraduates of other types of institutions, on indicators of career orientation (Table 14). Very high proportions (73 percent) of undergraduates at the major research universities plan to pursue studies beyond the bachelor's degree (Table 15). More than half of the undergraduates at research universities anticipate graduate studies.

The majors of undergraduates in research universities follow patterns that are similar in certain respects to those of both doctoral degree-granting universities and liberal arts colleges. Business and engineering majors are relatively popular, attracting 13 and 12 percent of the undergraduates, respectively (Fig-

ure 12). Ten percent of the undergraduates major in biological
sciences, and 8 percent major in each of three fields—health
sciences, humanities, and social sciences (Catalog Study, 1976).

Figure 12. Percentages of undergraduates majoring in professional
programs and other subject fields in research universities in 1976

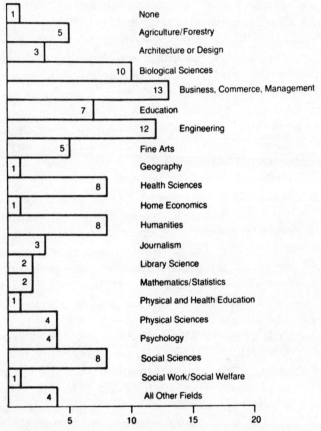

Note: Percentages do not add to 100 because of rounding.

Source: Carnegie Council Surveys, 1975-1976.

Summary

In this review of the five main classifications of colleges and universities in the United States, we have seen that their curricula
are influenced by the academic ability, high school preparation,

and educational objectives of their students, and the comprehensiveness of their programs. Community colleges have high proportions of students who enter with low ability and minimal preparation. Many of their students are occupation and career oriented, and these colleges give more attention to occupational subjects than do any of the other colleges and universities. At liberal arts colleges and research universities, large proportions of the students have high academic ability and enter college well prepared. They are less career oriented than are community college students and are slightly more likely to consider themselves intellectuals. Comprehensive colleges and doctoral degree-granting universities fall in a mid-range position with respect to student ability and aspirations.

In terms of comprehensiveness, the community colleges and liberal arts colleges have the fewest offerings, and the research universities have the largest number. This characteristic is influenced by size and also by function and history. Institutions that were established with responsibilities for teacher education or with the responsibilities for agricultural and technical education under terms of the Land-Grant College Act tend to be more comprehensive than liberal arts colleges. Graduate work and intensive specialization are concentrated in doctoral degree-granting and research universities.

Some caveats are in order. The differences among types of institutions are not necessarily based on quality. There are bright, highly motivated students in almost all colleges and universities, and institutions deserve high ratings for planning programs and adopting policies that serve their particular students, whatever their previous preparation or aspirations, were. And, finally, there is enormous variety within classifications.

7

The Mission of
Undergraduate Education

The founders of the first American colleges needed few words to describe their intentions. Harvard's rules stipulated that "Every one shall consider the Mayne End of his life & Studyes to know God & Jesus Christ, which is Eternall life." In 1701, Yale was said to be a place "wherein youth may be instructed in the arts and sciences, who through the blessing of Almighty God, may be fitted for public employment, both in Church and civil State." Queens College (Rutgers) was founded "for the education of youth in the learned languages, liberal and useful arts and sciences, and especially in divinity, preparing them for the ministry and other good offices."[1]

The curricula of modern colleges and universities can no longer be governed by the unified cultural objectives of colonial times. Instead, our heterogeneous society and the extraordinary increase in specialized knowledge since the founding of Harvard pose genuine dilemmas. Ancient Harvard and Yale could impose a totally required program of studies on their students, but our modern undergraduate institutions must offer a variety of ways of achieving the bachelor's degree. Originally, the aims of collegiate instruction that were phrased in the general principles

[1] All of these statements of purpose are taken from Brubacher and Rudy, 1968, p. 8.

enunciated by Harvard and Yale were consonant with the accepted values of society. Today, in a pluralistic society, our degree requirements are stated in terms of specific courses or areas of study and are seldom accompanied by a rationale for the selection of courses offered. Consequently, the student has no coherent guidelines from the institution on what his or her undergraduate education is supposed to accomplish. Nor do undergraduates know, as their early predecessors did, how course and degree requirements relate to the nature of their society.

Although our intellectual world no longer permits the assured prescription that was appropriate for colonial programs, it nevertheless does permit the emergence of some clear understanding about what colleges intend to accomplish. Articulating these understandings and providing for their continuing reassessment are the responsibilities of those who provide the academic leadership for every institution—a group that includes the president and principal academic officers, leaders involved in faculty policies relating to the curriculum, and perhaps those trustees who may have committee assignments in this area. The task of these leaders will be difficult, because the understandings that could be chosen and emphasized are numerous and are not available in ready-to-wear versions. They have to be institutionally tailored. The task will also require courage, for the priorities involved are often surrounded by controversy.

The result of the labors of the college's academic leadership should be a statement of the institution's mission that takes into account not only what the intended consequences of its educational efforts should be but also its traditions and resources. Because situations change, the statement should also allow for future amendment. Perhaps most importantly of all, since its object is to guide planning and action, the statement should be made in clear language that avoids the sales rhetoric often encountered in the introductions to college catalogs and recruiting brochures.

Although the development of the mission statement is properly the work of a college's academic leaders, its influence will be institution-wide and will ultimately need the weight and

authority that can be given to it only by those legally entrusted
and morally bound to exercise responsibilities for the long-run
welfare of the college. We therefore believe that the final definitions of the broad educational missions of colleges should be
officially adopted by the colleges' governing boards. Uniformity
of institutional missions will not be the result of these activities,
but we do not believe it should.

Responding to Individual and Societal Needs

Education consists of a series of events and activities that are
designed to help individuals to increase their intellectual, social,
personal, and moral potentials. At its best, it confronts people
of all ages with the realities of their environment, the human
condition, and the ideals toward which human beings have
striven throughout history. It prepares them for productive activity. It opens their minds to alternative ways of thinking and
living. It acquaints them with ways of learning and makes it possible for them to educate themselves. It provides a foundation
for making judgments, for determining personal and cultural
values, for choosing appropriate courses of action. It builds consensus and therefore can be an instrument of socialization and
social control. It also increases the tolerance individuals have for
diversity and therefore can enlarge freedom. The work of education is to make a positive difference in people's lives and also to
change society, over time, through the works of those it edu-
cates. But within that orientation there is considerable room for
institutional diversity, because the educational needs of both
individuals and society are multifaceted.

The needs of the individual. There are two ways of defining the
educational needs of men and women. One way is to regard the
"educated person" as an idealized type of human being and to
attempt to identify criteria for membership in that category.
Over the centuries, these criteria have constantly changed. His-
torian William Bouwsma has traced models of the educated man
that began with the evolution of the ancient warrior from pred-
ator to hero and came to include, over time, attributes of the
aristocrats who were concerned with prestige, achievement, and
leadership; of the scribes who could read and write and who

therefore possessed skills for improving the mind and for teaching others; of the educated citizen who subordinates individual talents to collective needs; the exponent of the Christian secular ideal, who distinguished between the concerns of religion and the concerns of education; and so on through to the present, when the notion that an educated man must be some kind of specialist has currency (Bouwsma, 1975, pp. 195-212). This analysis deserves attention because it helps to explain why many people, even today, persist in talking about idealized characteristics that anyone who wishes to be recognized as an educated person needs to have. But the ideal educated person is a complicated abstraction about which few people can agree at any given time and is by now a composite of many historic concepts.

A more useful way of talking about the qualities of the educated person is to stress learned capacities for dealing with life and the world today. Very broadly, these include the skills and knowledge people need at different times of their lives to cope with the voluntary and involuntary tasks of everyday living, with the chores and challenges of work, and with the activities associated with self-improvement. It also suggests a need for an education that serves people "within the context of a series of political, economic, and social systems" (Bailey, 1976).

In 1954, a special committee was appointed at the University of California at Berkeley to formulate, among other things, a statement defining the objectives of its College of Letters and Science. The committee approached its task by developing a series of statements that became decreasingly abstract and led directly into programs of the college.

From the committee's *Report to the Faculty,* issued in 1957, we note these six levels:

1. The fundamental aim of the College of Letters and Science is to increase man's understanding of nature and of himself. But this is a high-level abstraction, and has little *direct* connection with immediate realities. What do we want our students to be like, when we have finished with them, so that they may possess understanding?

2. In order that our students may have the understanding re-

ferred to above, we believe that they should have (a) a comprehension of abstract thought, (b) an appreciation of the structure of ideas, (c) a feeling for style, and (d) a basis for forming value judgments. But these are also high-level abstractions, and they are the result of certain abilities which the student must develop. Hence we must go to a still less abstract level.

3. On the third level, upon which the qualities listed above are built, we may put those abilities which we believe can be developed by the educational process; (a) the development of intellectual curiosity and the awakening of new intellectual interests; (b) the development of the ability to recognize facts and their relationships, with consequent liberation from uncritical loyalties evidenced by prejudice and provincialism; (c) the development of mature habits of reading and observation; (d) the development of esthetic appreciation; and (e) the development of appreciation for the responsibilities and satisfactions arising from the exercise of free choice.

4. Underlying the abilities just specified and forming the foundation upon which they must be built, is the considerable stock of knowledge which the student must have if he is to be, in any meaningful sense of the term, *an educated person.* The Committee does not believe that education can be divorced from knowledge, even though we meet now and then with unusual people who have the qualities of the educated person without the formal training.

5. At the fifth level, we come to a general statement of the program by which the student gains the knowledge specified in (4) above. It is the belief of the Special Committee that the present program of the College, *in its general characteristics,* can be the instrument by which the higher objectives can be reached. These general characteristics are two: (a) the experience of various different types of intellectual experience represented by the *breadth requirement* and (b) the advance in depth in a particular subject or field represented by the *major requirement.*

6. Finally, at the level of the completely specific, we have the particular programs which our students take.

In one of its major reports, the Carnegie Commission on Higher Education (1973c, pp. 13, 14) identified as a first purpose of higher education "The education of the individual student and the provision of a constructive environment for development growth." It specifically suggested that campuses could aid in the development of students by providing opportunities for

- Acquiring a general understanding of society and of the place of the individual within it
- Making a choice among diverse intellectual environments so that the student has a better chance of finding one that matches his or her interests and talents
- Developing a "critical" mind in the sense of the capacity to "test and challenge . . . previously unexamined assumptions" (Keniston and Gerzon, 1971) and also unexamined new ideas
- Training that will aid in obtaining suitable employment
- Surveying and intensifying cultural and creative interests to enrich life; enhancing the expressive as well as the verbal and mathematical talents
- Studying ethical issues and forming values and life goals
- Working out problems in connection with their "emotional growth"
- Meeting with and working with diverse types of people and thus "learning to get along with people"
- Participating in work and service activity that provides contacts with aspects of society
- Trying many interests and possible talents and even failing at some without heavy consequences
- Gaining access to advice and counsel from professional experts and from qualified adults in the campus community on both a formal and informal basis

In order to develop a schematic foundation for his extensive study of the consequences of American higher education, Howard Bowen examined more than 1,000 goal statements in "writings of noted educational philosophers and critics of the past and present, reports of public commissions and faculty

committees, and statements of leading educators in speeches, articles, and institutional reports" (H. Bowen, 1977, p. 53). From these statements, he has compiled a "catalog" that includes more than a score of categories of "goals for individual students" (see Appendix B). Among them are goals associated with verbal skills; quantitative skills; rationality (ability and disposition to think logically on the basis of useful assumptions); intellectual tolerance; esthetic sensibility; lifelong learning; personal self-discovery; morality; refinement of taste, conduct, and manner; citizenship; and traits of value in practical affairs (need for achievement, future orientation, adaptability, and leadership). Of particular interest in connection with the concerns of this commentary is Bowen's discussion of "substantive knowledge" as a goal for individual students. It includes "acquaintance with the cultural heritage of the West and possibly of other traditions, awareness of the contemporary world of philosophy, natural science, art, literature, social change, and social issues, and command of vocabulary, facts, and principles of one or more selected fields of knowledge."

We submit these examples from the Carnegie Commission and from Howard Bowen's analysis without suggesting that they necessarily form the basis of any specific institutional mission statement of a college. They do, however, suggest the range of subject matter that deserves consideration in framing such a statement.

In his annual report for 1975-76, Henry Rosovky, dean of the Faculty of Arts and Sciences at Harvard, approached the question of mission (which he discussed in terms of "standards") by suggesting that "Welcoming our graduates to the company of educated men and women makes sense to me only if it expresses our belief that their mental skills and powers have met a reasonable standard. Can that standard for undergraduate education be articulated at this time? I believe that it can." He then set forth six criteria:

1. An educated person must be able to think and write clearly and effectively. . . . Our students, when they receive their bachelor's degrees, must be able to communicate with precision, cogency, and force.

2. An educated person should have a critical appreciation of the ways in which we gain knowledge and understanding of the universe, of society, and of ourselves. . . . He or she should have an informed acquaintance with the mathematical and experimental methods of the physical and biological sciences; with the main forms of analysis and the historical and quantitative techniques needed for investigating the workings and development of modern society; with some of the important scholarly, literary, and artistic achievements of the past; and with the major religious and philosophical conceptions of man.

3. An educated American, in the last third of this century, cannot be provincial in the sense of being ignorant of other cultures and other times. It is no longer possible to conduct our lives without reference to the wider world or to the historical forces that have shaped the present and will shape the future. Perhaps few educated people will ever possess a sufficiently broad perspective. But it seems clear to me that a crucial difference between the educated and the uneducated is the extent to which one's life experience is viewed in wider contexts.

4. An educated person is expected to have some understanding of, and experience in thinking about, moral and ethical problems. While these issues change very little over the centuries, they acquire a new urgency for each generation when it is personally confronted with the dilemmas of choice. It may well be that the most significant quality in educated persons is the informed judgment which enables them to make discriminating moral choices.

5. We should expect an educated individual to have good manners and high esthetic and moral standards. By this I mean the capacity to reject shoddiness in all its many forms, and to explain and defend one's views effectively and rationally.

6. Finally, an educated individual should have achieved depth in some field of knowledge. Here I have in mind something that lies between the levels of professional competence and superficial acquaintance. In Harvard terminology, it is called a "concentration." The theory is straightforward: Cumulative learning is an effective way to develop a student's powers of

reasoning and analysis. It is expected that in every concentration students will gain sufficient control of the data, theory, and methods to define the issues in a given problem, develop the evidence and arguments that may reasonably be advanced on the various sides of each issue, and reach conclusions based on a convincing evaluation of the evidence.

At Western Washington State College, President Paul J. Olscamp approached the question of goals by asking "What then should a student be like, and what should he be able to do, after (and presumably partially as a result of) four years of undergraduate instruction here?" His answers concentrate on graduates of a single institution and on characteristics that concern them at the present time and are not tied to their idealized status. Two examples (Olscamp, 1977):

- The student should be able to contrast the origins and development of our culture and nation with at least some other nations and cultures, and he should be able to understand and describe past causal forces that are still at work in our present society.
- Graduates should have a basic understanding of the structures and properties of living beings, about the history and development of our planet and solar system, and about the relative place of humanity in it.

These are sweeping statements, to be sure, but they have one virtue. Should they be formally adopted as a part of an institution's mission statement, it would be reasonably easy to determine whether the curriculum provided for students at the institution did, in fact, make a contribution to their realization.

The educational needs of society. In 1852, Cardinal John Newman said, "If . . . a practical end must be assigned to a University course, I say it is that of training good members of society" (1927, p. 177). We concur, and believe that a college must therefore be concerned with what college-educated people must know in order to make a distinctive and constructive contribu-

tion to the progress and improvement of the general society. We identify five basic needs:

- For its political well-being, society needs wise and effective leadership and an informed citizenry.
- For its economic well-being, society needs able and imaginative men and women for the direction and operation of its institutions (broadly defined), for the production of goods and services, and for the management of its fiscal affairs. It also needs alert and informed consumers.
- For its cultural advancement, society needs creative talent and appreciative and discriminating readers, viewers, and listeners. It also needs people who understand the common culture and its antecedents in other parts of the world.
- For its survival, society needs members who understand the dependence of human beings on the resources provided in their natural environment and on one another.
- For its moral and ethical integrity, society needs tone-setting models and persons who, as parents and teachers and in other capacities, are able to pass the nation's ideals and heritage along to future generations.

In his study of the goal of higher education, Howard Bowen (1977, pp. 58-59) identified 11 general goals for society that could be achieved through instruction, through research, and through public service. Four of these had reasonably clear-cut implications for the curriculum:

- Preservation and dissemination of the cultural heritage
- Discovery and dissemination of knowledge and advancement of philosophical and religious thought, literature, and the fine arts—all regarded as valuable in their own right without reference to ulterior ends
- "Improvement" in the motives, values, aspirations, attitudes, and behavior of members of the general public
- Over the long periods of time, exerting a significant and favorable influence on the course of history as reflected in the evaluation of the basic culture, including the fundamental social institutions

For examples of how one's perception of educational needs of society can be translated into educational goals for college graduates, we can again cite passages from President Olscamp's statement (1977):

- "The graduate ... should ... comprehend the importance of practicing his citizenship rights, and of the necessity of remaining informed about issues pertinent to that practice."
- "He should be curious about his physical environment, and solicitous of its quality, and he should understand that an environment which provides the opportunity to test his intelligence as well as his body is not a luxury but a necessity."

But every institution should have its own missions that relate to the needs of society, and we cannot stress too strongly that those we have cited are only examples.

Capitalizing on Institutional Strengths

In developing mission statements, colleges may choose to incorporate special goals that are related to whatever natural, permanent features of the institution may make unique educational activities possible. Just before the turn of the century, the Berkeley campus of the University of California exploited its location across from the "gateway to the Orient" to create, with foundation help, a department of commerce that was the precursor of its present school of business administration. Colleges in coastal locations might also add educational missions that relate to scientific exploration of the seas or to marine biology. Some urban institutions might incorporate concerns for certain problems of the cities or might take advantage of the city's cultural facilities as centers of learning. Institutions in rural areas might have special concerns for the quality of life in areas dominated by small towns and a farm-based economy.

Colleges and universities might also consider the special characteristics of their students in framing their mission statements. Colleges for women or for men, colleges for blacks and other racial minorities, and colleges that serve students who are financially disadvantaged obviously will be aware of special

needs and interests of their student bodies when they determine their missions.

The Missions Statement

It would be quite possible to devote an entire volume to the educational philosophy of a college. But the task we suggest is much less ambitious. What we believe is needed is a concise series of statements that

1. Guide the academic leadership of a college in determining what educational programs are appropriate for accommodation in the institution's curriculum
2. Provide students with information about the institution's intentions so that they can compare them with their own interests and needs
3. Provide the college's governing board, accrediting agencies, and others who might have a legitimate reason to evaluate the performance of the college, the criteria by which the institution chooses, at least in curricular matters, to be governed

We would caution against including missions that aim beyond the institution's reach. Speaking at a convocation on her campus recently (1977), Helen Kelley, president of Immaculate Heart College in Los Angeles, referred to a statement of the characteristics that a distinguished American university had just announced as appropriate for its graduates. She said,

> I know a few people like that and, for the most part, I find them pleasant, if a little awesome, and seldom very young. I myself received an education the desired outcome of which would be all of those attributes.
>
> What remains, I am sad to report—and in spite of the fact that I have spent all of the intervening years in a scholastic setting—is the ability to think and write fairly clearly in a very limited area and good manners and moderate esthetic and moral standards. (That is to say, I know what I like, and I still recog-

nize a sin when I commit it.) It should be added that I was well on the way to acquiring those attributes by the time I began high school.

In the meantime, I have gained *and lost* some minimum understanding of mathematical and scientific principles and some moderate usage of French, German, and Spanish. My awareness of other cultures is limited to what I can read and see on the screen, expanded by the powers of imagination.

These observations remind us that although preparing a mission statement can be an awe-inspiring task, it should be approached with realism and humility. They also suggest that in committing a college to a mission, it is perhaps difficult, but still imperative, to distinguish between changes that result from the work of the college and those that one might hope would take place as the grand total of any student's educational and life experience.

One statement of mission we have seen, that of DeAnza College in California, states its mission in less than 25 words and supports it with five statements of "purposes," each of which is also less than 25 words in length. The purposes are, in turn, elaborated by brief statements of "Relevant Functions." The whole document is "intended to guide the activities of specific programs and to set criteria of accountability for the use by the selected Board of Trustees" ("The Mission of DeAnza College," n.d.). Under a heading of "Accountability," this document concludes with the following summary: "As a primary outcome of the functions performed under this mission, a student should be able to construct for himself:

- Essential academic skills
- Competency to choose and then enter a career
- Basic capacity to perform his citizenship responsibilities
- Creative interests and capacities

"As a subsidiary outcome—with the college aided by such other social institutions as the media, the peer group, and the

church—the student should develop an overall ethical orientation, competency in social situations, and a sense of identity, of autonomy, of personal integrity."

This example may be too terse and too modest in intent for the taste of some academic leaders. But in its execution it comes very close to the kind of statement we have in mind.

Need for Periodic Review

By stressing the importance of mission statements as points of reference for curricular policy, we do not pretend that, as difficult and time consuming as preparing them might be, such statements alone will solve all of a college's curriculum problems. By themselves, they constitute only a beginning for establishing sound programs and procedures. Moreover, the educational needs of individuals and society change over time. Colleges also change with the loss and replacement of faculty members and leadership, changes in the availability of financial support, shifts in the interests of students, changes in the environment surrounding the institution, and the development of new facilities —to mention only a few of the possible reasons. Colleges should therefore review their missions periodically—preferably as part of regularly scheduled evaluations to determine their general effectiveness and long-term budgeting priorities.

8

General Education:
An Idea in Distress

No curricular concept is as central to the endeavors of the American college as general education, and none is so exasperatingly beyond the reach of general consensus and understanding.

At the heart of the current confusion is the disappearance from higher education of a uniform liberal education for all college students. Liberal arts, rooted in concerns for civilization and a common heritage, were once the theme of the total undergraduate curriculum. Some colleges continue to devote their entire curricula to liberal studies today and often provide an excellent education for students who wish to spend their undergraduate years acquiring an understanding of their own interests and potentials and exploring their relationship to the world and to human endeavors. We believe that these institutions deserve encouragement and support. But in its comprehensive totality the knowledge suitable for a liberal education is now beyond the grasp of even these institutions. About the best that any college can do is introduce its students to historic benchmarks and great ideas or provide as broad an array of learning as its resources allow so that students can select their own liberalizing education and provide the advanced skills and background its graduates need for continuing to learn throughout their lives.

Seen in this perspective, *general education* is a mediating influence that, through institution-wide requirements, ensures

that all students obtain, from the many courses and programs an institution may make available, some knowledge of the ideas and culture that were once themes of the total liberal arts college. It does so by providing learning that:

1. Builds skills for advanced studies and lifelong learning
2. Distributes time available for learning in such a way as to expose students to the mainstreams of thought and interpretation—humanities, science, social science, and the arts
3. Integrates learning in ways that cultivate the student's broad understanding and ability to think about a large and complex subject

These are times in which the nation is confused about how our people, particularly our youth, are to be educated. Colleges too often respond with the easy answer: "Give the students whatever they want, with, perhaps, special attention to the training they need to enter gainful employment." But undergraduate education can do more than that. Through general education, colleges also have an opportunity to formulate an educational response to their own perceptions and interests of their students and society.

General education is important for other reasons:

- People need more learning skills throughout their lives, and, to gain access to unfamiliar subjects and ideas, they must be skillful users of libraries and other informative systems. Because increasing amounts of information about matters affecting their comfort and well-being are offered in quantitative terms, they need to be familiar with more sophisticated analytical tools, particularly statistics.
- We all need to prepare for the uncertainties of the future, and that involves, above all, fallback alternatives—for earning a living, for acquiring different skills, for adjusting to new human relationships, for pursuing new interests.
- There is growing recognition of how people are affected by broad problems of the world. We all need to understand the importance of reconciliation among nations and ideologies

for the sake of lasting peace; of the intricate balances necessary to sustain a healthful and attractive environment; of the
limits of available resources; of the aggregated impacts of
individual actions on the quality of our civilization and on
the safety and freedom of ourselves and of others.
• We have a new appreciation for the quality of our total lives.
We live longer and should expect to have many more experiences than were available to the generations that preceded us.
We also have to make more choices. So we need to develop
intellectual resources for developing a philosophy of life, for
choosing a life-style, for using leisure time in constructive and
satisfying ways, for understanding the cultural tradition not
only of our own community and nation but also of distant
and dissimilar parts of the world.
• We also need to understand and participate in the life of the
world as citizens—to acquire a more total view of where we
and the world stand in the grand structure and history of the
universe. We also need, as part of our education, knowledge
that will help us to plan and direct our lives for self-fulfill-
ment, to understand people and work with them for common
goals, and to obtain and analyze information in a way that
leads to effective decisions.

Fortunately, we are better able now than we have been for
many years to offer effective general education programs to
meet such needs.

• The capacities of colleges to offer stimulating instruction in a
variety of subjects is being extended by the development of
new technology and learning materials of high quality. Earlier
we noted the increased use of videotapes in college classrooms. Many of these programs were originally developed for
the general public and thus serve as excellent introductions to
some subjects for nonspecialists. There has also been a resur-
gence of efforts on the part of intellectuals with broad interests and vision to communicate to a nonspecialized audience
on complicated subjects of massive scope that must be viewed
from multiple perspectives. William H. McNeill's *The Rise of*

the West, Jacob Bronowski's essays on the development of science in *The Ascent of Man* (originally written for television), Edward O. Wilson's *Sociobiology: The New Synthesis,* and Carl Sagan's *Dragons of Eden: Speculations on the Evolution of Human Intelligence,* are perhaps representative of the best of the new books that have resulted from such efforts. That intellectuals of solid reputation are undertaking the preparation of interpretive works of this kind could have a salutary effect on general education on many of the nation's campuses.

• There is also evidence that faculty members are more identified with their current positions than they were seven or eight years ago. They appear to be less mobile and may, therefore, be more interested in the contributions they can make to their own institution and in the development of a special identity that will attract students. If it continues, this trend, too, could lead faculty members to take more interest in general education.

In view of these benefits and opportunities, as well as the prevailing confusion that surrounds it, general education deserves especially close attention from curriculum planners.

Advanced Learning Skills

The most common advanced learning skill subjects included among general education requirements are English composition, mathematics, foreign languages, and physical education. But studies made by Blackburn and his associates (1976) indicate that there has been a decline in the number of institutions requiring some of these subjects. The percentage requiring English declined from 90 to 72 between 1967 and 1974 (although a new countermovement in English composition, inspired by a highly publicized drop in student abilities to write, may have developed). During the same period, the percentage of institutions requiring a foreign language dropped from 73 to 53, the percentage requiring mathematics dropped from 33 to 20, and the percentage of colleges requiring physical education declined from 86 to 55 (Blackburn et al., 1976, p. 34).

A case is sometimes made that some of the skills that now are acquired in college should be provided by high schools. Although it is doubtful that all instruction that provides a foundation for general education can or should be shifted to secondary schools, we are encouraged by the fact that some high schools are already providing such instruction and some colleges are awarding college-level credit for it. Among the subjects particularly suited for advance credit are English composition, mathematics, and foreign languages.

The matter cannot be left entirely to chance, however. Colleges have an obligation to make clear to the high schools which skills they expect their students to acquire before they are admitted. In addition, they should make clear which of the skill subjects they offer might also be taught at high schools and what the criteria are for recognizing completion of such instruction as satisfying college requirements.

Once students are enrolled in college, they should have ample opportunities to use the advanced learning skills obtained in their general education in the instruction given in all departments throughout their undergraduate years. Few courses of instruction could not incorporate writing assignments, for example, and many subjects have at least some dimensions that can be appropriately explored with mathematics. Use of the visual, literary, and performing arts to express one's understanding of a subject is sometimes appropriate. A thoroughly articulated general education program accommodates students' needs to exercise all of their learning skills frequently.

We have also observed that the literature and methods of many disciplines outside the sciences increasingly involve analysis based on statistics and large data bases that can be developed only with the use of computers. Statistics and computer science are therefore certain to become absolutely essential for the functionally literate undergraduate in coming decades. Introduction to such subjects, preferably in high school, but in any event early in undergraduate college years, is urgently needed.

We recognize that foreign languages help to expand one's understanding of other cultures and of one's own native tongue, but we do not believe that it is essential to require all students

to study them to meet general education requirements. They should continue to be available, however, to students who need one or more languages for successful completion of a major—for example, in comparative literature, area history, intellectual history, certain international studies, and some sciences—or who wish to satisfy personal interests in one or more languages.

Physical education and nutrition are sufficiently important to one's individual welfare that their inclusion as required studies could be justified, at least in high school, and possibly in colleges as well. In college, we particularly favor emphasizing physical education activities that students can cultivate as individuals and use throughout their lifetimes.

Finally, the advanced learning skills components of general education are particularly well-suited to instruction in nontraditional modes. Such programs can be competency-based even when other parts of the curriculum are not. Many of them also can be adapted easily for personalized self-instruction, audiotutorial presentation, and presentation in a series of brief learning modules.

Distribution

The object of distribution requirements (which some people refer to as *breadth* requirements) is to assure that every student has some exposure to the content, traditions, and methods of the main subject fields (humanities, social sciences, natural sciences, and—too infrequently—the creative and performing arts). Such breadth is a counterweight to concentration. It provides students with a threshold of common knowledge that facilitates communication with other students and with professors in different disciplines. It also gives students an opportunity to explore several subject fields before choosing their majors.

At some colleges, every course acceptable for meeting distribution requirements is specified, and students are given little opportunity to make substitutions. Increasingly, however, colleges are becoming more flexible in this regard. Students at many colleges now meet distribution requirements by enrolling in courses selected from literally scores of offerings in the various subject fields. Within the totality of undergraduate educa-

tion, such generosity of choice is not necessarily unhealthy. In fact, it increases the ability of colleges to satisfy specific needs of a heterogeneous student body. But there is little or no coherence in such distribution, and with too much free election general education becomes fragmented and superficial.

To serve students who wish to satisfy distribution requirements, some departments simply encourage students to take the courses they designate as introductory for their own majors. Unfortunately, such courses seldom are broad enough to introduce students to an entire subject field or provide any understanding of the history and approach of the discipline itself. Departments may also offer "double-duty" courses, which satisfy distribution requirements while in effect intensifying the major. Examples might include "Statistics for Psychologists" or "German for Scientists." Far too many colleges make no effort to tailor departmental offerings to the distribution requirements of the general education program.

One way to improve that part of general education that is drawn from the subject fields is to develop for each one an introductory course for nonmajors that is devoted to the history, concerns, and methods of inquiry used in the field. In making this suggestion, we are aware that there is widespread criticism of what are often called "survey courses." It is true that when they are badly handled introductory courses deteriorate into superficial "appreciation" courses. We do not believe, on the other hand, that the flaw is in the concept. The flaw is in execution, which, in turn, is subject to college control.

To improve the quality of introductory courses, a college might urge two or more departments within each subject field to prepare and audition introductory programs. The college could then reserve the right to recognize the successful course for meeting general education requirements and, in doing so, provide budgetary and staff augmentation for the department sponsoring the accepted course. This augmentation could continue as long as the quality of the course remained high and could be curtailed if quality declined. If two departments within a subject field prepare equally sound courses and if financial resources permit, both might be recognized, thus giving students choices between sound alternatives.

It is tempting to suggest that in instances where it is impossible for subject fields to design high-quality introductory courses students should be permitted to take a specified number of any regular undergraduate courses within the subject field instead. Harvard's faculty has approved this option. The difficulty with the policy is that it effectively excuses the faculty from responsibility for developing an acceptable introductory course. It also endorses the doubtful proposition that any two or three unspecified courses in a subject field adequately introduce students, particularly nonmajors, to a field.

In 1969, the faculty at Brown University took a slightly different approach to the problem of introducing students to the various disciplines. It introduced, as an option, "modes-of-thought" courses that "place major emphasis on the methods, concepts and value systems required in approaching an understanding of a specific problem, topic or issue in a particular field of inquiry" (Brown University, 1975, p. 377). By "field of inquiry," the faculty meant "a general category of scholarly activity such as Humanities, Social Studies, Natural Sciences, or Formal Thought, that transcends departmental disciplines." Among the 36 modes-of-thought courses were: "Biology and the Nature of Man," "The Irrational in Society: Freud, Weber, and Simmel on Emotion and Charisma," and "The Process of Decision Making as Applied to Gliding and Scientific Research," and "Continental Drift." Characteristically, these courses are offered in small group situations. As first proposed, Brown students would be required to take five modes-of-thought courses to meet general education requirements, and it is conceivable that such a combination could provide a relatively well-rounded introduction to the main subject fields. As options, however, they differ from other courses in the various disciplines chiefly in their concentration on the use of distinctive modes of thought on specific topics.

As an alternative to subject field distribution, the University of Michigan gives students an opportunity to distribute general education according to "Approaches to Knowledge" (Commission on Graduation Requirements, 1974). The four approaches are the analytical approach (mathematics, syntax, philosophy); the empirical approach (social and natural sci-

ences); the moral approach (philosophy, religious studies, classical studies), and the esthetic approach (history of art, music, literature, and drama).

When there is resistance to required courses of any kind, it may be futile to suggest that there is an area of study that is inadequately represented in the breadth requirements of many colleges. But one omission deserves special attention. In the development of general education programs, the arts are often overlooked. Viewed not only for their own sake but also as a means of experiencing and communicating reality, the arts have a legitimate place among other subject fields in any education that claims to be human in its orientation and truly broad in its total dimension. Ideally, all students not only should have an opportunity to learn how artists perceive the world and translate their perceptions into visual representations and performance but also should participate in the arts. Realization of that ideal will require that the traditional "academic" disciplines become more hospitable to the arts, not only on the campuses generally but also at points where they touch subjects of concern within the disciplines themselves. For art departments, realization of the ideal means a willingness to provide educational programs for both prospective professionals and non-majors.

One final thought on distribution: It may well be that a little bit of distribution, well planned and presented, is a good and useful thing but that a lot of it left to chance and whim is useless or worse. Abraham Flexner (1930, p. 100) expressed a justifiable concern when he said "atomistic training—the provision of endless special courses, instead of a small number of opportunities that are at once broad and deep—is hostile to the development of the intellectual grasp."

Fragmentation that may be justifiable in free electives is difficult to defend in general education, which, of all components of the curriculum, should most clearly reflect institutional objectives. In the general education component of the undergraduate curriculum, definition and coherence should take priority over diversity. For that reason, we believe students might, in many cases, be confronted with somewhat fewer

requirements for distribution and more opportunities for integrating what they learn.

Integrative Learning Experience

The third component of general education is one that provides a means by which colleges help their students overcome the incoherence of distribution and electives (see Figure 13) and take

Figure 13. Distribution versus integrated learning experience

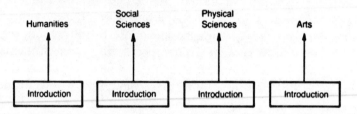

Distribution pattern: Introductory courses for nonmajors are given in each subject-field within first two years

Humanities	Social Sciences	Physical Sciences	Arts
Introduction	Introduction	Introduction	Introduction

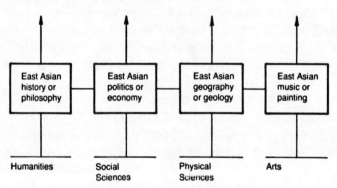

Integrated learning experience: Courses relevant to integrating theme are taken at any time they may be available in each subject-field

East Asian history or philosophy	East Asian politics or economy	East Asian geography or geology	East Asian music or painting
Humanities	Social Sciences	Physical Sciences	Arts

broad approaches to understanding their personal relationship to time and place and the development of civilization and their responsibilities as citizens. It also cultivates abilities to think about broad, general subjects rather than highly specialized topics. Integrative learning experiences may take many forms:

1. *Special requirements.* At many colleges, students may be required to take courses in world history, Western civiliza-

tion, or American literature to improve their general understanding of American life. (Many public colleges offer general education courses in American government and institutions in compliance with state laws.) Colleges with denominational affiliations may include religious studies among their general education courses.

Presumably, American institutions requirements are imposed as a guarantee that all persons who graduate from college will have a fundamental understanding of the structure, operations, and philosophy of their own states and nation. For this reason, it is difficult to understand why the basic requirements of this type should not be met at the high schools where much larger percentages of young Americans could be exposed to them. Such courses are not inappropriate to college, but we believe that states should consider permitting some students to "test out" of government and institutions' requirements (as some now do) or should authorize colleges to permit students to satisfy the requirement by taking college-level courses in these subjects either in high schools or adult and continuing education centers.

2. *Central subjects.* Actually, it is difficult to identify many courses or subjects that are so useful to students that they deserve to be studied by everyone without exception. Knowledge defies organization into hierarchical patterns. Daniel Bell, however, makes a strong case for the restoration of history as a central subject (1968, p. 172) on the grounds that "the senses of the past and the knottiness of fact are the necessary means of transcending contemporaneity and 'actualizing the universal' " (Bell, 1968, p. 173). In its broadest scope, including physical and social and intellectual history and not restricted to any one specific civilization, history may well deserve a central role in undergraduate general education. No other single discipline has its built-in orienting and integrating capacity.

Another approach to general understanding might be to concentrate on a civilization other than our own. A program in East Asian civilization, for example, might include history, literature, art, and philosophy of the people of East Asian countries.

Still another approach might be one that concentrates on humans and their total environment—natural, social, and cultural.

3. *Core courses and programs.* Resisting the trend from heavily prescribed to predominantly elective general education curricula, some colleges offer a fully prescribed "core" curriculum for all students. In pure form, such courses are prescribed for all students. St. Joseph's College in Indiana, for example, replaced a general education program that relied heavily on distribution requirements with an eight-semester core course that gives the entire student body, and as many members of the faculty as possible, "a common experience in reflecting on man, his situation, civilization, and culture, his achievements and problems, his meaning and purpose" (St. Joseph's College, n.d.). In the freshman year, students take courses on "The Contemporary Situation," and "Hebrew and Graeco-Roman Heritage." As sophomores, they take "Middle Ages" and "The Modern World." Juniors take courses on "Man in the Universe" (heavily oriented to the sciences) and "Nonwestern studies." Seniors study "Toward a Christian Humanism." In reporting on the eighth year of the program, the college notes, "Professors from up to 10 different departments have to sit down together and come up with a single set of readings and lectures for the semester of Core with which they are charged. The same group has to listen to one another lecture to the entire Core class (300+ students and 12 or so professors). These experiences have made the faculty come to know and respect one another much more than before Core" (St. Joseph's College, n.d.). Massachusetts Institute of Technology offers a core curriculum, Concourse, designed primarily for freshmen as an alternative to the traditional or dominant general education offering. In recent years, it has been oriented to the theme of "Men and Machines" and takes the place of courses in humanities, mathematics, chemistry, and physics in the freshman year.

4. *Survey courses.* On a somewhat more ambitious scale, integration of learning is achieved by introducing instruction that covers very broad subjects from the perspectives of several

disciplines. Columbia's pioneering "Contemporary Civilization" course, which began after World War I, had an integrated format and, although not without difficulty, continues today.

5. *Interdisciplinary programs.* University of Wisconsin at Green Bay had 20 thematically integrated "packages" in 1976. Among them were "Environmental Action and Legal Cultures," "Black and White Americans," "How We View Ourselves and Each Other," "Individual and Social Consequences of Sex Roles," "Coping with Uncertainty," "Language as a Human Resource," "Policy, Planning and Recovery," "Artists as Analysts," and "Prophets and Preachers" ("News from University of Wisconsin . . . ," 1976, p. 2). At the John Jay College of Criminal Justice, City University of New York, which has open admissions and a highly diverse student body, freshmen can enroll in "The Exceptional Person: A Study of Genius, Creativity, Deviance, and Differentness," a thematic course combining psychology, anthropology, police science, drama, and literature. Such programs are sometimes called "now" programs because they draw on the concerns of modern society rather than on the classical themes of some of the more traditional courses colleges might offer. We would hope that the pejorative implications of the term *now programs* will soon vanish. It is important that general higher education touch the past and the traditional, but it is also important that it touch the present. It is also conceivable that general education could touch the future, for those who seek to project and predict find that their attention must go to trends in many fields.

Entire experimental colleges have been organized around interdisciplinary themes. One, organized by Alexander Meiklejohn at the University of Wisconsin in the 1920s, devoted a year to the study of an ancient civilization and a second to the study of American civilization. A study of the student's own home community was required between the first and second year of the program. New Charter College—Oakland University (which is the product of a merger of two subcolleges) offers more than a dozen interdisciplinary general education programs each year.

6. *Emphasizing the perennial.* One way to think about

what should be taught to undergraduates is to ask what every person, regardless of his or her intended career, should know as a result of the general education experience. This approach provides the rationale for the "Great Books" curriculum that bases general education on the enduring wisdom of great men and women as expressed in their own major writings. The curriculum originated at Columbia University after World War I, was further developed at the University of Chicago, and was introduced in its purest form at St. John's College (Annapolis, in 1937, and Santa Fe, 1964). It survives at St. John's as fully prescribed undergraduate education.

7. *Integrating themes.* We would advocate more opportunities for students to use instruction obtained from several departments and organized around significant themes and problems to provide an integrated learning experience. A few of the many themes, each of which might draw upon history, philosophy, art, economics, or politics, and, in many cases, the sciences (see Figure 13), that might be considered for this purpose are:

Historical periods
    The classical era
    The medieval period
    The Renaissance
    The industrial revolution
    The modern era

Characteristics of civilizations
    Asian civilization
    Western civilization
    Primitive civilization
    Muslim civilization

Alternative world views
    Judaic
    Christian
    Moslem
    Far Eastern
    Marxist
    Modern liberal

An example of a problem-oriented general learning experience might be

Man and the Environment
    Resources
    Rural life
    Urban life
    Pathologies of industrial society
    Environmental planning

The characteristic feature of such learning experiences is that they provide a focus for instruction that draws on a variety of subject disciplines. They are therefore closely related to interdisciplinary programs. The subjects may be interesting in their own right, but their value is enhanced by bringing to bear whatever the sciences, humanities, social sciences, and the arts can contribute to their full understanding.

In addition to thematic learning experiences developed by institutions, students might be given opportunities to construct such programs of their own. The principle would be the same as that observed by colleges—the experience would focus on a subject or theme addressed from the point of view of several disciplines. But the student would determine the central theme and would select, from elective courses offered by the faculty of various departments, instruction related to the theme. Where insufficient electives were available for this purpose, the student might be encouraged to fill out the experience with courses offered at neighboring colleges or in independent study. If such programs were accepted in fulfillment of institutional integrative learning requirements, they should be approved in advance by appropriate officers of the student's college.

Interdisciplinary courses, core courses, and most other offerings that cross disciplinary boundaries are often introduced against a strong tide of faculty resistance. These kinds of courses tend to take faculty interests further afield from their specialties than do the more narrowly conceived courses that may satisfy distribution requirements on an ad hoc, elective basis, and they often call on unusual teaching talents that very few faculty members possess.

Most of the faculty's difficulties with interdisciplinary offerings arise when instructors are asked to leave the departmental environment to participate in such programs. To overcome this difficulty, a special program has been proposed at Drake University that involves asking departments to devise one-unit minicourses in such topics as "history and goals," "methodology," "ethics and values," and "social response" as they are addressed by their own discipline. To obtain the equivalent of a full course of credit, a student would take one "minicourse" on the same topic in each of three departments. To satisfy general education requirements, students would have to complete three units in three of the topics and perhaps a capstone, integrative course, that would involve small group discussion.

We hope that such ideas will be encouraged. Interdisciplinary programs are so admirably suited to the needs of general education, particularly at upper-division levels, that an effort to overcome the difficulties in offering them is very much worthwhile. A substantial part of the solution is for the college to acknowledge the difficulties involved and to provide special incentives and rewards for individual faculty members who are willing to confront them.

Timing of General Education

Most institutions expect their students to complete general education requirements within their freshman and sophomore years. In practice, such expectations are not realistic. They cannot be achieved, for example, unless colleges adopt policies that exclude transfer students from admission—a policy in the best interest of neither students nor colleges. At selective liberal arts colleges, 20 percent of the students have attended at least one other college; at other colleges, the proportion is 30 percent or more. In states where there are large numbers of community colleges and policies that facilitate transfer from such institutions to four-year colleges and universities, community colleges may provide much of the general education undergraduates receive. California is one such state, and at the State University at Long Beach, to give an example, only 20 percent of the students have had all of their general education on the campus.

Presumably, similar situations exist on other state college and university campuses in the state. Under such circumstances, a four-year college can exert control only over the general education that takes place during the later years of a student's undergraduate career.

In general, we would encourage colleges to keep general education as free of time restraints as possible. However, there are logistical reasons for suggesting that the components of general education have time priority in the following order:

1. Advanced learning skills
2. Distribution
3. Integrated learning experiences

We would expect advanced learning skills and most distribution requirements to be satisfied in the first two years of college. Courses meeting such requirements in four-year colleges should have counterparts in two-year colleges to facilitate transfer of credit. First priority is assigned to advanced learning skills because these must be acquired if further academic progress is to be made. Second priority is assigned to distribution because many students will use distribution courses to sample subjects from which they might choose majors. However, students who enter college with firm commitments to a specialty could defer meeting distribution requirements until later in their college careers. Most integrative learning experiences might be most effective in the junior and senior years. Until that time, many students will not have sufficient background in the different subject fields to make the most effective use of the instruction integrative experiences provide. We should point out, however, that some integrative learning experiences actually serve the purpose of exposing students to different subject fields or approaches to knowledge as well as integration. Students who participate in such programs may well be able, therefore, to compress the time required for their total general education program.

We would also point out that an inevitable consequence of postponing integrative learning experiences to the last two years

of college is the opening of opportunities for more students to begin majors earlier than the junior year. Whether this is desirable or not depends on the extent to which a student has made an early commitment to specialize in a subject. Those who have not done so should not be forced to start their majors too soon; instead, they should utilize some of their electives during the first two years of college to try out subjects that may prove acceptable as majors. In the long run, it may be preferable for students to utilize electives for this purpose than it is for them to seek a major from the more restricted offerings of a planned, discrete general education program.

Some possible variations of general education patterns are presented in Figure 14. They do not attempt to present all of the arrangements that are possible and do not represent the cur-

Figure 14. Variations of use of general education components in the undergraduate curriculum

Variation A				Year
				Fourth Year
				Third Year
	Distribution	Advanced Skills		Second Year
Integration	Distribution	Advanced Skills		
Integration	Distribution	Advanced Skills		First Year
Integration	Distribution	Advanced Skills		

Variation B				Year
Integration				Fourth Year
Integration				
				Third Year
Integration				
	Distribution	Advanced Skills		Second Year
	Distribution	Advanced Skills		
	Distribution	Advanced Skills		First Year
	Distribution	Advanced Skills		

Variation A. Representative present pattern

Eleven general education courses (one-third of the curriculum), 1 semester each. 4 advanced skills courses, 4 distribution courses, 3 integration courses. All in first two years.

Variation B. First preferred alternative

Eleven general education courses (one-third of the curriculum), 1 semester each. 4 advanced skills courses, 4 distribution courses in first two years. 3 integration courses in last two years.

(continued on next page)

Figure 14 *(continued)*

Variation C

Integration				Fourth Year
Integration				Third Year
Integration	Distribution			Second Year
	Distribution	Advanced Skills		
Integration	Distribution	Advanced Skills		First Year
	Distribution	Advanced Skills		

Variation D

Integration			Major	Fourth Year
		Major	Major	
Integration		Major	Major	Third Year
		Major	Major	
Integration	Distribution	Advanced Skills	Major	Second Year
	Distribution	Advanced Skills	Major	
	Distribution	Advanced Skills	Major	First Year
	Distribution	Advanced Skills	Major	

Variation C. Second preferred alternative

Eleven general education courses (one-third of the curriculum), 1 semester each. 3 advanced skills courses, 4 distribution courses in first two years, 4 integration courses spread over four years.

Variation D. Third preferred alternative

Eleven general education courses (one-third of the curriculum), 1 semester each. 4 advanced skills courses, 4 distribution courses in first two years, 3 integration courses in each of three years, 11 major courses beginning in freshman year.

(continued on next page)

ricula of any specific institution. They do, however, suggest some basic arrangements and show how they may relate, quantitatively, to the rest of the undergraduate curriculum.

Challenges and Opportunities

In colleges and universities that are not exclusively devoted to liberal education, the concept of general education is in trouble today, for several reasons:

- Its function and character are not well understood.
- Students come to college with diverse prior educational experiences, and it is impossible to build general education programs on a common foundation.
- As we noted in Section Five (Figure 6), there has been an

Figure 14 *(continued)*

Integration	Distribution			Fourth Year
	Distribution			
Integration				Third Year
	Distribution			
Integration	Distribution			Second Year
		Advanced Skills		
	Distribution	Advanced Skills		First Year
		Advanced Skills		

Variation E. Random distribution pattern

Eleven general education courses (one-third of the curriculum). 1 semester each. 3 advanced skills courses. 2 distribution courses. and 1 integration course in the first two years. 3 distribution and 2 integration courses in last two years. Suitable for student who is committed to major before the end of first year.

				Fourth Year
				Third Year
	Distribution			Second Year
	Distribution			
Integration	Distribution	Advanced Skills		First Year
Integration	Distribution	Advanced Skills		

Variation F. Minimal requirements

Eight general education courses (one-fourth of the curriculum). 1 semester each. 2 advanced skills courses. 4 distribution courses. 2 integration courses. All in first two years.

increase in the percentage of the total curriculum allotted to electives, and most of that increase has been achieved at the expense of general education.

- An increasing emphasis on career education and on preparing undergraduates for graduate and professional schools has encouraged both students and colleges to give higher priority to specialization and less to liberal education. In 1976, more students (68 percent) considered it essential to obtain "a detailed grasp of a special field in college" than considered it essential to get a "well-rounded education" (57 percent).
- The faculty reward system and peer pressures within faculty ranks discourage many professors from taking general education too seriously: Instruction in such courses is considered a distraction from specialization, research, and writing; new

faculty members are often unprepared to handle the broad subjects offered in general education; faculty participation is sometimes involuntary—and almost universally resisted.

In two-year colleges, general education encounters the same difficulties found in four-year institutions—and more. Many of the students in these institutions are in either non-degree vocational programs, for which general education is not required, or are planning to enroll in four-year colleges eventually and may not feel as bound by their community college graduation requirements as they are by those of whatever institution they may transfer to. Community college students may, therefore, ignore general education.

Conclusion

Faculty and student preference now seems to move toward specialization and atomization of the curriculum and away from integration and coherence. It is the pull toward a command of a narrow subject matter in great depth at the expense of familiarity with the principles and methods of thought and inquiry that makes it impossible for educated persons to deal with a variety of subjects on a fundamental level.

The erosion of general education on America's college campuses is even more severe than its share of curricula might indicate, for in many cases it is poorly defined and is so diluted with options that it has no recognizable substance of its own. We believe that the general education idea continues to have a place in American colleges and universities. We would hope that colleges could make greater efforts to define it and set limits on the extent to which further erosion will be permitted. It would be encouraging if colleges could define at least one-fourth and preferably a third of their undergraduate curriculum in such terms, but a coherent program involving even a smaller fraction of the curriculum would be preferable to the vagueness of general education offered by many colleges at the present time. If colleges cannot define what they intend to accomplish in general education, cannot specifically describe how it will benefit the students who engage in it, and cannot deliver an effective

general education component, they should seriously consider eliminating it entirely. They should not, however, use their incapacity to provide a well-defined and coherent general education program as an excuse to require students to fill out their graduation requirements with additional electives. Instead, they should question the necessity of requiring students to spend the time in college that meeting ineffective general education requirements now frequently demands.

General education is that part of the undergraduate curriculum that permits a college or university, as an institution, to make a unique contribution to the education of its students. Unlike the major, which is largely shaped by the various academic disciplines and professions and is designed by departments, or electives, which are subject to the free choice of students, general education can and should be under the control of the college. There may be no single best way to provide it for all students everywhere, but, from the many alternative arrangements that are possible, colleges should be able to design the general education that is best for their own students. No other effort to define the quality and character of the education to be offered is nearly as important as this one.

9

The Major—
A Success Story?

The case for specialization is concisely made by Philip Phenix in *Realms of Meaning* (1964, p. 272), where he points out that in a complex civilization "each person concentrates his energies upon doing a few things well rather than many things poorly." From an academic point of view, specialization is advocated because it exposes students to special systems of thought, special symbolic systems, and to opportunities to acquire special skills in a discipline. On a pragmatic level, specialization in college also can prepare one for advanced learning in a chosen field or for a job.

The literature of the curriculum seldom bothers with such advocacy and takes the importance of specialization as it is represented by the major (or subject concentration) for granted. Historically, the major is viewed to be part of the compromise between totally unspecialized undergraduate education that was offered by the first American colleges and the specialization of the curriculum that characterized German universities by the mid-nineteenth century and was greatly admired by leading American educators of that time. It was introduced into the United States at about the same time that elective courses were introduced to bring to American students the new knowledge that was being generated by scientific inquiry and was expected to flow in profusion from what were then very young universities. Without either the presence of the major or the rise of uni-

versities, the elective principle by itself might have created a totally formless college curriculum. But the major served to control the use of the new curricular freedoms, and, as universities were created, it provided a link of curricular specialization to ease the transition students were to make from old colleges to the advanced levels of education that became available in the new institutions.

The major has been one of the instruments, therefore, that persuaded Americans neither to concentrate general education entirely in the secondary-level institutions, as the Germans did with their *Gymnasien,* nor to develop dual college and university degrees, as the English once did with their unspecialized "ordinary" and specialized "honors" degrees.[1] It has served the additional function of identifying a level of specialization that is appropriate for entry into occupational fields that do not require the extraordinary depth of study needed by professional scholars and practitioners.

Of the three components found in the prevailing format of undergraduate curricula in the 1970s, the major appears to be the most stable. It occupies about the same percentage of the undergraduate curriculum now (between 25 and 41 percent in 1974) as it did in 1967 (27 to 40) (Table 16). During the same period, other components of the curriculum changed significantly. More than three-fourths of the juniors and seniors enrolled in college in 1976 were either "very satisfied" or "satisfied" with their majors (Carnegie Council Surveys, 1975-1976). In many ways, majors provide the true core of the undergraduate's experience (Little, 1974, p. 99). Each student engages in his or her particular major by choice and tends to make the major department a home on campus. At many institutions, it is a source of social contacts, personal advice and encouragement, and provides focus for undergraduate life.

Majors are not, however, an unqualified success. We note three major weaknesses:

---

[1]In this instance, *honors* has a different meaning than in American colleges, where it applies to ranking within the student body determined by academic achievement. In Great Britain, the term is associated with specialization.

Table 16. Percentages of undergraduate programs requiring
varying amounts of the undergraduate curriculum for the major
by degree type

Percentage of time spent on major	Degree				
	A.A.	A.S.	A.A.S.	B.A.	B.S.
1-10					
11-20	2	3		4	3
21-30	23	7		36	17
31-40	23	6	7	32	18
41-50	18	20	9	17	19
51-60	8	14	9	7	18
61-70	13	18	26	3	13
71-80	7	12	21	1	9
81-90	4	15	19		3
91-100	2	6	9		

Note: All of the programs require a major, or at two-year institutions, at least a pre-major. It should also be noted that bachelor and associate degrees should not be compared as the associate degree is usually two years in duration and the bachelor degree is typically four years.

Source: Catalog Study, 1976.

1. They are too oppressive, because they take too much of a student's time. Although the formal major requirements of a college may demand no more than a third of a student's time in some fields, the fact is that many students use substantial parts of their electives to intensify specialization beyond that which is officially required (Blackburn et al., 1976, pp. 28, 29). This practice not only intensifies the major beyond the expectations of most colleges (though not, perhaps, of most departments) but also results in a misuse of the electives that are basically provided to encourage students to sample many different subjects during their undergraduate years.

2. They are too narrow and single-minded. By definition, majors involve specialization. It is therefore difficult for them to accommodate students' interdisciplinary interests. Relatively untraditional ways of overcoming this weakness are discussed

subsequently in this section, but they are not yet widely used.
3. They lead to the neglect of courses that are designed and provided for nonmajors. Too often, the courses that departments offer for nonmajors are regarded as having low priority.

Typically, majors take up more of a student's time in upper-division than in lower-division studies. In some institutions and departments, majors start only in the junior year, on the assumption that it will take students two years to complete prerequisites for specialization. Another reason for the concentration of the major in the upper division is that many two-year college transfers are unable to commence major studies before that time. One effect of this practice is that students often spend at least 60 percent of their last two years on their majors —many spend much more. Some time during the last two years of college should always be available for general education and electives outside the subject field of the major. For that reason, we believe that students should not spend 100 percent of their time in the major in any one college year.

The Weights of Major Requirements

The major's share of the curriculum varies with the level of degrees sought and the subjects in which they are offered (Tables 16 and 17). The median percentage for the associate of arts is 41 to 50; for the associate of sciences, it is 60 to 61; and for the associate of applied science, it is 61 to 70. For the bachelor of arts, a smaller proportion of a student's time (a median of 31 to 40 percent) is required for the major than in any of the majors for associate's degrees (over four years the actual time is usually more) or for the bachelor of science degree. Occupational and professional areas of business, education, engineering, health sciences, and trade and technical areas generally require more time for the major than do arts and science subjects (Tables 17 and 18).

Within the five major types of institutions—community colleges, liberal arts colleges, comprehensive colleges, doctoral degree-granting universities, and research universities—there is

Table 17. Percentages of bachelor's degree programs in eight different
subject areas requiring varying amounts (in deciles) of the undergraduate
curriculum to be spent on the major

Percentage of time spent on major	Subjects							
	Humanities	Social science	Science	Business	Education	Engineering	Health science	Trade and technical arts
1-10								
11-20	5	9	2	1	2		1	
21-30	39	49	21	18	18	7	4	5
31-40	39	26	28	30	18	7	8	
41-50	12	12	29	22	23	6	17	5
51-60	2	2	14	20	25	12	19	23
61-70	2	2	5	9	12	24	25	23
71-80	1		1	1	3	24	24	27
81-90						20	2	18
91-100						1		

Source: Catalog Study, 1976.

little variation. In the arts and sciences, the one subject area
common to all institutions, the median percentage of the undergraduate curriculum spent on the major was 31 to 40 for each
(Catalog Study, 1976).

Ideally, the undergraduate concentration should be designed primarily for students who do not intend to pursue graduate studies. Undergraduates who plan to continue in their specialization after completing their bachelor's degree will have
ample opportunities to take advanced courses in their field and
related studies after they are admitted to graduate school. In
some graduate departments, it is not necessary, and in others it
is not even considered desirable, for students to enter with advanced specialization. Such preparation is not usually possible,
for example, in medicine, law, and many schools of education.
Moreover, it is questionable, as one faculty member has put it,

Table 18. Percentages of associate's degree programs in eight different subject areas requiring varying amounts (in deciles) of the undergraduate curriculum to be spent on the major

Percentage of time spent on major	Subjects							
	Humanities	Social science	Science	Business	Education	Engineering	Health science	Trade and technical arts
1-10								
11-20	12			2	4			2
21-30	24	26	23	13	12	9	4	9
31-40	24	32	15	11	40	3	5	2
41-50	29	13	18	23	8	13	8	22
51-60	6	16	15	11	4	6	13	7
61-70	6	13	13	17	12	20	20	20
71-80			13	11	12	22	17	11
81-90			3	8	8	19	25	15
91-100				5		3	9	11

Source: Catalog Study, 1976.

that formal instruction in any academic specialty really needs to be eight years deep. For students who do not plan to go to graduate school, majors intended mainly as preparation for post-baccalaureate study could actually be harmful, because they fail to take into account such students' needs to use their educations immediately on graduation for, among other things, earning a livelihood.

We realize that it will be difficult for colleges to resist student pressures to provide majors as introductions to graduate work. More than 57 percent of the undergraduates of all types of institutions and nearly three-fourths (73 percent) of undergraduates at selective liberal arts colleges and at the universities that are most heavily oriented to research expect to pursue education beyond the bachelor's degree level. But about two out of five undergraduates in all of higher education still expect their

bachelor's degree to be a terminal degree. To accommodate these different groups, some institutions should seriously consider developing an undergraduate curriculum that is either exclusively or mainly for undergraduates who do not intend to pursue graduate studies. There is apparently a void in the higher education spectrum that needs to be filled by such institutions. Other institutions should consider encouraging some departments to offer two types of undergraduate majors. One major would be intended primarily as a program for students planning to obtain no higher degree than a bachelor's; the other would be intended as specialized preparation for graduate school. The precedent for this approach is already offered by some chemistry departments in which there are now not only majors designed for future professional specialists but also majors for persons who do not need professional preparation in the subject. Such options should exist in both bachelor of arts and bachelor of science programs.

A principal finding of the study of the curriculum and its use that was conducted by Blackburn and his associates (1976, p. 29) was that in institutions where the percentage of electives available to students has increased, the greatest share of the electives is being used to achieve more depth rather than breadth in undergraduate studies. The effect of this use of electives is to increase the proportion of the student's curriculum actually used for the major. For whatever purpose the major is to serve, it should not require so much of a student's time that general education and free electives are overly constricted. The present average of the share of the curriculum devoted to the major—between 30 and 40 percent—seems not to be unreasonable. Such majors are roughly equivalent to 1 or 1½ years of the four spent in earning a bachelor of arts degree. Departments that impose major requirements that are either less than 25 percent or more than 50 percent of the total requirement for graduation should be challenged to prove that the content of such levels of concentration is justified. When the major exceeds 50 percent, departments should be particularly challenged to demonstrate that the major courses and major cognates included within that proportion of the curriculum are genuinely undergraduate

courses and are not duplicated by offerings at the graduate level at other institutions. One way to control the size of the major's share of the curriculum is to stipulate, as does Oberlin College, to give one of many examples, that out of the total number of courses or credit hours required for graduation at least 50 percent must be taken outside any one department or program. Under such regulations, the student who elects to take more than the maximum number of courses within his or her major department may do so, but only by taking more than the minimum number of courses required for graduation.

Variations of the Traditional Major

Of the catalogs of 270 institutions studied by the Carnegie Council staff in 1976, only three[2] described undergraduate curricula that either did not include disciplinary majors or discouraged students from taking them. The single-subject majors are still dominant in American colleges, but only 26 percent of the institutions represented in the catalog study required that all majors be based on a single discipline. The remainder offered options involving one or more variations.

These variations included the double major, involving full-scale concentrations in two different departments or subject fields; interdisciplinary (joint) majors in subjects such as psychobiology, social psychology, and medieval studies; self-created majors, which are devised by students, usually with faculty advice and consultation; and minors, which involve concentrations of lesser magnitude than the major and are taken in addition to the major. Among colleges of arts and sciences offering these options, the interdisciplinary major was more prevalent as an option (at 79 percent of the colleges) than any other variation, but all of the variations were optional at one-third or more of all institutions (Table 19). This pattern is unique to colleges of arts and sciences, however. As we shall see in the next section of this commentary, professional schools tend to offer only the traditional major.

[2] The three colleges were Spertus College of Judaica, Friends World College, and Goddard (Catalog Study, 1976).

Table 19. Percentages of different types of colleges and universities
requiring varying amounts (in deciles) of the undergraduate curriculum
to be spent on the major

Percentage of degree program required for major	Types of colleges and universities				
	Research universities	Doctorate-granting universities	Comprehensive colleges	Liberal arts colleges	Community colleges
1-10					
11-20	2	5	7	7	5
21-30	28	44	36	37	23
31-40	29	27	33	35	23
41-50	23	16	18	17	22
51-60	8	6	5	4	14
61-70	7	29	2		7
71-80	3				6
81-90					
91-100					

Source: Catalog Study, 1976.

Were it not for the facts that American college students
have an aversion to required subjects and that room must be
made in the curriculum for general education and electives,
double majors and major-minor combinations might be more
common. In this regard, the example of the Scottish universities
might be useful. In some colleges in that country, students may
study one subject throughout three years at the university and
two related subjects for one year each. In other programs, students may study three subjects to equal depth over three years.
And in still other cases, students may study three courses in
parallel for two years and choose one of them to study exclusively in a third year (Hajnal, 1972, pp. 78-79). In cases where
the three subjects chosen are in separate subject fields (rather
than in related disciplines within a subject field), such a scheme
provides elements of built-in distribution. In none of the three
possible arrangements does the heaviest concentration take up
more than one-third of the total curriculum.

Jacquelyn Mattfeld, formerly dean of academic affairs at Brown University and now president of Barnard College, has observed that of all of the available variations, "Perhaps the student-oriented or independent concentration has the greatest promise for the future, as it challenges the student to determine exactly what it is that he or she wishes to derive from an undergraduate education and to construct a course of study to achieve that end. . . . At Brown, for instance, students have developed concentrations in Mathematical Genetics, Public Policy Making, Neural Studies, Electronic Engineering and Music, Dance and the Urban Community, Philosophy of Biology, and many others. With this kind of imagination and enthusiasm on the part of students, it is curious that almost universally the percentage of students who take advantage of the independent concentration is quite small (only 5 percent at Brown)" (Mattfeld, 1975, pp. 543-544).

Many colleges have created special divisions or subcolleges to help students develop alternative curricula that often include self-designed majors. The University Colleges at the University of Ohio and University of New Mexico are examples of such units. Another is the College of General Studies at the University of South Carolina.

Nevertheless, what President Mattfeld observed about the small percentage of students at Brown who had used the option of a self-designed major follows the national pattern. In the Carnegie Council's survey of undergraduates in 1976, only 6 percent of those who responded said that they had majors of this type. To some extent, this reflects the fact that the option itself is available to undergraduates at only one-third of colleges of arts and sciences and at much less of the other divisions (Table 20).

One reason why so few of these programs are offered may be that not all colleges have the personnel and resources it sometimes takes to provide instruction in such majors. Another possibility is that, because some academic departments are very large and have within their ranks specialists in many fields, it is possible for some students to create what amount to interdisciplinary majors within their own major department. Still another reason is that undergraduates may find the traditional majors

Table 20. Percentages of subcolleges and schools offering variations
on the departmental disciplinary major

	Depart-mental, disci-plinary major	Inter-disci-plinary major	Double major	Self-created major	Minor	No major
Arts and sciences						
Required	26	1		1	12	1
Optional	73	79	35	33	42	4
Not offered	1	20	65	66	46	95
Business						
Required	60				2	
Optional	39	30	28	7	44	
Not offered	1	70	72	93	54	100
Education						
Required	38				6	
Optional	62	56	29	7	43	1
Not offered		44	71	93	51	99
Engineering						
Required	67					1
Optional	32	32	26	3	21	
Not offered	1	68	74	97	71	99
Health sciences						
Required						
Optional	78	27	25		27	
Not offered	22	73	75	100	73	100
Trade and technology						
Required						
Optional	63	35	6		38	
Not offered	37	65	94	100	62	100

Source: Catalog Study, 1976.

lying on the line of least resistance, because they require no
planning effort on the part of the students themselves. In contrast, self-designed majors not only require thoughtful planning

but also are unknown quantities—there may be unforeseen obstructions on the path to their completion, and there may be uncertain rewards (or penalties) for success. Students are often warned by advisors that such programs might not be recognized by graduate school admissions officers or prospective employers. As long as they are exceptions to general practice, alternatives to the major may be attractive mainly to students with well-defined self-perceptions and personal goals and, perhaps, even unusual courage.

Another reason for students staying within the confines of traditional concentrations, the one President Mattfeld describes as "most telling," is "a lack of interest and even hostility (toward alternatives) in some cases on the part of the faculty" (1975). Developing interdisciplinary majors may require faculty members to devote enormous amounts of time to student consultations and research in unfamiliar fields. In fear of "burning out" in such activities, many faculty members prefer to teach within more traditional, departmentally defined majors.

Despite these difficulties, we do not believe that students should have only one type of major available to them. Alternative majors may not be for everyone, but then, neither are traditional concentrations.

Some Special Problems

The undergraduate major is often criticized on three counts that have not been discussed previously in this section:

1. *There is no guarantee that the majors available at a college will match every student's interests.* Some colleges are simply too small to offer a wide range of majors. For example, 9 percent of the less selective liberal arts colleges (about 50 institutions) offer fewer than 10 majors. Even large institutions may not be able to match every possible student interest. This problem can be partially avoided by the creative use of available resources through good advising and use of independently designed major options. Interdisciplinary majors may also be created to expand the offerings available. There is a limitation on these possibilities, however, that is imposed by the availability of faculty for such programs. But this

problem is not insurmountable. Where a number of institutions are located near one another, agreements might be made to permit cross registration, for purposes of providing a range of major opportunities that no one institution can provide alone. One advantage of such arrangements would be that they would enable institutions with limited resources to concentrate on building certain departments to levels of distinction or developing special competence and expertise within subdisciplines without depriving their students of access to more generalized majors or to alternative specializations within a major subject.

2. *Majors vary in quality and substance.* Majors can be simply a collection of courses lacking in depth or cohesion. For example, majors such as "prelaw" or "serendipity" have been discovered. Furthermore, some departments specify only the number of courses or credits required for the major, without reference to content. Majors can also be too narrow in their conception and lack sufficient breadth or depth to challenge able undergraduates. Where such problems occur because institutional resources are limited, an argument can again be made for encouraging departments to avoid spreading themselves too thin and to build strengths in certain subspecialties in which they can acquire regional or even national superiority.

3. *Some majors that may be intellectually challenging and rewarding have no obvious value on the job market* (except in those academic fields where teachers and scholars are in short supply). In 1976, 13 percent of the nation's undergraduates said they had changed their majors because of the state of the economy or the job market. Another 17 percent took a second major or a minor for the same reasons (Carnegie Council Surveys, 1975-1976). In reporting this criticism, we do not contend that all majors should, in fact, be career oriented. On the other hand, it also is not necessary for majors to be so designed that the career orientations that may be possible are not, insofar as practicable, exploited. Within language majors, for example, special courses might be included that emphasize uses of language in business, education, science, or other fields.

Conclusion

To keep the major in perspective as one part and not the totality of undergraduate education, colleges should move in four main directions. They should:

1. Limit the total number of hours that may be invested in the major without extending the number of hours that must be completed for graduation.
2. Encourage departments to develop more courses for non-majors.
3. Encourage development of two major options in each department: one for students who do not intend to pursue their undergraduate majors in graduate school and another for those who do.
4. Provide more opportunities for students to take double majors, minors, interdisciplinary majors, and self-created majors.

The major is the most stable element in the undergraduate curriculum and will undoubtedly remain so for the foreseeable future. It gives the baccalaureate degree specificity. It ties the preeminent academic interests of students to faculty members who have similar interests and concerns. In preprofessional or occupational fields, it links undergraduate education at once to the "outside" world of nonacademic careers and, through their professors, to the world of advanced scholarship (although differentiation of undergraduate education to prepare students for these two worlds should, perhaps, be clearer). And it satisfies a prevailing sentiment, in and out of colleges, that all educated persons should know at least one subject in depth.

The traditional department-based major is stable and secure and is not threatened by any of the variations that are currently available in concentration options, because, if anything, these options strengthen it by accommodating students for whom it is plainly inappropriate.

*   *   *

For more information on the major, see the chapter "Major or Concentration" in the Carnegie Council on Policy Studies in Higher Education, *Handbook on Undergraduate Curriculum.*

10

Electives—Abundant for What Purpose?

There are many good reasons for reserving a part of the undergraduate curriculum for students to use as they choose. In doing so, colleges provide opportunities to:

- Sample widely the intellectual offerings of a college and benefit from the experience of being taught by stimulating and challenging teachers one might not be exposed to in any other way
- Sample subjects that may not be covered in distribution requirements of general education but might be interesting to concentrate on as either majors or minors
- Sample "broad learning experiences" that may be offered to undergraduates (see Section Eight)
- Acquire learning skills that might not be taught in required subjects
- Develop interests and talents in music, painting, or the other arts, and to keep fit and well exercised through physical education programs
- Satisfy curiosity about unfamiliar subjects and learn new things

Electives are also subject to misuse, however. Some students who are confronted with many choices seek out those that appear to be the least demanding and promise the highest

grades. Others may make random choices that have no discernible relationship to their main interests or to the rest of their studies.

When he became president of Harvard University in 1869, Charles W. Eliot announced his advocacy of electives as a way of opening the curriculum to subjects that had been historically ignored in the heavily prescribed programs of early American colleges. Within six years, most of the required courses in the Harvard curriculum were concentrated in the freshman year, and that pattern persisted until 1909, when President Lowell introduced a system of majors and general education distribution requirements. At most institutions, electives now represent about one-third of the total curriculum, but there was until recently some pressure for making them the dominant component of undergraduate education. In 1969, a majority of American undergraduates (53 percent) agreed[1] that "undergraduate education would be improved if all courses were elective" and so did 20 percent of the faculty (Carnegie Surveys, 1969-70). A totally "open" curriculum, free of requirements, facilitates design of a self-created, individualized undergraduate education, and some institutions, such as Hampshire College, provide such opportunities for all of their students. At such institutions (although not at Hampshire College), the student's program is usually approved by an advisor who can help impose some order on an education that is based on the diverse offerings available. At other institutions with open curricula, structure is imposed by a formal contract between the student and his or her faculty advisor.

At over 100 institutions, a new degree has been developed for students whose educational objectives are best met by sampling broadly from all available courses. In the community colleges, the *associate of general studies* degree recognizes completion of such a program. It is estimated that 10 percent of all four-year colleges and universities offer a *bachelor of general studies* (B.G.S.), or comparable degrees with other names, for students who complete a specified number of hours of course

---

[1] "Strongly" or "with reservations."

work. There is usually no major or general education requirement.

At the University of Michigan, the bachelor of general studies was introduced in the late 1960s in response to pressures for two curricular changes—to remove the language requirement from bachelor's degree programs and to create more flexibility in distribution requirements. The new degree accomplishes both objectives. It also eliminates the major as a graduation requirement. However, students in the B.G.S. program may, in fact, concentrate at least as deeply as other undergraduates, although they are not permitted to concentrate in more than 60 hours of a 120-hour undergraduate program. Many students who do concentrate in a subject and who take care to include substantial amounts of upper-division work in such studies, often obtain letters from their advisors or faculty members in the department of their concentration that certify their accomplishment. They find that such certification of individual "majors" is usually recognized by employers and graduate schools. It is technically feasible for students in bachelor of general studies programs to acquire as many as three "majors" in this way—but few of them do. The program is quite popular, and about 20 percent of the undergraduates at the University of Michigan take advantage of the option.

Nationally, however, student and faculty enthusiasm for a totally elective program has declined since 1969 to the point where it is preferred to the traditional curriculum by only 35 percent of the undergraduates and 13 percent of the faculty (Carnegie Council Surveys, 1975-76). The loss of popularity of the totally elective undergraduate curriculum is particularly interesting when one realizes that since 1967 the trend among colleges has been to increase opportunities for free election. The proportion of the undergraduate education devoted to the major has remained almost constant, the proportion devoted to general education has decreased, and the average range of proportions of the curriculum colleges devote to electives increased from a range of 17 to 31 percent in 1967 to 25 to 41 percent in 1973-74 (Blackburn et al., 1976, p. 11).

Perhaps many students now feel that the recently in-

creased number of electives is enough—or at least that some un-specified limit on electives is preferred. Perhaps faculties, the times, and undergraduates themselves are now somewhat more academically conservative than they were in 1969. It may also be that greater restriction is welcomed by students who encounter difficulty finding a sense of direction when they are confronted with total freedom of study and therefore gravitate toward the familiar and the regimented.

The recent drift of conventional college curricula toward increased availability of electives may be, in part, a response to the perceived trends of student demand in the 1960s. If so, we might expect a decrease in the electives available during the next few years as a result of the reported shifts in student interest. But the willingness of colleges to allow the size of the elective component to respond so easily to demand suggests that there may be a substantial part of the time colleges define as necessary for the completion of undergraduate education that no one knows specifically what to do with.

It is doubtful that a need for more electives in the undergraduate curriculum can be justified. Such offerings now constitute only one of many rapidly increasing sources of undesigned learning. More and more, colleges are making virtually all of their courses available to part-time students—with or without college credit. Under these circumstances, adult or continuing education can, for many former college students, be regarded as the use of "postponed electives" (foregone during undergraduate education but picked up in later years). This use of the curriculum may do a better job of satisfying serendipitous educational needs and providing certain kinds of skill involvement than options that are currently available to enrolled undergraduates. The richness of such offerings is further enhanced by their availability not only on college campuses but also in the adult education programs of high schools and colleges, libraries, museums, cultural organizations, and, in recent years, even in newspapers and on television.

The abundance of electives in the undergraduate curriculum might be more defensible if colleges made the function of such options more explicit, issued guidelines for their use, and

took steps to assure that the intended functions were not ignored or diminished in practice. That does not now appear to
be the case. Undergraduates are, in fact, using electives to increase the depth of their studies within major departments and
in the academic divisions within which the majors are found.
Blackburn and his associates found that at nine institutions
where transcripts were studied in detail the use of electives for
increasing depth increased by almost 1 percentage point at one
institution and between 12 and 15 percentage points at four
other institutions (Table 21). If such trends are truly representative and continue, acquiring breadth through "postponed electives"—adult and continuing education—rather than through
electives that provide breadth of learning during college years
may be less an option than the norm for students in the future.

Table 21. Percentage point changes in the proportion of increased depth
electives spent in depth-within-depth and breadth-within-depth
in 10 selected institutions, 1967 to 1974

	Increase in major-department electives (depth-within-depth) (1)	Increase in major-division electives (breadth-within-depth) (2)	Total increase in depth electives (1) + (2)
Institutions with large elective increases			
1	+3.9	+11.4	+15.1
2	+6.7	+ 5.6	+12.4
3	+1.6	+ 6.8	+ 8.5
4	+5.0	+10.3	+15.3
5	+4.9	+ 8.3	+13.2
Institutions with small elective change			
6	−0.1	+ 3.3	+ 3.2
7	−0.2	+ 2.8	+ 2.7
8	+0.2	+ 0.6	+ 0.8
9	+2.8	− 5.5	− 2.8
10	+1.2	+ 4.7	+ 5.9

Source: Blackburn et al., 1976, p. 30.

We do not intend to imply that undergraduates should use none of their electives to increase the depth of their majors. There are certain circumstances under which such use of electives seems wise. For example, undergraduates who do not intend to pursue graduate studies may wish to sample subfields within their major discipline both in undergraduate and graduate courses. Since they may not have another chance to do so, we believe they should not be prevented from using a limited number of electives for such purposes. Of greater concern is the possibility that departments may increasingly assume that their undergraduates will use electives for specialization and will plan the contents of the major on that assumption. It would be much preferable and more forthright to increase the number of courses to be included in the major requirements but designate some of the additional courses as electives *within* the major.

More fundamental, however, is the relationship of electives to the total curriculum. If the proportion of the curriculum devoted to electives continues to increase without efforts by colleges to define their function and offer guidance to students on their appropriate use, perhaps students should be given the opportunity to elect not to include them in their undergraduate education at all. Under such circumstances, students who have completed their major and general education requirements and demonstrate no need for additional studies could at least be given the opportunity to petition for exemption from all or part of the degree requirements represented by electives.

Elsewhere in this commentary, we have suggested that a new form of transcript be devised to indicate not only what courses were taken by students but also how those courses represent different components of the curriculum. It would be particularly useful to employers, directors of admissions, and deans of graduate schools if transcripts clearly indicated which courses on the transcript were electives. Such information would serve two constructive purposes. First, it would indicate which courses on the transcript that *appear* to be part of one's studies for the major or for general education are actually electives. Secondly, it would indicate more clearly the instances in which a student voluntarily took an academic risk in pursuing a difficult subject.

In general, when the number of electives available to students is clearly out of balance with other components in the undergraduate curriculum, we would prefer some reduction in the number of electives and an increase in the content and options available in general education. Exceptions to that policy might be acceptable in instances where students devise their own curricula in close cooperation with a member of the faculty and draw widely from the courses available to serve some specifically agreed-on purposes. A downward adjustment in the availability of electives is particularly needed, on the other hand, in institutions where the general education component is now loosely defined.

In the event that colleges may find the reduction of electives impossible, efforts should be made to make their advanced-level skill courses and broad learning experience sequences sufficiently attractive to encourage students to use their electives to participate in them. Such programs and courses should be given special attention in college catalogs and should be called to the attention of students by their faculty advisors.

*   *   *

For further information on degree programs that emphasize student election, see the chapter "Credits and Degrees" in the Carnegie Council on Policy Studies in Higher Education, *Handbook on Undergraduate Curriculum*.

11

Basic Skills—Where Does College Begin?

For purposes of this commentary, basic skills are defined as those that a student needs in order to embark on a college education. Among them are skills in reading, mathematics, and English composition, and students who arrive at college without them are usually considered in need of compensatory education. However, what is meant by "college-level" skills is ill defined and varies considerably from college to college.

For example, in mathematics, instruction in anything below the level of Calculus I is compensatory at Lehigh University. At Moravian College, a liberal arts college two miles away, instruction in anything less than college algebra and trigonometry is compensatory. At Kutztown State College, 20 miles from Moravian, the initial mathematics course is called "Fundamentals of Mathematics" and is at least a step below the entering level of mathematics at Moravian (Richardson, 1977, p. 7). Chemistry, biology, and physics are all offered as laboratory courses in many high schools, and most colleges accept any one of them as meeting their admissions requirements in science. But a student who has taken biology in high school and must take chemistry as a prerequisite for a major in college is considered in his chemistry class to be involved simply in beginning or introductory study, not compensatory work. Several foreign languages are offered in high school, but any study of them for

the first time in college is regarded as introductory study, not remediation.

These examples reveal general indecision about where the schools' responsibilities for teaching elementary skills end and where the colleges' responsibilities for teaching advanced-level skills begins. Overcoming this indecision is a joint responsibility of state boards of education and state college and university systems. State boards of education have an obligation to make clear what the minimum standards of graduation from high school will be. We shall see later in this section that several states are now taking action in this direction. But the minimum level of achievement deemed suitable for high school graduation may be substantially lower than the minimum level suitable for college admission.

Determining the latter level is, first of all, the responsibility of each college, and there is an enormous range of requirements found in almost all states. The lower level is represented by institutions that accept all high school graduates for admission. The upper level usually restricts admission to students who have studied specified subjects and compiled high scholastic records or who are ranked well within the top 15 percent of their high school graduating class. Since individual colleges may locate themselves at any point within this range of selectivity, it is difficult for either the high schools or the college and university systems to speak unequivocally about a state standard of scholastic achievement that should be met by all students planning to enter college. After careful scrutiny of the undergraduate programs of colleges and universities, however, it should be possible for state systems of higher education to at least identify:

- The proficiency levels in reading, writing, and mathematics a student needs to begin a college career
- Those subjects on which a college curriculum builds and to which every entering student should have had at least some exposure

For many years, the University of California, for example, has required that all entering students have (a) one year of his-

tory, (b) three years of English, (c) two years of mathematics, (d) one year of laboratory science, (e) two years of a foreign language, and (f) one or two years in advanced courses in mathematics, foreign language, or science.[1] We by no means advocate that this listing be adopted by all colleges, but it does usefully illustrate the concept that a college might aim for a presumption of some common background of educational preparation on the part of its entering students. It not only provides the college faculty with clues about the appropriate level of beginning instruction in their various courses but also informs the high schools of the subject matter they should offer to students who intend to enter college after receiving their high school diplomas. Obviously, colleges should have options to depart from state norms, both in terms of the levels of achievement expected of their entering students and in terms of the breadth of their studies in the subjects identified as part of the foundation of college-level education. But in choosing such options with standards in mind they may be more conscious than they are likely to be now of the limitations, burdens, or opportunities their policy creates for their own educational programs.

The Decline of Basic Skills

Indecision about the levels of preparation that are appropriate for college entrance is aggravated by the fact that there is some evidence that student skills, on the average, have been declining for several years. Placement tests at Ohio State University in 1975 showed that 26 percent of the freshmen at that university had not mastered what was regarded as high school mathematics and 30 percent did not have acceptable college-level writing skills (Maeroff, 1976, p. 1). At Columbia University, an instructor reported that her students "can't write and won't read." At Harvard, a senior staff member in the English program told our interviewer that students "show less facility in reading and do not know grammar." Tests at Sterling College reveal that half of the entering students there have difficulty with texts written at the freshman level. And in the General College at the

---

[1]These requirements are widely known as the University of California's "A to F requirements."

University of Minnesota, a terminal, two-year liberal arts program with open admission, only 10 percent of the students are capable of studying college algebra or trigonometry at the time of entrance (Levine, 1976b, p. 9).

The best-documented area of deficiency is that of English composition. In an investigative report on the decline of test scores and skills, for the *Los Angeles Times,* Jack McCurdy and Don Speich reported that 40 to 65 percent of the incoming freshmen at the University of California were required to take remedial English classes in 1975; within the California State University and Colleges, "as many as 60 percent of the students currently enrolled are estimated by system officials to be deficient in writing skills" (McCurdy and Speich, August 15, 1976).

To counter such trends, the College Entrance Examination Board has added two measures of writing skills to its college-admission testing program; Columbia University recently replaced a required literature course with a composition course (Maeroff, 1976); Cornell appointed an associate dean for writing; and a number of institutions that did not have them before the decline in scores attracted national concern, opened writing centers to which students could come voluntarily or on referral by their professors for special assistance with writing deficiencies. Several colleges that had given them up reinstated remedial writing programs, and a number of experimental projects designed to correct writing deficiencies were announced (Scully, 1976, pp. 1, 12).

Five years ago, university writing specialists at the University of California at Berkeley began to work with over 80 high school teachers in the San Francisco Bay Area in the study of writing problems, remedies, and teaching. Preliminary results of these efforts were impressive. In 1976, writing scores in project schools jumped 50 points as compared to a 13-point increase for students in nonproject schools. Twenty-four percent fewer graduates from the participating schools were required to take the university's remedial English class in 1976 than did so the previous year. Writing programs patterned on the Berkeley project are now being introduced in the Los Angeles, San Diego, and Sacramento areas of California and in four other states ("The Bay Area Writing Project . . . ," 1977, p. 87).

But the decline in skills has not been limited to English composition. Results of the Scholastic Aptitude Test (SAT) and American College Testing Program (ACT) presented in Table 22

Table 22. ACT and SAT score averages for college-bound seniors, 1960-61 to 1975-76

	ACT composite	*SAT verbal*	*SAT mathematical*
1960-61		474	495
1961-62	20.2	473	498
1962-63	20.4	478	502
1963-64	20.4	475	498
1964-65	19.9	473	496
1965-66	20.0	471	496
1966-67	19.4	467	495
1967-68	19.0	466	494
1968-69	19.4	462	491
1969-70	19.5	460	488
1970-71	18.9	454	487
1971-72	18.8	450	482
1972-73	18.9	443	481
1973-74	18.7	440	478
1974-75	18.3	437	473
1975-76	17.9[a]	429	470

[a]10 percent random sample.

Sources: American College Testing Program; College Entrance Examination Board.

show an overall drop in average scores between 1966-67 and 1975-76, with a significant slowing of the rate of decline between 1974-75 and 1975-76. The average nationwide SAT verbal and mathematics scores dropped 34 and 20 points respectively over the entire period, but because the forms of the tests have changed over the years, the actual drop may be much greater (McCurdy and Speich, August 15, 1976). The decreases are encountered in all geographical areas of the country, in all student ability groups, and in all family income groups. In its own report on the phenomenon, the Hudson Institute said,

"Declining academic achievement is not confined to the poor, the immigrants, the Negroes, or school districts where these children are found. It is a nationwide event" (Armbruster, 1977).

　　　Several frequently-advanced explanations for the test-score decline—including bad diets, birth control pills, and the drop in high school enrollments in Latin—were put to rest fairly early by Harold Howe II, vice-president of the Ford Foundation ("College Test Score," 1976, p. 3). A comprehensive study of the matter was made by the Advisory Panel on the Scholastic Aptitude Test Score Decline, created by the College Entrance Examination Board and headed by Willard Wirtz. This panel identified two categories of causes for the test score decline. The first reflects changes in the composition of persons taking the tests. The second reflects a variety of influences involving changes "in the practices of the schools and in the American social fabric" (Advisory Panel on Scholastic Aptitude Test Score Decline, 1977, p. 31).

　　　The panel found that between two-thirds and three-fourths of the score decline between 1963 and 1970 were related to changes in the composition of the group taking the examinations. Larger percentages of students with relatively lower high school grade averages began to go to college (and take the tests) during this period. There were also increases in the proportionate numbers in the test-taking group who had traditionally scored low on the test. These included students from lower socio-economic families, members of minority ethnic groups, and (on the mathematical but not the verbal tests) women (ibid., p. 11). There were decreases during the period in the number of students planning to attend highly selective colleges, and in the number of students who repeated the tests to improve their scores. The panel considers the "compositional" factors less as evidence of lack of inherent ability of certain groups within our society, than of the fact that our national efforts to extend educational opportunity to larger portions of our population is still unfinished business.

　　　Among the second group of factors identified by the panel are the following:

- A dispersal of learning activities and emphasis in the schools and a reduction in the number of courses that all students alike are required to take—particularly in English and the verbal skills area
- Diminished seriousness of purpose and attention to mastery of skills and knowledge in the learning process in the schools, at home, and in society generally; among the specific symptoms are automatic grade-to grade promotions, grade inflation, tolerance of absenteeism, lowering of the demand levels of text books and other teaching and learning materials, the reduction of homework, lowering of college entrance standards, and the inclusion of compensatory or "remedial" courses in colleges
- Increases in the amount of children's learning that develops through viewing and listening rather than through traditional modes
- Decline of the role of the family in the educational process
- Disruption of the life of the country generally during the time when the students tested in 1972 through 1975 were getting ready for college entrance examinations
- Diminution in young people's learning motivation

But the panel concludes: "There is no *one* cause of the SAT score decline, at least so far as we can discern, and we suspect no single pattern of causes. Learning is too much a part of Life to have expected anything else" (ibid., p. 33).

The Response of the Schools

The well-publicized decline of scores that measure student skills is leading educators and legislators throughout the country to initiate corrective action. Virginia, California, and New York are among a growing number of states that have legislation requiring that high school students prove they can read, write, and perform basic arithmetic computations before they graduate from high school. Arizona now requires that students graduating from high schools must read, write, and compute on at least the ninth-grade level. In Nebraska, elementary and secondary schools are required to establish a minimal performance level in

reading, writing, and arithmetic and to administer tests as many times as may be necessary for all students to prove mastery in these skills (Phipho, 1977).

Some of these actions and proposals aim at a distinction between achievement represented by surviving the educational process for specified amounts of time and at competence in the subjects that are studied. One implication is that school systems could ultimately have what amounts to multiple graduation procedures. Missouri is considering supplementing the high school diploma with a certificate indicating competency in the everyday application of basic skills. A county in Nevada is reportedly studying the award of special diplomas indicating student academic excellence (Phipho, 1977). Four kinds of certification for high school completion are conceivable: one indicating that a student "tested out" early, another indicating that a student attended high school for the required number of years with a satisfactory academic record, another indicating that a student has not only survived high school but has more than minimal skills for survival in modern society (as evidenced, say, by receiving a diploma and, in addition, passing a standardized test of competence), and yet another indicating that a student is prepared for and commended to higher education. Suggestions that two types of certification be used in Florida were made by a team of Educational Testing Service (ETS) consultants in 1976 (Fremer, Scudder, and Willingham, 1976, p. 17). Although every student record of precollege education should make proper note of special achievements, commendations, and competences, we would hope that multiple certification would be introduced in the nation's high schools with great care. It could be unnecessarily divisive and could encourage tracking of a kind that would seem to justify depriving students with early-diagnosed low ability of the level or kind of education suitable for their potential.

Despite these reservations, every effort should be made throughout the schools to make an early diagnosis of learning difficulties and to correct deficiencies in elementary skills as soon as possible after they are discovered. For the student who reaches college without such skills, even the best of remedial education programs may be too little and too late. We therefore

urge all states to take such measures as may be needed to ensure that elementary and high school students acquire proficiencies consistent with their abilities and grade levels in reading, computation, and written English.

Colleges should not leave the responsibility entirely with the schools, however. With the University of California's Bay Area Writing Project as a useful example, colleges and universities should become active participants in cooperative school and college programs to improve elementary skills of high school graduates.

We also favor the use of tests of competence as supplements to the currently prevailing methods of measuring students' educational progress. For over 30 years, by passing General Educational Development (GED) tests, persons who have not received high school diplomas have been able to receive certification of having acquired functional command of the knowledge acquired in high schools. These tests are now recognized by all 50 states, and many employers prefer hiring students who have passed such tests over those who only have the diploma (Fremer, Scudder, and Willingham, 1976, p. 5). Although such tests can be used for college admissions purposes, they do not test proficiencies defined by the colleges but instead test educational outcomes normed by the performance on the tests of high school seniors. In May 1977, Educational Testing Service administered the first tests in its Basic Skills Assessment Program. This program is designed both as a diagnostic instrument and as a means of helping secondary schools decide whether students have sufficient basic skills to meet the requirements for high school graduation. It may be administered first in the eighth and ninth grade and again in the last half of the eleventh grade so that a student with diagnosed weaknesses may engage in remedial work before graduation. During a visit to one of the nation's largest testing agencies, one of the Carnegie Council's staff representatives was told that perhaps a dozen or more tests to measure the competences people need to perform effectively in different capacities—as adults, as members of a profession, or as students in colleges and universities—would be widely available within five years.

One model for such assessment has been provided by the

Adult Performance Level (APL) materials developed at the University of Texas at Austin. These are based on systematically determined indicators of competence in basic skills required in the world of work, consumer economics, matters involving the government and law, and other adult concerns. Using these performance indicators, those developing the APL assessment assert they can predict whether persons will be "proficient," "functional," or "functional with difficulty" in the contemporary adult world (*Adult Functional Competency*, 1975). The APL procedure and some of its "performance indicators" are already in use in New York and Texas as the basis of external high school diploma programs. They also may be adaptable to tests that could be used in certifying persons as having competences comparable to those of persons graduating from high school, and the American College Testing Program is currently engaged in efforts to develop such instruments.

A major benefit of current efforts to develop performance indicators and other components of tests of this sort is that they force educators and evaluators to define more explicitly than before what a person should be able to do as a result of the school experience. If such tests are administered frequently throughout the school years, they will supplement methods now available for alerting teachers to the needs of some students for early special attention. It will not, however, define the threshold of college education.

That task really belongs to the colleges themselves and should be performed with great care. Too sharp a demarcation will reverse the clock on such constructive recent developments as the provision of opportunities for students to satisfy college requirements while they are still in high school, "testing-out" procedures that enable high school students to graduate early in order to enter college early, and concurrent enrollment procedures that enable students to be enrolled simultaneously in high school and college. These kinds of programs not only should continue but should become more widely available. But the historic demarcation between school and college suggested by the end of secondary schooling is no longer, by itself, satisfactory. One very good reason is that high schools no longer concentrate entirely on preparing students for college.

If it is possible to determine the characteristics and skills needed by people to function effectively in society at large with procedures such as those used in developing the APL program, perhaps it is also possible to determine by means other than high school transcripts the characteristics and skills of people who function well in college. One promising approach would be to ask groups of college faculty members to identify the skills and other attributes entering freshmen need if they are to successfully complete their initial college years. Using such predictors, high schools could give better guidance to their students, not only in their choice of colleges but also in their need for special studies in order to succeed in the college they choose to attend. The process would make school advising and college admissions the practice of foresight instead of hindsight. It would also define the threshold of the college curriculum without any unintended or unwarranted compromises of the college mission and curricular policy.

Compensatory Education

Before public high schools became common in the United States, colleges and universities frequently operated preparatory schools in conjunction with their collegiate programs. In fact, many colleges themselves had curricula that were not much above the level of secondary schools. As public high schools were developed, colleges gradually came to rely on these institutions instead of on their own departments for fulfilling the preparatory function.

But the standards met by high schools are not uniform, and neither are the entrance requirements of the nation's colleges and universities. Under such conditions, it is inevitable that some students graduate from high school without the basic skills and knowledge many colleges consider necessary for entering freshmen. At most community colleges, for example, many students cannot read at the seventh-grade level. Even at selective four-year institutions, students may enroll who need opportunities to overcome what promise to be troublesome deficiencies. To meet the needs of students who are inadequately prepared for college-level work, colleges and universities may offer compensatory education. Among community colleges, for example,

such instruction is available for credit in 78 percent of the arts and sciences programs and 88 percent of the trade and technical divisions. At the same colleges, noncredit compensatory instruction is available in 53 percent of the arts and sciences programs and 47 percent of the trade and technical divisions (Catalog Study, 1976). In four-year colleges, remedial instruction for credit is available in 39 percent of the arts and sciences divisions and in about half of the undergraduate professional schools. It is available without credit in 48 percent of the arts and sciences divisions of four-year colleges and in an average of 60 percent for five professional schools, with the highest (71 percent) in education and the lowest (46 percent) in engineering and trade and technical schools or divisions (Catalog Study, 1976). In all, we estimate that between 100,000 and 150,000 students participated in such programs in 1976 (Carnegie Council Surveys, 1975-1976).

To some extent, all education is compensatory because it corrects deficiencies in skills and understanding that prevent one from undertaking more advanced studies. There is a fine but perhaps important distinction to be made, however, between deficiencies that are shared by all students who approach a certain level of study equally prepared and those of students who, for one reason or another, have missed an important part of the necessary preparation. The problem is particularly acute in colleges and universities when the part of the preparation that has been missed is normally provided by elementary and secondary schools. Students with deficiencies of that type can make satisfactory progress in college only if the missing preparation is in some way provided early in the undergraduate years.

In some situations, providing missing preparation does not require special arrangements. These are cases in which introductory instruction is provided in both high schools and colleges as a matter of course—as mentioned earlier, foreign languages provide the most clear-cut example, but elementary chemistry or physics might also fall into this category. Another example might be relatively advanced mathematics—calculus, for example—that is offered as an option in many high schools but may be required in college as a prerequisite for advanced studies in

mathematics or the sciences. Students are able to begin such studies in college with relatively little difficulty. It is normally available to all students at all times. If their missing preparation is in fact usually available only as a precollege subject, however, their need for instruction to overcome deficiencies is at once more acute and possibly more difficult for many colleges to provide. Such instruction may not be offered routinely as a part of the curriculum that leads to a baccalaureate degree.

Where the need for special instruction to overcome deficiencies in preparation normally provided by high schools is widespread, states should make even greater efforts than they do now to assure that our schools give all students skills and proficiencies that are consistent with their abilities and grade levels in reading, computation, and written English. In addition, adult and evening schools that do not now do so should develop special programs designed to help people overcome deficiencies in basic skills required for successful performance in college. In its report on the relationship between higher education and the cities, the Carnegie Commission on Higher Education (1972a) recommended that city governments create "metropolitan educational opportunity counseling centers" designed to encourage more effective use of the educational resources of an area. Although the basic role envisioned for these centers was one of providing educational and vocational advice to citizens in metropolitan areas, they might also play a role, wherever they are established, in providing college preparatory opportunities. Colleges should not, however, shirk their responsibilities for creating special programs to help students overcome academic deficiencies if high schools or local communities fail to provide them.

The question of awarding credit for compensatory education taken at a college is troublesome, because of the variety of educational missions of our colleges and the differences in their admissions practices. For example, community colleges and other institutions that are required by law to accept for admission all high school graduates, regardless of the particular skills and knowledge they may have acquired with their diplomas may have broader missions in the provisions of college-level

instruction than other types of colleges. Under these circumstances, giving credit for any course of instruction included in the curriculum may well be regarded as appropriate. We would concur, however, with the recommendation of the Carnegie Commission on Higher Education (1970, p. 14) that "every student accepted into a program requiring compensatory education (for making up subject and skill deficiencies normally required for admission or continuation in higher education) receive the necessary commitment of resources to allow his engagement in an appropriate level of course work by the end of no more than two years." We would also suggest that, where credit for such instruction is given, credits should be counted toward meeting graduation requirements other than those for general education or the major.

Colleges should not only be concerned with providing compensatory education in the elementary skills but should also be concerned with helping students who wish to improve the more advanced-level skills they may have. For this purpose, several colleges, including the University of California, Berkeley, San Antonio College, and Colorado State College, have created skill development centers to help students overcome difficulties in writing, computing assignments, and analysis of written materials. Such centers are usually provided as a student service and do not offer academic credit for their instruction. Because teaching skills of this kind, often in a one-to-one tutorial relationship, can be time consuming and exhausting, colleges should draw on the full resources of the college community in finding personnel for such centers. Among such resources are new Ph.D.'s who have not as yet found full-time appointments, advanced undergraduates participating in work-study programs, and the volunteer and part-time assistance that can be provided by spouses of faculty members, retired faculty members or secondary school teachers, and others readily available in the campus community. In planning the work of such centers, the staff should concentrate on deficiencies or problems that are clearly correctable with relatively short-term investments of time and effort. They should also utilize, to the fullest possible extent, instructional technologies and materials that help students teach themselves.

Helping students overcome learning problems or skill deficiencies need not always be regarded as an institution-wide responsibility. Departments and schools within the college can take initiatives on their own. For example, at the University of Massachusetts, Amherst, the school of engineering and department of physics have been developing a freshman-year program for 350 engineering students. At the beginning of each year, students take a diagnostic test. On the basis of the results, a series of one-credit modules designed to overcome weakness in, for example, ratio relationships, "if . . . then . . . reasoning," separation and control of variables, and other "cognitive structures" are prescribed. Courses are also offered on problem solving, learning strategies, and understanding mathematical relations.

Writing skills are susceptible to improvement through frequent practice and evaluation. For that reason, writing assignments should be made regularly in as many courses in a college as possible, and faculty members outside departments of English should not feel restrained in criticizing and correcting writing as part of the evaluation they make of student work. Students cannot be expected to try to improve their own writing if they are allowed to believe that the majority of their professors and instructors do not think it is important for them to do so.

Conclusion

College curricula must be planned on the assumption that all of the new students on campus each year have acquired a certain minimum amount of learning skill and knowledge. Although high schools cannot be expected to tailor their curricula to meet the entrance requirements of every college and university in their region, they do have an obligation to provide instruction that prepares students for college-level work. This will normally involve skills in reading, composition, and mathematics at levels consistent with the number of years their students have been in school and exposure to certain subject matter that is drawn on as a foundation of what, by common practice, may be determined to be the academic undergraduate college curriculum.

At the same time, colleges, which are typically involved in a certain amount of introductory education in any event,

should be prepared to offer special instruction to students who, for one reason or another, find themselves in need of help in overcoming specific deficiencies in their preparation for college. Once students have been admitted, a college has an obligation to give them any support it can to help them succeed in meeting educational goals. Colleges should not, on the other hand, be expected to accept permanent responsibility for overcoming universal or widespread deficiencies in college preparation that result from systematic inadequacies of elementary and secondary schools.

To prevent widespread deficiencies in college preparation from occurring, colleges should:

- Train teachers of elementary skills and introductory academic subjects, with particular attention to the diagnosis and remediation of deficiencies early in students' learning careers
- Conduct research on the causes of learning problems and propose reforms
- Work with teachers and schools in the improvement of instruction in elementary skills and academic subjects
- Determine and publicize their own expectations of the level of preparation needed by high school graduates who are admitted for undergraduate studies on their campuses
- Maintain records of the performance of high school graduates who come to them for undergraduate education and periodically advise the high schools of patterns of consistent high performance or deficiencies encountered in their graduates
- Create remedial programs to assist students who come to them with specific deficiencies in elementary learning skills and subject matter preparation
- Develop learning centers to assist undergraduates in the improvement of more advanced learning skills whenever it is needed throughout their college careers

*   *   *

For further information on elementary skills and the undergraduate curriculum, see the chapter "Basic Skills and Knowledge" in the Carnegie Council on Policy Studies in Higher Education, *Handbook on Undergraduate Curriculum*.

12

Undergraduate Education
and the World of Work

In the view of many Americans, preparing people for work is
becoming the dominant function of education. R. Freeman
Butts (1975, p. 21) has observed that "Despite the concern of
the 1930s and 1940s for the values of nonvocational liberal education, the rush to the professions and the technical specializations has proceeded pell mell, interrupted for a time by the
downgrading of scientific and professional training by the youth
culture of the 1960s, but by common agreement now in full
flood tide among college students of the present generation."
By 1976, 95 percent of America's undergraduates considered
training and skills for an occupation to be either "essential" or
"fairly important" goals of their college education (Carnegie
Council Surveys, 1975-1976).

There are two possible consequences of this interest that
could distort the purposes of the college curriculum. One is that
students may become so single-minded in their studies aimed
toward specific jobs that they become overspecialized and perhaps inflexible. The other is that students and employers alike
might overemphasize the importance of degrees and other certification for employment. The result of this emphasis is that the
level of credentialing for the positions that are available spirals
upward beyond the actual demands of the work to be performed. Those people caught up in this trend can become
underproductive and dissatisfied employees, discontented citi-

zens, and frustrated alumni who feel that their education has
somehow failed them (O'Toole, 1974, pp. 19, 20).

For this reason, we believe that any discussion of the relationship between education and the world of work must go beyond specific job preparation and manpower needs of the
moment. Although graduates of American colleges can, and
hopefully will, derive independence and satisfaction in careers
with promising futures, it is equally, if not more important that
they match their skills and competences with a thorough understanding of work as a characteristically human enterprise. They
should appreciate its role in building self-esteem and a sense of
accomplishment; in ordering one's personal life; in contributing
to the welfare and comfort of others; in participating in the productive activities of the enterprise, the profession, the community, and the nation. Only by understanding the role of work in
all of its forms and in all of its many contexts can one fully
understand humanity and some of the basic forces that shape
our society. Failure to understand it could leave one oblivious
to the full significance of what goes on in at least one-third of
the lives of most adult Americans.[1]

A thorough introduction to the world of work will also
give students a sense of reality that may not always come
through their academic studies and campus experiences. It will
introduce them to the costs as well as benefits of activities and
programs and will introduce them to the importance of basic

[1]Relatively few sources for a broad introduction to the world of work
now exist. A brief investigation by the staff of the Carnegie Council on
Policy Studies in Higher Education yielded information on four books that
make a contribution, however. One is the *Occupational Outlook Handbook* issued and updated every two years by the U.S. Bureau of Labor
Statistics. Richard Nelson Bolle's *What Color is Your Parachute? A Practical Manual for Job-Hunters and Career-Changers* (Berkeley, Calif.: Ten
Speed Press, 1974) is considered by some to be especially helpful to
women reentering the job market and to be strong on values clarification
and practical tips on how to find out about employment possibilities.
C. R. Powell's *Career Planning and Placement for the College Graduate of
the '70s* (Dubuque, Iowa: Kendall/Hunt, 1976) emphasizes careers in business and contains information on career ladders. H. E. Figler's *A Career
Workbook for Liberal Arts Students* (Cranston, R.I.: Carroll Press, 1975)
is reportedly appropriate for either college or high school students.

processes that are encountered directly in the world of work but have implications for other parts of life as well. Among them would be planning, budgeting, supervision of the work of others, scheduling, and maintaining inventories and quality controls. Although it may be difficult to teach these processes in the classroom, they can be taught and learned as a part of an undergraduate experience that effectively combines classroom studies with experiences in work situations.

Increasingly, undergraduates may also need to know more about the distinction between jobs and careers and the importance of keeping individual options open. As we have seen within the present decade, the demand for educated men and women in the employment market can shift abruptly. Colleges cannot, with any assurance, educate students today for participation in occupations guaranteed to have a high demand for them three or four years from now. At any future time, there will be occasions when students may have to accept positions that do not immediately utilize the preparation their colleges gave them. Both students and the general public need to understand that this is not necessarily a matter for great alarm. As a recent study of Harvard graduates of the class of 1971 shows, some of the students who accept what might be regarded as underemployment right after graduation do so with the expectation that they will return to a university to acquire advanced learning in their chosen career fields (Fisher, 1976, p. 26). Their employment of the moment does not represent derailment from a career line—only switching to a temporary siding. Moreover, what some may regard as underemployment may be regarded by others as undervaluation of certain occupations. An example cited in the Harvard study involves five graduates working as carpenters, not, apparently, as interim employment, but as a result of "a heightened evaluation of a job with variety, physical involvement, craft, and independence" (Fisher, 1976, p. 37).

The Need for Counseling

In the past, students have voluntarily adjusted to labor market demands with remarkable speed. Their ability to adjust might be even greater if they had available to them better information

about career opportunities. The National Manpower Institute recommended that special community councils be established "to ease the transition back and forth between classrooms and the workplace" and that high school and college students receive at least five hours of career guidance and counseling each year (Wirtz, 1975, p. 172).

We are informed by the College Placement Council that offices that assist students find employment in business, government, and industry[2] exist at 1,503 (79 percent) of the nation's four-year colleges and 863 (76 percent) of its two-year colleges. Most of these services offer student counseling. But from our survey of undergraduate attitudes and experience we learn that the students' appraisals of career advising are not consistently high. In 1976, 8 percent of the undergraduates rated their vocational advising as "highly adequate," and 54 percent said they had "never sought this type of advising" (Carnegie Council Surveys, 1975-1976). These data suggest that there may be a need to improve career advising services on the campuses and to encourage more students to take advantage of the advising that is available to them. But that conclusion is not entirely justified. The findings from the Carnegie Council surveys (1975-1976) may also mean that students feel no need for such counseling or that it is not available to them.

In some professional schools, undergraduates often receive counseling and advice on career matters in conjunction with academic advising. At other colleges, advising for the two different purposes is kept separated. But there are exceptions. At La Verne and Coe Colleges, for example, academic and career counseling are not, strictly speaking, combined, but they share space and, to some extent, personnel. Faculty members provide academic counseling in conventional ways, but there is also a center for academic and career planning, where students file the academic plans they intend to pursue throughout their college

[2]The College Placement Council does not specifically represent career planning and placement officers devoted to the teaching field. That activity is represented by the Association for School, College, and University Staffing. But there is considerable overlap in the membership of both organizations.

years, their plans for satisfying concentration requirements, and each term's schedule of courses. At the same center, undergraduates can take inventories and exercises that assist them in clarifying work-related values, explore career fields with the help of a network of college alumni, develop a "credentials file" of letters of recommendation, resumés, and transcripts, and get assistance in preparing resumés, writing letters of application, and interviewing prospective employers. The advantages of the physical proximity of the various advising services are that it creates opportunities and inducements for students to seek career counseling as they utilize the advising services provided for all students and that it does not treat vocational counseling as an activity extraneous to the educational concerns of the institution.

Often overlooked by educators is the opportunity that a quest for an appropriate career provides for relating personal development to occupational preparation. The choice of a career, after all, should be made on the basis of one's own values and personality. Programs that assist students in identifying those aspects of their own lives may have educational as well as career benefits.

With that possibility partly in mind, the Educational Testing Service has developed a computer-based guidance system that was introduced into several colleges (most of which were community colleges) in 1975. Called a System of Interactive Guidance and Information (SIGI), the program places individual students in communication with a very large data base and a system of analysis that enables them to assess their own career statuses and values, locate and compare occupational alternatives appropriate to their situations and needs, estimate the difficulty of achieving alternative career goals, and plan strategies for entering the occupations they choose.

After a trial of the system in 1973, groups using it were compared with control groups on three criteria regarded as important elements in "rational decision making: the number of occupational constructs the student could volunteer in an appropriate context, the amount of information the student had about preferred occupations, and the extent and nature of the

student's planning. . . . The experimental group scored highet than the control group on all three criteria, although the differ- ences were statistically significant only for planning and for the total scores" (Katz and Kroll, 1975, p. 7).

Attempts to link the educational process with career guid- ance in colleges and universities is likely to encounter resistance from some faculty members and officials who fear that the re- sulting centers will cost money that ought to go to departments of instruction or that they may open the door to more speciali- zation or the devaluation of an already beleaguered general edu- cation. At institutions with sound educational policies, such fears are unfounded. There is, in fact, perhaps greater danger to the integrity of undergraduate education when the linkage be- tween learning and work is de facto but unrecognized than there is when it is placed in proper perspective.

The Roles of General Education

The fact that students place a high value on career preparation while they are still in college does not mean that the specialized studies involved in such preparation are all employers should care about. They should also value the results of the total undergraduate educational experience. If it is effective, it in- creases the likelihood that a prospective college-educated em- ployee will be:

- Appreciative of the local, national, and international contexts in which his or her occupational endeavors are pursued
- Aware of fields of knowledge that offer data and insights rele- vant to his or her occupation
- Capable of communicating effectively with coworkers, supe- riors, customers, and the general public
- Resourceful in adjusting personally and professionally to problems and unexpected developments and opportunities
- Able to learn quickly and independently
- Able to recognize excellence in products, performance of as- sociates and competitors, and plans for future developments
- Experienced in working to meet specified standards and per- severing to the conclusion of assigned tasks

• Able to set and meet standards of ethical behavior and morality

These are not outcomes colleges should strive to realize solely, or even mainly, to satisfy prospective employers. They are consequences of a good total undergraduate experience that should be valued for their own sake and should "come with the deal" when employers hire college graduates.

Improving Chances for Employment

Undergraduates typically acquire the particular knowledge and skills they hope to offer to prospective employers in their major studies. But there is not always a close correlation between one's major and one's ultimate career. Opportunities may arise that lead one into an occupation for which one has not specifically prepared, and college-educated people may change careers several times during their working lives. Moreover, some students deliberately choose majors that prepare them for specific roles in careers or professions outside their major field. The student who plans to become a salesman and majors in psychology rather than business administration or the student who plans to become an attorney and majors in speech might be examples. Such uses of the curriculum are consistent with the fact that, in 1971, nearly two-thirds of American business administrators who were college graduates had not majored in business administration (Bisconti, 1975, p. 7). Virtually all academic disciplines provide an educational base for teachers, including (with advanced training) college faculty members, and some teacher-training institutions do not permit undergraduates to major in education. On the other hand, teaching careers may be among the few that are really compatible with the educational preparation of large proportions of graduates in the social sciences and humanities (which explains why the 1970s, with their reduced opportunities for educators at all levels, have been particularly difficult for graduates in these fields).

Colleges might improve the employment prospects of such students by offering, in addition to departmental major options, certain interdisciplinary majors defined by broad areas of occu-

pational and professional endeavor. A major in ecology or environmental management, for example, could draw on the biological sciences, physical sciences, forestry, agriculture, geography, urban management, and other disciplines related to occupations in land management, environmental protection, urban and regional planning, irrigation development, and other such fields. A major in communications could draw on English, journalism, languages, art, music, mathematics, and electronic and computer technology and could prepare persons for employment in news and information media, data processing and analysis, publishing, advertising, and public relations. A major in public service could draw on political science, psychology, biological sciences, law enforcement, and business administration and could prepare persons for a wide range of positions in government and public service organizations. If such majors were more extensively available, concentrations offered by single departments could become, more frankly and perhaps more effectively, what many of them are now—preparation for advanced education or for narrowly defined occupations and professions. Such majors might also be beneficial to students who plan to become members of college or university faculties.

Students should have options to take joint majors and major-minor combinations that permit them to concentrate on subjects of special interest to them and, at the same time, to increase their potential value to employers. Joint majors in business education and a foreign language, or education and a foreign language are examples of combinations for which there is some demand at the present time.

At some institutions, it may not be possible for students to obtain the courses they need in order to balance majors that are in low demand on the job market with instruction that will increase their employability. For example, some liberal arts colleges may not have any technical or professional courses available. Universities may not have any occupational instruction in their curricula. In such cases, colleges might explore the possibility of cooperating with other institutions, including two-year colleges, universities, technical institutes, or professional schools, to provide such courses for their students.

The principle to be observed is not that every student should be encouraged to acquire a specialized marketable skill before graduation from college but that no student should be involuntarily penalized in the job market for electing to concentrate in college on a subject that is of great personal interest but has no obvious demand by employers.

In the absence of interinstitutional cooperative arrangements, undergraduates should themselves seek ways to enhance the attractiveness of low-demand majors to prospective employers by supplementing them with technical and vocational education or work experience during summers and stop-outs. Such experiences will be particularly valuable if they demonstrate to employers a student's early interest in certain long-term career goals.

Work Experiences

In 1976, 19 percent of the undergraduates in American colleges worked full-time, and 34 percent worked part-time, while enrolled in higher education (Carnegie Council Surveys, 1975-1976). Many educators believe that such experience should be made available to all students and that its educational potential should be more fully utilized. In a discussion of secondary education, the Harvard "red book" indicated that "experience in actual work" is "beneficial for all, even more so for those who expect to enter business or a profession than for those who will engage in some form of manual or craft work" (Harvard Committee, 1945, p. 175). Torsten Husen (1974, p. 26) has urged that "efforts should be made to investigate at length the extent to which it would be possible to let the vast majority of young people enter the job world for longer periods —to give them training for responsibility and the much-needed opportunity to grow into adult roles. For instance, what about permitting young people to practice in certain rapidly expanding and highly labor-intensive service occupations, such as child welfare, sick care, and old-age care?"

This is not a new idea. As is the case for most colleges, Berea College in Kentucky provided employment for its neediest students even before it decided to accept only students who

could not otherwise afford college. But in 1906 President William G. Frost and the college's trustees became concerned about the fact that students were dividing into two groups—those who were needy and had to work and those who were less needy and did not. To bridge the widening gap, they required that all students work, and the policy continues today. All 1,400 students at the college are employed either in institutional jobs, such as working on the college newspaper, in janitorial work, campus security, and the library, or in student industries, such as woodworking, needlecraft, Boone Tavern Inn, or ceramics. About 25 percent work in academic departments, and 6 percent do social service in the surrounding communities. Labor program payments take the forms of credit against the cost of education (there is no tuition) and of direct payment of 80 cents to $1.68 per hour.

Also in 1906, the University of Cincinnati introduced what is generally regarded as the first cooperative education program in the United States. It provided engineering students an opportunity to alternate periods of work and study. Three years later, a similar program was launched at Northeastern University in Boston, which now has the largest cooperative program in the country. In 1975, approximately 14,000 undergraduates were involved in it (Wooldridge, 1975, p. 10).

In 1921 Arthur E. Morgan built jobs into the curriculum of Antioch College at regular intervals so that students could come face to face with "practical realities in all their stubborn perplexity" (Rudolph, 1962, p. 474). This was the first time that the idea of alternating studies with work experience was utilized for all students in a liberal arts college. In this setting, the emphasis was on work as a means of personal development, not as job training. Since September 1975, Antioch's education-work mix has had both general education and concentration functions (Levine, June 1976b, pp. 26, 27). Faculty members at Antioch react positively to this program, because it enables them to reduce time spent on applied aspects of their subjects. It also keeps students up to date on current developments in some fields.

At LaGuardia Community College in Long Island City,

New York, every student is required to participate in an "internship" during one quarter in the freshman year (there are four quarters in the college's year-round operation) and during two quarters in the sophomore year. In 1975, more than 250 employers participated in the project. Two-thirds of the college's 1974 graduating class of 437 students applied for transfer to senior colleges, and within six months after graduation an additional one-fourth of the class had accepted full-time employment. Of those employed full time, three-fourths were employed by firms and organizations that had participated in the cooperative education program.

This example is particularly appealing because it effectively integrates the work experience with classroom education. While the seminars that make this possible are inevitably oriented to career planning, they also involve value questions (What is important in a working relationship?) and management questions (How can employers motivate workers?). The seminars for the third internship involve independent research on topics related directly to the internship experience, to industry-wide issues, or issues pertaining to work in general. This element of formal education is crucial, and it ought to be a feature of any cooperative education program that benefits from state or local financing based on enrollments in such programs. It is also doubtful that any academic credit should be given for work components of undergraduate education that do not include some faculty involvement, requirements for seminars, student logs, or a written report that relates the work experience to the student's on-campus studies.

Whether or not credit should be given for work experience itself depends to a considerable extent on the ability of colleges to assess such experience in terms of their own educational goals. In 1974, Cooperative Assessment of Experiential Learning (CAEL), a project involving the Educational Testing Service and 10 colleges and universities, was formed to address this and related problems. Of particular relevance to college-sponsored work programs is a guide CAEL has developed for students who plan to participate in such arrangements. It outlines 11 steps the student should take, ranging from taking stock of goals and con-

sidering available work options to assessing learning outcomes
after the work experience and identifying new learning objectives (Cooperative Assessment of Experiential Learning, 1975).

Cooperative education jobs (often called "internships")
provide practical training that can be related to students' majors
and long-term career objectives, opportunities to test out career
fields, add a dimension of life experience to the general education of students, and afford students an opportunity to earn
money for the partial support of their education. They are now
available in one form or another at approximately 900 (almost a
third) of all colleges in the country (Wooldridge, 1975, p. 175).
Within four-year colleges, cooperative education is available in
16 percent of the colleges of arts and sciences, 25 percent of
business schools, 29 percent of schools of education, 26 percent
of engineering schools, 17 percent of schools of health sciences,
and 27 percent of trade and technology schools. Nationally, 9
percent of the nation's undergraduates have "had an apprenticeship, internship, or a job for academic credit or to meet graduation requirements" (Carnegie Council Surveys, 1975-1976). The
percentage of students involved in such instruction could be
much higher. Fifty-two percent of all undergraduates state that
they wish they had had such an experience (Carnegie Council
Surveys, 1975-1976).

It is not likely that cooperative education will be universally available for all students very soon. Start-up costs are quite
high, and, although such programs afford an opportunity for
institutions to increase enrollments without increasing services,
such savings may be substantially offset by high costs of administration. Some institutions would have to change their calen-
dars radically to accommodate staggered terms of alternating
work and study. For the same reason, planning the sequence of
highly formal instruction in general education or the major (for
example in the sciences) could become more complicated. The
number of jobs that would be required would be quite high—
perhaps 3 million nationally, if one assumes that one-third of
the undergraduate student force would be in an employment
situation at all times. Students who have to work to stay in
school might feel threatened. In a sense, they would have to

compete for jobs not only with other students who have to work but also with their colleges and, through those institutions, with many students who would not have to work if they did not need jobs to complete college requirements. Introducing the concept of voluntary service as a part of the cooperative education idea might avoid that problem, but if working for pay were removed totally from the programs, many of the important educational objectives (that is, practical demonstration of the economic principles that apply to the job situation) would be compromised or obviated. Competition among institutions for cooperative education contracts with employers could create administrative and public relations problems for both colleges and employers unless the programs were coordinated through voluntary regional arrangements.

Despite these difficulties, many institutions that do not now do so should give serious consideration to the development of cooperative work-study programs, apprenticeships, and internships as a part of their undergraduate curricula.

Conclusion

America's colleges have been reluctant to make explicit commitments to an education that is designed to help their students acquire a full understanding of the world of work. At some institutions, particularly two-year community colleges, students are able to obtain intensive, short-term training in skills needed for specific types of jobs. For a more general education, they must rely heavily on what they learned in high schools or from their families or peers. At other colleges, students find great concern for the life of the mind, for individual adjustment to life experiences, to uses of leisure, and for preparing them for more advanced learning but little interest in relating all of that to the great bloc of time men and women devote to earning a living. For many, integration of education and the world of work does not really begin until after they graduate.

To fill this gap in undergraduate education, we believe colleges should become more explicit about their role in preparing students for occupations and professions. In addition, we support:

- More study of the place of work in human lives and in society and experimentation with courses and seminars that explore various aspects of the world of work
- Provision of opportunities for students to stop out of college periodically to alternate educational and work experience
- Scheduling of classes and courses to accommodate needs of students who work part-time
- Development of cooperative work and education programs, particularly when they include features that give students a chance to integrate work and classroom experiences
- Development of work-study programs on the campuses and in the neighboring communities
- More extensive use of computer technology for assessing student skills, interests, and aptitudes and for matching them with career fields and appropriate educational programs
- Improvement of occupational counseling services and making their availability better known on campuses
- Introduction of some of the instruction generally encountered only in general education into the courses offered in vocational programs and professional schools, so that students will become familiar with the human problems and ethical issues specifically encountered on the job or in practice

13

Values and
the Academic Tradition

Early American colleges assumed responsibility for moral training and value development as a matter of course. As Bernard
Murchland points out, liberal education "was from the beginning a perfective process, a shaping of human sensibility toward
desirable and rationally justified patterns of action. It was quite
frankly an ethical enterprise, involving nothing less than the
transformation of the individual" (Murchland, 1976, p. 22). For
many years, colleges were regarded as extensions of the religious
denominations with which they were affiliated and were expected to conduct themselves in a missionary capacity for
youth (some of whom were regarded as victims of parental
neglect where moral training was concerned). In the early nineteenth century, colleges and students alike were at the forefront
of the revivalist movement and subscribed to its teaching and
values (Sloan, 1971, pp. 227-231). And, until very recently, all
colleges, whether religious or secular in their control, were expected to assure that the behavior of their students would be at
least no worse in the college community than what would be
tolerated by their own parents at home.

But a time soon came when colleges could no longer pre-
sume to know with certainty which standards their students'
parents—or society at large, for that matter—would condone or
condemn. The churches that for so long had set the moral tone
for Americans declined in influence as the separation of church

and state became more pronounced. Many of the new colleges created in the nineteenth century were built and supported not by churches, but by state governments, and eventually many of the colleges that had been founded by religious organizations disengaged themselves from denominational controls. Moreover, Americans rapidly became people of many different denominations and faiths, and the primacy of any single, religiously based code of conduct could not be established.

Families, too, lost their influence as public school systems expanded and the population moved from rural isolation to the close quarters and diversions of the cities. The development of convenient transportation and instant communication and entertainment also drew young people away from traditional family guidance and controls. At every turn, particularly in the cities, but increasingly in rural areas as well, people are exposed to alternately value-challenging and value-sustaining experiences provided by libraries, museums, concert halls, theatres, sports arenas, conferences and meetings, books, periodicals, and television sets.

Among intellectuals, the emergence and development of science had a pervasive effect on how the world was perceived and on which authorities were to be trusted. Revealed, or dogmatic truth and values became suspect and reliance was placed instead on what could be believed or logically proved on the basis of observation and experimentation. The new sciences had their own morality and value systems, rooted in an openness to alternative ideas, obligation to be skeptical of what was not proved, respect for a conscientious search for truth, diligence and thoroughness of scholarship, and fair use of the ideas and work of others. But this morality, for the most part, has been uncodified and is observed mainly in the laboratory and the study.

Efforts of colleges to exert a moral influence on their students have also been affected by new philosophies. In the view of the logical positivists, for example, no assertion can be accepted as fact unless it can be verified empirically; statements about moral, esthetic, or religious values are therefore considered unverifiable and thus without meaning. Relativists cannot accept the notion of universally applicable morals and values

because they believe that such concepts are true only for the individuals and groups that ascribe to them. Similarly, the existentialists, who emphasize the importance of being and the responsibilities of individuals to exercise free, personal choice in all aspects of their lives, find the idea of externally imposed morality and values untenable. Expectations that colleges play a greater role in the value formation of students is also thwarted by the single-minded dominance of an orientation to cognitive rationality that is sometimes found in American colleges and universities. Bernard Murchland (1976, p. 24) describes the effect of that orientation as follows: "The principal trait of cognitive rationality, and what most sets it off from the liberal arts tradition is its stance of value neutrality. It is nourished by an ideology and supported by a methodology that shields it from the domain of values with a veritable arsenal of carefully worked-out distinctions: subjective-objective, rational-emotive, ought-is, and so forth. These distinctions are guaranteed to keep what counts as truly knowable on one side of the hyphenations, with what is merely felt on the other." The regrettable implication of such distinctions is that values have no legitimate place in institutions concerned primarily with knowledge that is acquired through science and learned cognitively.

The new philosophies and the attitudes they engender have not totally eliminated or replaced the older, more traditional views of what is virtuous and valuable. But they severely complicate the role that colleges might play in helping their students develop values of their own. Beginning in the early 1900s, faculty members gave up responsibility for supervising student conduct and such matters became administrative concerns, thus separating moral and ethical behavior of students from academic concerns of the educational enterprise. And finally, in the face of challenges to college authority that were part of the student dissent of the 1960s, what remained of the influence that colleges once exercised over the personal values of students *in loco parentis* were often either compromised or greatly diminished. Edward Eddy (1977, p. 8) sums up the consequences this way: "New values have emerged—autonomy, tolerance, personal freedom. Old values—responsibility, community,

integrity have declined. But more important, the new values are not well understood and defined."

Many of the new values came with changes in the general society. As the population became concentrated in the cities, individuals had to make more accommodations to the needs and demands of others. To the extent that such accommodations have limited people in their ability to satisfy personal preferences, they have placed a premium on personal autonomy and freedom. With the growth of the nation, it has become difficult for people to identify, much less adopt, national values. Instead, the country and its large cities are cut down to personal size by each individual through affiliation with neighborhoods, clubs, associations, churches, and other less massive units. It is to these associations and, although less often than in the past, to their own families that men and women turn for value orientation and reinforcement.

It is not surprising, then, that the American people are confused by multiflanked assaults on their convictions about who they are, what they should cherish, and what they can do without. Helping people to overcome that confusion, to acquire a sense of their own humaneness, to say nothing of an appreciation for an inherent order in the universe, has been a charge to America's colleges and universities from the beginning. Although they are now themselves more diverse, the knowledge that they draw on for their instruction is still regarded as sufficiently unified to somehow anchor fundamental values that can be relied on as we continue efforts to build a humane, modern society.

Renewed Interest

There are increasing signs that an explicit concern for values in education is missed. Last year, 84 percent of the parents of public school children favored instruction in the schools that would deal with morals and moral behavior (Gallup, April 18, 1976), and colleges are increasingly also being asked to play a more active role in helping undergraduates to shape their values.

For 62 percent of the undergraduates participating in the 1976 Carnegie Council Survey, for example, "formulating

values and goals of my life" were "essential" outcomes of their education, and for an additional 31 percent (for a total of 93 percent) that outcome was "very important" (Carnegie Council Surveys, 1975-1976). In rating outcomes of college education, 83 percent of the faculty members checked "firm moral values" as "essential" or "very important" (Carnegie Council Surveys, 1975-1976).

These student and faculty interests notwithstanding, do colleges really have a role to play in the development of student values? Increasingly, educational leaders say they do. Derek Bok, president of Harvard, points out that "every business man and lawyer, every public servant and doctor will pass through our colleges, and most will attend our professional schools as well. If other sources of ethical values have declined in influence, educators have a responsibility to contribute in any way they can to the moral development of their students" (Bok, 1976, p. 26).

Morality and Values of the College Campus

All of the major controversies on American college campuses are centered on moral issues. Charges of the abridgment of personal freedom, of physical abuse of persons, of the misuse of resources or authority, of prejudice or discrimination in student admissions or faculty appointments and advancement, of cheating, or of misappropriating work and credit that belong to others are some of the many campus issues that are morally based. Some of them are uniquely relevant to the college itself, but many involve standards that are appropriate both to a college and to any democratic, pluralistic society.

To meet such standards, members of the college might be encouraged to cultivate certain traits and abilities. The following are examples:

In scholarship, they should
> Respect facts and know how to get them
> Recognize and practice logical analysis
> Develop an obligation to explore alternative explanations
> Recognize consequences of facts for the survival and quality of life of humans

In relationships with one another, they should
  Be sensitive to the feelings and sensitivities of others
  Be tolerant of other points of view
  Be civil in discussion
  Be honest in the presentation of facts, goals, and explanations
  Be supportive of individual freedom of expression

They should avoid
  Simplification of complicated issues
  Evaluating individual persons on the basis of stereotypes

They should value
  Merit in the personality and performance of others
  Fair play in competition for credits, awards, and honors
  Fairness in debate
  The cultural heritage of our civilization

A college's contributions to the development of student values is not made just by faculty members in front of classrooms or even by faculty members as living models of ideal educated men and women. A more profound influence is made by the character and life of the college itself. In his surveys of students and alumni of Haverford College, Douglas Heath (1968) found that they counted as one of the college's great strengths its insistence that students integrate both the intellectual and moral components of their education. The insistence was not manifested by edict. Instead, it was a part of the atmosphere of the total college environment. This finding led Heath to speculate that "A community that has an ideal or vision has, in effect, expectations of what its members are to become. Such ideals or expectations, so out of fashion nowadays, may be more silent than vocal; they may work their effects outside of awareness; they may constitute the invisible college. . . . And when such expectations are consistently expressed in all structures and activities of the institution, then different communal experiences may mutually reinforce one another" (Heath, 1968, pp. 242, 243).

The creation of the kind of community Heath described involves, first of all, a clarity of institutional mission. If certain

values are to be emphasized, they, too, need to be well understood by everyone in the college. A religiously supported college such as Haverford will have a much easier time identifying such values than a public college or a private college with either no or very loose ties to a denomination, but the task is probably not totally impossible at any institution. Creating the kind of community Heath has in mind also requires some attention to scale. It cannot evolve readily in institutions where students are not able to communicate with one another or with their professors easily and with some regularity. Large institutions, therefore, may have difficulty creating and sustaining a communal atmosphere unless they find ways to develop effective subcolleges or other small units that make close daily person-to-person contacts possible.

Values of the Academic Tradition

American higher education does have intrinsic potentials for exerting wholesome, nonreligious influences on students' values fully in keeping with the highest intellectual traditions.

At the center of college and university value systems is truth, sought not only as an end in itself but also because it leads to other truths and because it can be used as the basis for making choices among a range of ideas, policies, and day-to-day decisions.

Related to the academic community's esteem for truth is its reverence for intellectual freedom and its tolerance for ideas that may threaten one's own beliefs or even welfare. In 1975, 85.6 percent of the faculty in the United States agreed that "Faculty members should be free to present in class any idea that they consider relevant, however much I may disagree with their views" (Carnegie Council Surveys, 1975-1976). Another large proportion (71.1 percent) agreed that scientists should publish their findings regardless of the possible consequences. Such attitudes are not expressions of status-related values, but rather of functional requirements for a society in which truth is to be discovered, tested, and defended. Off the campus, these attitudes foster tolerance, open-mindedness, civility, and courage in confronting unfamiliar or disturbing ideas.

Another set of values that are integral to the academic

enterprise involves rewarding persons on the basis of the merits of their work above any other consideration. Thus 74.5 percent of the faculty participating in the Carnegie Council's 1975 survey disagreed with the proposition that "the only basis for salary differentiation among faculty in the same rank should be seniority," and 88.1 percent disagreed with the notion that "the normal academic requirements should be relaxed in appointing members of minority groups to the faculty here." Related to these values are concepts that one should be rewarded only for work one performs, that the rules for grading and faculty evaluations should be clear and even-handedly applied, and that procedures for evaluation and determining rewards do not disadvantage specific learners or groups of learners.

Such values as these—truth, freedom, and fairness in the award of honors and material benefits—if strictly observed, can exert strong and important influences over undergraduates' lives. But "can" is not "will," and it would be unfortunate for colleges to assume that because they have opportunities and capacities for moral influence they need do nothing more about it. They should not mistake the ideal for reality. The search for truth is the reigning activity of academic life, but truth, like many other virtues, can, without vigilance, become an end that justifies any means. Both inside and outside of American colleges, there is growing concern that there may be limits to the justification of seeking truth without due regard to social and moral consequences. Out of such concern, scientists decided to discuss with citizens representing the community of Cambridge appropriate means for defining limits on genetic research at Harvard and M.I.T. And, at annual meetings of the American Sociological Association and American Psychological Association last fall, many participants reportedly expressed concern for "deception, deceit, manipulation, disguise, covert operations, and misrepresentations" resorted to by social scientists to get "honest" answers to their questions. They also expressed a need for "increased ethical scrutiny" to ensure that the human subjects of research would be protected from possible harm as a result of such research ("A Moral Crusade," 1976). Rewards commensurate with merit are advocated, but the summer of

1976 was marked by reports of widespread cheating in the national military academies, and competition for the few open places in some graduate and professional schools is cited as explanation for high incidences of cheating elsewhere in higher education. Independence is heralded as a virtue of the educated mind but is not fully honored. Perry (1968) reports that "where independence of mind is demanded of authority, its forms can be mastered and 'handed in' while the spirit remains obediently conformist. As a student said of his performance on an examination, 'Well, I decided to be in favor of that book they asked about, but I did not forget to be balanced.' " In 1976, 61.3 percent of the nation's college undergraduates agreed that "It is possible to get good grades without really understanding the material." And 47.5 percent agreed that "Many successful students make it at my college by 'beating the system' rather than studying" (Carnegie Council Surveys, 1975-1976). Such lessons may be more enduring than those found in lectures or textbooks.

We believe that, although the members of academic communities are human and have no corner on the morality market, the ideals of the academic tradition, particularly those concerned with respect for truth and intellectual freedom, provide a reasonable basis for an influence worthy of being generated by our nation's colleges. But if colleges are to assume a major role in the value development of undergraduates they need to be more vigorous than ever before in articulating the ideals of the academic tradition (with due regard for appropriate nonacademic issues and concerns) and in insisting that those ideals be honored to the fullest extent possible by all members of the college community.

In its report *Dissent and Disruption* (1971a), the Carnegie Commission on Higher Education advocated that every college should adopt, with the participation of all of its parts, a clear statement of the rights and responsibilities of the members of the institution. More broadly, Eric Ashby has advocated a "Hippocratic Oath" for the academic profession that might make faculty members more fully aware of the importance of their responsibilities as teachers (in Urban, 1977, p. 213). Such

efforts are overdue in American colleges and universities, and we would urge, first of all, that the American Association of University Professors, which has been relatively successful in defining the rights and privileges of faculty members of American colleges and universities, renew efforts of its members to develop an academic code of ethics. Such a code would be an essential, if modest, first step in generating faculty awareness of their responsibilities to their profession and to the influence of their own attitudes and conduct on the values of their students.

We also urge individual colleges and universities to adopt some basic principles that will be observed relative to the rights and responsibilities of faculty, students, administrators, staff, and trustees on their own campuses in matters involving the educational process and requirements of the search for truth. We would not expect every college to express the same values as a result of such activity—at least not in the same way. But among those that might be included would be:

- Fair and accurate representation to the public and to students of the mission, offerings, facilities, and resources of the college
- Freedom of speech, press, peaceful assembly and association, and political beliefs; and freedom from personal force and violence, threats of violence, and personal abuse
- The right of each member of the institution to organize his or her own personal life and behavior, so long as it does not violate the law or agreements voluntarily entered into and does not intervene with the rights of others or the educational process
- Admission to, employment by, and promotion within the campus in accord with provisions against discrimination
- Obligation to respect the freedom to teach, to learn, and to conduct research and publish findings in the spirit of free inquiry
- Freedom from institutional censorship and individual or group intolerance of the opinions of others
- The right of members to be judged on the basis of individual merit and character, not as representatives of a race, sex, na-

tional heritage, religious denomination, or any other grouping that can be stereotyped
- The right of the teacher to determine the specific content of his or her course, within defined course objectives
- Responsibility of the teachers not to depart significantly from their areas of competence or to divert significant time to material extraneous to the subject matter of their courses
- Obligation of faculty members to meet their classes regularly and on time
- Responsibility of faculty members to set aside certain hours each week for consultation with students and to be present and available to students at the times thus designated
- Obligation not to interfere with any member's freedom to hear and to study unpopular and controversial views on intellectual and public issues
- Recognition and awards based on the merit and amount of each member's own individual efforts
- Fair use of the time, services, and resources of college and obligation to avoid conflict of interest and improper or dual compensation for effort and time in pursuit of external interests

The development of a statement of rights and responsibilities is at once functional, in the sense that it makes the expectations of an institution with respect to the conduct of its members explicit, and instructional, in the sense that it reflects the values considered important to the educational enterprise and the life of the college. For both purposes, it is essential that such statements be accompanied by the development of fair and effective procedures for handling charges of violations. The lessons to be learned from the existence of such statements that are ignored or unfairly enforced are unworthy of any college that presumes to academic respectability.

In line with suggestions made by the Carnegie Commission in *Dissent and Disruption* (1971a), the appropriate procedures would be to handle minor infringements of standards of personal conduct by advice and admonitions from students, faculty members, department chairmen, deans, and presidents. In more

serious cases, judgment and recommendation of penalties should be made by committees of students or faculty or both.

Values and Instruction

There is congruence of moral- and value-oriented education advocated in this section of our commentary and the advantages of broad learning experiences and interdisciplinary study that should be recognized. Earl McGrath and Derek Bok both argue for the introduction of problem-oriented courses into the curriculum on grounds that such courses inevitably require students and their teachers to consider moral consequences of solutions and the value ranking of competing objectives. McGrath (1976, p. 13) offers as one example, public policy related to ecological matters: "One has only to follow the controversial debates on [this subject] to observe that although a large body of technical knowledge is usually involved the decisions rest on issues involving human values. After all the facts are presented, some intelligent persons will believe it more important to preserve for future generations the natural beauty of our forests, fields, and streams, while others will place a higher value on the immediate satisfaction of our energy needs at low cost through the practice of strip mining. Similar alternate categories of priorities could be made for each issue on which society must reach a decision. They would reveal the fact that as indispensable as it may be, factual knowledge is not enough."

The values and moral development of students are also strongly influenced, as Martin Trow (1976, p. 21) points out, by "the teacher as a person, both through his personal relationships with students and in his role as a model of the seeker of knowledge, for understanding, and for the truth (with a small *t*)." It is difficult and perhaps unwise to attempt to institutionalize this faculty influence. It is most effective and valid when it results from the quality of institutional performance and student-teacher interactions. However, colleges should pay some attention to two problems. One is that students may actually be too distant from their professors much of the time, and such distance makes it impossible for them to acquire more than a superficial impression of the character of their professors and

the attitudes they have toward their discipline, their work, their colleagues, and their students. (Of course, when professors are mediocre or deficient in qualities worthy of emulation, such distance may be beneficial.) The other problem is that because faculty members rarely teach outside of their own departments some of those who have the most to offer to their students in terms of personal influence and example may be known to relatively few undergraduates. To overcome the first of these problems, undergraduates should be given ample opportunities to experience the values of academic tradition at close range. Such opportunities ideally would include working closely with faculty members in independent learning projects, tutorials, and seminars. To partially solve the second problem, we suggest that the example of a campus tradition once observed at the University of California at Davis be considered for adoption by other colleges. Each year, students invited a member of the senior faculty to present for the entire student body a "last lecture"—the lecture one would give if it were the last one he or she would present to undergraduates. The topic was left open, but the object was to allow particularly popular lecturers to share their personal beliefs and attitudes with undergraduates throughout the student body.

To some extent, every academic discipline has its own value system. Moreover, most academic disciplines inevitably raise issues that ought to be confronted in a balanced fashion as a part of undergraduates' education. Ideally, we believe that, in courses where it is relevant, material should be provided that identifies the moral issues raised by research and practice within the discipline providing the course and explores the relationship between the discipline and the world at large. Every major should ideally offer a capstone course oriented to the moral and ethical concerns of the discipline. But in expressing this ideal, we have some hesitation, for we realize that such courses would be immensely difficult to prepare and that they could easily degenerate into doctrinaire platitudes. They should be the departmental or divisional equivalent of the courses in "moral philosophy" offered by college presidents in the early years of American higher education. Therefore, if they are offered at all,

they should be presented by a senior faculty member within a department who is widely respected by undergraduates and recognized as a thoughtful and provocative lecturer or discussion leader.

Conclusion

Although the pluralistic society outside the campus no longer can be identified with a single set of values and principles that might be instilled in American youth, colleges are by no means relieved of a continuing responsibility for helping students to identify and adopt values of their own. The resources of the campuses for such efforts are very rich. The basic data is found in abundance in the history and literature that fills the shelves of every college library and in the experience and values of the people whom students see every day as professors, administrators, and fellow students. Beyond this data, there is a tradition of academic life, centered on the search for truth, that imposes codes of conduct on the campuses that have application in other situations as well.

Those who assert that colleges should exert no influence on the personal values and morality of their students are, therefore, in error. Colleges cannot help but have an influence. They have such influences because they immerse their students in value-laden experience and teaching every day. The problem is that students do not always have proper guidance in taking advantage of the lessons on values and morality that are there to be learned. Too often they must learn them on their own. Often they do not learn well, or they reach the wrong conclusions from the data at hand. What is needed now is for colleges and universities not only to appreciate the extent of the influence they inevitably exert on the value orientation of youth but also to accept responsibility for consciously incorporating that influence into their educational endeavors.

14

Implementing Curricular Policy and Change

The curriculum is very much a part of the daily life of a college or university. It determines many of the things students and faculty members do and takes much of its character from their private hopes and dreams and the limits of their personal interests, talents, and energies. Just describing the curriculum and its components leaves this daily life undisturbed. Suggesting from the outside that it needs evaluation or change, on the other hand, is an intrusion likely to be resisted. And those who make such suggestions need to understand in advance that the feasibility of anything they propose depends almost totally on the acquiescence of those personally affected by whatever recommendations may be made.

Measuring Effectiveness

In addition to their need to establish missions and goals for their educational programs, institutions need to determine appropriate measures of their effectiveness in meeting those goals. While many institutions are under frequent assessment by accrediting, licensing, and other external agencies, they also need measurement criteria of their own.

Measuring the effectiveness of education has become a subject of growing interest[1] and will be the subject of a forthcom-

[1]See, for example, Dressel and Associates (1961), Withey (1971), Juster (1975), Taubman and Wales (1974), Hodgkinson, Hurst, and Levine (1975), Dressel (1976), and H. Bowen (1977).

ing report on the benefits of college attendance that is being
prepared by the Carnegie Council on Policy Studies in Higher
Education. In his work on consequences of higher education,
Howard Bowen (1977, p. 27) describes six kinds of sources of
information that are often used for this purpose:

1. Investigations of changes in the achievements, personalities,
   attitudes, and behavior of students during the college years
2. Surveys of the view of students and alumni about their college experiences
3. Censuses, public opinion polls, and other explorations of attitudes, economic status, and behavior of adult respondents
4. Multiple regression studies for particular populations incorporating many variables and designed to sort out the separate
   impact of education in income, career choice, health, voting
   behavior, religion, and so on
5. Case histories of individuals
6. Critical and analytical studies without empirical data

Virtually all of these studies have shortcomings. Bowen says
"some of the studies are out of date or limited to atypical single
institutions. Some, for want of better data, use inappropriate
statistics or rely on inadequate or biased samples. Some draw
upon verbalizations of attitudes, opinions, and behavior that
rely on uncertain memory and unreliable subjective evaluations
of respondents. Some use tests or survey instruments that are
cruder than they purport to be. Some studies, especially in the
public opinion field, are inadequate because the methods were
chosen for purposes other than the study of higher education.
Finally, interpretations of results are questionable, because the
studies are not solidly based on widely accepted theory about
the causation of change during college" (H. Bowen, 1977, pp.
27-28).

    For purposes of individual colleges, many of these ap-
proaches are unacceptable in another respect—they are expensive. Techniques that might be more readily available for institutional measurement of effectiveness are:

1. Comparing students' performance on comprehensive examinations administered by neutral agencies or institutions at the time students enter with performance on appropriate examinations at the time they graduate (not inexpensive, but a relatively uncomplicated procedure)
2. Making annual comparison of rates of student admission, retention and attrition
3. Collecting basic information concerning alumni:
    a. Occupational choices
    b. Participation in governmental, community, and voluntary activities
    c. Admission to graduate schools
    d. Publication of writings
    e. Awards and honors received
    f. Number of children and their educational status
    g. Self-perceptions as to happiness and satisfaction with education

In utilizing these techniques, colleges should attempt to collect comparable data at relatively frequent intervals over long periods of time. And, where surveys are used, some effort should be made to include the same people (or same types of people) in each consecutive survey and to use the same questions as long as they are relevant or significant.

Colleges might also consider forming visiting committees of alumni and faculty from other institutions to participate in evaluation efforts, but for most institutions the margin of benefit provided by such committees over the reviews conducted in accrediting procedures may be small.

Evaluation of the effectiveness of an institution is an essential part of the management function. It should be carried out continuously on behalf of a college's governing board by its president and academic leadership.

As we have indicated earlier in this commentary, large academic units within the institution should conduct periodic reviews of their own effectiveness and the effectiveness of the departments within their purview. These evaluations may well

entail such matters as the effective utilization of faculty and budget, enrollment and attrition, and, where it may be appropriate, research achievements. But they should, above all, compare the activities and outcomes of educational programs with their stated objectives. At present, adequate measures for such comparisons may not be available at most campuses and may need to be developed jointly by the units to be evaluated and the officials making assessments.

At the course level, evaluation should be made by departments, taking into account as much evidence as can be collected, including review of course objectives, assignments to students, examinations, and grading. Consideration should also be given to student evaluations of professors and their courses.

Administering General Education

The general understanding and advanced-level skill requirements for graduation are specified institution-wide—by the governing board or the faculty senate or council. The number of distribution or breadth courses included in general education is also prescribed institution-wide. Where general education is a fully prescribed component of the curriculum, it is typically the responsibility of the principal academic officer of the college. Where it involves only one or two general understanding requirements and distribution requirements, administration of general education is decentralized or shared by a college-wide academic officer and the departments that offer courses that are accepted as meeting distribution requirements. As a general rule, no general education courses are offered directly by a college-wide division.

Some institutions might experiment with separate administrative units for general education. The advantages of such units are that they can give general education more coherence, can develop instruction exclusively for meeting general education objectives, can encourage interdisciplinary programs, and can evaluate general education activity on its own terms, and not as a part of departmental offerings. The Chicago College was one example of such a unit.

As we have mentioned in another context, the almost in-

surmountable obstacle is that general education is not highly regarded by discipline-oriented faculty members, and faculty members who participate in it outside their own department are sometimes at a disadvantage when they are considered for promotion by their departmental colleagues. Yet general education courses generate enrollments and are therefore important factors in departmental budgeting.

One way to overcome these problems would be to centralize the budgeting, financing, and evaluation of general education programs in an academic unit that has authority to:

- Approve or disapprove any new general education courses given in a department
- Allocate funding to departments or other academic units in amounts determined as general education's prorated share of the department's total instructional expense
- Periodically review all departmental courses or programs that undergraduates use to meet general education requirements and withdraw support for offerings that do not adequately meet general education objectives
- Initiate interdepartmental and extradepartmental instructional programs that meet general education objectives, compensating departments for their contributions to such programs
- Allocate funds to departments that wish temporarily to release faculty members from other instructional responsibilities in order to plan and develop new general education courses or programs

Initiating such procedures may be quite difficult on established campuses that have not already moved in this direction. To achieve it, the central administration must, in effect, assess each department's educational program and recapture departmental funds that are found to be utilized for general education instruction.

In its report *Reform on Campus,* the Carnegie Commission on Higher Education (1972d) noted that deans of graduate divisions in American universities have played key roles over the

years in setting standards and encouraging innovation for postgraduate education. Increasingly, colleges have assigned similar
functions to deans of undergraduate education, deans of instruction and the curriculum, and officers with other titles suggesting responsibilities at the undergraduate level. Such officers
could provide important centers of educational administration
wherever they exist, and, where they do not already exist, such
officers may be particularly essential as a counterbalance to the
sometimes unwarranted influence graduate divisions can exercise over the undergraduate curriculum.

Changing the Curriculum

Historically, there have been five major types of change in
American higher education (Levine, March 1976a).

1. *The establishment of new colleges.* This was the strategy used
   in the creation of Bennington College, Oakland University,
   Hampshire College, and Metropolitan State University.
2. *The development of innovative enclaves within existing institutions.* This involves setting aside a specific place in the curriculum for experimentation. The enclave may be an experimental subunit, such as the Meiklejohn College at the University of Wisconsin, the Chicago College developed at the
   University of Chicago in the 1930s and 1940s, and the General College at the University of Minnesota. It might be a
   period in the calendar reserved for experimentation, as is the
   case of the month-long winter term at Hampshire College.
   Such enclaves are relatively inexpensive, serve as institutional
   laboratories for experimentation, are easy to implement, and
   can be a source of institutional self-renewal if useful enclave
   programs diffuse throughout a campus, or if large numbers of
   faculty and students participate in both the enclave and the
   rest of the college. New College at the University of Alabama
   provides a more recent example. The disadvantage of innovative enclaves is that they can become isolated from the rest of
   the campus so that the changes they seek to realize may be
   prevented from becoming institution-wide.
3. *Holistic change.* This involves adoption of a major curriculum

change characterized by a unifying and coherent philosophy of education. Charles W. Eliot achieved it at Harvard, particularly in the establishment of the elective system, and Frank Aydelotte succeeded in reorienting Swarthmore to concern for the nonaverage student in the 1920s and 1930s. Examples are the Great Books program at St. John's, the reform of undergraduate education attempted with mixed success at Brown University in the 1960s, and the introduction of the competency curriculum at Sterling College. Of all forms of change, the holistic reform is the least common, the most efficient (since it involves substitution rather than adaptation or addition of new curriculum), the most difficult to get adopted, the least successful (particularly at large universities), and the most risky. If the change does not succeed, there is nothing else within the institution to fall back on.

4. *Piecemeal change.* This involves the adoption of minor curriculum changes, such as the elimination of language requirements, the adoption of an advanced placement program, and the mounting of new courses. It is the most common form of curriculum change and the easiest to implement. It is rarely undertaken as a part of a comprehensive, integrated educational philosophy. The initiation of core courses, adaptation of general education requirements, and development of interdisciplinary courses and broad learning experiences are examples of such change.

5. *Changes on the periphery.* These involve experimentation and alternatives provided in educational institutions off the campus. An autonomous "free university" or counseling service are examples. Such programs help to identify new needs of undergraduates and may provide unusual examples of ways in which such needs can be met. They can also provide competition to traditional colleges and, where they are successful, provide incentives for introducing new approaches and programs.

Curriculum change typically involves four stages—recognition of need, planning and formulation of a solution, implementation and initiation of the plan, and institutionalization of the

change (Levine, March 1976a). Unfortunately, these processes cannot, in all cases, take place in an orderly fashion. Those who perceive the need may not be the same as those who initiate a plan or formulate a solution. The outcome ultimately depends on how well a change fits the institutions in which it is attempted. When the change offers significant advantages, it will be incorporated into a college either through diffusion or through the efforts of a formally recognized academic or administrative unit. In general, quiet, continual, orderly change is usually more effective than highly publicized extensive change attempted all at once.

Who Does What?

Responsibility for curricular policy and change resides with many different individuals and units within and without the college.

Governing Boards

Governing boards have a responsibility for making the institutional mission an explicit instrument of educational policy for institutions of higher education. They may also:

- Have responsibility for making a periodic review of the educational programs of their institutions and determining ways in which the effectiveness of the curriculum and instruction are to be measured
- With the assistance of the faculty government and academic leadership, adopt a statement of objectives for the general educational programs of their institutions, and consider creating a centralized administrative unit to approve new courses and programs proposed for inclusion in general education, periodically review courses and programs offered for that purpose, and allocate funds to departments and academic divisions that provide general education instruction
- Select academic and administrative leaders who have demonstrated an interest in undergraduate instruction and curricular development
- Ask the administration and faculty where the institution

stands with respect to the seven areas of activity and concern we identified in Section One

Academic Leaders

Academic leaders, including college presidents, academic deans, and other members of the institution with significant responsibility for institution-wide educational policy, can define and periodically review the institution-wide mission, secure its adoption by governing boards, and encourage academic divisions and departments within the institution to develop statements of educational objectives appropriate to their endeavors. In addition, academic administrators may:

- Periodically review the educational programs of every academic division or department to discover programs that deserve special support and weaknesses that need correction.
- Identify current and emerging needs of individuals and society for special new educational programs that cannot be easily initiated by single academic divisions or departments, seek financial resources for developing such programs, and coordinate the cooperative efforts that may be required within the college to make the new programs effective.
- Attempt to realize savings of between 1 and 3 percent each year from existing programs to be used as a self-renewal fund for new expanded undergraduate education programs.
- Once new programs are introduced, give them ample time to prove their effectiveness. Too often, changes are judged ineffective before they have had a chance to prove themselves or adjust to unanticipated conditions.
- Exercise great care in the review of recommendations for faculty appointment and promotion, giving due consideration not only to personnel policies that may be involved in such matters but also to the effect of personnel decisions on curriculum and educational policy.
- Wherever it is feasible to do so, initiate cooperative efforts between the faculty of their colleges and neighboring high schools that will help to improve the elementary skills of high school graduates and entering college students.

- Explore the feasibility of cooperative arrangements with neighboring educational institutions for the purpose of broadening the availability of skill and occupational training that can be made available to their students, either as a supplement or as part of their undergraduate education.
- Make efforts to improve and give greater visibility to career and academic counseling services for undergraduates.
- Seek out opportunities to achieve desired long-term, institution-wide changes in educational policy by encouraging the efforts of individuals and small groups who can contribute to the realization of such objectives through the successful initiation and development of promising small-scale experiments and changes. On the whole, small incremental efforts may achieve more than large-scale reforms attempted all at once.

Working with faculty senates, councils or other groups with authority and responsibility for educational policy, the administrators and academic leaders of the college can also:

- Encourage the development of a "Bill of Rights and Responsibilities" for all members of the campus community.
- Permit students to petition for exemption from any graduation requirement for which specific objectives and/or educational content cannot be defined explicitly by the faculty.
- Grant exemptions to students who have satisfactorily demonstrated that they have met institution-wide requirements for graduation at another institution or through independent study. Where such requirements are normally met in degree-credit courses, exemption should be accompanied with the granting of college credit.
- Minimize time restraints in specifying requirements for graduation and for completion of general education components of the curriculum.
- Recognize majors created by students themselves with the advice of members of the faculty and majors that involve interdisciplinary perspectives. They might particularly encourage interdisciplinary majors that provide a basic foundation for groups of related occupations or professions.

- Systematically encourage improvement of teaching in colleges and keep faculty members informed of resources available to them for improving teaching skills and helping them to make effective use of new instructional methods and technology.
- Encourage graduate schools to offer doctor of arts or similar degrees for persons who intend to emphasize teaching rather than research during their professional careers and provide positions and opportunities for advancement to persons who hold such degrees.
- Encourage establishment of learning centers that can assist students in the improvement of the foundation skills for college-level learning and provide opportunities for independent, self-paced learning of the fundamentals of certain subjects that are taught in several different departments (for example, the first principles of statistics).
- Adopt a new form of transcript that indicates not only the courses and grades students receive but also how courses taken are distributed among the various components of the undergraduate curriculum.
- Provide pass-fail and pass-no credit grading options in addition to letter grades in any course involving the teaching of specific skills and competences whose mastery can be determined by performance or in courses that students who are not specializing might be afraid to enroll in if doing so would involve risking a good academic record.
- Provide on-campus compensatory education for students who need help in overcoming weaknesses in basic skills.
- In the absence of a central administrative division responsible for general education, faculty senates or councils should coordinate development of introductory courses for nonmajors in each broad subject field—for example, the social sciences or humanities. Such courses should cover the history, major concerns, and methods of inquiry that are characteristic of the subject field.
- Encourage development of broad learning experiences that draw on more than one discipline as alternatives to some or all discipline-based distribution requirements.

Departments of Instruction and Single-Subject Colleges

Departments of instruction and single-subject colleges can define the objectives of their majors and require members of their faculty to specifically define the objectives of their courses. They can also:

- In cases where they have approximately equal numbers of majors who plan to attend graduate school and majors that plan to terminate their formal education at the baccalaureate level, develop alternative majors to meet the needs of each group
- Develop introductory courses in their disciplines for non-majors
- Give adequate recognition to the contributions of members of their faculty who engage in general education programs or interdisciplinary instruction, participate in faculty development programs (as masters or learners), or develop courses that effectively utilize new methods of instruction or instructional technology
- Resist pressures to include in their majors more courses than constitute a reasonable share of the students' total undergraduate curriculum

Students

Students can take advantage of the resources not only of their own colleges but also of nearby institutions that can supplement their studies with skill and occupational training or other instruction that may be useful to them after graduation. They might also:

- Define and frequently review the personal objectives they hope to reach by going to college
- Take advantage of increasing opportunities to participate directly in the improvement of undergraduate education as members of committees developing curricular policy and by making contributions to the evaluation of teaching and faculty members at their institutions
- Consider the advantages of double majors or major-minor

combinations (if they are available) when the number of electives offered to them exceed the number they need for sampling the curriculum widely or for developing special personal skills and interests
- Make greater use than many of them now do of academic, vocational, and personal advising services offered by their institutions
- Take advantage of opportunities to combine education and work through cooperative education programs or internships
- Plan off-campus experiences that supplement or enrich classroom instruction

States

States that require public or private colleges to offer specific courses to undergraduates can, if they do not already do so, permit undergraduates to satisfy such requirements by passing an examination on the material to be covered, or by taking approved courses in such subjects in high schools or in authorized adult and continuing education programs.

State legislators should be sensitive to the possibility that legislation affecting college and university budgets and personnel policies also may impose undesirable restrictions on the development of the undergraduate curriculum. They should consult with college and university officials before passing any legislation that would even inadvertently result in the impossibility that certain subjects could be taught in at least some institutions in the state's system or would impair curricular flexibility through excess regulation or inadequate funding.

Accrediting Agencies

Accrediting agencies should continue to observe policies opposing standardization and conformity in higher education in the United States. In the interests of that policy, they should avoid unnecessary specificity in the description of programs that meet their standards. In their guides to institutions for self-evaluation, they should also avoid describing the process in terms that imply preference for dominant existing arrangements. The interest of these agencies in developing standards for evaluating nontraditional programs should be encouraged.

Learned Societies

Learned societies should follow the leadership of those organizations within their midst that have already made substantial efforts to improve undergraduate teaching, develop new educational materials, and stimulate discussion and improvement of the undergraduate curricula in their fields. In such efforts, they deserve the support of governmental agencies and of private foundations, but if such support is not forthcoming they should try to find resources of their own to use for such improvements.

Conclusion

If the undergraduate curriculum is a success in the United States —and in some respects it is—it is impossible to decide who should get the credit. Inside and outside the colleges, those responsible are numerous and often exert their influence in subtle but important ways. If the undergraduate curriculum is in trouble and needs reform—which in some instances is also the case—it is equally difficult to decide who has the biggest responsibility for making it better. In the preceding pages, we have attempted to suggest some of the things that certain people and certain groups are most able to do, or, for various reasons, have the clearest obligation to do. The major tasks are few but important. They are (1) to formulate more clearly the advanced learning skills necessary in college and provide better training in them; (2) to give more attention and use greater ingenuity in improving distribution requirements; (3) to make integrative courses a more central feature of intellectual activity—concentrating on broad structures of thought as well as on areas of more specific analysis; (4) to assist the primary and secondary schools in teaching basic skills and providing compensatory training in them, when necessary, at the college level; (5) to bridge the gap between thought and action and create more opportunities for students to understand the world of work; (6) to clarify and apply more precisely the essential moral principles of academic life for the sake of the integrity of campus life and for the contribution that can be made to the skills of citizenship more generally; and (7) to assert the corporate interests of the

academic community in the quality of the curriculum in its totality as well as in its component parts.

By performing these tasks, our colleges and universities can reassume initiatives and roles of leadership that may have been lost in an era of accommodation and reaction to rapid growth and change. They can assume a more active and less passive role in the development of the national character. And they can play an even more vital part in the life and learning of their undergraduates.

Appendix A

Special Studies and Consultation Relevant to This Commentary

*1. Special Studies Sponsored by the Carnegie Council
on Policy Studies in Higher Education*

To obtain historical perspective on our subject, the Carnegie Council on Policy Studies in Higher Education has commissioned a history of the undergraduate curriculum by Frederick Rudolph, Mark Hopkins Professor of History at Williams College. Entitled *Curriculum,* his book traces the development of undergraduate instruction and programs since 1636. The Carnegie Council also sponsored an analysis of the undergraduate curriculum directed by Robert Blackburn, with the assistance of Ellen Armstrong, Clifton Conrad, James Didham, and Thomas McKune, at the University of Michigan. This study involved an examination of the bachelor of arts degree requirements at 270 colleges and universities and a subsequent analysis of student transcripts at 10 selected institutions. The results of this study (cited in this commentary as *Blackburn et al.*) were published in 1976. The Council is also sponsoring work in progress by David Riesman, Henry Ford II Professor of Social Sciences at Harvard, who is preparing a handbook for students on the undergraduate curriculum and will write an essay assessing the prospects of recent curriculum developments in American higher education.

2. *Publications of the Carnegie Commission on Higher Education Related to the Undergraduate Curriculum*[1]

Reports of the Commission

Less Time, More Options: Education Beyond the High School. January 1971.

Reform on Campus: Changing Students, Changing Academic Programs. June 1972.

The Fourth Revolution: Instructional Technology in Higher Education. June 1972.

Toward a Learning Society: Alternate Channels to Life, Work, and Service. October 1973.

Sponsored reports and essays

Eric Ashby. *Any Person, Any Study: An Essay on Higher Education in the United States.*

Joseph Ben-David. *American Higher Education: Directions Old and New.*

Joseph Ben-David. *Centers of Learning: Britain, France, Germany, United States.*

Howard R. Bowen and Gordon K. Douglass. *Efficiency in Liberal Education: A Study of Comparative Instructional Costs and Different Ways of Organizing Teaching-Learning in a Liberal Arts College.*

Earl F. Cheit. *The Useful Arts and the Liberal Tradition.*

Everett C. Hughes, Barrie Thorne, Agostino M. DeBaggis, Arnold Gurin, and David Williams. *Education for the Professions of Medicine, Law, Theology, and Social Welfare.*

Carl Kaysen (Ed.). *Content and Context: Essays on College Education.*

Dwight R. Ladd. *Change in Educational Policy: Self Studies in Selected Colleges and Universities.*

Alexander Mood. *The Future of Higher Education: Some Speculations and Suggestions.*

Jack Morrison. *The Rise of the Arts on the American Campus.*

---

[1] All publications of the Carnegie Commission are available from McGraw-Hill Book Company, Box 402, Hightstown, New Jersey, 09520.

Herbert L. Packer and Thomas Ehrlich. *New Directions in Legal Education.*

Edgar Schein. *Professional Education: Some New Directions.*

Stephen H. Spurr. *Academic Degree Structures: Innovative Approaches—Principles of Reform in Degree Structures in the United States.*

Alain Touraine. *The Academic System in American Society.*

3. Individuals and Members of Advisory Groups Consulted in the Preparation of this Commentary

Dorothy Abrahamse
Department of History
California State University at Long Beach

Alison Bernstein
Fund for the Improvement of Postsecondary Education

Merle Borrowman
Dean, School of Education
University of California, Berkeley

Paul E. Bragdon
President
Reed College

Marvin Bressler
Professor of Sociology
Princeton University

Charles Bunting
Fund for the Improvement of Postsecondary Higher Education

John H. Chandler
President
Scripps College

Earl Cheit
Dean, Graduate School of Business Administration
University of California, Berkeley

Arthur M. Cohen
President
Center for the Study of Community Colleges
Professor of Higher Education
University of California, Los Angeles

Marty Corry
Nexus

Joseph P. Cosand
Director
Center for Higher Education
University of Michigan

K. Patricia Cross
Senior Research Psychologist
Educational Testing Service

Eugene E. Dawson
President
University of Redlands

A. Robert Dehart
President
DeAnza College

William B. Fretter
Chairman, Academic Senate
University of California, Berkeley

Donald R. Gerth
President
California State College at
Dominguez Hills

Virgil W. Gillenwater
Executive Vice-President
Northern Arizona University

John Gillis
Academic Vice-President
Chapman College

Richard Gilman
President
Occidental College

Richard Hendrix
Fund for the Improvement of
Postsecondary Education

Richard L. Hoffman
Vice-President for Academic
Affairs
Mars Hill College

Stephen Horn
President
California State University, Long
Beach

David Justice
Fund for the Improvement of
Postsecondary Education

Helen Kelley
President
Immaculate Heart College

J. Terrence Kelly
Dean of Administration and
Open College
Miami-Dade Community College

John Laster
Nexus

R. Jan Lecroy
Vice-Chancellor for Academic
Affairs
Dallas County Community
College District

Jane Lichtman
Nexus

R. A. Lombardi
President
Saddleback Community College

T. R. McConnell
School of Education
University of California, Berkeley

Frederick W. Ness
President
Association of American Colleges

Paul J. Olscamp
President
Western Washington State College

Roderic B. Park
Provost and Dean of the College
of Letters and Science
University of California, Berkeley

Gertrude K. Patch
Lone Mountain College

Richard C. Richardson, Jr.
Professor and Director
Center for Higher and Adult
Education
Arizona State University

David Riesman
Henry Ford II Professor of Social
Sciences
Harvard University

Sheldon Rothblatt
Professor of History
University of California, Berkeley

Arman Sarafian
President
La Verne College

Edwin F. Taylor
Massachusetts Institute of
Technology

Michael Scriven
University of California, Berkeley

Neil Smelser
Department of Sociology
University of California, Berkeley

Martin Trow
Director
Center for Research and
Development in Higher
Education
University of California, Berkeley

Virginia B. Smith
President
Vassar College

Barbara M. White
President
Mills College

James K. Sours
President
Southern Oregon State College

James Q. Wilson
Professor of Government
Harvard University

4. Surveys and Catalog Analyses Used in the Preparation of This Commentary

Throughout the commentary, we have relied heavily on the Carnegie Commission Surveys of 1969-70 and the Carnegie Council's 1975-1976 surveys of faculty, graduate students, and undergraduates in the United States. All of these surveys were conducted under the direction of Martin Trow, now Director of the Center for Research and Development in Higher Education at the University of California, Berkeley. The 1975-1976 surveys produced tabulated responses of 25,000 faculty members, 25,000 undergraduates, and 25,000 graduate students. The 1969-70 surveys were conducted by the Carnegie Commission on Higher Education with the cooperation of the American Council on Education and the support of the Office of Education, U.S. Department of Health, Education and Welfare. They yielded tabulated responses from 60,000 faculty members, 70,000 undergraduates, and 30,000 graduate students. In this commentary, the surveys are cited as *Carnegie Council Surveys, 1975-1976, Carnegie Surveys, 1969-70,* and *Carnegie Surveys, 1975-76.*

The Carnegie Council Staff has also conducted a detailed

analysis of the catalogs of 270 colleges and universities to identify curriculum differences between associate and bachelor degrees, and curriculum differences among professional schools and other major academic divisions within institutions. In this study, the staff was able to identify institutional practices in such matters as admissions, uses of alternative instructional methods, and grading. This study is cited as *Catalog Study, 1976.*

Much of the Council staff's research will be included in another major work on the undergraduate curriculum. This is a *Handbook on Undergraduate Education,* which will be issued as a companion to this commentary and to the history of the curriculum by Professor Rudolph. References to the chapters of the *Handbook* relevant to subjects discussed in this commentary are noted at the end of each section of the commentary. The *Handbook on Undergraduate Education* will be available early in 1978.

5. Institutions Visited and Campus Hosts

To gather information for uses in this commentary and the forthcoming *Handbook on Undergraduate Curriculum,* visits were made to the following campuses. At each campus, many administrators, faculty members, and students were interviewed.

Amherst College
    Arnold Collery, Dean of the Faculty

Antioch College
    Robert Parker, Director, Cooperative Program

Bennington College
    Tom Parker, formerly of Bennington, now Chicago, Illinois

Brown University
    Margie Abbot, Office of Dean of the Faculty

Capitol Higher Education Service, Hartford, Connecticut
    Donald Barnes

University of California, Berkeley
    Edward L. Feder, Executive Officer, Budget and Planning, College of Letters and Science

University of California, Santa Cruz
    Dean McHenry, Chancellor Emeritus

University of Chicago
    Charles D. O'Connell, Jr., Vice-President and Dean of Students
    Charles Oxnard, Dean of the College

Claremont Colleges
    Joseph Platt, President
    E. Howard Brooks, Provost

Coe College, Iowa
    J. Preston Cole, Dean of the College

Columbia University
    Eugene Rice, Chairman, History Department

Flathead Valley Community College
    Bruce Johnson, Dean of Instruction

Hampshire College
    Barbara Turlington, Dean

Harvard College
    David Riesman, Henry Ford II Professor of Social Sciences
    Paul Doty, Wallinckrodt Professor of Biochemistry
    Henry Rosovsky, Dean of the Faculty
    Edward Wilcox, Director of General Education Programs and Freshman Seminars
    Francis Pipkin, Associate Dean of Faculty

University of Iowa
    May Brodbeck, Vice-President, Academic Affairs

Fiorello H. La Guardia Community College
    Martin Moed, Dean of Faculty
    Janet Lieberman, Assistant Dean of Faculty

University of Michigan
　　Marc Ross, Director, Residential College
　　Zelda Gamson, Co-Director, Residential College

University of Minnesota
　　Richard P. Bailey, Dean, General College

Minnesota State College System
　　Emily Hannah, Vice-Chancellor for Academic Affairs

Oakland University
　　Frederick Obear, Vice-President for Academic Affairs

Princeton University
　　Neil Rudenstine, Provost
　　Marvin Bressler, Chairman, Sociology Department

Simon's Rock
　　A. Perry Whitmore, formerly of Simon's Rock

University of South Florida
　　Carl D. Biggs, Vice-President for Academic Affairs

Sterling College
　　Carol Gene Brownlee, Dean

Swarthmore College
　　Theodore Friend, President

Technical Career Institutes
　　Nathan Buch

Appendix B

A Catalog of Goals
of Higher Education

The following catalog of goals was developed by Howard Bowen for his study on *Investment in Learning: The Individual and Social Value of American Higher Education.*[1] The goals have been identified in a reading of more than 1,000 goal statements in the writings of noted educational philosophers and critics of the past and present, reports of public commissions and faculty committees, and statement of leading educators in speeches, articles, and institutional reports.

I. Goals for Individual Students

    A. Cognitive Learning

        1. *Verbal skills*. Ability to comprehend through reading and listening and to speak and write clearly and correctly. Effectiveness in the organization and presentation of ideas in writing and in discussion. Possibly some acquaintance with a foreign language.

        2. *Quantitative skills*. Ability to understand elementary concepts of mathematics and to handle simple statistical data and statistical reasoning. Possibly some understanding of the rudiments of accounting and the uses of computers.

3. *Substantive knowledge.* Acquaintance with the cultural heritage of the West and possibly of other traditions. Awareness of the contemporary world of philosophy, natural science, art, literature, social change, and social issues. Command of vocabulary, facts, and principles in one or more selected fields of knowledge.

4. *Rationality.* Ability and disposition to think logically on the basis of useful assumptions. Capacity to see facts and events objectively—distinguishing the normative, ideological, and emotive from the positive and factual. Disposition to weigh evidence, evaluate facts and ideas critically, and to think independently. Ability to analyze and synthesize.

5. *Intellectual tolerance.* Freedom of the mind. Openness to new ideas. Willingness to question orthodoxy. Appreciation of intellectual and cultural diversity. Intellectual curiosity. Ability to deal with complexity and ambiguity. Historical perspective and cosmopolitan outlook. Understanding of the limitations of knowledge and thought.

6. *Esthetic sensibility.*[2] Knowledge, interest, and responsiveness to literature, the fine arts, and natural beauty.

7. *Creativeness.* Imagination and originality in formulating new hypotheses and ideas and in the producing of new works of art.

8. *Intellectual integrity.* Understanding of the idea of "truth" and of its contingent nature. Disposition to seek and speak the truth. Conscientiousness of inquiry and accuracy in reporting results.

9. *Wisdom.* Balanced perspective, judgment, and prudence.

10. *Lifelong learning.* Love of learning. Sustained intellectual interests.

---

[2] Esthetic sensibility is often classified under affective development rather than cognitive learning. It contains elements of both.

B. Emotional and Moral Development
   1. *Personal self-discovery.* Knowledge of one's own talents, interests, values, aspirations, and weaknesses. Discovery of unique personal identity.
   2. *Psychological well-being.* Progress toward the ability to "understand and confront with integrity the nature of the human condition" (Perry, 1968, p. 201). Sensitivity to deeper feelings and emotions combined with emotional stability. Ability to express emotions constructively. Appropriate self-assertiveness, sense of security, self-confidence, self-reliance, decisiveness, spontaneity. Acceptance of self and others.
   3. *Human sympathy.* Understanding of human beings. Humane outlook. Capacity for empathy, thoughtfulness, compassion, respect, tolerance, and cooperation toward others including persons of different backgrounds. Democratic and nonauthoritarian disposition. Skill in two-way communication with others.
   4. *Morality.* A valid and internalized but not dogmatic set of moral principles. Moral sensitivity and courage. Sense of social consciousness and social responsibility.
   5. *Religious interest.* Serious and thoughtful exploration of purpose, value, and meaning.
   6. *Refinement of taste, conduct, and manner.*

C. Practical Competence
   1. *Traits of value in practical affairs generally.* Virtually all of the goals included under cognitive learning and emotional and moral development are applicable to practical affairs. In addition, the following traits, which are more specifically related to achievement in practical affairs, may be mentioned:
      a. *Need for achievement.* Motivation toward accomplishment. Initiative, energy, drive, persistence, self-discipline.
      b. *Future orientation.* Ability to plan ahead and to be prudent in risk taking.

       c. *Adaptability.* Tolerance of new ideas or practices. Willingness to accept change. Versatility and resourcefulness in coping with problems and crises. Capacity to learn from experience. Willingness to negotiate and compromise. Keeping options open.

       d. *Leadership.* Capacity to win the confidence of others, willingness to assume responsibility, organizational ability, decisiveness, disposition to take counsel.

2. *Citizenship.* Understanding of and commitment to democracy. Knowledge of governmental institutions and procedures. Awareness of major social issues. Ability to withstand propaganda and political argumentation. Disposition and ability to participate actively in civic, political, economic, professional, educational, and other voluntary organizations. Orientation toward international understanding and world community. Ability to deal with bureaucracies. Disposition toward law observance.

3. *Economic productivity.* Knowledge and skills needed for first job and for growth in productivity through experience and on-the-job training. Adaptability and mobility. Sound career decisions. Capacity to bring humanistic values to the workplace and to derive meaning from work.

4. *Sound family life.* Personal qualities making for stable families. Knowledge and skill relating to child development.

5. *Consumer efficiency.* Sound choice of values relating to style of life. Skill in stretching consumer dollars. Ability to cope with taxes, credit, insurance, investments, legal issues, etc. Ability to recognize deceptive sales practices and to withstand high-pressure sales tactics.

6. *Fruitful leisure.* Wisdom in allocation of time among work, leisure, and other pursuits. Development of tastes and skills in literature, the arts, nature, sports, hobbies, community participation, etc. Lifelong edu-

cation, formal and informal, as a productive use of leisure. Resourcefulness in overcoming boredom, finding renewal, and discovering satisfying and rewarding uses of leisure time.

7. *Health.* Understanding of the basic principles for cultivating physical and mental health. Knowledge of how and when to use the professional health care system.

D. Direct satisfactions and enjoyments from college education.
1. During the college years.
2. In late life.

II. Goals for Society[3]

A. Preservation and dissemination of the cultural heritage.
B. Discovery and dissemination of knowledge and advancement of philosophical and religious thought, literature, and the fine arts—all regarded as valuable in their own right without reference to ulterior ends.
C. "Improvement" in the motives, values, aspirations, attitudes, and behavior of members of the general population.
D. Progress in the broad social welfare as reflected in religion, health, order, justice, information, care of the underprivileged, etc. Progress toward the identification and solution of social problems.
E. Economic efficiency and growth.
F. Enhancement of national prestige and power.
G. Progress toward human equality.
H. Progress toward personal freedom and autonomy.
I. Rendering of useful services to various groups of society.
J. Direct satisfactions and enjoyments received by the population from living in a world of advancing knowledge, technology, ideas, and arts.

[3]These goals may be achieved through instruction, through research and related activities, or through public services.

K. Over the long periods of time, exerting a significant and favorable influence on the course of history as reflected in the evaluation of the basic culture including the fundamental social institutions.

Not for Everyone: Ideas to Consider— One Place or Another

Because of the diversity of undergraduates and of the colleges that provide their education, not all ideas for change can be applied to all institutions. Some might be appropriate to small colleges but not to large ones; others may be appropriate to universities but not to liberal arts or community colleges.

Here we submit 69 such ideas. Some of them have been tried or proposed at specific institutions. Many are untested. *None are offered as recommendations.* What follows is not a short list of priority ideas, but instead, is the beginning of a long list of possibilities. It is presented here merely to suggest some of the many ideas that have been expressed in discussions and studies of the curriculum and may be worth consideration by at least some colleges.

Planning

- Academic divisions within colleges might be required to make thorough self-studies on a staggered basis every five years. Such a procedure will give every division the opportunity to reassess goals and programs systematically at regular intervals.
- Visiting committees consisting of departmental alumni and members of similar departments at other institutions might be helpful in evaluating departmental objectives.

- Faculty members and students might be given access to the college's governing board or academic leadership when educational policy questions are considered. Faculty and students experience the curriculum directly, and their experiences and observations in such matters should carry special weight in the deliberations of college policy makers.
- The difference an education is intended to make in a student's knowledge and abilities might be made a more prominent basis of curriculum planning. Knowing such differences in advance provides a basis for evaluating both learning and teaching that is more significant than measures of time spent in class and subjects covered.
- Minimodules of instruction, extracted from full courses, could be adapted for presentation in alternative learning formats. Such modules can be made available on tape (video or audio), in work sheets, or in other formats a student can use independently. At some institutions, such modules are now made available in the residence halls and libraries. Such modules could have two basic functions: (1) they provide alternate ways of teaching key information that may be more effective for some students than the predominant method of teaching—that is, they acknowledge learning differences among individual students; and (2) they provide a convenient means of acquiring basic instruction that may have been missed or inadequately understood when initially presented in the classroom.
- The college registrar and librarian might be appointed to membership on academic policy committees and encouraged to participate in faculty meetings. This would give the registrar an opportunity to inform faculty members of the practical implications of proposed curricular changes. It would also give the faculty an opportunity to explain the intent of proposed changes so that the registrar could help them make the changes work effectively. Librarians can offer information about the capacity of available information systems and learning resources to support anticipated changes. If they participate in decisions, they can also respond quickly to new kinds of information demands.

Preparing for College and the Admissions Process

- High school students might be encouraged to study mathematics and English sequentially from grades 9 through 12 in order to keep options open to college programs, jobs, and other careers that require such skills.
- More colleges than now do might experiment with admission of students one or two years prior to high school graduation as a means of reducing the overlap of instruction offered between high school and college.
- High school students might be permitted to delay entrance to college for a predetermined period (a term or year, say) after having been admitted. Students who might need such a break between high school and college are sometimes deterred because they fear such a "stop-out" would impair their chances for being admitted to college.
- Colleges could recruit, admit, and serve older students more actively. Doing so could help to break up the "youth ghetto" on many campuses and encourage a sharing of values and interests across age groups.
- Many courses in the undergraduate curriculum are intrinsically interesting and valuable whether they are taken as a part of a degree program or not. Unless a course is too crowded, no restrictions should be raised to prevent nondegree students planning to take only a few courses from enrolling.

Advising

- New faculty members and students could be invited to participate in a joint orientation program that begins before the start of regular classes and continues with occasional seminars and special meetings throughout the first term. This foundation period could help students acquire knowledge of the resources and programs of the college before they have to make decisions about their academic programs. It could also provide opportunities for students who feel they need special help in improving their elementary skills to arrange for assistance in such matters in advance of entering their first classes. The foundation period could make the faculty more knowledgeable about their college, more active in its affairs, and better advisers.

- Four-year colleges might develop special orientation programs for transfer students.
- Off-campus educational advisory services in public agencies might be established with the support of one or more colleges to provide information, counseling, and referral services.
- If not all students, then particularly freshmen and seniors might be informed of the courses they have been able to register for before classes begin. At small colleges, this might be achieved by initiating preregistration enrollment periods for members of these classes. At some institutions, it might be facilitated by inaugurating on-line, immediate registration-enrollment procedures in which computers keep track of class openings and registrations. Without such assistance, students sometimes do not find out that certain courses they applied for are closed until after they arrive for the first day of classes. The time lost finding second- and third-choice alternatives can be costly and discouraging.
- Colleges might try designating instructors of such very small classes (under 12 students) as may be offered to freshmen as the faculty advisors of all members of those classes during the year. This could assure that, on some campuses, every freshman will come to know at least one faculty member reasonably well.
- Underclass students might be paired with upper-division peer advisors. In this way, freshmen and sophomores could have access to the advice of students who have already completed the work they are beginning.
- Advanced students, teaching assistants, or even young faculty members might be enrolled as "master students" in some introductory courses or seminars for freshmen. These students would attend all classes, do all of the assigned reading, and take all examinations. In addition, they would meet regularly on a voluntary basis with other students in the class to discuss study techniques, research methods, note taking, and other classroom skills.

General Education

- All students could be required to participate in a senior seminar, prepare a senior thesis, or pass a senior comprehensive

examination. This would make it possible for the culmination of undergraduate education to involve an independent, synthesizing, or integrating experience.

- Different programs of general education might be offered for different types of learners. The cooperative experience at Antioch places freshmen who are abstract (idea-oriented) learners in situations where they can develop skills for learning by experience. A college that stresses vocational preparation might offer an interdisciplinary seminar that integrates work experience and vocational concerns with literature or history.
- Colleges might stress the value of physical education courses such as tennis, bowling, golf, or swimming that give students lifelong recreational skills.
- All students might be encouraged to work in the creative arts. A few institutions do this by requiring that all students take a course in art, music, the dance, or "creative" writing to satisfy general education requirements. Others provide open studios with paid directors and instructors to assist students who choose to engage in the arts on an informal, recreational basis.

Interdisciplinary Instruction

- More use might be made of interdisciplinary, problem-based studies, such as environmental studies, conservation of energy, and urban studies in organizing the faculty and the curriculum. Such approaches emphasize the unity of knowledge and the cooperative contributions of individual disciplines in problem solving.
- Colleges might offer all students an opportunity to study the commonality and differences in world cultures. This is the theme on which Friends World College is based. Other colleges might introduce it as a topic either for broad learning experiences or as a component of general education.
- Large colleges or universities with more than 2,500 students might be subdivided into thematic college units. Small college units can enrich the learning environment and give students a chance to work closely with faculty members and fellow students.

• Several institution-wide nondisciplinary faculty positions might be created. This would permit colleges to appoint faculty members who do not fit comfortably into any single discipline and ensure the existence of at least a few interdisciplinary courses on campus.

Teaching

• Colleges might officially publish student evaluations of faculty teaching in the form of student course guides. Where such guides have been developed responsibly, often with student initiative, they have become helpful to students who want to know more about courses than the name of the professor and a description of the course content. Faculty members may also use them for feedback on their teaching effectiveness.

• To supplement college catalogs, faculty members might be encouraged to file abstracts of every course they teach, providing information about their personal philosophies and their approach to the instruction and subject matter to be offered. Such abstracts should be made available through the campus library to all students.

• Efforts might be made to guarantee each freshman at least one class with 12 or fewer students during his or her first year at college. Such classes will give students a chance to work closely with a faculty member early in their undergraduate years.

• Colleges might form consortia to share costs of instruction in esoteric teaching areas, in courses with relatively low enrollments, and in programs requiring large capital expenditure. Consortia of this kind make possible a diversity of offerings that could not be offered by individual institutions on their own.

• Older adult students might be trained to serve as educational resource persons qualified to assist in teaching certain subjects. Older adults sometimes come to college after completing rich and successful careers. This experience and insight can be tapped for the benefit of younger undergraduates.

• Reorientation and renewal programs might be established for

faculty in departments with underemployed instructional staff. Such programs could train some faculty members to teach in new areas. It might involve further graduate education, team teaching with faculty in allied fields, or internships in business, professions, and government.

• Departments might designate certain faculty members as "master teachers" to provide guidance to new faculty members and teaching assistants and to serve as consultants to all members of the department in dealing with special teaching problems. Where such appointments are made, they might be officially recognized by the college and the persons thus designated might be given special salary augmentation. Since the object of such appointments would be to provide models of teaching ability, they would not be rotated, might be limited in number, and might be recognized by the university or college only after careful institution-wide review of qualifications.

• Colleges that emphasize the teaching abilities of their faculty might follow the example of some two-year colleges by recruiting outstanding secondary school teachers and helping them to upgrade their subject matter competence through graduate study. It may be easier to improve a good teacher's subject matter competence than it is to train a research-oriented Ph.D. to become a good teacher.

• Greater use might be made of the college library's resources for undergraduate education. Information specialists on the library staff can be particularly useful in assembling illustrative material and reading lists. In some instances, they are qualified to give seminars as guest lecturers on subjects in which they have had research or practical experience.

• Faculty development centers could be established by more colleges to aid faculty members in improving teaching; to develop seminars, colloquia, or minicourses on pedagogy and educational technology; to share research and grant information; and to help faculty members find out about instructional techniques and approaches that have worked well in departments other than their own.

• English department faculty and graduate students might be

assigned to work in a consulting capacity with professors teaching lecture courses for freshmen and sophomores. English composition should be an element of all instruction, rather than an isolated course. English department consultants can help lecturers plan writing assignments, evaluate the composition strengths of students, and assist readers and teaching assistants in diagnosing difficulties and suggesting improvements.

• Universities might encourage graduate students who are planning teaching careers to take special courses or seminars in pedagogy and engage in practice teaching.

• Graduate students who are planning careers in college teaching might be encouraged to minor in a discipline that is compatible with their major field and provides them with high-demand skills and knowledge. This will facilitate the development of an interdisciplinary orientation and guard against faculty overspecialization.

• "Educational" art might be developed as a component of the arts on a footing with commercial art or the fine arts. Kenneth Boulding (1975, p. 10) points out that the arts are increasingly used for educational purposes on television, in publishing, and in development of educational materials. They are also used effectively by students to express what they have learned—through creative writing, films, musical composition, and painting. He suggests that there is latent educational power in the arts that ought to be harnessed.

Independent Learning

• Colleges might establish Independent Learning Centers or Learning Pavilions (see Carnegie Commission, *Toward a Learning Society,* 1973d). These could be used by students to pursue instruction at their own pace and, in some cases, in formats other than that used in the prevailing course structure. Such centers should provide access to programmed textbooks, reading lists, language laboratories, films, audiotapes and videotapes, and computer terminals. Counselors should be available to assist with the planning of self-instruction and use of equipment. Where a number of colleges are located near one another, they might share such a facility.

- More undergraduates might be given opportunities to perform research under the supervision of faculty members. At research universities, early experience with research could enhance the undergraduate's understanding of the regimen of scholarship. It could also help to stimulate interest in the student's research-related studies. It would also give undergraduates an opportunity to work closely with professors, to understand academic work, and become aware of the values that are respected by scholars.
- Individualized curricula based on short one-unit modules organized around single concepts or topics might be developed. In such a program developed at Grand Valley State College in Michigan, the modules are designed for mastery learning and are augmented by integrative seminars and other programs. The availability of such modules, at least theoretically, makes it possible for students to study only those parts of a subject they actually need and gives them more flexibility in the use of their time since all of their instruction is not in modules of uniform size.

Innovation

- Experimental subunits specifically charged with filling gaps in a college's curriculum and serving as a laboratory for curricular experimentation might be created. Such units could enable institutions to respond quickly to new curriculum needs. One such unit at Tufts University provides freshmen seminars, guided student teaching, interdisciplinary courses, guest lecturers, student-research opportunities, and self-paced instruction among other programs. Regular departments have adopted several successful programs from the experimental unit that they would not have tried themselves.
- For all programs, fixed expiration dates that are subject to periodic review and extension might be established. This allows academic programs to exist only as long as they are needed and to be phased out without being declared failures.

Grading and Certification

- Some small colleges might supplement degrees and certificates with a cumulative, written record of the student's edu-

cational accomplishment. College degrees and certificates no longer have reliable normative or substantive meaning and often certify no more than "seat time." A cumulative written record would be more informative both for students and for persons using the record for employment and other purposes.

- In essay examinations, instructors might include at least one question that requires students to integrate what they have learned in a course with other learning experiences in college. Students need constant practice in expressing ideas coherently and relating what they learn in class to what they have learned in other courses or in their life experiences. Term papers can also be used for this purpose.

- Where the criteria for graduation with honors or the dean's list fail to distinguish extraordinary achievement, such honors might be eliminated or redefined. During the academic year 1974-75, 83.4 percent of the seniors at Harvard graduated with honors. Other colleges reported similar percentages. Unless changes are made, present "honors" procedures deepen the embarrassment of the small percentage of graduates who have done poorly without bestowing appropriate rewards on a similar proportion of students who have done extraordinarily well.

Degrees and Certification

- Colleges might simplify the undergraduate degree structure by reducing the number of degrees offered to no more than seven. The most appropriate degrees might be the associate in arts, associate in science, associate in applied science, associate in general studies, bachelor of arts, bachelor of science, and bachelor of general studies.

- Colleges and universities could recognize the progress and achievement of students every two years with the awarding of appropriate degrees or certificates.

- Some colleges might consider reducing the amount of time required to earn a bachelor's degree by one year, particularly for students who plan to attend graduate school or for students for whom the major is now the only well-defined component of the undergraduate curriculum. Much of the time

spent by many students as undergraduates is now spent on specialized studies that could as well be pursued at the graduate level.

Transition from Undergraduate to Graduate Education

- Undergraduates might be encouraged to obtain a broad general education prior to admission to graduate school. Undergraduates frequently overconcentrate because they feel that doing so will improve their chances for graduate and professional school admission. Perhaps they should be advised that, after becoming a graduate student, it is often easier to intensify concentration than it is to sample subjects outside of their specialization.
- Universities might offer feedback to institutions about the strengths and weaknesses of their former students who enroll in graduate school. Colleges also need up-to-date information about graduate and professional school admissions standards and the job market for holders of advanced degrees.

Education for New Kinds of Students

- Community resources such as libraries, museums, galleries, ethnic neighborhood organizations, social agencies, and government facilities might be utilized in planning the curriculum. Every community offers resources that can complement on-campus facilities and that sometimes can substitute for such facilities.
- Instruction at other than normal class times—summer, weekends, evenings, and early mornings—might be offered to students who work and cannot attend college during regular class hours.
- To bring education to new student clienteles, colleges might offer instruction in labor union meeting halls, community centers, local schools, churches, fraternal facilities, or other places where groups of people congregate. Providing instruction in such locations might be a convenience for persons who are unable to commute long distances or who might be fearful of feeling out of place in the college environment.
- What British educators call "sandwich" programs, which

alternate periods of work and education, might be introduced more widely. Such programs not only enable undergraduates to gain experience in the "world of work" but also enable some students who would otherwise be unable, for financial reasons, to attend college to do so.

- Special support services might be provided for women, members of minority groups, part-time students, and students with learning difficulties who are now entering colleges. Such services may include child care, tutorial assistance, or alternative cafeteria menus. HELP (Higher Education for Low-Income People), a unit of the General College, a two-year terminal liberal arts program at the University of Minnesota, is an example of a comprehensive program of this type.

Coordinating Education with Other Institutions

- Closer ties might be established between community colleges and four-year institutions. This could be done by providing community college students with more information about four-year college programs, admissions requirements, and career opportunities that require bachelor's degrees. Increasingly, four-year colleges are seeking out technical and occupational programs in two-year colleges to be used for supplementing their liberal arts or highly specialized undergraduate education.
- Four-year colleges might systematically report on the status, strengths and weaknesses of their students who are community college transfers.

Communications with Students

- Serious consideration could be given to revamping the catalogs of many institutions. There is no reason for course catalogs to be unattractive and visually difficult to read. But good graphics need to be accompanied by clear, well-organized descriptions of the college program that can be easily understood by persons who have never been on an institution's campus. It would be helpful to prospective students if all colleges would attempt to organize their catalogs in a similar sequence of presentations to facilitate comparison

of institutions. Every possible effort should be made to weed out of any current catalog courses of instruction that will not actually be given. Failure to do so not only misrepresents an institution's offerings to its students but also can give an impression that an institution's curriculum is over-inflated.

For Schools

- More instruction and practice in the use of computers might be offered. Computer technology is increasingly essential to all fields of knowledge. Moreover, it provides powerful instructional tools for students to use independently or in projects assigned by instructors. One barrier to such use is a concern of faculty members that too few students feel comfortable working with such systems independently.
- Schools might offer lectures, counseling, and written information on postsecondary education, financial aid, and careers to parents while their children are still in grade school. Major decisions, which sometimes involve a break with past family tradition, require years of planning and good information.
- Recent high school graduates might be invited back to their schools to share their postgraduate experiences with students and faculty. This will help to provide the secondary school with up-to-date information about the suitability of the education offered to the life demands on young graduates.
- Beginning in the first year of secondary schools, students might be given seminars, lectures, counseling, and information on postsecondary education, financial aid, and careers during school hours. This would enable students to make better decisions regarding high school programs and postgraduation plans, whether they are college bound or not.
- More career and college information systems might be created to help high school students make sound decisions. A computerized "career information system" with terminals in many Oregon high schools provides students with information about manpower needs, job descriptions, education needed for jobs, and names of postsecondary educational institutions that offer training in different fields.

For Government

- States might establish learning pavilions or centers for guided adult independent study in areas that may be geographically remote from existing campuses. Libraries, shopping malls, museums, or high school campuses might be advantageous locations. Such centers could not only provide counseling and tutoring but also could have available an extensive range of learning materials and modern instructional technology.
- States could develop examinations like the one currently in use in California that permits high school students to "test out" of high school early. Such programs give advanced students an opportunity to accelerate their education. They also make it possible for qualified students to avoid what is often an academically soft final year of high school.
- Metropolitan governments might establish brokerage organizations in urban areas to provide potential students with information about postsecondary education opportunities, counseling, and advocacy services for gaining credit for prior learning at educational institutions. In surveys of adults, 71 percent have indicated a desire to learn more about some subject (Cross and Jones, 1972, p. 51). These students need information and advising.

Appendix D

Evaluating Student Work

There is a story about a new college graduate who picked up his transcript at the registrar's office of his college, looked it over, and observed in some dismay, "To think that after 16 years of education and a bachelor's degree, the most important things I got out of it were the first few letters of the alphabet I learned in kindergarten!"

For many students, faculty members, admissions officers, and employers, the symbols used to grade student work have inordinate importance and are interpreted as an absolute judgment on the quality of a student's efforts. One problem with that is that the symbols mean different things at different times. As Ohmer Milton and John Edgerly (1976, p. 47) point out, "(1) Unidimensional symbols report multidimensional phenomena. A given grade can reflect level of knowledge, attitudes, procrastination, interest or lack of it, and other factors. The lone symbol specifies none of these things. Perhaps each professor assumes every other interpreter will see in the lone symbol all of the nuances he or she intended. (2) The symbol, by itself, reveals nothing about the quality of the test or tests through which it has been derived."

To complicate matters further, grades are determined in different ways. Some professors utilize norm-referenced grading that evaluates students in comparison with each other. This approach is based on assumptions about how individuals within a group will sort themselves out in scores on certain measures. It makes no allowance for the general ability of the total group. Other professors utilize criteria-referenced grading that evaluates

students in comparison with a maximum possible number of specified tasks that can be or should be performed correctly. Criteria-referenced grading is becoming increasingly widespread because it is used extensively in colleges with competency-based curricula and in classes that utilize "mastery learning" instructional strategies.

There are also differences in the instruments used to measure student performance. Some professors use "objective" examinations, usually of the multiple-choice variety, which may be difficult to prepare but which yield reasonably clear-cut, easily measurable results. Others use essay examinations, which are somewhat easier to prepare but more difficult to score. Then, depending on the individual practice of professors, course grades may also be influenced by a student's class attendance, performance on written work or experiments, evidence of supplemental study, and, occasionally, on even more intangible fac tors. It is this diversity of professorial practice that makes grading a curricular concern, for there is strong anecdotal evidence that grading practices affect student choices of professors and thus, indirectly, courses.

Grading practices are also a concern, because grades themselves are used for two purposes that are not fully compatible. They are used to inform students about their progress and achievements, and in that sense they are diagnostic. They are also used by people who have some reason to evaluate the student's achievement and abilities—and who rely on grades as predictors of success in another college or graduate division, or as indicators of skills, knowledge, and personal qualities employers are interested in. Because of this second use, students tend to regard grades more as rewards than as diagnostic information— in the job market or in competition for places in graduate school grades are considered coin of the realm. "Good" grades may also be regarded as the students' "payoff" to their parents and others who supported and encouraged them during the college years.

Grade Inflation

Because grades are used as a sorting device by prospective employers and graduate school admissions officers, norm-referenced

grading is often preferred by professors and students. But there recently has been serious deterioration in the rigor with which such grading has been used.

In a study of 50 universities conducted by the office of institutional research at the University of California at Berkeley, it was found that from the early 1960s to the early 1970s, the percentage of A grades awarded more than doubled, from 16 to 34 percent, while the percentage of C grades had diminished not quite by half, from 37 to 21 percent (Suslow, 1976, p. 1). In the same study, it was found that the mean grade-point indices for 16 universities rose from 2.47 to 2.94 on a scale in which A equals 4 and F equals zero (Suslow, 1976, p. 10). The Carnegie survey of undergraduates confirms these trends (see Section Three).

Reasons advanced for this "grade inflation" are many. They include the timidity of professors faced with student demands for "grading reform" in the 1960s (in 1969, 58 percent of the undergraduates participating in the Carnegie survey agreed that undergraduate education would be improved if grades were abolished); the widely reported use of lenient grading to hold or expand class enrollments; tendencies of some faculty members to give "compensatory" grades to members of minority groups or to students with low ability; fears in the 1960s that giving male students bad grades would result in their being sent to the battlefields of Vietnam; diffusion of graduate school grading practices to the undergraduate level; fears of giving students grades that would deprive them of good jobs or entry to law or medical school; the introduction of undergraduate seminars in which students work together to promote higher grades; the introduction of mastery learning instruction; and increased use of pass-fail and other grading options that have no numerical value that can be used in computing grade-point averages.[1]

In response to the rising grade-point averages, Dickinson

[1]In 1969, 19 percent of the undergraduates responding to the Carnegie survey had taken a pass-fail course, and in 1976 the percentage had increased to 32 (Carnegie Surveys, 1969-70; Carnegie Council Surveys, 1975-1976).

College (among others) eliminated its "dean's list," because too many students acquired the 3.5 grade-point average that qualified them for the honor. Chicago State University, which had substituted an "R" or "repeat" grade for an F in 1972, restored the failing grade in 1975, expelled 130 students for making unsatisfactory progress, and sent nearly 1,000 others notices of warning or probation ("Stanford Finds Less Inflation," January 23, 1975, p. 5).

For reasons that are not totally clear, but possibly as a reaction to grade inflation and increased grading options in the interim, fewer students were as attracted by the idea of abolishing grades in 1976 than were in 1969. Moreover, in response to the 1976 Carnegie survey, over half (57.2 percent) said they were either "satisfied" or "very satisfied" with the methods of grading and evaluation used at their college, and the percentage of students who thought undergraduate education would be improved if grades were abolished decreased to 32 in 1976. But the percentages of students who are disaffected remain sufficiently large to encourage colleges to explore a variety of grading practices and options, including pass-fail grading, written evaluation, raising the ceiling on grades, and adjusting grades to reflect a student's performance compared to others in his or her class.

The pass-fail option. One option for overcoming grade inflation involves use of a system in which letter grades are abolished and students are given either a passing or failing grade. A variation on this alternative is to list only the courses on a student's transcript he or she has passed without recording those failed. Philosophically, the pass-fail option is regarded as a means of putting more emphasis on learning and less on competition for grades. Colleges also offer pass-fail grading as an option to encourage students to try courses that they might otherwise avoid for fear that they might not succeed in them and spoil an otherwise good academic record.

After making a special study of grade inflation, Michael Scriven at the University of California, Berkeley, concluded that

pass-fail systems were still subject to inflation and too uninformative to be helpful to students or persons evaluating the students' transcripts. Professors and others who engage in such reviews sometimes complain of "sanitized transcripts" that fail to indicate how many times a student tried a course before he or she passed, or fail to indicate a student's standing in a class. For similar reasons, pass-fail grades could conceivably be a burden to students looking for a job. Despite such complaints, Scriven's conclusions do not apply, it seems to us, when all of the students' achievements that are being compared are assessed in the same way.

We believe, on the other hand, that while institutions that choose to use pass-fail systems in their undergraduate programs should not be discouraged from doing so, they should indicate what the minimum passing level in a course is. That is, is it comparable to a "C" or a "D" in terms of letter grades? Or does it indicate minimally accepted performance of certain specific tasks?

Written evaluation. The Carnegie Commission on Higher Education (1973d) defined as one objective for the future, replacing degrees with an accumulative written record of students' educational progress. One component of such records conceivably could be written evaluation of student performance in courses. As is the case with pass-fail transcripts, written evaluation may be frustrating to persons who wish to know how qualified a student is for certain tasks or responsibilities in comparison with other students. They are also time consuming to prepare, may be almost impossible for professors at large institutions or classes to provide, and may become standardized in time. These criticisms have validity but should not rule this option out completely. Written evaluation is certainly appropriate in small classes and in evaluating independent study. And it makes more sense as a supplement to letter grades than do proposals for "super" or "star" grades (see the section "Raising the ceiling" below). From the standpoint of the student, such evaluation may be the fairest and most helpful of all, and the college has a

much stronger responsibility for informing its students about their progress than it has for informing future employers and graduate schools about their achievement.

Grade quotas. This option involves limiting the number of high grades to be given in a class. For example, in a class of 50 students a professor may restrict the number of A's to be awarded to 5. This option could reverse grade inflation, but it is not particularly useful in giving a student a clear assessment of the intrinsic quality of his or her work.

Raising the ceiling. In this option, new grades are added at the top end of the A-F scale. Specifically described by Scriven is a "star" grade with a value of 5 or 4.5 on a four-point scale. A variation (which can be combined with the "star" grade option) is the A+ grade with a value calculated at 4.3 In both cases, Scriven says the number of the new grades awarded must be restricted. The star grades should be no more than 5 percent of an instructor's grades, and the A+ grades should be limited to 10 percent of the instructor's grades if the "star" grade is not also used, and to 5 percent if it is.

Adjusted grades. This option, which is being adopted in part by the College of Letters and Sciences at the University of California, Berkeley, involves (1) recording course average grades to show, adjacent to the grade awarded to an individual undergraduate student, the average undergraduate grade given in a course and (2) the number of undergraduate students enrolled. Reports for courses enrolling less than 10 students would not include average grades. Thus a student enrolled in Psychology 1 might receive a report: "Psychology 1: B— (B+) 355." This would indicate that the student was below the class average (B+) in a course enrolling 355 students. This option provides the external users of grades with a more realistic picture of the meaning of a student's transcript, does not penalize students for taking a "tough graded" course, and provides a strong incentive for instructors to develop and apply criteria that will recognize differ-

ences in performance. It could be very unfair, however, in a class in which all or most students were preselected for high ability.

Another version of this system would be to take the difference between the student's grade-point average and the average course norms and add it to the average of the course norms to produce an adjusted grade-point average. If the student's grade-point average were 3.1, the average course norm were 2.8, and the average of course norms were 2.9, the student's adjusted grade-point average would be $(3.1 - 2.8) + 2.9$, or 3.2. The student's adjusted grade-point average would then reflect the extent of his or her superiority to others taking the same work. The procedure would create an advantage to the students who choose courses and instructors that have C averages (that is, grade on a curve). This system could also be unfair in a class in which all students were highly intelligent and diligent.

An adaptation that could apply to several of these procedures involves publication of course, department, and instructor norms that can be taken into consideration by administrators and promotion committees.

Many of these suggestions are possible only where the recording of grades is computerized. For schools without sophisticated facilities of this kind, Scriven suggests a transcript that shows, on the reverse side, the average grade of majors in each department, and, adjacent to the student's grade-point average, the average grade-point average of students graduating at the same time. Such transcripts might also state that all of these averages can change from year to year.

To Improve Understanding

Grading procedures can be a source of confusion, dissatisfaction, and frustration on college campuses. Individual faculty members grade differently, and the whole procedure is often highly subjective. Colleges should therefore make special efforts to keep faculty members and students well informed about the meaning and limitations of the grading options that are available on their campuses. One way colleges can achieve that objective

is to prepare written materials and organize special seminars on the consequences of alternative grading procedures for students, for departments, and for the institution. Such programs should be provided for both faculty members and students.

References

Ackerman, J. S. "The Arts in Higher Education." In C. Kaysen (Ed.), *Content and Context: Essays on College Education*. New York: McGraw-Hill, 1973.

Adult Functional Competency: A Summary. Austin, Tex.: Adult Performance Level Project, University of Texas, 1975.

Advisory Panel on the Scholastic Aptitude Test Score Decline. *On Further Examination*. New York: College Entrance Examination Board, 1977.

American Chemical Society. "Objectives and Guidelines for Undergraduate Programs in Chemistry." Pamphlet. Washington, D.C.: American Chemical Society, 1972.

American Institutes for Research. *Safeguarding Your Education: A Student's Consumer Guide to College and Occupational Education*. Santa Ana, Calif.: Media One, 1977.

American Psychological Society. *Directory of Teaching Innovations in Psychology*. Washington, D.C.: American Psychological Society, 1973.

Armbruster, F. *Our Children's Crippled Future—How American Education Has Failed*. New York: Quadrangle/New York Times Book Co., 1977.

Arts, Education and Americans Panel, The. *Coming to Our Senses: The Significance of the Arts for American Education*. New York: McGraw-Hill, 1977.

Ashby, E. *Any Person, Any Study: An Essay on Higher Education in the United States*. New York: McGraw-Hill, 1971.

Astin, A. W. *Preventing Students from Dropping Out: A Longitudinal, Multiinstitutional Study of College Dropouts*. San Francisco: Jossey-Bass, 1975.

Bacon, F. "De Haeresibus." *Meditationes Sacrae*. In J. Spedding and D. D. Heath (Eds.), *The Literary and Professional Works of Francis Bacon*. Vol. 1. London: Longman, 1861. (Originally published 1597.)

Bailey, S. K. *The Purposes of Education*. Bloomington, Ind.: Phi Delta Kappa, 1976.

"The Bay Area Writing Project Expands in California and Starts in Other States." *University Bulletin*, 1977, *25* (17), 87.

Bell, D. *The Reforming of General Education*. New York: Columbia University Press, 1966. (Anchor Books edition, 1968).

Ben-David, J. *American Higher Education: Directions Old and New*. New York: McGraw-Hill, 1972.

Ben-David, J. *Centers of Learning: Britain, France, Germany, United States.* New York: McGraw-Hill, 1977.

Bisconti, A. S. *College Graduates and Their Employers.* Bethlehem, Pa.: College Placement Council Foundation, 1975.

Blackburn, R., Armstrong, E., Conrad, C., Didham, J., and McKune, T. *Changing Practices in Undergraduate Education.* Berkeley, Calif.: Carnegie Council on Policy Studies in Higher Education, 1976.

Blake, E., Jr., Lambert, L. J., and Martin, J. L. *Degrees Granted and Enrollment Trends in Historically Black Colleges: An Eight Year Study.* Washington, D.C.: Institute for Services to Education, 1974.

Bok, D. C. "Can Ethics Be Taught?" *Change*, October 1976, *8* (9), 26-30.

Booth, W. C. "Is There Any Knowledge That a Man Must Have?" In W. C. Booth (Ed.), *The Knowledge Most Worth Having.* Chicago: University of Chicago Press, 1967.

Boulding, K. E. "A Technology for Education Art." *Technology Review*, 1975, *77* (7), 10.

Bouwsma, W. J. "Models of the Educated Man." *American Scholar*, 1975, *44* (2), 195-212.

Bowen, H. R. *Investment in Learning: The Individual and Social Value of American Higher Education.* San Francisco: Jossey-Bass, 1977.

Bowen, H. R., and Douglass, G. K. *Efficiency in Liberal Education: A Study of Comparative Instructional Costs and Different Ways of Organizing Teaching-Learning in a Liberal Arts College.* New York: McGraw-Hill, 1971.

Bowen, W. G. *Report of the President.* Princeton, N.J.: Princeton University Press, 1977.

Bowles, F., and DeCosta, F. A. *Between Two Worlds—A Profile of Negro Higher Education.* New York: McGraw-Hill, 1971.

Bronowski, J. *The Ascent of Man.* Waltham, Mass.: Little, Brown, 1974.

Brown University. *The Bulletin of Brown University: Catalogue for the Years 1975-1977.* Providence, R.I.: Brown University, 1975.

Brubacher, J. S. *The Courts and Higher Education.* San Francisco: Jossey-Bass, 1971.

Brubacher, J. S., and Rudy, W. *Higher Education in Transition: A History of American Colleges and Universities, 1636-1968.* New York: Harper & Row, 1968.

Brubacher, J. S., and Rudy, W. *Higher Education in Transition: A History of American Colleges and Universities, 1636-1976.* (3rd rev. ed.). New York: Harper & Row, 1976.

"Business (as usual) is Top Major." *Higher Education Daily*, 1976, *4* (46), 3.

Butts, R. F. "European Models for American Higher Education (1636-1860)." *Viewpoints* (Bulletin of School of Education, Indiana University), 1971, *47* (5), 9-43.

Butts, R. F. "The Search for Purpose in American Education." Paper presented at the 75th anniversary forum of the College Entrance Examination Board, Plenary Session, New York, October 27, 1975.

Byrom, F. L. "Frustration or Fulfillment?" Paper presented at the annual meeting of the Association of American Colleges in New Orleans, February 11, 1977.

Cannon, H. C. "Foreign Languages and the Humanities." In D. R. Jankowsky (Ed.), *Language and International Studies.* Washington, D.C.: School of Languages and Linguistics, Georgetown University, 1973.

Carnegie Commission on Higher Education. *A Chance to Learn: An Action Agenda for Equal Opportunity in Higher Education.* New York: McGraw-Hill, 1970.

Carnegie Commission on Higher Education. *Dissent and Disruption: Proposals for Consideration by the Campus.* New York: McGraw-Hill, 1971a.

Carnegie Commission on Higher Education. *Less Time, More Options: Education Beyond the High School.* New York: McGraw-Hill, 1971b.

Carnegie Commission on Higher Education. *The Campus and the City: Maximizing Assets and Reducing Liabilities.* New York: McGraw-Hill, 1972a.

Carnegie Commission on Higher Education. *The Fourth Revolution: Instructional Technology in Higher Education.* New York: McGraw-Hill, 1972b.

Carnegie Commission on Higher Education. *The More Effective Use of Resources: An Imperative for Higher Education.* New York: McGraw-Hill, 1972c.

Carnegie Commission on Higher Education. *Reform on Campus: Changing Students, Changing Academic Programs.* New York: McGraw-Hill, 1972d.

Carnegie Commission on Higher Education. *A Classification of Institutions of Higher Education.* Berkeley, Calif.: Carnegie Commission on Higher Education, 1973a.

Carnegie Commission on Higher Education. *Continuity and Discontinuity: Higher Education and the Schools.* New York: McGraw-Hill, 1973b.

Carnegie Commission on Higher Education. *The Purposes and the Performance of Higher Education in the United States: Approaching the Year 2000.* New York: McGraw-Hill, 1973c.

Carnegie Commission on Higher Education. *Toward a Learning Society: Alternative Channels to Life, Work, and Service.* New York: McGraw-Hill, 1973d.

Carnegie Commission on Higher Education. *Tuition: A Supplemental Statement on the Report of the Carnegie Commission on Higher Education on Who Pays? Who Benefits? Who Should Pay?'* Berkeley, Calif.: Carnegie Commission on Higher Education, 1974.

Carnegie Council on Policy Studies in Higher Education. *Handbook on Undergraduate Education.* (See Appendix A-4.)

Carnegie Council on Policy Studies in Higher Education, Garbarino, J., Feller, D., and Finkin, M. *Faculty Bargaining in Public Higher Education.* San Francisco: Jossey-Bass, 1977.

Carnegie Council Surveys, 1975-1976. (See Appendix A-4.)

Carnegie Foundation for the Advancement of Teaching, The. *More than Survival: Prospects for Higher Education in a Period of Uncertainty.* San Francisco: Jossey-Bass, 1975.

Carnegie Foundation for the Advancement of Teaching, The. *The States and Higher Education: A Proud Past and a Vital Future.* San Francisco: Jossey-Bass, 1976.

Carnegie Surveys, 1969-70. (See Appendix A-4.)

Carnegie Surveys, 1975-76. (See Appendix A-4.)

Cartter, A. M. *Ph.D.'s and the Academic Labor Market.* New York: McGraw-Hill, 1976.

Catalog Study, 1976. (See Appendix A-4.)

Centra, J. A. *Faculty Development Practices in U.S. Colleges and Universities.* Princeton, N.J.: Educational Testing Service, 1976.

Cheit, E. F. *The Useful Arts and the Liberal Tradition.* New York: McGraw-Hill, 1975.

Chronicle of Higher Education Deskbook, 1976-77. Washington, D.C.: *Chronicle of Higher Education*, 1976.

Cohen, A. M. "Political Influences on Curriculum and Instruction." In W. M. Birenbaum (Ed.), *New Directions for Community Colleges: From Class to Mass Learning*, no. 7. San Francisco: Jossey-Bass, 1974.

Cohen, A. M. "The Politics of Enrichment: Re-Establishing a Professional Birthright." Speech to the National Humanities Faculty meeting, Miami, March 12, 1977.

"College Test Score Decline Pooh-Poohed." *San Francisco Chronicle*, October 27, 1976, p. 3.

Commission on Graduation Requirements. *Report of the Commission on Graduation Requirements.* Ann Arbor: College of Literature, Science, and the Arts, University of Michigan, 1974.

Commission on Institutions of Higher Education. *Standards for Membership, Institutions of Higher Education.* Burlington, Mass.: New England Association of Schools and Colleges, 1974.

Commission on the Future of the College, The, Princeton University. *Final Report.* Princeton, N.J.: Princeton University Press, 1973.

Cooperative Assessment of Experiential Learning (CAEL). "Prospectus for Institutional Participation in the Tryout of CAEL Materials." Princeton, N.J.: Educational Testing Service, 1975.

Cross, K. P. *Accent on Learning: Improving Instruction and Reshaping the Curriculum.* San Francisco: Jossey-Bass, 1976.

Cross, K. P., and Jones, J. Q. "Problems of Access." In S. G. Gould and K. P. Cross (Eds.), *Explorations in Non-Traditional Study.* San Francisco: Jossey-Bass, 1972.

Dickey, F. G., and Miller, J. W. *Current Perspective on Accreditation.* Washington, D.C.: American Association for Higher Education, 1972.

Doty, P., and Zinberg, D. "Science and the Undergraduate." In C. Kaysen (Ed.), *Content and Context: Essays on College Education.* New York: McGraw-Hill, 1973.

Dressel, P. L. *College and University Curriculum.* Berkeley, Calif.: McCutchan, 1971.

Dressel, P. L. *Handbook of Academic Evaluation: Assessing Institutional Effectiveness, Student Progress, and Professional Performance for Decision Making in Higher Education.* San Francisco: Jossey-Bass, 1976.

Dressel, P. L., and Associates. *Evaluation in Higher Education.* Boston: Houghton-Mifflin, 1961.

Dunham, E. A. *Colleges of the Forgotten Americans: A Profile of State Colleges and Regional Universities.* New York: McGraw-Hill, 1969.

Eddy, E. D. "What Happened to Student Values?" *Educational Record*, 1977, *58* (1), 7-17.

Fisher, F. D. *One Thousand Men of Harvard: The Harvard College Class of 1971 Five Years Later.* Cambridge, Mass.: Office of Career Services and Off-Campus Learning, Harvard University, 1976.

Flexner, A. *Universities: American, English, German.* London: Oxford University Press, 1930.

Frank, A. C. *The 1975 Seniors at Berkeley.* Berkeley: Office of Student Affairs Research, University of California, 1976.

Frankel, C. *The Democratic Prospect.* New York: Harper & Row, 1962.

Fremer, J., Scudder, H., and Willingham, J. "Graduating Early: The Question of an Equivalency Examination for Florida High School Students." A report prepared for the Florida Department of Education by the Educational Testing Service, Princeton, N.J., 1976. (Mimeograph.)

Furniss, W. T. *American Universities and Colleges.* (11th ed.) Washington, D.C.: American Council on Education, 1973.

Gallup, G. "Public Favors Teaching Morals in Public Schools." The Gallup Poll. Chicago: Release dated April 18, 1976.

Glazer, N. "The Social Sciences in Liberal Education." In S. Hook, P. Kurtz, M. Todorovich (Eds.), *The Philosophy of the Curriculum: The Need for General Education.* Buffalo, N.Y.: Prometheus Books, 1975.

Glenny, L., Shea, J. R., Ruyle, J. H., and Freschi, K. H. *Presidents Confront Reality: From Edifice Complex to University Without Walls.* San Francisco: Jossey-Bass, 1976.

Gordon, M. S. "The Changing Job Market for College Graduates in the United States." Paper presented at a conference on youth, Ditchley, England, November 1, 1976.

Greeley, A. M. *From Backwater to Mainstream: A Profile of Catholic Higher Education.* New York: McGraw-Hill, 1969.

Greenberg, D. S. "The Coming Crisis in Academic Science." *Chronicle of Higher Education*, 1977, *14* (14), 1, 12.

Hajnal, J. *The Student Trap, A Critique of University and Sixth Form Curricula.* Middlesex, England: Penguin Books, 1972.

Handlin, O., and Handlin, M. F. *The American College and American Culture—Socialization as a Function of Higher Education.* New York: McGraw-Hill, 1970.

Harcleroad, F. F. *Institutional Efficiency in State Systems of Public Higher Education.* Tucson: Higher Education Program, University of Arizona, 1975.

Harvard Committee. *General Education in a Free Society.* Cambridge, Mass.: Harvard University Press, 1945.

Heath, D. H. *Growing Up in College: Liberal Education and Maturity.* San Francisco: Jossey-Bass, 1968.

Hodgkinson, H. L. "Evaluation to Improve Performance." In D. W. Vermilye (Ed.), *Learner-Centered Reform—Current Issues in Higher Education 1975.* San Francisco: Jossey-Bass, 1975.

Hodgkinson, H. L., Hurst, J., and Levine, H. *Improving and Assessing Performance: Evaluation in Higher Education.* Berkeley: Center for Research and Development in Higher Education, University of California, 1975.

Hofstadter, R., and Metzger, W. P. *The Development of Academic Freedom in the United States.* New York: Columbia University Press, 1955.

Hughes, E. C., Thorne, B., DeBaggis, A. M., Gurin, and Williams, D. *Education for the Professions of Medicine, Law, Theology, and Social Welfare.* New York: McGraw-Hill, 1973.

Husen, T. *The Learning Society.* London: Methuen, 1974.

Jacobson, R. L. "Undergraduate Averages Dip for the First Time in Decade." *Chronicle of Higher Education,* 1976, *13* (1), 1.

Jencks, C., and Riesman, D. *The Academic Revolution.* Garden City, N.Y.: Doubleday, 1968.

Juster, F. T. (Ed.). *Education, Income, and Human Behavior.* New York: McGraw-Hill, 1975.

Karp, G. "Catchy Course Titles Catch Students." *The Christian Science Monitor,* Jan. 17, 1977, p. 84.

Katz, M. R., and Kroll, A. M. "Evaluating a Computer-Based Guidance System." *Findings,* 1975, *2* (3), 5-8.

Kaysen, C. (Ed.). *Content and Context: Essays on College Education.* New York: McGraw-Hill, 1973.

Kelley, H. Address given at convocation of Immaculate Heart College, Los Angeles, February 14, 1977.

Keniston, K., and Gerzon, M. "Human and Social Benefits." In *Universal Higher Education Costs and Benefits.* Background papers for annual meeting of American Council on Education, Washington, D.C., 1971.

Knott, B. "What Is a Competence-Based Curriculum in the Liberal Arts?" *Journal of Higher Education,* 1975, *46* (1), 25-40.

Ladd, D. R. *Change in Educational Policy: Self-Studies in Selected Colleges and Universities.* New York: McGraw-Hill, 1970.

Lee, R. "Reverse Transfer Students." *Community College Review,* 1976, *4* (2), 64-70.

Levine, A. "Why Innovation Fails: The Institutionalization and Termination of Innovation in Higher Education." Unpublished doctoral dissertation, State University of New York, Buffalo, 1976a.

Levine, A. "Reflections of an Itinerant Interviewer: A Sketch of Undergraduate Curriculum Trends." Prepared for the Carnegie Council on Policy Studies in Higher Education, 1976b. (Mimeograph.)

Little, R. D. "Beyond Careerism: The Revival of General Education." *The Journal of General Education,* 1974, *26* (2), 83-110.

Lowell, A. L. *What a University President Has Learned.* New York: Macmillan, 1938.

McCurdy, J., and Speich, D. "Drop in Student Skills Unequaled in History." *Los Angeles Times,* August 15, 1976, pp. 1, 3, 23, 26.

McCurdy, J., and Speich, D. "School Standards Also Decline, Fewer Basics, More Electives Lead to Drop in Student Scores." *Los Angeles Times,* August 16, 1976, pp. 1, 3, 18, 19.

McCurdy, J., and Speich, D. "Answers to Decline of Student Skills Sought." *Los Angeles Times,* August 17, 1976, part 2, pp. 3, 4, 5.

McGrath, E. J. *Liberal Education in the Professions.* New York: Teachers College Press, 1959.

McGrath, E. J. *Values and American Higher Education.* Topical Paper No. 2. Tucson: Higher Education Program, University of Arizona, 1976.

McHenry, D. E., and Associates. *Academic Departments: Problems, Variations, and Alternatives.* San Francisco: Jossey-Bass, 1977.

McNamara, W. "The Disciplines Get It Together." *Change,* 1976, *8* (11), 22.

Maeroff, G. I. "Rise in Remedial Work Taxing Colleges." *New York Times,* March 7, 1976, p. 1.

Mattfeld, J. "Toward a New Synthesis in Curricular Patterns of Undergraduate Education." *Liberal Education,* 1975, *61* (4), 531-547.

Mead, M. *Coming of Age in Samoa.* Gloucester, Mass.: Peter Smith, 1928.

Meiklejohn, A. *The Liberal College.* Boston: Marshall Jones, 1920.

Milton, O., and Edgerly, J. W. *The Testing and Grading of Students.* New Rochelle, N.Y.: Change Magazine and Educational Change, 1976.

"The Mission of DeAnza College." Pamphlet. Los Altos Hills, Calif.: De Anza College, 1976.

Modern Language Association. *Options for Teaching of English: The Undergraduate Curriculum.* New York: Modern Language Association, 1975.

Mood, A. M. *The Future of Higher Education: Some Speculations and Suggestions.* New York: McGraw-Hill, 1973.

" 'A Moral Crusade' is Raging Within the Social Sciences." *Chronicle of Higher Education,* 1976, *13* (2), 9.

Morison, S. E. *The Founding of Harvard College.* Cambridge, Mass.: Harvard University Press, 1935.

Morrison, J. *The Rise of the Arts on the American Campus.* New York: McGraw-Hill, 1973.

Muhlenberg College Catalog 1975/1976. Allentown, Pa.: Muhlenberg College, 1975.

Muller, S. "Higher Education and Higher Skilling." *Daedalus,* 1974, *103* (4), 148-158.

Murchland, B. "The Eclipse of the Liberal Arts." *Change,* 1976, *8* (10), 22-26, 62.

National Center for Education Statistics. *Education Directory: Colleges and Universities, 1975-76.* Washington, D.C.: U.S. Government Printing Office, 1976a.

National Center for Education Statistics. *Digest of Educational Statistics, 1975.* Washington, D.C.: U.S. Government Printing Office, 1976b.

National Center for Education Statistics. *Education Directory: Colleges and Universities, 1976-77.* Washington, D.C.: U.S. Government Printing Office, 1977.

Newman, J. *The Idea of a University.* New York: Longmans, Green, 1927.

"News from University of Wisconsin—Green Bay." *Change in Liberal Education,* 1976, *2* (9), 2.

New York Times, Nov. 14, 1976, section 12, pp. 3, 11.

O'Hara, W. T., and Hill, J. G. *The Student, The College, The Law.* New York: Teachers College Press, 1972.

Olscamp, P. J. "Quality, Quantity and Accountability." Bellingham: Western Washington State College, 1976. (Mimeograph.)

Olscamp, P. J. "Does Our Undergraduate Curriculum Create Educated Persons?" Bellingham: Western Washington State College, 1977. (Mimeograph.)

Orlans, H. *Private Accreditation and Public Eligibility.* Lexington, Mass.: Heath, 1975.

O'Toole, J. (Ed.). "Work and the Quality of Life." Resource papers for Work in America, a special task force, Massachusetts Institute of Technology. Cambridge, Mass.: M.I.T. Press, 1974.

Pace, C. R. *Education and Evangelism: A Profile of Protestant Colleges.* New York: McGraw-Hill, 1972.

Packer, H. L., and Ehrlich, T. *New Directions in Legal Education.* New York: McGraw-Hill, 1972.

Patterson, F. *Colleges in Consort: Institutional Cooperation Through Consortia.* San Francisco: Jossey-Bass, 1974.

Perry, W. G., Jr. *Forms of Intellectual and Ethical Development in the College Years: A Scheme.* New York: Holt, Rinehart and Winston, 1968.

Phenix, P. H. *Realms of Meaning.* New York: McGraw-Hill, 1964.

Phipho, C. "Update III: Minimal Competency Testing." Denver, Colo.: Education Commission of the States, 1977. (Mimeograph.)

Piaget, J. *To Understand Is to Invent.* New York: Grossman, 1973.

Raubinger, F. M., Rowe, H. G., Piper, D. L., and West, C. K. *The Development of Secondary Education.* New York: Macmillan, 1969.

Richardson, R. C., Jr. Letter to V. A. Stadtman, February 14, 1977, from the president of Northampton County Area Community College.

Rosovsky, H. "Undergraduate Education: Defining the Issues." Excerpts from the *Dean's Report 1975-1976,* reprinted from the *Report of the President of Harvard College and Reports of Departments, 1975-76.* Cambridge, Mass.: Harvard University Press, 1976.

Rothblatt, S. *Tradition and Change in English Liberal Education.* London: Faber & Faber, 1976.

Rudolph, F. *The American College and University: A History.* New York: Knopf, 1962.

Rudolph, F. *Curriculum: The American Undergraduate Course of Study Since 1636.* San Francisco: Jossey-Bass, 1977.

Russell, B. *Wisdom of the West.* Garden City, N.Y.: Doubleday, 1969.

Sagan, C. *Dragons of Eden: Speculations on the Evolution of Human Intelligence.* New York: Random House, 1977.

Saint Joseph's College. "The Core Curriculum at Saint Joseph's College." Rensselaer, Ind.: Saint Joseph's College, n.d.

Schein, E. H. *Professional Education: Some New Directions.* New York: McGraw-Hill, 1972.

Scully, M. G. "Plainer Talk for Textbooks." *Chronicle of Higher Education,* 1974, *9* (4), 11.

Scully, M. G. " 'Writing Crisis' Spurs Big Corrective Effort." *Chronicle of Higher Education,* 1976, *15* (7), 1, 12.

Seattle Pacific College Bulletin, 1974/76. Seattle, Wash.: Seattle Pacific College, 1974.

Semas, P. W. "Does Accreditation of Business Schools Maintain Quality or Protect Monopoly?" *Chronicle of Higher Education,* 1977, *13* (25), 3.

Shattuck, R. "Contract and Credentials: The Humanities in Higher Education." In C. Kaysen (Ed.), *Content and Context: Essays on College Education.* New York: McGraw-Hill, 1973.

Shils, E. "The Academic Ethos Under Strain." *Minerva*, 1975, *13* (1), 1-37.

Sloan, D. "Harmony, Chaos, and Consensus: The American College Curriculum." *Teachers College Record*, 1971, *73* (2), 221-251.

Smelser, N. J. "The Social Sciences." In C. Kaysen (Ed.), *Content and Context: Essays on College Education*. New York: McGraw-Hill, 1973.

Special Committee on Objectives, Programs, and Requirements. *Report to the Faculty of the College of Letters and Sciences*. Berkeley: College of Letters and Sciences, University of California, 1957.

Spurr, S. H. *Academic Degree Structures: Innovative Approaches*. New York: McGraw-Hill, 1970.

Spurr, S. H. "American Higher Education and the Bachelor's Degree." Paper prepared for U.S.-U.S.S.R. Seminar on Higher Education, Princeton, N.J., March 15-18, 1976. (Mimeograph.)

"Stanford Finds Less Inflation." *Higher Education Daily*, 1975, *3* (16), 5.

"Student Sues University: Says She Learned Nothing." *Chronicle of Higher Education*, 1975, *10* (3), 2.

Suslow, S. "A Report on an Interinstitutional Survey of Undergraduate Scholastic Grading, 1960s to 1970s." Berkeley: Office of Institutional Research, University of California, 1976. (Mimeograph.)

Taubman, P., and Wales, T. *Higher Education and Earnings: College as an Investment and a Screening Device*. New York: McGraw-Hill, 1974.

Taylor, E. F. "What to Ask of a College." Unpublished monograph, 1974. (Mimeograph.)

Tewksbury, D. G. *The Founding of American Colleges and Universities Before the Civil War*. New York: Arno Press and New York Times Book Co., 1969.

Thwing, C. F. *History of Higher Education in America*. New York: Appleton-Century-Crofts, 1906.

Toffler, A. *Future Shock*. New York: Random House, 1971.

Touraine, A. *The Academic System in American Society*. New York: McGraw-Hill, 1974.

Trivett, D. A. *Competency Programs in Higher Education*. ERIC/Higher Education Research Report no. 7. Washington, D.C.: American Association for Higher Education, 1975.

Trow, M. "The American Academic Department as a Context for Learning." *Studies in Higher Education*, 1976, *1* (1), 11-22.

Trow, M. "Higher Education and Moral Development." *AAUP Bulletin*, 1976, *62* (1), 20-27.

Urban, G. R. *Hazards of Learning*. La Salle, Ill.: Open Court, 1977.

U.S. Bureau of the Census. "School Enrollment—Social and Economic Characteristics of Students: October 1974." *Current Population Reports*, series P-20, no. 286. Washington, D.C.: U.S. Government Printing Office, November 1975.

U.S. Bureau of the Census. "Educational Attainment in the United States: March 1975." *Current Population Reports*, series P-20, no. 295. Washington, D.C.: U.S. Government Printing Office, June 1976a.

U.S. Bureau of the Census. "School Enrollment—Social and Economic Characteristics of Students: October, 1975." *Current Population Re-*

ports, series P-20, no. 294 (Advance Report). Washington, D.C.: U.S. Government Printing Office, June 1976b.

U.S. Department of Health, Education and Welfare. *Digest of Educational Statistics.* Washington, D.C.: U.S. Government Printing Office, 1976.

"U.S.O.E. Drops the Chemical Society." *Chronicle of Higher Education,* 1974, *9* (5), 7.

U.S. Office of Management and Budget, Executive Office of the President. *Social Indicators, 1973.* Washington, D.C.: U.S. Government Printing Office, 1973.

Walters, E. "Professional Education." In A. Knowles (Ed.), *Handbook of College and University Administration.* Vol. 2. New York: McGraw-Hill, 1970.

Warren, J. R. "Alternatives to Degrees." In D. W. Vermilye (Ed.), *Learner-Centered Reform: Current Issues in Higher Education 1975.* San Francisco: Jossey-Bass, 1975.

Western Association of Schools and Colleges. *Handbook of Accreditation.* Oakland, Calif.: Western Association of Schools and Colleges, 1975.

Whitehead, A. N. *The Aims of Education.* New York: Macmillan, 1929.

Whitehead, A. N. *Modes of Thought.* New York: Macmillan, 1938.

Wilson, E. O. *Sociobiology: The New Synthesis.* Cambridge, Mass.: Harvard University Press, 1975.

Wirtz, W., and the National Manpower Institute. *The Boundless Resource, A Prospectus for an Education/Work Policy.* Washington, D.C.: New Republic Book Co., 1975.

Withey, S. B. *A Degree and What Else?* New York: McGraw-Hill, 1971.

Wooldridge, R. L. *Analysis of Student Employment in a Cooperative Education Program.* Boston: Center for Cooperative Education, Northeastern University, 1975.

Index

Hurst, J., 251n, 307
Husen, T., 231, 308

I

Implementation: of curricular policy and change, 251-265; recommendations on, 255, 264-265; responsibility for, 258-264
Individuals, needs of, and education, 152-158, 275-280
Innovation: ideas for, 289; instructional, faculty role in, 76-78
Institutions: changes in, 23-24; characteristics of, 128-149; competition of, 29, 60-62; consumerism responded to by, 4-5; cooperation by, 62; coordination of, 292; functions of, 5-6; interaction of, 29, 58-62; internal dynamics of, 96-99; mission of, 150-163; number of, 1, 23, 60; secularization of, 33-34; strengths of, and missions, 160-161. *See also* Higher education
Integrative or synoptic courses: characteristics of, 173-179; core courses in, 175; general education role of, 9; improvement of, 12-13; interdisciplinary programs for, 176; recommendations on, 18; requirements in, 173-174; in sequence of general education, 14; subjects central to, 174-175; survey courses at, 175-176; themes in, 177-178; timing of, 180-183
Interdisciplinary programs: and faculty, 178-179, 183-184, 197; ideas for, 285-286
Ithaca College, new course at, 48

J

Jacobson, R. L., 37, 308
Jencks, C., 73, 308
John Jay College of Criminal Justice, and interdisciplinarity, 176
Jones, J. Q., 294, 306
Juola, A. E., 37
Juster, F. T., 251n, 308

K

Karp, G., 48, 308
Katz, M. R., 228, 308
Keller, F. S., 76

Kelley, H., 161-162, 270, 308
Keniston, K., 155, 308
Knott, B., 124, 308
Knowledge, new, influence of, 29, 39-40. *See also* Learning
Kroll, A. M., 228, 308
Kutztown State College, basic skills at, 207

L

La Guardia Community College, Fiorello H., work-study at, 232-233
Lambert, L. J., 24, 304
La Verne College, academic and career counseling at, 226-227
Leaders, academic: and curricular change, 259-262; and institutional mission, 151. *See also* Presidents, influence of
Learned and professional societies. *See* Societies, learned
Learning: independent, ideas for, 288-289; uses of, 119-121. *See also* Knowledge
Lee, R., 58, 308
Lehigh University, basic skills at, 207
Levine, A., 210, 232, 256-257, 258, 308
Levine, H., 251n, 307
Lewis, R. W., 77
Liberal arts colleges: characteristics of, 134-141, 149; competency-based curriculum at, 125; course/faculty ratio at, 72, 96; curriculum allocation at, 130, 140-141; degrees from, 135, 138; faculty degrees at, 85; faculty satisfaction at, 83; faculty workload at, 81; general education at, 14n; humanities at, 104; majors at, time spent on, 194; professional education at, 114, 115; student characteristics at, 133-140; student satisfaction at, 80, 82, 83, 84, 90, 91, 92-93; subject fields at, 140; transfer students at, 179
Liberal education: as curricular focus, 3; defined, 9n. *See also* General education
Lincoln University, founding of, 24
Little, R. D., 187, 308
Locke, J., 39
Long Beach, California State University: curricular review at, 10; transfer students at, 179
Louisburg College, advertisement of, 88

THE CAMBRIDGE ANCIENT HISTORY

THIRD VOLUME OF PLATES

THE
CAMBRIDGE
ANCIENT HISTORY

EDITED BY

S. A. COOK, Litt.D., F.B.A.

F. E. ADCOCK, M.A.

M. P. CHARLESWORTH, M.A.

VOLUME OF PLATES III

PREPARED BY

C. T. SELTMAN, M.A.

CAMBRIDGE
AT THE UNIVERSITY PRESS
1966

PUBLISHED BY
THE SYNDICS OF THE CAMBRIDGE UNIVERSITY PRESS
Bentley House, 200 Euston Road, London, N.W.1
American Branch: 32 East 57th Street, New York, N.Y. 10022
West African Office: P.M.B. 5181, Ibadan, Nigeria

First printed 1930
Reprinted   1962
1966

Printed in Great Britain at the University Printing House, Cambridge
(Brooke Crutchley, University Printer)

2713

PREFACE

The illustrations collected in this volume contrast in many respects with those of its predecessor. The latter was devoted almost entirely to Greek art; here will be found objects ranging from Britain to India, from Spain to Central Asia. This altered aspect is due to the fact that the volume provides illustrations for volumes vii and viii of the *Cambridge Ancient History,* which are concerned with that greatly extended horizon of which men became aware through the conquests of Alexander and the westward expansion of Rome. Yet the Mediterranean holds the centre of interest; hence the products of the Hellenistic Age, sculpture, painting, architecture and the minor arts, occupy the chief place. But, in addition to the plates illustrating such subjects, there will be found illustrations of Celtic, Iberian, Thracian, Bosporan and Carthaginian products, and of numerous coins which have been mentioned in the text of the *History.* If Italy and Rome appear to have received scant notice this is because the discussion of their art is reserved for volume ix and for the plates which will illustrate it.

For the selection of the subjects illustrated and for the commentaries on them the volume is indebted to the writers of the several chapters concerned. Mr de Navarro has dealt with the Celtic products, Professor Schulten with the Iberian, Professor Kazarow with the art of the Thracians. Professor Rostovtzeff has described the plates illustrating his chapters on the Bosporan kingdom, Pergamum, Rhodes, Delos and Hellenistic commerce. The commentary on Hellenistic sculpture, painting and architecture is the work of Professor Ashmole; Mr Charlesworth has selected the illustrations of Carthaginian handicraft. For the descriptions of the coins the compiler of the volume is responsible.

The main purpose of this book will be achieved if it proves helpful to readers of volumes vii and viii. Yet it may have an interest of its own. The first volume of plates, it was suggested, might indicate many of the influences which contributed to the formation of Greek art; the second showed the growth of that art to full maturity; the third depicts the civilized world and its barbarian fringes eagerly borrowing, selecting, modifying the artistic ideas of the Greeks.

PREFACE

Acknowledgments are gratefully made to Professor Ashmole, Dr A. B. Cook, Professor Ebert, Monsieur Goury, Professor Kazarow, Professor Rostovtzeff and Professor Schulten for the use of photographs in their possession, and to the Directors of the British Museum and of the Austrian Archaeological Institute for permission to reproduce numerous pictures. The Directors of the Museums in Berlin, Cologne, Copenhagen, Munich, Oxford, Paris and Rhodes have either generously supplied photographs or sanctioned the reproduction of antiquities under their care. To Dr G. F. Hill, Keeper of Coins and Medals in the British Museum, to Professor K. Regling and Monsieur J. Babelon of the Cabinets of Coins in Berlin and Paris, as well as to Monsieur R. Jameson and Mr E. T. Newell, thanks are due for the provision of plaster casts and photographs of coins.

Professor Ashmole desires to thank Mr E. S. G. Robinson of the British Museum for selecting the coins illustrating portraiture on p. 164; Mr de Navarro thanks Professor and Mrs Chadwick for assistance on various points. The volume is, in particular, indebted to Professor Rostovtzeff for the use of eight of his pictures of Hellenistic terracottas. Messrs F. Bruckmann of Munich have generously supplied a photograph (p. 178 [b]) which is due to appear in a forthcoming publication (Hermann, *Denkmäler der Malerei des Altertums*).

Reproduction from the books specified has been sanctioned by the following publishers:

C. A. Beck, Munich (Furtwängler, *Kleine Schriften*).

E. de Boccard, Paris (*Bulletin de Correspondance Hellénique*, 1884).

F. Bruckmann A.G., Munich (Brunn, *Denkmäler*; Pfuhl, *Malerei und Zeichnung der Griechen*; Schulten, *Numantia*).

The Clarendon Press, Oxford (Rostovtzeff, *Iranians and Greeks in South Russia*; ib. *History of the Ancient World*).

W. de Gruyter and Co., Berlin (Ebert, *Reallexikon der Vorgeschichte*; Humann, *Magnesia am Maeander*; Knackfuss, *Das Rathaus von Milet*; Wiegand and Schrader, *Priene*).

Propyläen-Verlag, Berlin (Rodenwaldt, *Die Kunst der Antike, Hellas und Rom*).

Seemann and Co., Leipzig (*Zeitschrift für Bildende Kunst*, 1903).

Société française d'Editions d'Art, Paris (*Pergame*).

PREFACE

The Staff of the University Press again deserve grateful acknowledgement for their accurate care.

Upon the outside cover is a design representing a bronze statuette in Berlin It is of the third century B.C. and represents a Gallic slinger with a horned helmet and wearing a torque and a belt.*

C.T.S.

October 1930

* This paragraph refers to a jacket design which has been superseded.

TABLE OF CONTENTS

ix

CONTENTS

CONTENTS

CONTENTS

CONTENTS

[a], [b] silver, and [c] bronze coins of the *Achaean League*, 280–146 B.C.
[a] Federal mint; head of Zeus. Rev. monogram **AX** in wreath.
[b] Corinthian mint; types as last, but Pegasus over the monogram.
[c] Argive mint, Zeus Amarios. Rev. **AXAIΩN APΓEIΩN**; Demeter
Panachaia seated. *Brit. Mus. Cat. Peloponnesus*, p. 2, 2, Wt. 2·59 g.;
p. 3, 28, Wt. 2·43 g.; p. 13, 155. (vii, 736.)

[d], [e] Regal coins of cities on the Black Sea after about 290 B.C.
[d] *Sinope*, tetradrachm with Alexander types (cf. *Vol. of Plates*, ii,
8 [n]), in the field **ΣI** and aplustre. *Newell Coll.* [e] *Byzantium*, gold
stater with Lysimachus types (cf. *Vol. of Plates*, ii, 8 [l]); below
Athena a trident. *Naville Catal.* xiii, 676. (vii, 90.)

[f] *Antigonus Gonatas.* Tetradrachm struck to commemorate his
naval victory over the Egyptian fleet off Cos in 258 B.C. Head of
Corinthian Poseidon. Rev. Apollo seated on the prow of the
"Isthmia," the king's flagship, which was dedicated at Delos; on
the prow **BAΣIΛEΩΣ ANTIΓONOY**. Formerly *Pozzi Coll.* Wt.
16·75 g. (vii, 714.)

[g] *Antigonus Gonatas.* Tetradrachm issued after his defeat of the
Gauls at Lysimacheia in 277 B.C. Macedonian shield on which head
of Pan and pedum. Rev. inscription as last; Athena Alkis, in field
Macedonian helmet. Formerly *Pozzi Coll.* Wt. 17 g. (vii, 107, 201.)

[h] *Abdera*, bronze coin. Portrait of Ptolemy III, diademed and
with aegis at neck. Rev. **ABΔHPITΩN**; griffin of Abdera. Struck
probably after 239 B.C. when Ptolemy's general occupied Abdera.
Formerly *Imhoof-Blumer Coll.* (vii, 719.)

[i] *Areus of Sparta*, 310–266 B.C. Tetradrachm with Alexander
types (cf. *Vol. of Plates*, ii, 8 [n]). Rev. inscription **BAΞIΛEOΞ** (*sic*)
APEOΞ. The earliest known Spartan coinage. Lambros, *Peloponnese*,
Pl. IA', 6. (vii, 99.)

[j] *Cleomenes III of Sparta*, about 228 B.C. Tetradrachm. Portrait
with diadem. Rev. **ΛA**; agalma of helmeted Apollo of Amyclae,
beside him a goat, in field wreath. *B.M.C. Peloponnesus*, p. 121, 1.
Wt. 16·56 g. (vii, 719.)

COINAGE OF BACTRIA, PERGAMUM, EGYPT AND SYRACUSE

[a], [b] *Bactria and Sogdiana* under *Diodotus*, about 250 B.C. Tetradrachms. A portrait of the same ruler appears on both coins. Rev. Zeus hurling a thunderbolt, eagle before him. [a] **ΒΑΣΙΛΕΩΣ ΑΝΤΙΟΧΟΥ**, [b] **ΒΑΣΙΛΕΩΣ ΔΙΟΔΟΤΟΥ**. *B.M.C. Seleucid Kings*, p. 15, 18. Wt. 16·65 g. *B.M.C. India, Greek and Scythic Kings*, p. 3, 3. Wt. 16·66 g. (vii, 719.)

[c] *Philetaerus*, ruler of *Pergamum* and vassal of the Seleucid House, 284–263 B.C. Tetradrachm. Portrait of Seleucus I. Rev. **ΦΙΛΕΤΑΙ-ΡΟΥ**; Athena seated. *B.M.C. Mysia*, p. 114, 28. Wt. 16·82 g. (vii, 709; viii, 590, 601, 612.)

[d] *Eumenes I*, king of *Pergamum*, 263–241 B.C. Tetradrachm. Portrait of his uncle Philetaerus. Rev. as last coin. *Ibid.* p. 115, 31. Wt. 16·99 g. (vii, 709; viii, 591.)

[e] *Arsinoe II*. Silver tetradrachm. Before 270 B.C. Head of the queen wearing diadem, stephane and veil. Rev. **ΑΡΣΙΝΟΗΣ ΦΙΛΑΔΕΛΦΟΥ**; eagle on thunderbolt. *B.M.C. Ptolemies*, p. 43, 7. Wt. 13·97 g. (vii, 97, 703.)

[f] *Syracuse* under *Agathocles* as *strategos autokrator*, 316–304 B.C. Tetradrachm with old Syracusan types. Head of goddess surrounded by dolphins. Rev. **ΣΥΡΑΚΟΣΙΩΝ**; four-horse chariot, triskeles above. *Bibl. Nat. Paris.* Wt. 17·2 g. (vii, 621.)

[g] *Syracuse* under *Agathocles* as king, 304–289 B.C. Tetradrachm. **ΚΟΡΑΣ**, head of Kore. Rev. **ΑΓΑΘΟΚΛΕΙΟΣ**; Nike erecting trophy, triskeles in field. *Bibl. Nat. Paris.* Wt. 17 g. (vii, 634.)

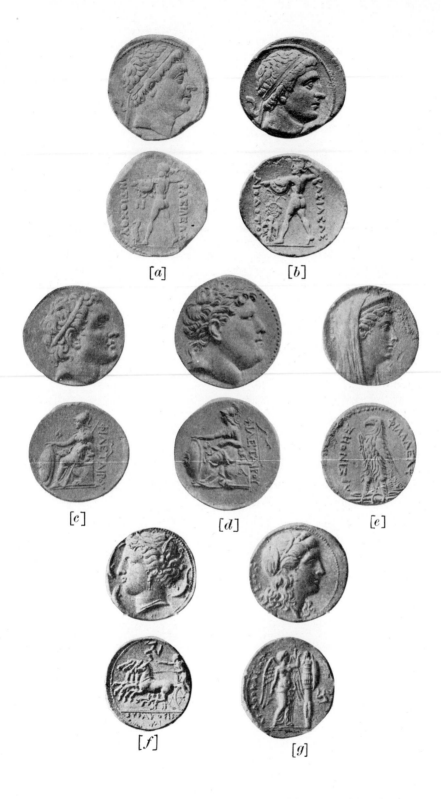

[a]

[b]

[c]

[d]

[e]

[f]

[g]

Rome, cast bronze libral *as,* about end of fourth century, or first half of third century B.C. Head of bearded Janus. Rev. prow of ship, above, (sign of value). *Brit. Mus.* The average weight of the Roman libral *as* is 327·45 g. (vii, 433, 607, 608, 662, 663.)

[a], [b] *Rome,* cast bronze libral *semis* and *uncia,* part of the same series as the *as* (p. 6). [a] Head of Jupiter, **S** (= semis) below. Rev. prow, **S** above. [b] Head of Bellona. Rev. • under prow. *Brit. Mus.* (vii, 662.)

[c] *Beneventum,* bronze coin struck after 268 B.c. **BENEVENTOD**, head of Apollo. **ΠROΠOM**, horse and pentagram. *B.M.C. Italy,* p. 68, 1. (vii, 608.)

[d] Silver didrachm, '*Romano-Campanian,*' having the same types as [c], but on the obv. **ROMANO**, and on rev. star instead of pentagram. *Brit. Mus.* Wt. 6·84 g. (vii, 608.)

[e] '*Romano-Campanian*' didrachm. Head of Heracles. Rev. **ROMANO**; she-wolf suckling twins. *Brit. Mus.* Wt. 7·06 g. (vii, 367, 608.)

[f] '*Romano-Campanian*' didrachm. Bearded head in crested Corinthian helmet. Rev. **ROMANO**; bust of horse, behind ear of corn. The head and ear of corn are Metapontine types; the horse's bust Carthaginian (cf. below, p. 20 [l]). *Brit. Mus.* Wt. 7·45 g. (vii, 608, 649.)

[g], [h], [i] *Roman silver* usually ascribed to 268 B.c. Denarius, quinarius and sestertius with marks of value **X**, **V** and **HS** behind the head of Roma. Rev. **ROMA**; Castor and Pollux on horseback, stars above them. *Brit. Mus.* Wts. 4·32; 2·24; 1·07 g. (vii, 489, 608, 663.)

[j] *Locri* as ally of *Rome,* about 275 B.c. Didrachm. Head of Zeus resembling that on coins of Pyrrhus. Rev. **ΛOKPΩN**; Locri as **ΓIΣTIΣ** placing a wreath upon the head of the seated **PΩMA**. *B.M.C. Italy,* p. 365, 15. Wt. 7·08 g. (vii, 654.)

[k] *Rome,* struck bronze *as* reduced to uncial standard after 217 B.c. Types like those of the libral *as* (p. 6), but over the prow **SAR**, the beginning of the mint-official's name. *Brit. Mus.* (vii, 433: viii, 112.)

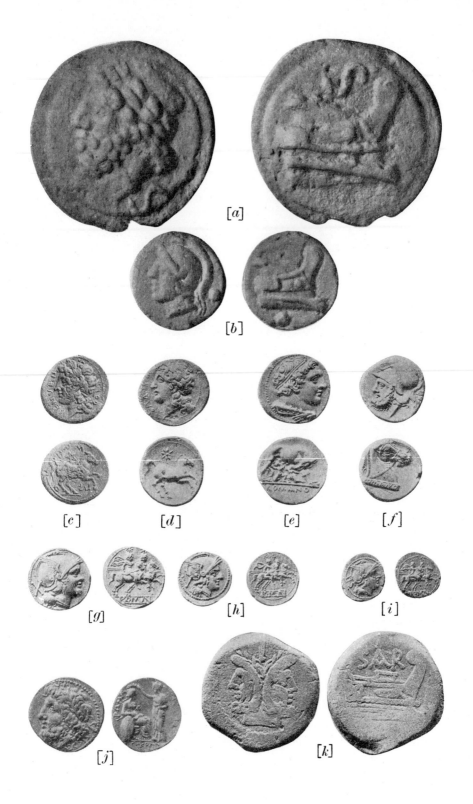

[a]

[b]

[c]   [d]   [e]   [f]

[g]   [h]   [i]

[j]   [k]

[a] *Roman denarius*, issued about 65 B.C. by a descendant of M. Aemilius Lepidus, to commemorate his legendary guardianship over Ptolemy V in 201 B.C. ALEXSANDREA; head of Tyche of Alexandria wearing turreted crown. Rev. M · LEPIDVS TVTOR REG · ΓONTF · MAX · S · C; M. Aemilius placing a wreath on the head of the boy-king who holds a sceptre. *Brit. Mus.* (viii, 166.)

[b] Gold stater, minted perhaps in Corinth, with the portrait of *Flamininus*. Rev. T · QVINCTI; Nike crowning the name. She resembles closely the figure on the gold staters of Alexander (cf. *Vol. of Plates*, ii, 8 [m], [o]). *Berlin Mus.* Wt. 8·55 g. (viii, 193.)

[c] *Philip V* of Macedon, 220–179 B.C. Tetradrachm. His head diademed. Rev. ΒΑΣΙΛΕΩΣ ΦΙΛΙΠΠΟΥ; Athena Alkis (cf. coin of Antigonus, p. 2 [g]). *Brit. Mus.* Wt. 16·78 g. (viii, 144.)

[d] *Nabis*, king of *Sparta*, 207–192 B.C. Tetradrachm. His portrait, with beard and shaven upper lip, wreathed and diademed. Rev. ΒΑΙΛΕΟΣ (*sic*) ΝΑΒΙΟΣ; Heracles seated. *Brit. Mus.* Wt. 17·04 g. (viii, 189.)

[e] *Orophernes*, pretender to the throne of Cappadocia, 158–157 B.C. Tetradrachm minted in *Priene*. Diademed head. Rev. ΒΑΣΙΛΕΩΣ ΟΡΟΦΕΡΝΟΥ ΝΙΚΗΦΟΡΟΥ; Nike crowning the name (cf. *Vol. of Plates*, ii, 8, [o]); in field, owl on base (mint-mark of Priene). *B.M.C. Galatia, Cappadocia, Syria*, p. 34, 1. Wt. 16·4 g. Found at Priene. (viii, 281.)

[f] *Spanish* silver coin of the weight of a denarius. Iberian legends. Male head. Rev. horseman. *Brit. Mus.* (viii, 309.) The types are derived from [g] below.

[g] Bronze coin of *Hiero II* of *Syracuse*, 274–215 B.C. His portrait diademed. Rev. ΙΕΡΩΝΟΣ; horseman. *Bibl. Nat. Paris.* (viii, 281.)

[h] Bronze coin, 'sextans,' of *Emporium*. Bust of Roma, with two dots as the mark of value on her helmet. Rev. EMPORI; Pegasus. *Naville Catal.* xii. (viii, 281.)

[i] Silver drachma of *Emporium*. Female head and dolphins copied from Syracusan coinage (cf. p. 4 [f]). Rev. ΕΜΓΟΡΙΤΩΝ; Pegasus copied from coins of Corinth (cf. *Vol. of Plates*, ii, 8 [e]). *Jameson Coll.* Wt. 4·56 g. (viii, 311.)

[j] *Gades*, silver coin. Head of Heracles. Rev. Phoenician legend; fish. *Mathey Coll.* Wt. 2·93 g. (viii, 311.)

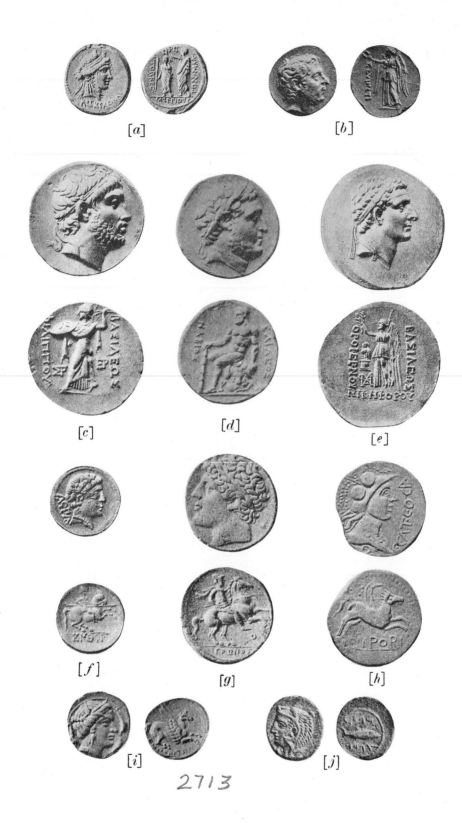

[a]

[b]

[c]

[d]

[e]

[f]

[g]

[h]

[i]

[j]

2713

[a], [b], [c] *Macedon* after division into four *Regiones*, coins issued 158–149 B.C. [a], [b] Tetradrachms of the first and of the second division. Macedonian shield (cf. p. 2 [g]), on which head of Artemis. Rev. club in oak-wreath; ΜΑΚΕΔΟΝΩΝ ΠΡΩΤΗΣ, or ΔΕΥΤΕΡΑΣ. [c] Bronze coin of the fourth division. Head of Zeus. Rev. as last, but ΤΕΤΑΡΤΗΣ. No coins of the third division have been found. [a] *Du Chastel Coll.* [b] *Allatini Coll.* [c] *Berlin Mus.* Wts. 17 g.; 16·75 g. (viii, 277.)

[d] '*Philip*' *Andriscus*, Macedonian Pretender, 149–148 B.C. Tetradrachm. Macedonian shield on which his head in the helmet of the hero Perseus. Rev. types as last coins; ΒΑΣΙΛΕΩΣ ΦΙΛΙΠΠΟΥ. Formerly *Pozzi Coll.* Wt. 17·17 g. (viii, 276.)

[e] *Juventius Thalna*, in Macedon. Tetradrachm, 149 B.C. Types as [a] but rev. legend ΜΑΚΕΔΟΝΩΝ, LEG(atus pro quaestore), above hand holding branch, θαλλός, probably the signet of Thalna. Formerly *Imhoof-Blumer Coll.* Wt. 16·94 g. (viii, 276.)

[f]–[i] Tetradrachms issued by *Antiochus IV Epiphanes*: [f] with the portrait of his nephew, the baby Antiochus; [g] with his own portrait. Both have the same reverse legend and type—'of king Antiochus,' Apollo seated on omphalos, a small tripod in the field, about 175–170 B.C. (viii, 498, 713 *sq.*); [h], [i] about 167 B.C., or later, have on the reverse Zeus Olympios Nikephoros: [h] has a portrait of the king; [i] of the king as Zeus laureate and disguised with a beard. The last bears the long inscription ΒΑΣΙΛΕΩΣ ΑΝΤΙΟΧΟΥ ΘΕΟΥ ΕΠΙΦΑΝΟΥΣ ΝΙΚΗΦΟΡΟΥ. (viii, 508.) The heads on all four coins are surrounded by fillet-borders. *B.M.C. Seleucid Kings*, p. 24, 3, Wt. 17·03 g.; p. 34, 4, Wt. 17·02 g.; p. 35, 15, Wt. 16·82 g.; p. 36, 22, Wt. 16·83 g.

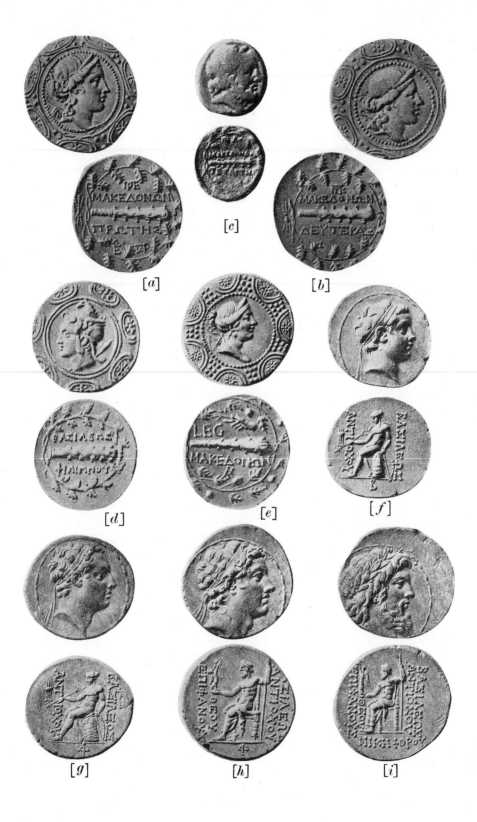

[a] [c] [b]

[d] [e] [f]

[g] [h] [i]

COINAGE OF BABYLON, SYRIA, JUDAEA AND ASIA MINOR

[a] *Timarchus*, satrap of Babylon, as Great King in Babylonia and Media. Tetradrachm, *ca.* 162 B.C. His portrait in Macedonian helmet. Rev. ΒΑΣΙΛΕΩΣ ΜΕΓΑΛΟΥ ΤΙΜΑΡΧΟΥ; the Dioscuri on horseback. The types are copied from those of Eucratides, Great King of Bactria. Formerly *E. F. Weber Coll.* Wt. 15·8 g. (viii, 518.)

[b] *Antiochus VI Dionysus.* Tetradrachm, 145–142 B.C. Head of the boy-king radiate and diademed. Rev. ΒΑΣΙΛΕΩΣ ΑΝΤΙΟΧΟΥ ΕΠΙΦΑΝΟΥΣ ΔΙΟΝΥΣΟΥ; Dioscuri on horseback, in field ΤΡΥ (for Tryphon).

[c] *Tryphon* as *Basileus Autokrator.* Tetradrachm, 142–138 B.C. Diademed head. Rev. ΒΑΣΙΛΕΩΣ ΤΡΥΦΩΝΟΣ ΑΥΤΟΚΡΑ-ΤΟΡΟΣ; Macedonian helmet and ibex-horn. *B.M.C. Seleucid Kings,* p. 63, 3, Wt. 16·53 g.; p. 68, 2, Wt. 15·99 g. (viii, 527.)

[d] The first *Jewish coinage* under *Simon Maccabaeus.* Bronze half-shekel of the year 136/5 B.C. Citron (*ethrog*) between two bundles of twigs (*lulab*), around 'In the fourth year—one-half.' Rev. palm-tree between two baskets, around 'The redemption of Zion.' *B.M.C. Palestine,* p. 184, 2. Wt. 15·07 g. (viii, 529.)

[e] *John Hyrcanus.* Bronze, 135–104 B.C. Crested helmet. Rev. double cornucopiae, around 'Jehoḥanan the High Priest and the Commonwealth of the Jews.' *B.M.C. Palestine,* p. 188, 1. (viii, 531.)

[f], [h] *Cistophoric tetradrachms, ca.* 200 B.C. onwards. Cista Mystica, with half-open lid, from which a serpent issues, ivy-wreath. Rev. bow-case between two coiled serpents. [f] Minted in *Pergamum*, has monogram ΠΕΡΓ and small torch. [h] From *Ephesus*, has ΕΦΕ and a bee in wreath upon the reverse. *B.M.C. Mysia,* p. 123, 90. Wt. 12·47 g. *B.M.C. Ionia,* p. 64, 152. Wt. 12·72 g. (viii, 612.)

[g] *Rhodes.* Tetradrachm, *ca.* 300–166 B.C. Radiate head of Helios facing. Rev. rose with bud between ΡΟ; above ΤΕΙΣΥΛΟΣ (magistrate), in field statue of a goddess. *B.M.C. Caria and Islands,* p. 242, 128. Wt. 13·22 g. (viii, 633.)

[a]

[b]

[c]

[d]

[e]

[f]

[g]

[h]

[a] Silver obol of *Phocaea* in Ionia, sixth century B.C. Found at *Saint-Remy de Provence*. Head of a seal, a little seal beneath it (cf. *Vol. of Plates*, i, 302 [b]). Wt. 0·6 g.

[b], [c], [d] A diobol and two obols from the *Hoard of Auriol* near *Marseilles*; the type a ram's head. The first like [a] may be of Ionian mintage, the second perhaps made by a Massiliote Greek, the third is a barbarous imitation struck by the pre-Celtic inhabitants of southern France. *Bibl. Nat. Paris.* Wts. 1·15 g.; 0·6 g.; 0·6 g. (vii, 46.) See de Navarro, *Antiquity* II, 1928, p. 431.

[e]–[j] The gold stater of *Philip of Macedon* and its *Celtic derivatives.* [e] Minted by *Philip* in Macedon (cf. *Vol. of Plates*, ii, 6 [o]). [f] An intelligent *Celtic* imitation. [g] Attributed to the *Raurici* (district around Bâle); [h] to the *Aulerici Diablintes* (Normandy). [i] A type characteristic of *Kent* (but found occasionally on the opposite French coast); the head of the god with elaborately stylized hair. [j] A broken-down version of the last, hair and lines on the obverse; the horse on the reverse reduced to lines and pellets. Occurs in *S.W. England* (Oxfordshire, Sussex, Cornwall). [e] *Seltman Coll.* Wt. 8·58 g. [f] *Brit. Mus.* Wt. 8·55 g. [g] *Dessewffy Coll.* Wt. 7·43 g. [h], [i] *Brit. Mus.* Wts. 6·67 g.; 7·68 g. [j] *Dessewffy Coll.* Wt. 6 g. (vii, 46, 47.)

[k], [l], [m] Coins of the *Eastern Celts* imitated from silver tetra-drachms of *Philip of Macedon* (cf. *Vol. of Plates*, ii, 6 [p]). [k] From *Pannonia*. Head of Zeus. Rev. horseman and indeterminate letters. [l] From *Dacia*. The head stylized into curves, spirals and alphabetic signs; the rider is bird-like. [m] From *Moesia*. A bearded Janiform head doubtless influenced by the Roman *as* (above, p. 6) and there-fore to be dated in the second century B.C. Rev. horseman. All in the *Dessewffy Coll.* Wts. 13·45 g.; 11·10 g.; 13·52 g. (vii, 46.)

[n] Gold *Regenbogenschüsselchen* of the type attributed to the *Boii.* Bird's head, torque and pellets. Rev. concave, a 'rainbow' and six pellets. Formerly *Pozzi Coll.* Wt. 7·48 g. (vii, 47.)

[o] *Massilia*. Drachma, fourth century B.C. Head of Artemis. Rev. MAΣΣA lion. *Brit. Mus.* Wt. 3·7 g.

[p] *Celtic imitation* of the last coin. *Dessewffy Coll.* Wt. 2·19 g. (vii, 46.)

[q] *Rhode*. Drachma; female head. Rev. open rose. *Brit. Mus.*

[r] *Emporium*. Drachma; female head, dolphin. Rev. Pegasus (cf. p. 10 [i] for a slightly later coin). *Brit. Mus.* Celtic imitations of these types are frequent. (vii, 46.)

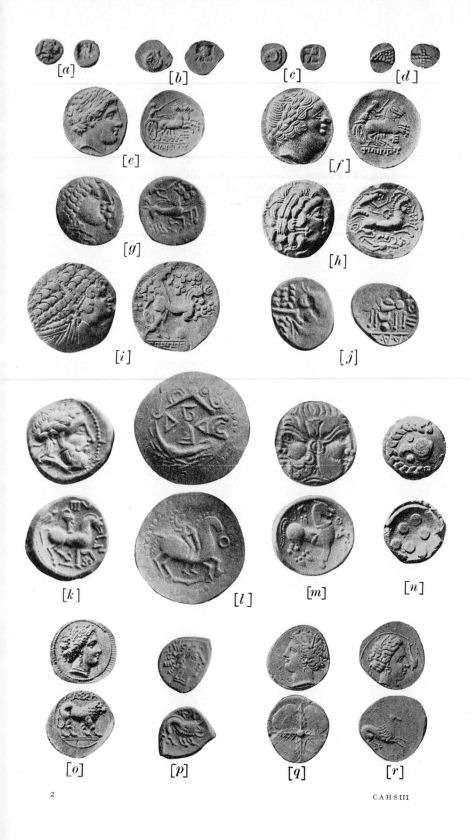

[a] [b] [c] [d]

[e] [f]

[g] [h]

[i] [j]

[k] [l] [m] [n]

[o] [p] [q] [r]

THRACIAN COINS

[*a*] *Sparadocus.* Tetradrachm, about 450–424 B.C. Cloaked horseman
with two spears. Rev. ΣΠΑΡΑΔΟΚΟ; eagle tearing serpent. *Bibl.
Nat. Paris.* Wt. 16·98 g. (On these coins [*a*]–[*r*] see viii, 556.)

[*b*], [*c*] *Seuthes I.* Silver, 424–410 B.C. Cloaked Thracian horseman.
Rev. [*b*] ΣΕΥΘΑ ΑΡΓΥΡΙΟΝ, [*c*] ΣΕΥΘΑ ΚΟΜΜΑ. *Bibl. Nat.
Paris.* Wt. 8·48 g. *B.M.C. Thrace*, p. 201, 1. Wt. 8·59 g.

[*d*], [*e*] *Maronea.* Bronze coins struck in the name of Thracian kings.
[*d*] *Amatocus I*, about 405–396 B.C. Double-axe; ΑΜΑΤΟΚΟ. Rev.
vine; ΕΠΙ ΚΛΕΑΝΤΟΣ (magistrate). [*e*] *Teres II* (about 400 B.C.).
Same types, ΤΗΡΕΩ. Rev. ΕΠΙ]ΚΕΑΝΔΡ[Ο. *Sofia Mus.* and
Vienna Mus.

[*f*] *Eminacus.* Silver, fifth century B.C. ΕΜΙΝΑΚΟ; Heracles in
lion-skin stringing his bow. Rev. wheel and four dolphins. *Brit.
Mus.*

[*g*] *Saratocus.* Silver, about 400 B.C. Probably minted in *Thasos.*
Silen kneeling holding kantharos. Rev. ΣΑΡΑΤΟ; amphora.
Brit. Mus. Wt. 1·11 g.

[*h*] *Bergaeus.* Silver, about 400–350 B.C. Perhaps minted in *Thasos.*
Silen and nymph. Rev. ΒΕΡΓΑΙΟΥ. *Berlin Mus.* Wt. 3·29 g.

[*i*], [*j*], [*k*] *Cypsela.* Bronze coins struck for dynasts. [*i*] *Hebryzelmis*,
386–384 B.C. Head of city goddess. Rev. ΕΒΡΥ, a vase (*Kypsele*).
[*j*] *Cotys I*, 384–360 B.C. Horseman. Rev. ΚΟΤΥΟΣ, a *Kypsele.*
[*k*] *Cersobleptes*, 360–341 B.C. Female head. Rev. ΚΕΡ, a *Kypsele.*
[*i*], [*j*] *Brit. Mus.* [*k*] *Sofia Mus.*

[*l*] *Cetriporis.* Bronze, about 356 B.C., probably minted in *Thasos.*
Head of Dionysus. Rev. ΚΕΤΡΙΠΟΡΙΟΣ, kantharos and thyrsus.
Bibl. Nat. Paris.

[*m*], [*n*] Bronze coins with types copied from those of *Philip of
Macedon* (cf. *Vol. of Plates*, ii, 6 [*p*]). [*m*] *Scostoces*, about 350 B.C.
Head of Apollo laureate. Rev. ΣΚΟΣΤΟΚΟΥ; horseman. [*n*]
Seuthes III, about 338–313 B.C. Head of Zeus. Rev. ΣΕΥΘΟΥ, as
last. *Sofia Mus.*

[*o*] *Lysimachus*, 323–281 B.C. Tetradrachm. Portrait of Alexander
with horn of Ammon. Rev. ΒΑΣΙΛΕΩΣ ΛΥΣΙΜΑΧΟΥ; Athena
Nikephoros (cf. *Vol. of Plates*, ii, 8 [*l*]). *Sofia Mus.* Wt. 17 g.

[*p*] *Cavarus.* Bronze, about 219–200 B.C. Head of Apollo. Rev.
ΒΑΣΙΛΕΩΣ ΚΑΥΑΡΟΥ; Nike crowning his name as on Alexander's
gold coins (cf. *Vol. of Plates*, ii, 8 [*o*]). *Sofia Mus.*

[*q*] *Mostis*, about 200 B.C. Tetradrachm. Portrait of king. Rev.
ΒΑΣΙΛΕΩΕ ΜΟΣΤΙΔΟΣ ΕΠΙ ΣΑΔΑΛΟΥ (magistrate) ΙΓ (date
year 13). *Berlin Mus.* Wt. 16·58 g.

[*r*] *Sadalas*, about 42 B.C. Bronze. Head of king. Rev. ΒΑΣΙΛΕΩΣ
ΣΑΔΑΛΟΥ; eagle. *Sofia Mus.*

18

[a]   [b]

[d]   [c]

[e]   [f]

[g]   [i]   [h]

[j]   [m]

[l]   [o]   [k]

[n]   [q]   [n]

[p]   [r]

[a] *Samos*. Tetrobol, sixth century B.C. Lion's scalp facing. Rev. rough quartered incuse square. *B.M.C. Ionia*, p. 350, 1. Wt. 2·02 g. [b], [c] *Bosporan coins* imitating the Samian type. Both with facing lion's scalp. Revs. [b] ΓΑΝΤ in the four raised quarters of an incuse square; [c] ΑΓΟΛ in a quartered incuse square; the first of *Panticapaeum*, second of *Apollonia*. *Naville Catal.* v. Wt. 1·9 g. Formerly *Pozzi Coll.* Wt. 1·42 g. (viii, 562, 586.)

[d] *The Sindians*. Silver, fifth century B.C. Eagle-headed griffin with curled wing, ear of corn. Rev. ΣΙΝΔΩΝ; head of horse. *Jameson Coll.* Wt. 1·26 g. (viii, 565.)

[e]–[j] Coins of *Panticapaeum*. [e], [f] Gold staters, fourth century B.C. Heads of bearded Silens with pointed ears (cf. the heads of the Scythians on gold and silver objects, *Vol. of Plates*, i, 252, 262). Rev. ΓΑΝ; lion-headed horned griffin, with curled wing, biting a spear, ear of corn below. *Jameson Coll.* Wts. 9·09 g.; 9·09 g. [h]–[j] Silver. [h] Head as on [e]. Rev. ΓΑΝ; bull's head. [i] Facing head of beardless satyr. Rev. lion biting a spear. [j] Head of satyr. Rev. lion's head. Formerly *E. F. Weber Coll.* Wts. 3·55 g.; 2·45 g.; 2·29 g. [g] Bronze. Head of satyr. Rev. lion's head, beneath it a sturgeon. (viii, 569, 586.)

[k], [l] Coins of *Carthage*, fourth to third centuries B.C. [a] Gold stater. Head of goddess copied from Syracusan coinage (cf. p. 4 [f]). Rev. horse. *Naville Catal.* xiii. Wt. 9·38 g. [b] Bronze, similar head. Rev. horse's bust. (vii, 608; viii, 488.)

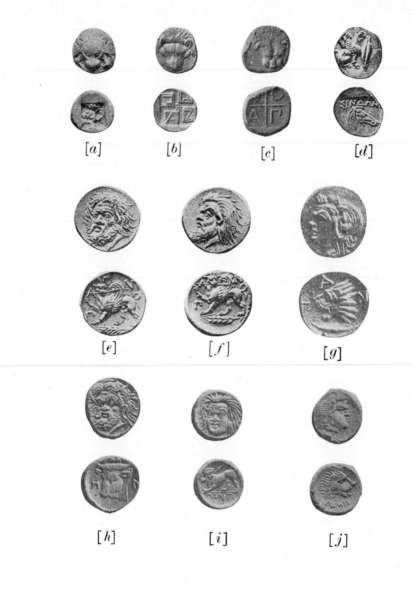

[a]　　　　[b]　　　　[c]　　　　[d]

[e]　　　　[f]　　　　[g]

[h]　　　　[i]　　　　[j]

[k]　　　　　　[l]

CHIEFTAIN'S GRAVE, *Weisskirchen*, Rheinprovinz, Barrow 2 La Tène A (see vii, 43 *sq.*). (*Bonner Jahrbücher*, XLIII, 1867, Pl. VII; Déchelette, *Manuel* (1914), II, 3, fig. 439; Jacobsthal and Langsdorff, *Die Bronzeschnabelkanne* (= J. and L.), 1929, p. 28, Pl. 36 *a* and *b*.)

[a] Bronze stamnos or vessel for mixing wine (height 40 cm.). Note beaded lip with two catches for lost lid. This vessel was found to contain white pitch. Pliny tells us that the Greeks mixed pitch, resin and other substances with their wines to give them briskness (*H.N.* XIV, 124). See de Navarro, *Antiquity*, 1928, p. 435.

[b] Handle with Silenus mask from same. Cf. Déchelette, *La Collection Millon* (1913), fig. 18, 3.

[c], [d] Bronze beaked flagon (*Schnabelkanne*). Height 42·5 cm. Jacobsthal (*op. cit.*) makes out a strong case for these flagons being of Etruscan, not Greek origin. They date for the most part from the opening decades of the fifth century B.C.

[e] Handle to same. Jacobsthal type 5 (see J. and L. pp. 45 f.). Associations of stamnoi with beaked flagons occur also on the following sites north of the Alps: Dürkheim, Rhenish Palatinate; Klein Aspergle, Wurtemberg; Weisskirchen, Barrow 2; Bouzonville, Lorraine (see p. 34). Another stamnos was found in the tumulus of La Motte St Valentin, Hte. Marne.

[f] Gold band, possibly an armlet. Diameter 4·7 cm. Zone of winged sphinxes in repoussé, above and below which a zone of lattice patterns between two beaded lines. Reinecke (*Mainzer Festschrift*, 1902, p. 74) considers that both in form and workmanship the sphinxes are faithful and competent copies of Greek models but that the barbaric origin of the object is betrayed by the mechanical repetition of the sphinxes and the ornamentation of the two zones framing them (vii, 48).

[g] Lower part of an iron dagger with remains of bronze sheath ending in a trefoil chape; note the gold foil rosettes. Length 7 cm.

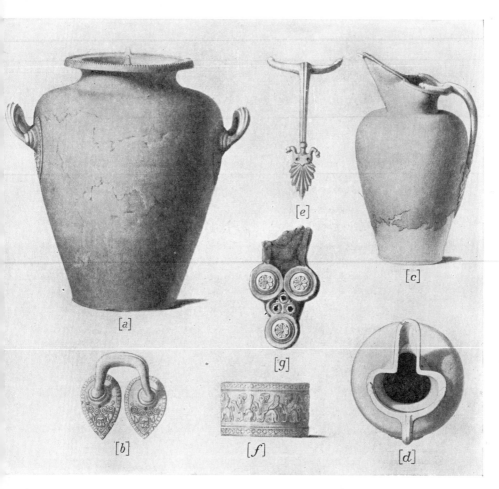

CONTENTS OF A RHENISH CHIEFTAIN'S GRAVE

CHARIOT-BURIAL, *Somme Bionne, Marne*. La Tène A (see vii, 43). (*Brit. Mus. Guide, Iron Age Antiquities*[2], Pl. III; Morel, *Champagne Souterraine*, Pl. VII *sqq.* and text, pp. 23 *sqq.*; also Ebert, *Reallex. der Vorgeschichte* (= *R.L.V.*), *s.v.* Wagengrab.)

The grave in question is a flat grave, surrounded by a circular ditch. The following are among the more important objects found (unless otherwise stated they are of bronze): a long iron Early La Tène sword in a bronze and iron scabbard ending in an enamelled trefoil chape (*B.M. Guide*, fig. 54); iron spits (Déchelette, *Collection Millon* (1913), p. 231); an embossed gold band; a gold finger-ring; a girdle clasp, confronted griffons type (*B.M. Guide*, Pl. IV right); a beaked flagon (*ib.* fig. 53, cf. above, Pl. II *c*). Apart from two iron tires and other parts of the chariot, the following horse-trappings: forked objects with trefoil terminals, pierced circular and semi-circular objects (*B.M. Guide*, Pl. IV); two iron bits with bronze rings. Pottery: a local pedestal urn (*B.M. Guide*, cf. fig. 64); a red-figure Attic kylix (J. and L. Pl. 34 *a*). In Jacobsthal's opinion this vase cannot date from before 450 B.C. (*ibid.* p. 62). In view of this, the Somme Bionne chieftain was probably laid in earth between 440 and 420 B.C., possibly a generation later than the chieftain in the second Weisskirchen barrow.

Apart from relatively numerous burials in France, chariots have been found in the La Tène A Rhenish Chieftains' Graves (see also *Mannus*, XXII (1930), pp. 103 f.). For S.W. Bohemia (La Tène A), see Schraníl, *Vorgesch. Böhmens-Mährens*, p. 212. Those from Yorkshire and most of those from Hungary (*B.M. Guide*, pp. 119 *sqq.* and *R.L.V.* XIV, p. 29) date from phase C. The Yorkshire chariot-interments differ from those of the continent in that the skeletons were contracted (buried seated in the chariot?) and that horses were found: in continental chariot-burials horses are exceptional. Hallstatt chariot-graves occur from S.W. Bohemia to the Marne (Jogasses grave 16) and even further west. Unlike those of the La Tène period, many of these earlier vehicles have four wheels.

There is an allusion to chariot-burial in the 'Destruction of Dind Rig,' an Irish prose epic referring to a period prior to that of the Ulster cycle (*Zeitschrift für Celtische Philologie*, III, p. 9).

MARNE CHARIOT-BURIAL

LA TÈNE A, EASTERN AREA (see vii, 43 *sq.*). (This and the following two plates are taken, respectively, from Lindenschmidt's *Altertümer unserer heidnischen Vorzeit* (= *AuhV.*), v, Pls. 50, 57, 51, which illustrate Reinecke's three papers, *ib.* pp. 281 *sqq.*, 330 *sqq.*, 288 *sqq.*, on which this text, pp. 26–30, is based. See Bibliography to Vol. vii, ch. 2, *s.v.* Lindenschmidt.)

Metal. (Unless otherwise stated the objects are bronze.)

Iron swords and scabbards with bronze chapes: [a–c] respective lengths 72 cm.; 20 cm. (length only of part illustrated); 72 cm.

Curved iron knife ('Hiebmesser')*:* [f] length, 31 cm.

Fibulae: [o]–[q] variants of the Certosa type; [w] mask-fibula; [m] bird-head fibulae; [s] stylized development of last-named type with knee bow. Lengths: 7 cm.; 7·2 cm.; 7·5 cm.; 9 cm.; 3 cm.; 4·8 cm.

Armlets: [d], [e], [u] types with three or four groups of knobs: [d] open and hollow cast, [e] and [u] closed; [l] open wire type with ring catch. Diameters: 7·5 cm.; 7·5 cm.; 7 cm.; 6·5 cm.

Torcs: [i] thin, open type, single group of knobs; [k] thin, angular in section, hook-and-eye catch; [j] thicker, cast, cast spiral ornament, and pin catch. Diameters: 14·5 cm.; 14 cm. and 15·5 cm.; 15·5 cm.

Pottery. (Monochrome; mostly dark in colour;
the finer vessels in bucchero technique.)

Lenticular flasks: [r] (with zoomorphic frieze, cf. *R.L.V.* vii, Pl. 193 d) found with [o]–[q]; [y] and [z] with geometric ornamentation. Heights: 24 cm.; 20·5 cm.; 19 cm.

Bottle-shaped vessel: [h] rounded shoulders, broad flat base. Height: 19·5 cm.

Pail-shaped vessel: [g] 'form perhaps influenced by archaic Greek vase types (such as archaic hydria and amphora forms).' Horizontal grooves and arc motifs on neck. Height: 25 cm.

Fragment of omphalos dish: [n] the inner side decorated with curvilinear motifs. Diameter: 16·5 cm.

Vessels with everted necks and broad, elliptical bodies, on the shoulders of which are curvilinear motifs: [a_2], [c_2]. Heights: 16 cm.; 10 cm.

Vessels with everted lips and broad, more or less carinated bodies, the shoulders decorated with mouldings and geometric motifs: [t], [v], [x], [b_2]. All save [b_2] made on the wheel. Note the dragonesque motifs on [b_2]. Heights: 12·5 cm.; 12 cm.; 14·5 cm.; 17 cm.

The following have *omphalos* bases: [n], [r], [t], [v], [y], [z], [a_2]–[c_2]. For the sites on which the above objects were found see *AuhV.* v, pp. 281 *sqq.*

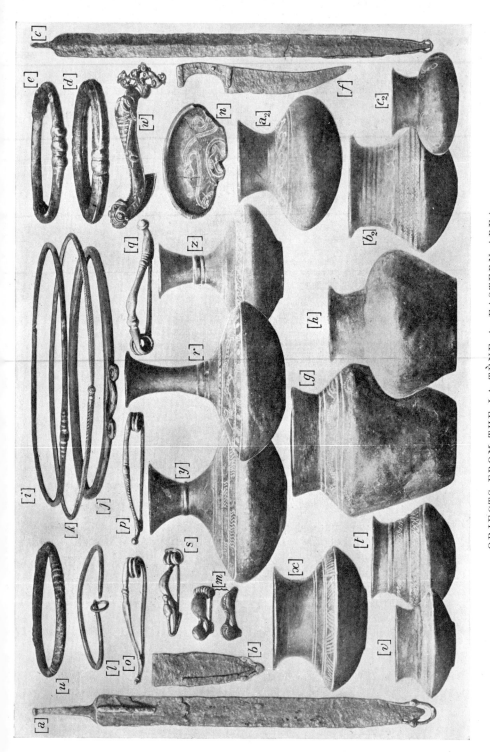

OBJECTS FROM THE LA TÈNE A, EASTERN AREA

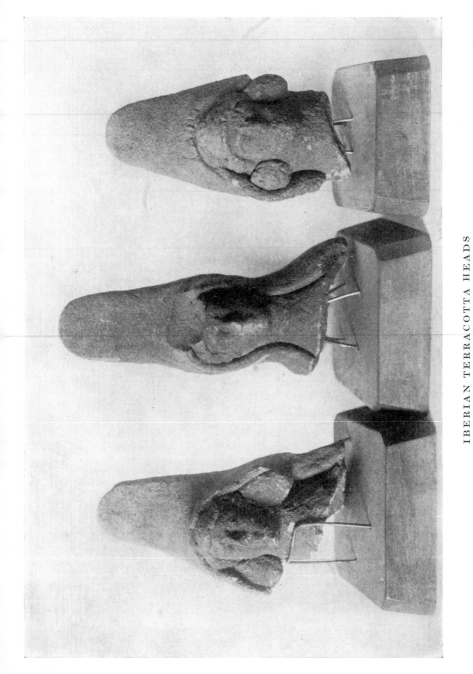

IBERIAN TERRACOTTA HEADS

THE CELTS

(Unless otherwise stated the objects are bronze.)

Iron swords: [a], [f] the latter with fragments of iron sheath, and chape with coral inlay. Respective lengths: 75 cm. and 70 cm.

Broken iron spear head: [b]. Length: 22·5 cm.

Fibulae: [d] foot and bow with inlay-discs; [g] iron, fragmentary; [i] with knee bow, end of foot lacking; [j] typical La Tène B form: bent-back foot touching bow; [k] bow with five borings; [l] band-shaped bow, foot lacking; [m] iron, foot with knobs; [w] red coral disc on foot. Respective lengths: 5·5 cm.; 6 cm.; 9·5 cm.; 7·5 cm.; 8 cm.; 9 cm.; 8·5 cm.; 6 cm.

Armlets: [o] two band-shaped, seal-top terminals with sunk beds for inlay; [r] knobbed, with small buffer terminals; [s] small, open, seal-top terminals; [u] fragment of large knobbed arm-ring, with *s*-motifs; [z] undulated wire type. Greatest diameters: 6·4 cm.; 7·3 cm.; 5·8 cm.; 10 cm. (length); nearly 6 cm.

Foot-rings: [v] foot- or arm-ring with saddle-shaped bend, four knobs and plug catch; [x] open, knobbed, seal-top terminals; [b₂] open, knobbed. Greatest diameters: 7 cm.; 10·5 cm.; 9·3 cm.

Torcs: [c] open, plain, seal-top terminals; [h] open, buffer terminals, coral ring-discs, etc.; [n] in two parts, buffer type, knobs, etc., with plastic decoration, plug catch; [q] closed, buffer type, plastic decoration on knobs etc., discs for inlay; [t] twisted wire, angular in section, hook-and-eye catch, glass rings on small wire rings; [c₂] plain, seal-top terminals, figurine on ring. Greatest diameters: almost 13 cm.; 15·5 cm.; 16·2 cm.; 18 cm.; 13 cm.; 13·5 cm.

Figurines (anthropomorphic)*:* [y], [d₂], see also [c₂]. Heights: 4 cm.; 3 cm.; almost 5 cm.

Smaller rings: [e] closed, four knobs; [e₂] triannular wire object. Diameters: 3·5 cm.; about 1 cm.

Girdle-hooks: [p] hook with bronze sheet mount for end of girdle, repoussé and punched decoration; [a₂] bronze hook with rivet-holes and 'terret' for end of leather girdle. Breadths: 4 cm.; 2·8 cm.

Rattle: [f₂] clay, double conic with stamped geometric motifs. Diameter: 4·5 cm.

[a]–[e], [h], [i], [w]–[y] from *Rhenish Palatinate*; [f], [g] *Alsace*; [u] (?), [v] *Rhenish Hesse*; [q]–[t], [c₂] *Starkenburg*; [z]–[b₂] *Upper Hesse*; [n]–[p] *Hesse Nassau*; [d₂], [e₂] *Wurtemberg*; [j]–[m] *Bohemia*. For Sites, see *AuhV.* v, pp. 330 *sqq.*

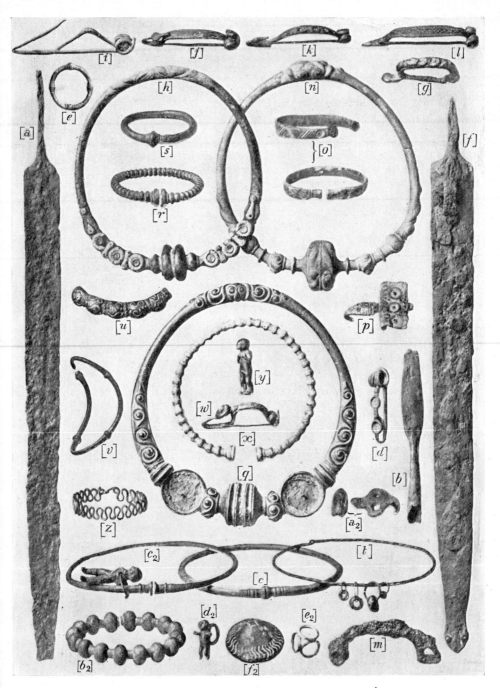

OBJECTS FROM NORTH OF THE ALPS, LA TÈNE B

LA TÈNE C IN THE BAVARIAN DANUBE VALLEY (see vii, 45 *sq.*).

Metal. (Unless otherwise stated the objects are bronze.)

Iron swords: [*a*], [*c*] (with iron sheaths); [*b*]. Note survival of earlier (B) forms in [*a*] and [*b*]; for typical La Tène C form, cf. [*c*]. Respective lengths: 74 cm.; 68 cm.; 86 cm. (sheath 74 cm.).

Twisted iron sword-chain and end-piece to same: [*e*]. Lengths: about 48 cm.; 15 cm.

Three hollow iron sword-strap rings: [*d*]. Diameter: 4·5 cm.

Iron spear-heads: broad-bladed: [*f*] with two iron spear-butts; and [*h*]; narrow-bladed: [*g*]; [*i*]. Lengths: 55 cm. (length of butts: 9 cm.; 11 cm.); 30 cm.; 33 cm.; 43 cm.

Iron shield boss: [*j*] 'trigger-guard' form and two iron 'shield-bindings.' Lengths: 33 cm.; 19 cm.; 17·5 cm.

Iron shears: [*x*]. Length: 23 cm.

Tweezer: [*y*]. Length: 5·7 cm.

Fibulae: [*u*], [*v*] (both iron), typical La Tène C forms (foot clasping bow); [*w*], [i_2] pseudo-La Tène B fibulae. Lengths: 11·2 cm.; 17 cm.; 7·9 cm.; 16 cm.

Armlets: [*n*] closed deep blue glass outer side with three rows of points; [*o*] hollow bossed type (*Nussarmring*) with hinge (arm- or foot-ring); [*p*] ditto, but larger bosses (arm-ring); [*q*] spiral wire, with two blue glass beads with orange yellow spirals, and zigzags; [*r*] closed, fluted, three rectangular plaques; [*s*] closed, three groups of pronounced triple knobbing; [*t*] open, 'cast torsion'; [g_2] closed, lignite. Greatest diameters: 9 cm.; about 12 cm.; 9·5 cm.; 6 cm.; 9 cm.; 8·3 cm.; 6·3 cm.; 7 cm.

Torc: [*k*] iron, 'omega' torc, button terminals. Greatest diameter: 17 cm.

Girdles, etc: [*l*] clasp- and suspension-hooks with pendants from big girdle-chain of ring, rod and cruciform members, red enamel on last-named and clasp-hook. Hooks with zoomorphic heads (cf. *Auh V.* v, p. 288, fig. 1); [*m*] end-pieces (zoomorphic clasp-hook and pendants) of a doubled girdle-chain (cf. *ib.*); [h_2] parts of a girdle-chain (on zoomorphic clasp-hook and end-piece, red enamel inlay). Total lengths of chains: about 154 cm.; 172 cm.; 123 cm.

Pottery. (Asterisk denotes wheel-made.)

Monochrome grey to grey-black ware: [*z*] bowl, incurving lip (diameter about 18 cm.); *[a_2] pedestal vase (height 20·5 cm.); *[b_2] pail-shaped vessel, curved profile, moulding on shoulder (height 26·5 cm.); *[c_2] pail-shaped vessel, strongly curved profile, moulding on shoulder (height 16·5 cm.); *[d_2] brown pedestal vase, curved profile (height 23 cm.); [e_2] pot, channelled walls, convex profile (height 16·5 cm.); [f_2] flat, sharp-angled dish (height 4·6 cm.); [j_2] pail-shaped, biconic vessel, channelled walls, stamped concentric circles on shoulder (height 12·5 cm.); [k_2] biconic vessel, foot-ring, moulding and grooves on shoulder (height 20 cm.).

[*a*] from *Straubing*; [*b*]–[f_2] *Manching*; [g_2]–[k_2] *Aislingen*.

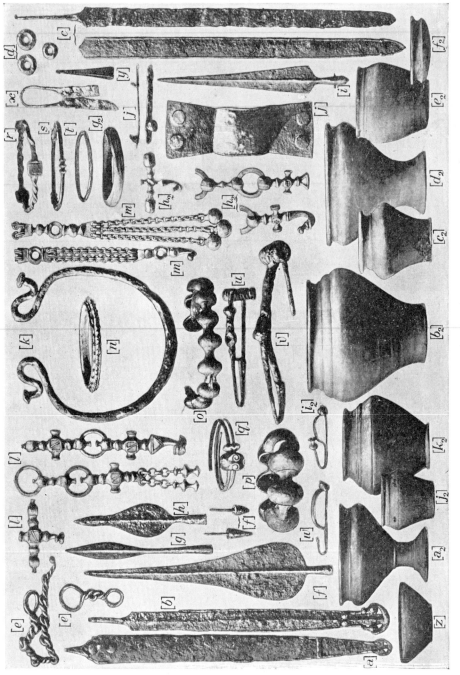

OBJECTS FROM THE BAVARIAN DANUBE VALLEY, LA TÈNE C

EXAMPLES OF LA TÈNE A ORNAMENTATION FROM THE MIDDLE RHINE AND MARNE AREAS (see vii, 47 *sq*.).

[*a*] Gold pierced mounting, possibly for a cup, from a Chieftain's Grave at Schwarzenbach (Barrow 1), Birkenfeld (= *Bonner Jahrbücher*, XXIII, Pl. IV, 3; cf. Baldes-Behrens, *Katalog Birkenfeld*, Pl. 5). The top frieze, framed by zones of beading, is mainly composed of 'Celtic' (three-leaved) and disintegrated palmettes. The middle, of stylized palmettes, the multifoliate articulation of their two lower side leaves contributing to the formation of the palmette derivatives with which they alternate. The lowest and narrowest frieze is composed of bud motifs, the neck of each bud being separated by a moulding from the crest of the undulated line on which it stands (cf. Déchelette, *Manuel*, fig. 664); two zones of beading.

[*b*] Engraved ornamentation on the bronze helmet from Berru, Marne (= *Rev. Archéologique*, 1875, I, Pl. X; cf. Déchelette, *op. cit.* figs. 656 and 490.2). (See vii, 48.) Top left hand corner: interlocking *s*-motifs with foliate 'insets.' Top right hand corner and middle: derivatives from the enclosed palmette alternately inverted and connected by curved almond-shaped motifs; on the projecting parts, palmette derivatives and palmettes. Lowest: degenerate derivatives of the enclosed palmette; similar connecting motifs. The engravings on this helmet (with which cf. Déchelette, *op. cit.* fig. 655) reveal a tendency towards a treatment of design fundamentally at variance with classical tradition: the abolition of the distinction between the pattern and its background, brought about by the covering of a given ornamental field with primary and complementary motifs. Not only did this practice open a whole range of fantastic curvilinear patterns, but it contributed very largely to the abstract, geometric treatment of ultimately naturalistic motifs. The origin of this innovation is perhaps to be sought in pierced metalwork (cf. [*a*]), or possibly in such inlay work as that on the throats of the Bouzonville flagons (cf. p. 35). On the helmet from Berru the contrast is heightened by the complementary motifs being carried out in *pointillé*. For an example of developed primary and complementary ornamentation, see the bronze mirror from Desborough (*B.M. Iron Age Guide*, fig. 133).

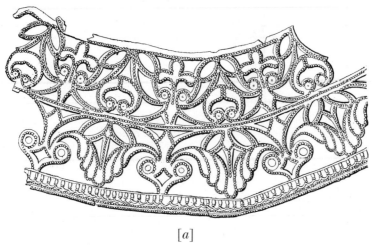

[a]

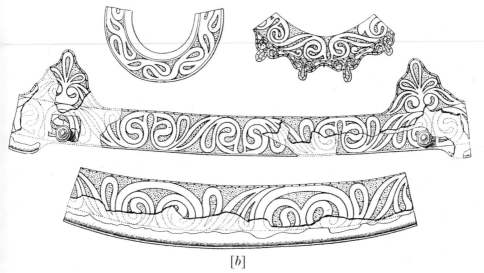

[b]

EXAMPLES OF LA TÈNE A ORNAMENTATION

BRONZE BEAKED FLAGON of Celtic workmanship from *Bouzonville,* near *Metz.* La Tène A. In the *British Museum.* (R. A. Smith,
Celtic Bronzes from Lorraine, in *Archaeologia,* LXXIX, pp. 1 *sqq.*; *Illustrated London News,* March 23rd and 30th, 1929; *The British Museum
Quarterly,* IV, No. 3, p. 66; J. and L. p. 99.) One of a pair of
bronze flagons (*oinochoai*) ornamented with coral and red enamel,
found with two bronze stamnoi (cf. above, p. 23 [a]). Greatest height:
about 39·4 cm. Patina, a dark lustrous green. For a full description
of this remarkable flagon see Smith, *op. cit.* pp. 3 *sqq.* (cf. *ib.* fig. 4).
The flagons from Bouzonville differ in many features from the usual
type of *oinochoe* (cf. above, p. 23 [c], [d]): the bodies of the former
are tall and high-shouldered and only paralleled by the clay *Schnabelkanne* from Hallstatt (J. and L. p. 99, Pl. 27, No. 138); the beaks and
the tops of the Bouzonville vessels are covered in (the wine was
poured in through a narrow hole, closed with an enamelled bronze
stopper, and out through a narrow tube, the point of egress lying
below the duck on the spout). They also differ in being embellished
with coral and red enamel, and in certain of their zoomorphic features: the duck on the covered spout, the ear- and thigh-spirals on
the beasts. The latter features have been attributed to Scythian influence (but see J. and L. p. 59 for thigh-spirals). Should this view
prove correct, the occurrence of such spirals on the Bouzonville
flagons—which also bear very early Celtic enamel work—would
lend colour to the view that the art of enamelling reached the Celtic
area from the Black Sea region. Owing to the dearth of connecting
links, it is not easy to determine the routes by which Scythian influence reached the Celtic area during La Tène A: although there is
undeniable evidence for the presence of Scythian raiders in Silesia
during the fifth century (see *Schlesiens Vorzeit,* N.F. IX, pp. 11 *sqq.*),
the Celtic invasion of that region did not occur until phase B
of the La Tène period. Ear-spirals are foreign to Greek and
Etruscan art; but, in comparing resemblances between the Scythian
and Celtic styles, one should not forget that they were both to a
great extent parallel but independent barbaric developments of a
common classical influence (vii, 48). Although this important new
find may reveal the existence of Scythian influence upon Celtic Art
as early as La Tène A, there is no reason to believe that influence
to have been of other than secondary importance.

BRONZE FLAGON FROM LORRAINE

3-2

OBJECTS from the DOUBLE BURIAL near *Waldalgesheim, Huns-rück*. La Tène B (vii, 45) (= *R.L.V.* xiv, Pl. 55–6; E. aus'm Weerth, *Der Grabfund von W., Bonner Winckelmannsprogramm*, 1870; *Führer durch das Provinzialmuseum, Bonn* (1915), p. 25, Pl. 9 (1, 2), Pl. 10; Behrens, *Katalog Bingen* (1918), pp. 25 *sqq.*). The lower of the two graves contained the remains of a man with his horse, chariot, table service [a], [b], etc.; the upper one that of his wife or concubine with rich objects of adornment (see [c]–[f]). (Cf. vii. 73.)

[a] The bronze flagon is a Celtic derivation from the earlier Etruscan *Schnabelkanne*. Instead of a beak it is furnished with a tubular spout, and differs still further from the usual beaked flagon in the shape of its body and its foot (cf. 23 [c]). The small horse surmounting the vessel in the photograph is thought to belong to the lid. Note the bearded figure with human ears and long pointed ears (horns?) at the foot of the handle, probably derived from the Achelous mask. For the ornamentation on the body of the vessel, not visible on this plate, see *B.M. Iron Age Guide*, fig. 11, p. 20 (cf. *Mainzer Festschr.* 1902, p. 82; J. and L. p. 44). Further examples of this type of flagon occur in France (2) and the Rhenish Palatinate (1), while a number of imitations in pottery came to light in the South Swiss (Ticino) cemeteries (cf. Behrens, *op. cit.* p. 28 *sq.*; Déchelette, *op. cit.* ii, 3, fig. 654, p. 1454 *sq.*).

[b] The bronze bucket is one of the only Greek works of art found in the transalpine Celtic area in a La Tène B context (cf. vii, 45). Outside of that area, apart from the example cited on vii, 45, one of these buckets was found at Kjeldby (Denmark). Cf. Déchelette, *op. cit.* pp. 1440–2. The free flower-tendrils (*frei bewegte Blüthenranken*) at the base of the drooping palmette on the Waldalgesheim bucket show that this vessel cannot be dated earlier than the closing years of the fifth century B.C. (cf. *Mainzer Festschr.* 1902, p. 81).

[c] Gold torc with buffer terminals. The ornamentation (forked flower-tendrils) is directly derived from the decoration on the bucket [b]. For full analysis of the ornamentation, see *B.M. Iron Age Guide*, pp. 19 *sqq.*

[d], [e] Two gold buffer-ended wristlets decorated with human masks, palmette decorations, free tendril motifs, etc.

[f] Closed, twisted gold ring for the upper arm.

The chief new classical contribution towards La Tène B art is the free tendril motif.

[a]   [b]

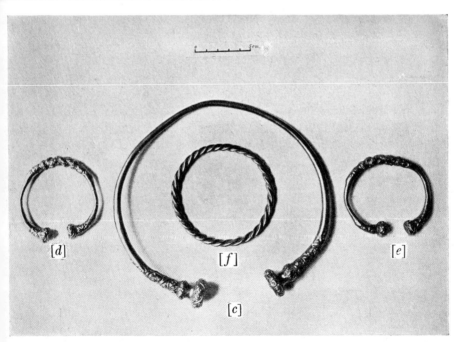

[d]   [f]   [e]

[c]

OBJECTS FROM WALDALGESHEIM

Types of BRONZE AGE CHIP-CARVED POTTERY, *Kerbschnitt-keramik* (= *RLV*. VIII, pl. 78). (vii, 55.) [*a*]–[*b*] From *Bavaria*. [*c*]–[*g*] From *Wurtemberg*. [*h*]–[*i*] From *Hesse*. Respective heights: 12·5 cm.; 8 cm.; 6 cm.; 5 cm.; 10·5 cm.; 12 cm.; 5·7 cm.; 8·5 cm.; 13·8 cm. Apart from the Lower Rhenish area chip-carved pottery practically disappears in Hallstatt A to re-emerge in Hallstatt C (see vii, 55 on recrudescence of the Bronze Age population in South Germany). Also cf. forms of funnel-neck globular-bodied vessels of Hallstatt B (*AuhV*. v, Nos. 1002, 1007) with fig. [*f*] and Behrens, *Bronzezeit Süddeutschlands*, Pl. XV). See Behrens, *op. cit.* for sites.

HARPSTEDT POTTERY (= *Mannus*, XVII (1926), p. 293). (See vii, 67, 56.)

The cradle of the Harpstedt style lay in the region between the Ems and the Weser, whence it spread [i] through the Lippe valley to the Lower Rhenish area, [ii] through Brunswick to East Havelland and parts of Saxony. The vessels, which vary in colour (light yellow, reddish, dark brown), are more or less pail-shaped with frilled lips and rough walls; the roughened appearance is obtained by smearing, or combing. According to Stampfuss' revised chronology (cf. *Mannus*, Ergänzungsband v (1927), pp. 50 *sqq*. with *Mannus*, XVII, 1926, pp. 287 *sqq*.), the vessels date from Northern Bronze Age V to Hallstatt C. Rhenish variants [*t*]–[*u*], often with finger-tip ornamentation, occur in the Middle Rhenish zone (cf. Rittershausen, *Nass.Annalen*,1926, Pl. IX,12,13, and the Coblentz region, *Mannus*, XXII, 1930, p. 109 *sq*.), where they overlap with the Mehren (Hallstatt C/D) and La Tène A cultures. The people who brought these vessels with them to the Lower Rhine area are held to be the first Teutonic invaders to settle in those parts.

Type I, [*j*]–[*k*], does not survive the Bronze Age; type II, [*l*]–[*m*], is more frequently found in the Bronze Age; types III, IV, V, [*n*]–[*o*], [*p*]–[*q*], [*r*]–[*s*], date from Hallstatt C, although a few examples of type III occur in Bronze Age V. Certain vessels of true Hallstatt C/D forms found in the Lower Rhenish area reveal in the roughening of their walls Harpstedt influence. (See Stampfuss, the two papers referred to above, and literature there cited; Kendrick, *The Druids*, p. 39 *sq*., for occurrence in England; cf. Childe, *The Danube*, p. 364 *sq*.)

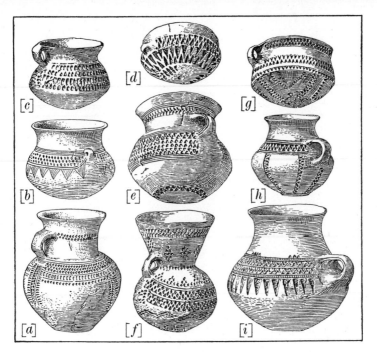

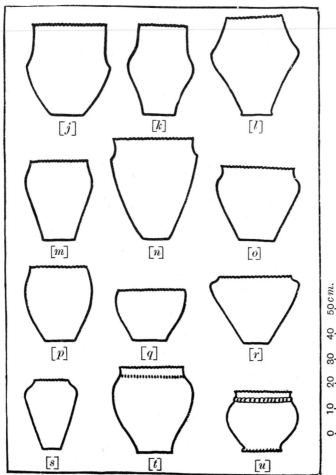

TYPES OF POTTERY

POTTERY FROM THE LOWER RHINE AND THE MARNE.
[*a*], [*b*] *Pail-shaped urns* (Eimerurnen) *with 'finger-nail' ornamentation.* [*a*] from *Hirzenberg* near *Siegburg*, Rhine Province; *Hallstatt* D
(= *R.L.V.* viii, Pl. 161 *c*). [*b*] from *Marson*, Marne; La Tène I
(= *B.M. Iron Age Guide*, Pl. v 8). Height: 16 cm.

[*c*], [*d*] *Broad paunched urns with tall incurving necks.* [*c*] with
triangular motifs on paunch, from *Hirzenberg* near *Siegburg*; Hallstatt D (= *R.L.V.* viii, Pl. 161 *f*). Also found in Mehren (Hallstatt
C/D) contexts (vii, 69). [*d*] slightly carinated variant of same, with
decoration in white, from *Haulzy*, Marne, grave 78; beginning of the
La Tène period (= Goury, *L'Enceinte d'Haulzy*...Pl. IV). Height:
22·5 cm. Further examples of this type occur at Étrechy, Marne
(Morel, *op. cit.* Pl. 19. 9 and 12). Cf. also Baldes-Behrens, *Katalog
Birkenfeld*, Pl. XII 9, and the more angular La Tène I variants
from the Trèves region (Déchelette, *op. cit.* fig. 669). [*a*], [*c*]
Cologne Museum, [*b*] *Brit. Mus.*, [*d*] Nancy Museum.

The distribution of these types of pottery supports E. Rademacher's
view of a migration of part of the Lower Rhenish 'Tumulus
peoples' into the Marne and Middle Rhine areas at the end of Hallstatt D (*R.L.V.* v, s.v. *Haulzy*, and viii, p. 497); (see also vii, 67 *sq.*).
Haulzy was cited (vii, 60) as an isolated link between the Lower
Rhenish Tumulus peoples and the Late Hallstatt Celtic invaders of
Spain. Since the publication of vol. vii, other sites of the Haulzy
type have been excavated by Chenet in the east Marne district.
Apart from these, Hallstatt influences reached the Marne (*Rev.
Arch.* 1927, Jogasses) presumably from the Swiss plateaux. What
is probably an earlier type of the Siegburg-Haulzy urn was found
at Can Missert (Terassa), Catalonia (*Anuari de l'Institut d'Estudis
Catalans*, vi, p. 584, fig. 335; still closer parallels are to be seen in
the Barcelona museum). Kraft and Bosch Gimpera (*Mannus*, Ergbd.
vi (1928), pp. 258 *sqq.*) and Kraft (*Stellung der Schweiz*...in *Anzeiger
f. Schweiz. Altertumskunde*, 1927/8, and *Antiquity*, 1929, pp. 33 *sqq.*)
show that there is reason to believe that the Celts invaded coastal
Catalonia as early as the Urnfield Period (vii, 55). These papers,
which only came into the writer's hands after vol. vii, chap. ii, was
in the Press, are important. Nevertheless, the location of the early
home of the Celts in the Rhone area is not borne out by the testi-
mony of river-names [vii, 54]. Further, 1100 B.C. seems too early a
date for this invasion: in spite of the occurrence of cylinder-neck
urns, other types of pottery from Can Missert and similar sites
point to the event in question not taking place prior to Hallstatt B,
circ. 900–800 B.C., and possibly being connected with Hallstatt
pressure on the Swiss lake-dwelling population. The finds from
Peralada show that Catalonia was also affected by the Late Hallstatt
Celtic invasions (*Anuari*, vi, p. 590 *sq.*; cf. vii, 59 *sq.*).

[c]   [a]

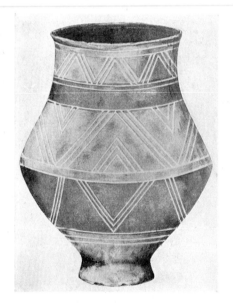

[d]   [b]

POTTERY FROM THE LOWER RHINE AND THE MARNE

SPAIN

IBERIAN POTTERY from South-eastern *Spain, Aragon.*

[*a*], [*b*] Bowls from *Sant Antoni* near *Calaceite*: [*a*] diameter: 21 cm.; [*b*] diameter: 26 cm.

[*c*]–[*f*] Goblets and bowls from *Azáila* in *Saragossa*: [*c*] height: 20 cm.; [*d*] height: 22·5 cm.; [*e*] diameter: 25 cm.; [*f*] diameter: 24 cm.

This pottery owes much to Greek influences. (vii, 785.)

[M. Ebert, *Reallexikon der Vorgeschichte,* x]

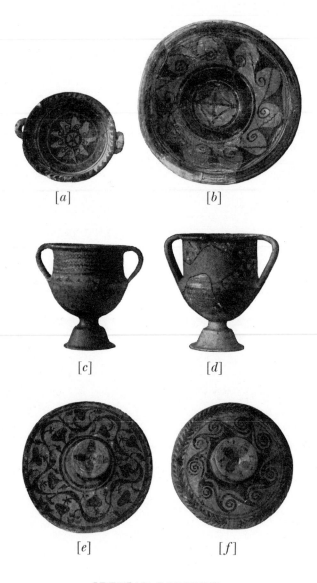

[a]   [b]

[c]   [d]

[e]   [f]

IBERIAN POTTERY

IBERIAN WEAPONS

[a] An iron *Pilum,* 70 cm. long. [b] An iron sword, *Falcata,* 57·4 cm. long. [c] Sword, La Tène C type. *Gladius Hispaniensis,* 68·6 cm. long. All from the cemetery at *Cabrera de Mataró,* Province of *Barcelona.* (vii, 784; viii, 86.)

[M. Ebert, *Reallexikon der Vorgeschichte,* x]

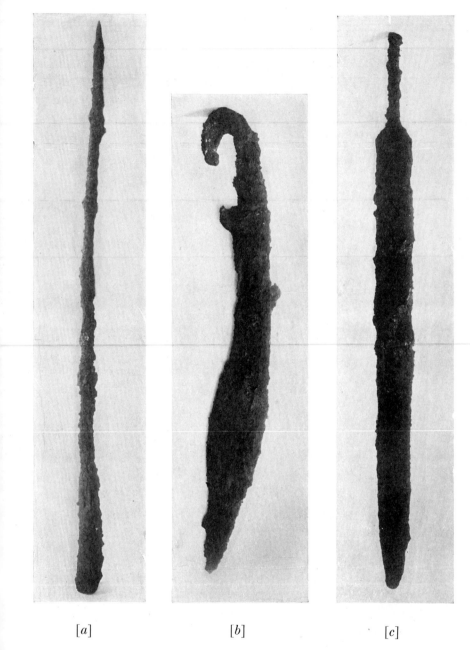

[a]　　　　　　　　[b]　　　　　　　　[c]

IBERIAN WEAPONS

SPAIN

HEADS OF IBERIAN TERRACOTTA FIGURINES

Two of the women wear large ornaments which cover the ears (cf. the head from *Elche* near *Alicante*, *Vol. of Plates*, i, 294 [b]), all three wear the mantilla. From the Iberian site *Serreta* near Alcoy (Province of *Alicante*). (vii, 785.)

[*Photograph Prof. Schulten*]

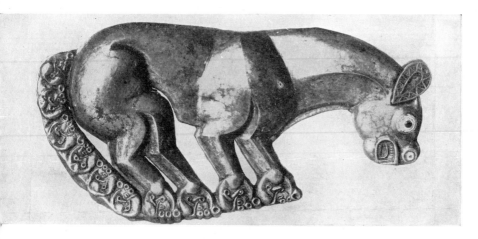

[a]

[b]

[c]

FANTASTIC ANIMALS

[*a*] Part of THE ROMAN CIRCUMVALLATION of *Numantia*. In the foreground, marked by an arrow, appears part of Scipio's vallum. (viii, 321.)

[*b*] HEADQUARTERS OF SCIPIO on *Castillejo* to the north-west of *Numantia*. The picture shows a room with six column-bases in the *praetorium* of Marcellus. (viii, 321.)

[*A. Schulten*, Numantia, III, Pl. 3, 1; Pl. 14, 2]

[a] A PART OF THE CIRCUMVALLATION OF NUMANTIA

[b] HEADQUARTERS OF SCIPIO

4

Two views of the HOUSE OF THE FAUN at *Pompeii*. Second century B.C.

[*a*] The large *atrium*.

[*b*] The two Corinthian columns of the *tablinum* in which was found the Alexander mosaic (cf. *Vol. of Plates*, ii, 110). The 'incrustation' type of mural decoration appears on either side of the *tablinum*. (viii, 347.)

[a]

[b]

HOUSE OF THE FAUN, POMPEII

[a] From an Attic red-figure column-crater by the Orpheus painter, found at *Gela*, now in *Berlin*. Orpheus singing to the accompaniment of his lyre, surrounded by Thracians; they wear long embroidered cloaks and fox-skin caps. Two lances are carried by each Thracian. (viii, 543, 544.)

[A. Furtwängler, *Kleine Schriften*, ii, Pl. 50.]

[b] Fragment of an Attic white-ground kylix by the Pistoxenos painter, found on the Acropolis in *Athens*. A Thracian woman; an animal appears tattooed on her arm. (viii, 543.)

[E. Pfuhl, *Malerei und Zeichnung der Griechen*, iii, 416. F. Bruckmann A.G., Munich.]

[a]

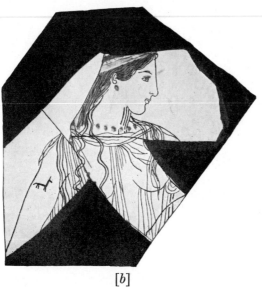

[b]

THRACIANS ON ATTIC VASES

[a] Relief of the fourth century B.C. Bendis, wearing a long-sleeved shortened chiton, covered by an animal's skin (*nebris*) slung over the left shoulder. A long cloak (*zeira*) falls behind, on her head a Thracian cap and on her feet high boots with tops turned over. Her right hand holds a patera, her left a spear. Facing her are two bearded men in chitons, the leader carrying a torch in his lowered right hand. They are followed by eight naked epheboi. In the *British Museum*. (viii, 549.)

[b] Relief from *Shapla-dere* (Mesembria on the coast of the Aegean). A four-wheeled cart drawn by a pair of mules or horses. The driver, wearing a sleeved chiton and cloak, sits on the box. In the cart behind is a passenger wearing a cloak clasped in front. An outrider, wearing short chiton and cloak, precedes the cart. About 450 B.C. Height 1·02 m. *Sofia National Museum*. (viii, 555.)

[c] A funeral stele from *Abdera*. A horseman wearing chiton, chlamys and baggy trousers riding to right; on his right hip, hung from a belt, is a sword, and his right hand once brandished a spear. His left arm raises an oval shield. Behind him (much mutilated) stands the figure of a soldier carrying two spears. Second to first century B.C. Height 1·23 m. *Sofia National Museum*. (viii, 543.)

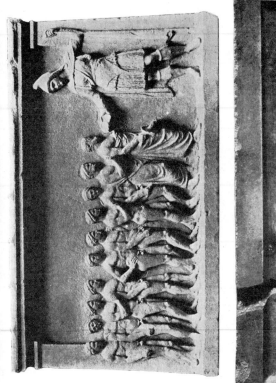

[a]

[b]

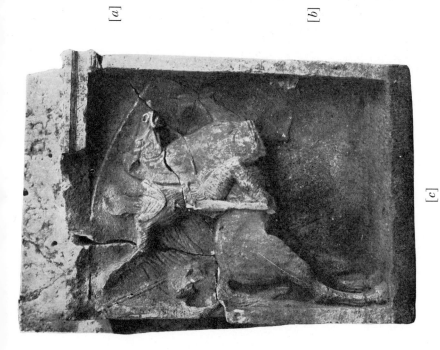

[c]

RELIEFS DEPICTING THRACIAN COSTUME

[a] BRONZE HELMET, Thracian shape, with cheek-pieces, from a grave near *Kovatshovitsa* (district of *Nevrokop* in northern Macedonia). Fourth century B.C. Height 39 cm. *Sofia Nat. Mus.* (viii, 546.)

[b] THRACIAN BRONZE HELMET found near *Karaagačh* (district of *Philippopolis*). Fourth century B.C. (?). *Sofia Nat. Mus.* (viii, 546.)

[c] IRON CURVED SWORD found near *Vinograd* (district of *Gorna-Orechovitza*, northern Bulgaria); La Tène type. Length 40 cm. *Sofia Nat. Mus.* (viii, 545.)

[a]

[b]

[c]

ARMS AND ARMOUR

[a] SILVER CHAIN from *Bukyovtsi* (district of *Orechovo* in northern Bulgaria). Attached to the chain are five (originally six) fibulae, each 8·5 cm. long. The chains depend from rosettes with heads (perhaps of Apollo) beneath them. From the shorter chains hang pellets shaped like poppy-heads.

[b] DECORATED SILVER VASE of oinochoe type, with tall foot and wide lip. Height 15 cm.

[c] SMALL SILVER VASE without decoration. Height 6·4 cm.

All in *Sofia Nat. Mus.* (viii, 557.)

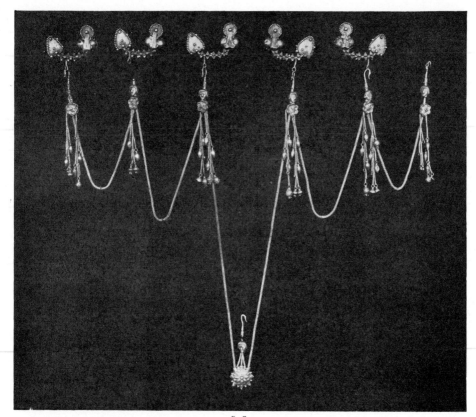

[a]

[b]

[c]

OBJECTS IN SILVER

[*a*] On the left a SILVER FIBULA, length 5·9 cm., engraved, from the district of *Vratsa* in northern Bulgaria; on the right another, length 4·5 cm., from a tumulus near *Tsareva-Livada* (district of *Gabrovo* in northern Bulgaria). La Tène A.

[*b*] POTTERY FUNERAL URN with four handles from *Pashaköi* (district of *Kizilagač* in southern Bulgaria). On it are incised four stylized animals, the one illustrated having upon its flank a design resembling the fibulae above [*a*]. La Tène. Height 29 cm.

All in *Sofia Nat. Mus.* (viii, 557.)

[a] SILVER FIBULA

[b] FUNERAL URN

[a] MASSIVE GOLD RING with swivelling bezel bearing an engraved Thracian inscription in Greek characters:

ΡΟΛΙϵΤΕΝΕΑϵΝ|ΕΡΕΝΕΑΤΙΛ|ΤΕΑΝΗϵΚΟΑ|
ΡΑϵΕΑΔΟΜ|ΕΑΝΤΙΛΕϵΥ|ΠΤΑΜΙΗΕ|ΡΑϵ|ΗΛΤΑ

From a tumulus near *Ezerovo* (district of *Borissovgrad,* southern Bulgaria). Fifth century B.C. Weight 31·3 grammes; the bezel 20 × 17 mm. *Sofia Nat. Mus.* (viii, 554.)

[b] TWO GOLD RINGS (diam. 2·3 cm.) with oval bezels. The one on the left is engraved with the design of a cock: the other was probably once enamelled, the ends of the hoop terminating in serpents' heads. Weights 16·2; 15·45 g.

[c] MASSIVE GOLD ARMLET ending in serpents' heads. Diam. 9 cm. Wt. 298·25 g.

[d] GOLD PENDANT, the central portion of a necklace.

[e] SILVER AMPHORA originally covered in gold-leaf; the lower portion fluted, around the shoulder a double zone of lotus-leaves linked together by volute-like stalks. The handles are winged Persian lion-griffins (cf. the Persian silver-gilt handle, *Vol. of Plates,* i, 324 [d]). The vase is perhaps of Ionian workmanship. Height 27 cm.

[b]–[e] from the tumulus near *Duvanli* in southern Bulgaria (cf. p. 64). Fifth century B.C. *Sofia Nat. Mus.* (viii, 557.)

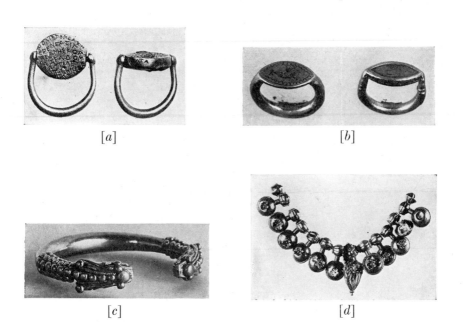

[a]

[b]

[c]

[d]

[e]

OBJECTS IN GOLD AND SILVER

[*a*] GOLD TORC of stout twisted wire, diam. 12·8 cm.; wt. 349 g.; hollow gold pyramidal pendant, height 2·5 cm.; and gold earring, diam. 2·5 cm., the thicker portion hollow.

[*b*] A pair of FISH of thin gold plate. Length 31·5, 28·2 cm. Wts. 45, 50 g. *Philippopolis Nat. Mus.* (viii, 557.)

All from the tumulus near *Duvanli* (cf. p. 62).

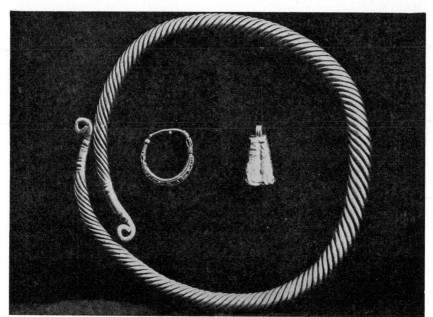

[a] GOLD TORQUE

[b] GOLD FISH

[a] SILVER JUG with handle and curved lip; round the shoulder runs an engraved band of vertical lines. Height 9 cm.

[b] SILVER PHALERA in repoussé work; Heracles strangling the Nemean lion. Diam. 8·8 cm.

[c] On the left, two HORSE-TRAPPINGS of silver heavily alloyed with copper. The upper specimen (length 6·5 cm.) consists of two lion's hind-legs (cf. 70 [a]), the paws ending in birds' heads, while the flank has a griffin's head upon it, the whole being framed in a cable border. The lower specimen (length 6·1 cm.) is shaped like a pair of fantastic monsters. On the right, a convex bronze orna-ment of SPIRALS and a PALMETTE, probably from the base of the handle of a bronze jug. Height 5·3 cm.

All from the tumulus near *Panagyurishte* (cf. p. 68). *Sofia Nat. Mus.* (viii, 558, 573.)

[a]   [b]

OBJECTS IN SILVER

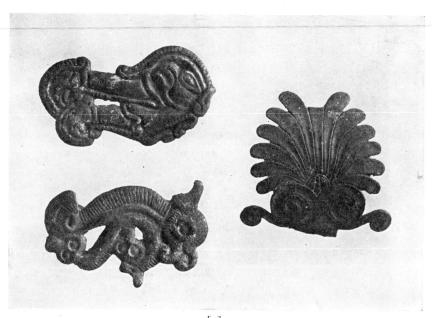

[c]

ORNAMENTS OF SCYTHIAN TYPE

5-2

[a] Three SILVER PHALERAE in repoussé work; on the first a rosette consisting of five lotus-buds (diam. 8·6 cm.); the others (diam. 8 cm.) engraved with a pair of symmetrically grouped animals (perhaps pigs); behind them is a bird and before them a palmette springing from a dotted volute.

[b] THIN SILVER PLATE shaped like a double-axe (probably a horse's frontlet): in the centre is a large rosette, above is Heracles, in barbarian garb, holding a club in his right hand and leading with his left an animal (the Nemean lion or Cerberus?); beneath him and under the rosette are two winged griffin-like monsters; at the bottom appears a siren with a lyre. Length 32 cm.

All from the tumulus near *Panagyurishte* (cf. p. 66). *Sofia Nat. Mus.* (viii, 558.)

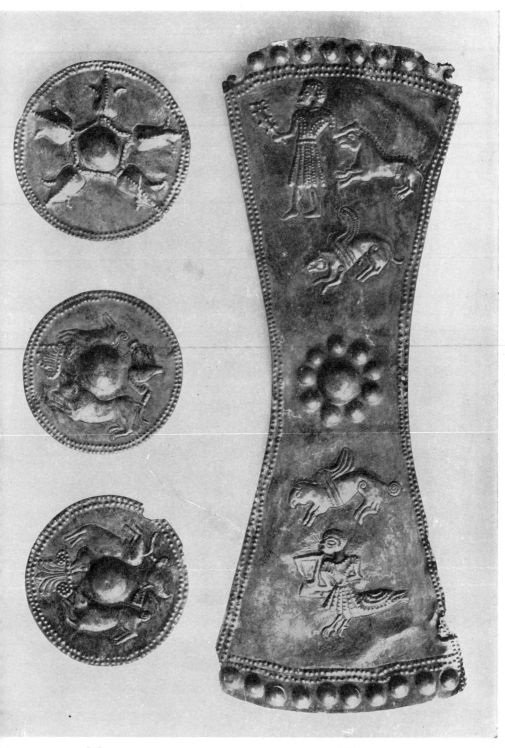

SILVER ORNAMENTS

[a] Above, a pair of SILVER ORNAMENTS, length 7·2 cm., in the form of stylized lion's hind-legs grown together (cf. 66 c). Below, a pair of griffin's heads, lengths 4·5, 4·8 cm. From the tumulus near *Brezovo*. Fourth to third century B.C.

[b] SILVER BOWL with central boss, diam. 10 cm., and a SILVER ORNAMENT, similar to those described above, length 6·5 cm. From *Radyuvene*, fourth to third century B.C.

[c] BRONZE BUCKET with ring-base and double-handle; an egg-and-tongue moulding runs round under the rim; the attachments for the handles are decorated with palmettes. From *Brezovo*. Height 22 cm.

[d], [e] Two SILVER ORNAMENTS worked *à jour*. [d] A design of interlinking spirals and circles round a central boss. Height 6·3 cm. [e] A long-necked stylized animal (horse or reindeer). 5 cm. across. From *Brezovo*.

All in *Sofia Nat. Mus.* (viii, 558, 573.)

[a]

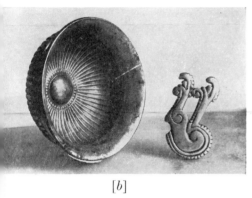

[b]

[c]

[d]

[e]

OBJECTS OF GREEK AND SCYTHIAN TYPE

[a] Two IRON SPEAR-HEADS and the SHEATH of a CURVED SWORD from *Vinograd*. Lengths 40·5 cm.; 37 cm.; 17·5 cm. La Tène (cf. p. 28 [b]).

[b] The upper part of a LONG IRON SWORD, length 38 cm., and the fragment of a SHEATH from a grave near *Popitsa* (district of *Bela-Slatina* in northern Bulgaria) (cf. p. 30 [c]).

[c] IRON BIT from *Vinograd*. Length 23 cm. La Tène.

[d] BRONZE FIBULA, length 8·6 cm., from the district of *Tirnovo* in northern Bulgaria. La Tène.

[e] IRON SPUR, width 9·6 cm., from *Vinograd*.

[f] IRON FIBULA, length 11·7 cm., found near *Pleven* in northern Bulgaria. La Tène C (cf. p. 30 [u], [v]).

All in *Sofia Nat. Mus.* (viii, 560.)

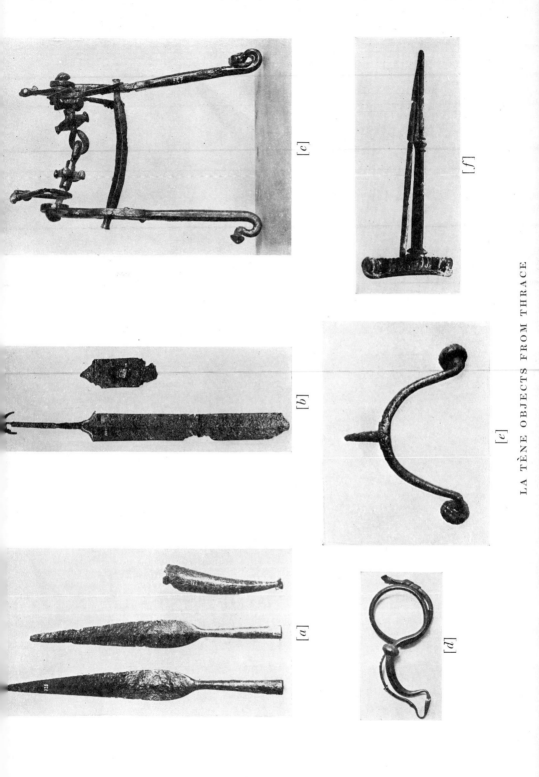

LA TÈNE OBJECTS FROM THRACE

THRACE

[a] A pair of GOLD EARRINGS terminating in lions' heads.

[b] ORNAMENT of twisted silver wire, the ends decorated with lyre-shaped plates. Length 23 cm.

[c], [d] A BRONZE JUG, height 11 cm., and detail of its handle.

All from a grave near *Kran* in the district of *Kazanlik* in southern Bulgaria. In *Sofia Nat. Mus.* (viii, 560.) La Tène B.

[*After drawings by R. Popov*]

[a]

[b]

[c]

[d]

OBJECTS FROM KRAN

A set of three SILVER-GILT PHALERAE in high relief; each has a triple frame consisting of a coarse leaf border, a striped border and a raised cable border.

[a] A horseman wearing trousers, top-boots and a stiff cloak, round his neck a collar of five spirals. He raises his right hand in a gesture of adoration (cf. *Vol. of Plates*, i, 264). Diam. 15·5 cm.

[b] Female bust facing. Two plaits of her thick hair hang down in front of her shoulders; round her neck is a collar of eight spirals and she wears armlets, each of five spirals, with triangular ornaments above and below each armlet; she is clad in a sleeveless woollen tunic with embroidered border, a plait (perhaps a gold ornament?) hangs between the breasts. Over each shoulder appears a bird (dove?). Diam. 18·3 cm.

[c] Elaborate rosette with central sunflower ornament. Diam. 12·5 cm. [cf. Rostovtzeff, *Recueil Kondakoff*, Pls. XXIII, XXIV; and p. 110 below].

All from *Galiče* (district of *Orechovo* in northern Bulgaria). *Sofia Nat. Mus.* (viii, 560.) Second to first century B.C.

[a]

[b]

[c]

SILVER-GILT PHALERAE

ENGRAVED and GILT SILVER MIRROR, probably imported from Aeolian Asia Minor. Greek workmanship. Found in a Scythian barrow-grave near *Kelermes* in the Kuban region. Adorned with various figures of gods and animals, the most prominent being the winged figure of the Great Goddess, mistress of animals, the πότνια θηρῶν, and opposite it a group of two Silens (forest-spirits) fighting a griffin. Sixth century B.C. In the *Hermitage.* (viii, 571.)

[Rostovtzeff, *Iranians and Greeks*, Pl. VI; Ebert, *Reallexikon der Vorgeschichte*, VI, p. 279, Pl. 81 *a*]

SILVER MIRROR

[*a*] GOLD CUP of Assyro-Phoenician or early Persian workmanship. Found in a Scythian barrow-grave near *Kelermes* in the Kuban region. Decorated with three rows of animals in repoussé work: a row of running ostriches, another of dogs chasing gazelles or antelopes, and a third with figures of male and female ibexes. The style of the last row recalls the Scythian animal-style. Sixth century B.C. *Hermitage.* (viii, 571.)

[Rostovtzeff, *Iranians and Greeks*, Pl. VII, 1; Ebert, *Reall. d. Vorg.* VI, Pl. 81 *b*]

[*b*] GOLD FISH, probably a horse-trapping or armour plate, of Ionian workmanship. Found in Germany in Brandenburg near *Vettersfelde* and forming part of a treasure which belonged originally to a Scythian chieftain or part of the furniture of a Scythian grave. The body of the fish is decorated with two rows of figures: lions attacking hoofed animals and fishes, headed by a Triton; the tail bears a figure of an eagle; all in repoussé work. The extremities of the tail end in ram-heads. Early fifth century B.C. *Antiquarium, Berlin.* (viii, 571, 587.)

[A. Furtwängler, *Der Goldfund von Vettersfelde,* im 73 *Berliner Winckelmanns-programm* 1883 (reprinted in Furtwängler, *Kleine Schriften,* II (1912); Ebert, *Reall. der Vorg.* XIV, pp. 156 *sqq.*, Pl. 44]

[a]

GOLD CUP

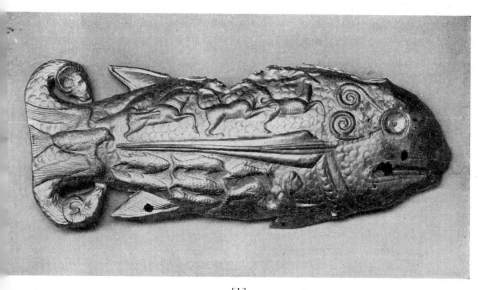

[b]

GOLD FISH

[*a*] GOLD EARRINGS of Greek workmanship. Found in a grave of the necropolis of *Theodosia* in the Crimea. Fourth century B.C. *Hermitage.* (viii, 585.)

[Minns, *Scythians and Greeks*, p. 401, fig. 294, 3; Rostovtzeff, *Iranians and Greeks*, Pl. XVIII, 1]

[*b*] GOLD NECKLACE of Greek workmanship. Found in a grave of the necropolis of *Nymphaeum* (El-Tegen) in the Crimea. Fifth century B.C. *Ashmolean Museum, Oxford.* (viii, 585.)

[Rostovtzeff, *Iranians and Greeks*, Pl. XVI, 4]

[a]

[b]

GOLD JEWELLERY

[*a*], [*b*] HANDLE and SHEATH of a SHORT SCYTHIAN SWORD
(*akinakes*). Plated with gold, made by an Ionian artist for a Scythian customer or by a Scythian artisan trained by an Ionian.
Found in a Scythian barrow-grave near the farm *Shumeiko, Romny,*
Poltava. The handle is adorned with geometric ornaments in
granulate work, like Ionian works of the same kind, and the sheath
with figures of animals treated both in the Near Eastern and in the
Scythian manner. The two heraldic ibexes above are orientalizing;
the vertical row of seven cat-like creatures is Scythian in style.
Sixth century B.C. In the *Museum, Kiev.* (viii, 571, 587.)

[Rostovtzeff, *Iranians and Greeks,* Pl. VIII, 3; W. Ginters, *Das Schwert der Skythen
und der Sarmaten,* Pl. 3 *c* and 69 *b* (reconstruction of this and contemporary and
related Scythian swords), cf. Ebert, *Rcall. d. Vorg.* xiv, pp. 156 *sqq.,* Pl. 15]

[*c*] SHORT SCYTHIAN BRONZE SWORD (*akinakes*), probably of
local Scythian workmanship. Found in a Scythian barrow near
Poltava. The handle is adorned with cast figures of animals treated
in the manner of the Scythian animal style (two feline and two
hoofed animals, probably female elks or reindeer). Sixth century
B.C. *Museum, Poltava.* Unpublished. (viii, 571, 587.)

[*d*] GOLD-PLATED SHEATH of a SCYTHIAN SWORD, probably of
Panticapaean workmanship. Adorned with a running design in the
Ionian animal style. The work is repoussé (lions and heads of a
stag or reindeer), with the exception of the chape which bears the
figure of a stylized mask or Medusa-head. Found in the side-grave
of the barrow of *Solokha* (left side of the lower Dnieper). Fourth
century B.C. *Hermitage.* (viii, 571, 587.)

[W. Ginters, *Das Schwert der Skythen und der Sarmaten,* Pl. 22 *b*; Ebert, *Reall. d. Vorg.*
xii, pp. 294 *sqq.,* Pl. 81 *b*]

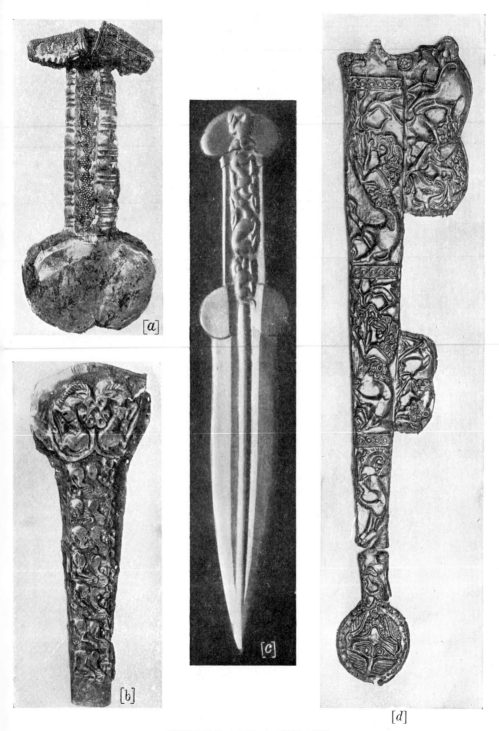

[a]

[b]

[c]

[d]

SWORDS AND A SHEATH

[a] Gold figure of a WILD BEAST (lioness?). Probably a decoration for armour. Scythian or Central Asiatic workmanship. Note in it traits which link this peculiar treatment of metal by the artist (the so-called *Schrägschnitt* or a peculiar kind of chip-carving) with the typical treatment of wood or bone; cp. 112 [b], [c]. Found in a barrow-grave near *Kelermes* in the Kuban region (cp. 78 and 80 [a]). The ears of the beast are inlaid with amber, the eye and the nostrils with enamel in proto-cloisonné technique. The paws of the animal, rendered in repoussé work, are shaped as cats curled up. The tail consists of six such medallions likewise in repoussé work. This treatment of extremities is one of the peculiarities of the Central Asiatic beast-style. Sixth century B.C. *Hermitage.* (viii, 571, 587.)

[Rostovtzeff, *Iranians and Greeks*, Pl. IX, 1; *idem, The Animal Style in S. Russia and China*, Pl. V, 2; Ebert, *Reall. d. Vorg.* xiii, Pl. 27 A (c); Borovka, *Scythian Art*, Pl. 12]

[b] Figure of an ANIMAL of FELINE species. Cast bronze, plated with gold. Scythian workmanship. Found in the grave of the *Zolotoj Kurgan* (Golden Barrow) near *Simferopol* in the Crimea. The gold sheath which covers the centre of the body of the beast is adorned with almond-shaped wire frames originally filled with enamel. Sixth century B.C. *Hermitage.* (viii, 571, 587.)

[Ebert, *Reall. d. Vorg.* xiii, Pl. 31 A (c); Borovka, *Scythian Art*, Pl. 13]

[c] Figure of an ANIMAL of FELINE species. Cast bronze, plated with gold. Scythian workmanship. Place of origin unknown. The shoulder of the beast is adorned with a stylized eagle, or eagle-griffin, head, which is a peculiarity of the Central Asiatic animal style (cp. 112 [b]). Sixth to fifth century B.C. *Louvre*, Department of Far Eastern Art. Unpublished.

[*a*] BRONZE POLE-TOP. Cast bronze. Scythian workmanship. Found in a Scythian barrow-grave near the *Ulski Aul* in the Kuban region. The pole-top shows the shape of an eagle-head reduced to a stylized beak (spiral) and an equally stylized eye (formed as a human eye). The eagle-head is adorned with other stylized eagle-heads reduced to beaks and eyes of varying sizes. Below, a figure of a crouched ibex. The pole-top is a typical product of the Central Asiatic animal-style. Sixth century B.C. *Hermitage.* (viii, 571, 587.)

[Rostovtzeff, *Iranians and Greeks*, Pl. X A; *idem, Animal Style*, Pl. VI, 1, 2; Borovka, *Scythian Art*, Pls. 24 and 25; Ebert, *Reall. d. Vorg.* Pl. VI, 1, 2. Cf. Rostowzew, *Skythien und der Bosporus*, p. 264]

[*b*] BRONZE POLE-TOP. Cast bronze. Scythian workmanship. Place of origin unknown. Shape of a mule-head. Sixth to fifth century B.C. *Louvre, Paris.* Cp. Rostovtzeff, *Iranians and Greeks*, Pl. X C; Borovka, *Scythian Art*, Pl. 26 (almost identical pole-top from Kelermes, Kuban region). (viii, 571, 587.)

[*c*] BRONZE PLAQUE from horse-trappings. Cast bronze. Scythian workmanship. Found in one of the graves of the *Seven Brothers Barrows* in the Kuban region. Stylized female elk-head. Fifth century B.C. *Hermitage.* (viii, 571, 587.)

[Rostovtzeff, *Iranians and Greeks*, p. 196, fig. 22 c: *Animal Style*, Pl. X, 7; similar plaques, Borovka, *Scythian Art*, Pl. 5]

[*d*] BRONZE PLAQUE from horse-trappings. Cast bronze. Scythian workmanship. Found in one of the graves of the *Seven Brothers Barrows.* Stylized boar's head. Fifth century B.C. *Hermitage.*

[Minns, *Scythians and Greeks*, p. 214, fig. 115; Rostovtzeff, *Animal Style*, Pl. X, 8; Borovka, *Scythian Art*, Pl. 170]

[a]　　　　　　　　　　　　　　[b]

POLE-TOPS

 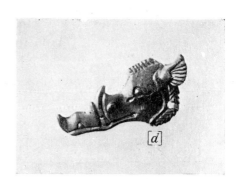

[c]　　　　　　　　　　[d]

PLAQUES

[*a*] SILVER RHYTON. Persian or Graeco-Persian workmanship. Found in one of the graves of the *Seven Brothers Barrows* in the Kuban region. The end of the rhyton is shaped as the forepart of a winged ibex (an animal typical of Persian art). Fifth century B.C. *Hermitage.* (viii, 571, 587.)

[Minns, *Scythians and Greeks*, p. 211, fig. 110; Rostovtzeff, *Iranians and Greeks*, Pl. XII A; Ebert, *Reall. d. Vorg.* XII, pp. 84 *sqq.*, Pl. 18 A]

[*b*] GOLD ARMLET. Greek or Graeco-Persian workmanship. Found in one of the graves of the *Seven Brothers Barrows*. The body of the armlet consists of two fine flexible chains; the ends terminate in snakes' heads. Fifth to fourth century B.C. *Hermitage.* (viii, 571, 587.)

[Rostovtzeff, *Iranians and Greeks*, Pl. XV, 1]

[*c*], [*d*] GOLD PLAQUES of roughly triangular form. Originally probably nailed to the rim of a wooden or horn rhyton. Persian, or Graeco-Persian, workmanship. Found in one of the graves of the *Seven Brothers Barrows*. One of the plaques is adorned with a figure of a winged panther or tiger killing an ibex, the other with that of an eagle killing a kid. Fifth century B.C. *Hermitage.* (viii, 571, 587.)

[Minns, *Scythians and Greeks*, p. 211, fig. 112; Rostovtzeff, *Iranians and Greeks*, Pl. XIII; Ebert, *Reall. d. Vorg.* XII, p. 87, Pl. 19]

[*e*] GOLD PLAQUE, probably nailed originally to the rim of a wooden or horn rhyton, produced in one of the Greek cities of the Black Sea. Found probably in a Scythian barrow near *Maïkop* in the Kuban region. Sea-eagle carrying a sturgeon. Cp. the coins of Sinope and Olbia. Fifth century B.C. *Antiquarium, Berlin.* Unpublished. (viii, 587.)

[Cf. Rostowzew, *Skythien und der Bosporus*, p. 346]

[*f*] ENGRAVED GEM, enlarged. Persian or Graeco-Persian workmanship. Found in a barrow of the necropolis of *Nymphaeum* (El-Tegen) near Panticapaeum. Horned Persian lion-griffin. Fifth century B.C. *Ashmolean Museum, Oxford.* (viii, 571, 587.)

[Rostovtzeff, *Iranians and Greeks*, Pl. XVI, 1]

[c]

[d]

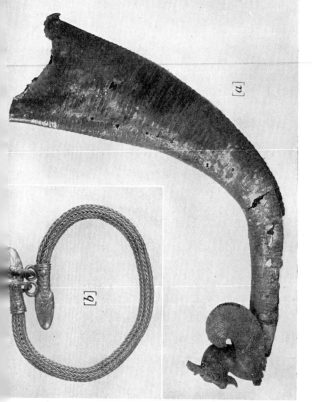

[a]

[b]

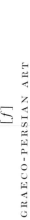

[f]

[e]

[*a*] BRONZE PATERA HANDLE of Greek workmanship. Found in one of the graves of the *Seven Brothers Barrows* in the Kuban region. A Hermes Kriophoros of ornamental character. Sixth to fifth century B.C. *Hermitage*. (viii, 563.)

[*Compte-rendu de la Comm. Arch.* 1877, Atlas, I, 9; Minns, *Scythians and Greeks*, p. 378]

[*b*], [*c*] GOLD PLAQUES, originally sewn on to garments, of Panticapaean workmanship made for Scythian customers. Probably part of the same find to which belongs the plaque 90 [*e*]. Some plaques have the shape of stags with stylized horns, the extremities of which end in eagle-heads, some that of eagle-griffins. Fifth century B.C. *Metropolitan Museum, New York*. (viii, 587.)

[Rostovtzeff, *Animal Style*, Pl. IX, 1]

[*d*] BRONZE STAG. Handle of a Scythian kettle. Greek workmanship. Found in a barrow of the *Ulski Aul* in the Kuban region. Sixth century B.C. *Hermitage*. (viii, 563.)

[Borovka, *Bulletin of the Academy of the History of Material Civilization*, II, 1922, pp. 193 *sqq.*, Pl. II; Ebert, *Reall. d. Vorg.* XIV, p. 2, Pl. 1 C]

[*e*] BRONZE MIRROR with wooden handle. Greek workmanship. Found in one of the graves of the *Seven Brothers Barrows*. The lower part of the surface of the mirror is adorned with an engraved palmette. Another engraved design, added probably later by a Scythian artisan, shows two wild beasts attacking a deer. (viii, 563.)

[Rostowzew, *Skythien und der Bosporus*, p. 301]

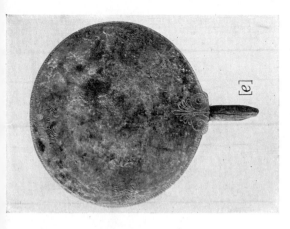

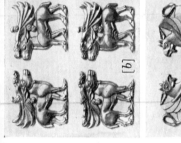

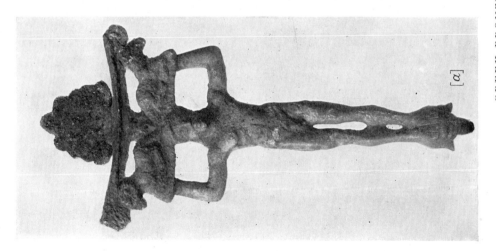

GREEK BRONZES AND SCYTHIAN GOLD PLAQUES

BOSPORUS

Two views of the TSARSKI KURGAN ('Royal' Barrow) near Kerch. First half of fourth century B.C.

[a] The interior, seen through the doorway. The courses up to the one numbered 7 are perpendicular, above that corbelled.

[b] The twelve courses of the vaults, corbelled out one above the other. (viii, 585).

[Reproduced from *Jahreshefte des oesterreichischen archaeologischen Instituts*, x, 1907, p. 236 *sq.* See Minns, *Scythians and Greeks*, p. 194]

[a]   [b]

THE 'ROYAL' BARROW

[*a*], [*b*] P A I N T E D C L A Y V A S E S of Greek, probably Athenian, work-manship; found in a Greek grave of the necropolis of *Phanagoreia*. [*a*] Birth of Aphrodite; [*b*] winged Sphinx. Late fifth century B.C. *Hermitage*. (viii, 585.)

[Minns, *Scythians and Greeks*, p. 345, fig. 251; p. 344, fig. 250; Rostovtzeff, *Iranians and Greeks*, Pl. XVII, 1; Pridik, *Zeitschrift für bildende Kunst*, 18, pp. 172 *sqq.*; Phar-makowski, *Three polychrome vases in the form of statuettes found in Phanagoreia*, Memoirs of the Academy of the History of Mat. Civ. i, 1921; Rostowzew, *Skythien und der Bosporus*, p. 225. Often discussed and reproduced in works on the history of Greek art. Bibliography in M. H. Swindler, *Ancient Painting*, p. 462]

GREEK VASES

ARYBALLUS OF XENOPHANTUS. Work of an Athenian artist, perhaps resident at Panticapaeum. Found in a Greek grave at *Panticapaeum*. The body of the vase is adorned with figures in relief and painting. The figures in relief are coloured white, red and blue, with gilt accessories; the end-figures are flat in red-figure technique. The scene represents Persians on a hunting expedition, their names being inscribed beside the figures. The animals hunted are partly real, partly fantastic. The vase bears the inscription: ΞΕΝΟΦΑΝΤΟΣ ΕΠΟΙΗΣΕΝ ΑΘΗΝ. Shortly before 400 B.C. *Hermitage.* (viii, 585.)

[*Compte-rendu de la Comm. Arch.* 1866, Atlas, Pl. IV; *Antiquités du Bosphore Cimmérien*, Pl. XLV (here reproduced); Minns, *Scythians and Greeks*, p. 343, fig. 249. Often discussed and reproduced. Bibliography in Pfuhl, *Malerei und Zeichnung der Griechen*, II, pp. 591 and 600; M. H. Swindler, *Ancient Painting*, p. 297]

[*a*] CLAY VASE painted with various colours in the distemper technique. Panticapaean workmanship. Found in a rock-cut grave of the necropolis of *Panticapaeum*. A Greek fighting an Amazon. Third century B.C. *Hermitage.* (viii, 585.)

[*Compte-rendu de la Comm. Arch.* 1878–9, Atlas, Pl. I, 5; Minns, *Scythians and Greeks*, p. 348, fig. 253; M. H. Swindler, *Ancient Painting*, fig. 565]

[*b*] CLAY AMPHORA with painted and plastic ornaments painted in various colours. Greek workmanship. Found at *Olbia*. Third century B.C. *Hermitage.* (viii, 585.)

[Trever, *Materials for the Archaeology of S. Russia*, xxxv, 1918]

[a]

VASES

[b]

Frieze of a LARGE SILVER AMPHORA. Panticapaean workmanship. Found in one of the graves of the *Chertomlyk Barrow* on the right bank of the lower Dnieper. Scythians in the prairies of S. Russia lassoing and saddling horses on the eve of a military expedition. Fourth century B.C. *Hermitage.* (viii, 571, 587.)

[Reproduced from *Antike Denkmäler*, IV, Pl. 46. (F. Bruckmann, A.G.) To the bibliography given there by Waldhauer add P. Jacobsthal, *Ornamentik griechischer Vasen*, Pls. 142, 143]

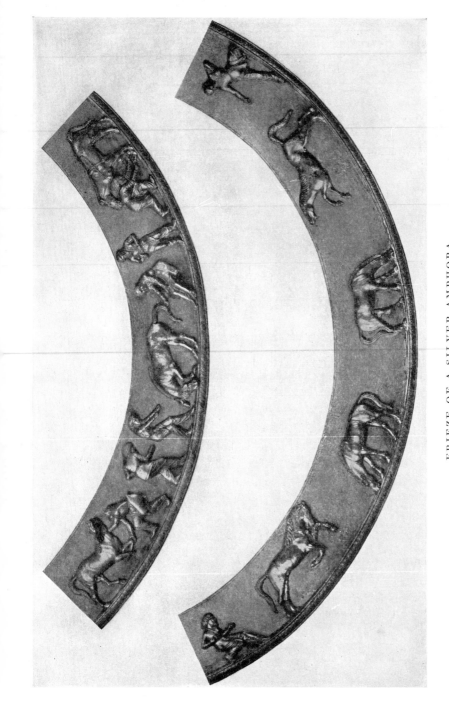

FRIEZE OF A SILVER AMPHORA

[*a*] GOLD PATERA. Panticapaean workmanship. Found in the side-grave of the *Solokha Barrow* on the left side of the lower Dnieper. The patera is adorned with figures in repoussé work: three rows of grouped animals showing wild beasts killing various creatures. Two Greek inscriptions probably give the name of the artist and that of the owner. Fourth century B.C. *Hermitage.* (viii, 571, 587.)

[Rostovtzeff, *Iranians and Greeks*, Pl. XX, 12; Ebert, *Reall. d. Vorg.* iv, Pl. 85; xii, p. 298, § 10]

[*b*] SILVER BOWL. Panticapaean workmanship. Found in the side-grave of the *Solokha Barrow.* Young Scythians on horseback hunting lions. Between them appear two lions playing with each other, and, on the opposite side, a group of two Molossian dogs. Fourth century B.C. *Hermitage.* (viii, 571, 587.)

[Rostovtzeff, *Iranians and Greeks*, Pl. XX, 12; Ebert, *Reall. d. Vorg.* xii, Pl. 83]

[a]

GOLD PATERA

[b]

SILVER BOWL

[a] GOLD PLAQUE sewn originally on to a belt. Local workmanship; found in a Scythian grave in a barrow near *Axjutinzy, Romny, Poltava*. A Scythian king, or chieftain, seated holding a battle-axe in his left hand and a drinking cup in his right. A bow-and-arrow case (*gorytos*) hangs on his right side. Repoussé work. Third century B.C. *Historical Museum, Moscow.* (viii, 571, 587.)

[Minns, *Scythians and Greeks*, p. 182, fig. 75 *bis*; Rostovtzeff, *Bull. de la Comm. Arch.* 49 (1913), p. 8, fig. 3; Ebert, *Reall. d. Vorg.* XIII, p. 95, Pl. 39 F (*a*)]

[b]–[n] GOLD PLAQUES originally sewn on garments. Panticapaean workmanship. Repoussé work. Found in various Scythian barrows of the steppes of S. Russia. [b]–[d] show ritual scenes: [b] 'sacramental draught' of a Scythian prince administered by the Great Goddess of the Scythians; [c] the Great Goddess and her sacred animals (dog and raven); [d] ritual wrestling. Plaques [g] and [j] recall contemporary Greek coin-types. The rest are purely ornamental. Some of the plaques belong to the fifth century B.C., the majority to the fourth, some to the third. *Hermitage* and *Museum, Kiev.* (viii, 571, 587.)

[Rostovtzeff, *Bull. de la Comm. Arch.* 49 (1913); *Iranians and Greeks*, Pl. XXIII; Minns, *Scythians and Greeks, passim*, esp. p. 208]

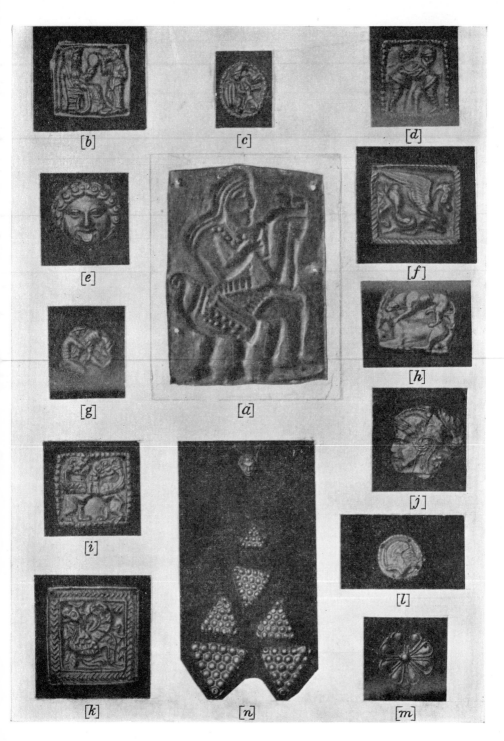

GOLD PLAQUES

[*a*]–[*d*] GOLD ORNAMENTS in open work. Probably ornaments for saddles. Scythian, or Graeco-Scythian, workmanship. Found partly in the earth, partly in the graves of the *Alexandropol Barrow* (Lugovaja Mogila) on right side of the lower Dnieper. Degenerate and geometricized Ionian and Scythian animal figures both single and in groups. Third century B.C. *Hermitage.* (viii, 587.)

[*Recueil d'antiquités de la Scythie*, Pl. XV; Minns, *Scythians and Greeks*, p. 155, fig. 42; Ebert, *Reall. d. Vorg.* XIII, pp. 87 *sqq.*, Pls. 36 A and 36 C]

[*e*] BRONZE POLE-TOP. Scythian workmanship in cast bronze. Found in the earth of the *Alexandropol Barrow*. Winged figure of the Great Goddess of the Scythians. Third century B.C. *Hermitage.* (viii, 584.)

[*Recueil d'antiquités de la Scythie*, Pl. I, 8; Minns, *Scythians and Greeks*, p. 154, fig. 40; Ebert, *Reall. d. Vorg.* XIII, Pl. 35 D (*c*)]

[*f*] IRON OPEN-WORK FIGURE, nailed originally on to a funeral chariot or on to a funeral canopy, plated with gold. Found in the earth of the *Alexandropol Barrow*. Figure of the winged Great Goddess of the Scythians, the πότνια θηρῶν, holding two stags. Third century B.C. *Hermitage.* (viii, 584.)

[*Recueil d'antiquités de la Scythie*, Pl. I, 3, 4; Ebert, *Reall. d. Vorg.* XIII, Pl. 35 D (*g*)]

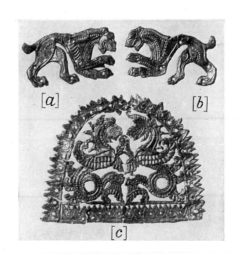

GOLD ORNAMENTS

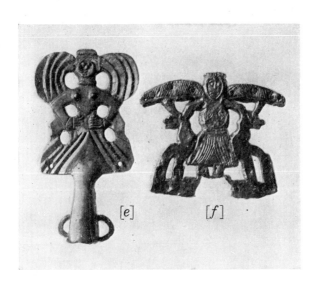

FIGURES OF THE WINGED GODDESS

Eight GOLD CIRCULAR PLAQUES (phalerae) from horse-trappings.
Repoussé work. Indo-Hellenic workmanship (?). Found in a horse's
grave of the *Alexandropol Barrow* on the lower Dnieper. [*a*] Single
figures of animals (eagle, winged horse, bull and lion): [*b*] bulls'
heads forming a solar wheel around a human face in front view,
four boars' heads forming a solar wheel around a rosette, and a
rosette of eight leaves; all probably symbols of a solar religion
(cf. p. 76 above). Third century B.C. *Hermitage.* (viii, 588.)

[*Recueil d'antiquités de la Scythie*, Pl. VII, 1, 3, 7, 6; Rostovtzeff, *Recueil Kondakoff*,
Pl. XXII; Ebert, *Reall. d. Vorg.* xiii, Pl. 36 C (*c*)–(*k*)]

[a]

[b]

GOLD PLAQUES

[*a*] GOLD PLAQUE nailed originally to the rim of a wooden or horn rhyton. Persian, or Graeco-Persian, workmanship. Repoussé work. Found in one of the graves of the *Seven Brothers Barrows*. Figure of a wolf-headed dragon with Asiatic wings and a tail ending in the head of a goose. Fifth century B.C. *Hermitage.* (viii, 571, 587.)

[Minns, *Scythians and Greeks*, p. 211, fig. 111; Rostovtzeff, *Iranians and Greeks*, Pl. XIII D; Ebert, *Reall. d. Vorg.* XIII, Pl. 19 D; Borovka, *Scythian Art*, Pl. 20 A]

[*b*] GOLD STAG, probably a decoration for armour, or a horse-trapping, and gold chain adorned with gold cylinders surmounted by figurines of lions. Scythian or Central-Asiatic workmanship. The stag in repoussé work has the eye and ear inlaid with enamel. Under the stylized horns is an eagle's head. Found in Hungary near *Zöldhalompuszta* in a cremation grave. Sixth century B.C. (viii, 571, 573.)

[N. Fettich, *La Trouvaille scythe de Zöldhalompuszta près de Miskolc, Hongrie*, in *Archaeologia Hungarica*, III, 1928, pp. 37 *sqq.*; G. Childe, *The Danube in Prehistory*, 1929, pp. 394 *sqq.*]

[*c*] GOLD STAG, probably a decoration for armour or a horse-trapping. Scythian or Central-Asiatic workmanship. Repoussé work. The eye and ear originally inlaid with enamel. Found in Hungary near *Tápios-Szent-Marten* in a cremation grave. (viii, 571, 573.)

[N. Fettich, *op. cit.*; G. Wilke, in Ebert, *Reall. d. Vorg.* XII, Pl. 66 *a*; Rostovtzeff, *Animal Style*, Pl. V, 1]

[a]

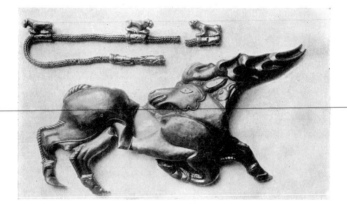

[b]

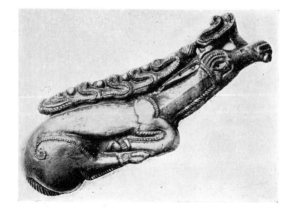

[c]

GOLD ORNAMENTS

MARBLE PORTRAIT HEAD, life size, perhaps of a Pergamene prince from *Pergamum*. Now in *Berlin*. (viii, 600.)

[*Altertümer von Pergamon*, VII, Pl. XXIV]

8-2

(*a*) MARBLE PANOPLY found in *Rhodes*; in the *Museum of Rhodes*. (viii, 637.)

[*Clara Rhodos*, I, 1928]

(*b*) A ROCK-CARVING at *Lindus* in Rhodes representing the stern of a Rhodian ship. One of the rudders is lashed to the side; the helmsman's seat is upon the deck under the curved *aphlaston*. (viii, 638.)

[*Bulletin de l'Académie royale des Sciences et des Lettres* (Copenhagen), 1907, p. 31]

[a] RHODIAN MARBLE PANOPLY

[b] SHIP'S STERN AT LINDUS

[*a*] ARIADNE, from the southern slopes of the *Acropolis at Athens*; *National Museum, Athens*. About 300 B.C. (viii, 670.)

[*Phot. English Photographic Co.*]

[*b*] MENANDER, terminal bust from neighbourhood of *Naples*; in *Boston*. Roman copy probably of an original by the sons of Praxiteles, set up in the theatre of Dionysus at Athens in the early third century B.C. (viii, 671.)

[Delbrück, *Antike Porträts*, Pl. 20]

[*c*] THEMIS by Chaerestratus, from *Rhamnus*; *National Museum, Athens*. Late fourth or early third century B.C. (viii, 670.)

[*Phot. English Photographic Co.*]

[*d*] SELENE descending to Endymion. Found in *Rome*; in the *Vatican*. Roman copy from a Greek original of the early third century B.C. The arms, right foot and other patches are modern. (viii, 670.)

[*Phot. Brogi*]

[a] ARIADNE

[b] MENANDER

[c] THEMIS

[d] SELENE

[*a*] DIONYSUS, from the choragic monuments of Thrasyllus and Thrasycles, southern slope of Acropolis, *Athens*; in the *British Museum*. 320 or 271 B.C. (viii, 670.)

[*Phot. Prof. B. Ashmole*]

[*b*] DEMOSTHENES, probably from the neighbourhood of *Tusculum*; in the *Vatican*: Roman copy in marble from a bronze original by Polyeuctus, 280 B.C. The most serious restorations are the forearms, and the hands, which in the original were clasped. (viii, 671.)

[*Phot. Brogi*]

[*c*] NILE, from a temple of Isis in *Rome*; in the *Vatican*. Copy of the first century A.D. from an original of the third century B.C. Many details restored, especially parts of the children. (viii, 671.)

[*Phot. Brogi*]

[a] DIONYSUS

[b] DEMOSTHENES

[c] NILE

[*a*] Head of a girl, *Taranto*. Roman copy from an Athenian original of the early third century B.C. (viii, 671.)

[*Phot. Prof. B. Ashmole*]

[*b*] Head of a MUSE; in the *Lateran Museum, Rome*. Roman copy from an original of the third century B.C. (viii, 677.)

[*Phot. Alinari*]

[*c*] Head of POLYHYMNIA; in *Dresden*. Roman copy from an original of the third century B.C. (See p. 142 [*c*].) (viii, 677.)

[*Phot. Dresden Museum*]

[*d*] Head of a statue of TYCHE. (See p. 124 [*d*].) (viii, 124.)

[*Phot. Faraglia*]

[a]   [b]

[c]   [d]

FEMALE HEADS

[a], [b] Small bronzes of TYCHE in *Florence* and in the *de Clercq* Collection. The swimming river-god, Orontes, appears beside the second, but is missing from the first.

[c] TYCHE of Antioch. Roman copy in marble from the bronze original by Eutychides. From *Rome*: in *Budapest*.

[*Photographs F. Bruckmann A.G., Munich*]

[d] YOUNG TYCHE. Roman copy in marble after a bronze original by Eutychides, early third century B.C. From the *Esquiline*; *Palazzo dei Conservatori, Rome.* (Cf. p. 122 [d].) (viii, 674, 675.)

[*Phot. Alinari*]

[a] [b]

[c] [d]

FIGURES OF TYCHE

The statue of VICTORY from *Samothrace*; in the *Louvre*.

By a Rhodian sculptor, set up to commemorate the battle of Cos, *c.* 258 B.C. It recalls an earlier (lost) statue dedicated by Demetrius Poliorcetes, as a memorial of the battle of Salamis in Cyprus, which is reproduced on certain of his coins. (Cf. *Vol. of Plates*, ii, 10 [*k*].) (vii, 714 *sq.*; viii, 675.)

[*Phot. Giraudon*]

VICTORY FROM SAMOTHRACE

[*a*] LAOCOON and his sons attacked by serpents. From the *Palace of Titus, Rome*; in the *Vatican*. By Agesander, Polydorus and Athenodorus of Rhodes, early first century B.C. Photograph from a cast in which one of the boys and other parts have been removed. (viii, 678.)

[*Phot. University of Berlin*]

[*b*] The punishment of DIRCE by Zethus and Amphion. From the *Baths of Caracalla, Rome*; in *Naples*. Roman version in marble of the bronze by Apollonius and Tauriscus of Tralles. The men's heads, legs and arms, the woman's head and torso, and many other parts, are modern. (viii, 678.)

[*Phot. F. Bruckmann A.G., Munich*]

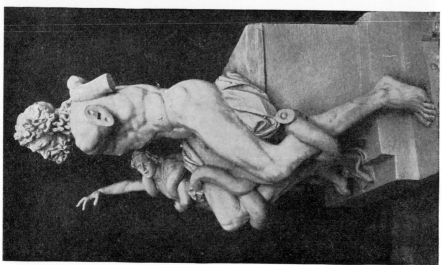

[a] LAOCOON

[b] DIRCE

[a], [b] Roman copies in marble from bronze originals of the late fourth century B.C. probably by Lysippus or his school. From *Herculaneum*; in *Dresden*. (viii, 677.)

[*Phot. Dresden Museum*]

[c] Figure from the balustrade of the altar of Athena Polias, *Priene*; in *Berlin*. Late fourth century B.C. (viii, 677.)

[*Phot. Berlin Museum*]

[d] Statue from *Magnesia*; in *Constantinople*. About 200 B.C. (viii, 677.)

[*Phot. Sebah and Joaillier*]

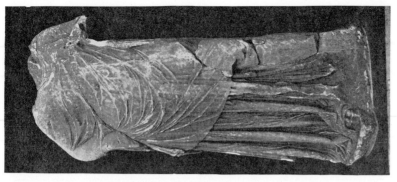

[d]

[c]

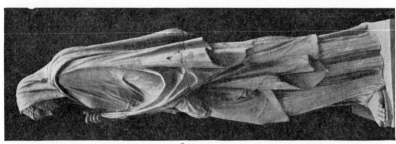

[b]

[a]

DRAPED FEMALE FIGURES

9-2

[*a*] HERMES resting while on a journey. Roman version in bronze of a bronze original of the third century B.C. Lysippic school. From *Herculaneum*; in *Naples*. (viii, 675.)

[*Phot. Anderson*]

[*b*] Boy praying. Bronze copy of a bronze original by Boedas, a pupil of Lysippus; early third century B.C. From *Italy*; in *Berlin*. (viii, 673.)

[*Phot. Berlin Museum*]

[*c*] Boy taking a thorn from his foot. Roman fountain-figure, a copy in marble after a bronze original of the third century B.C. From *Rome*; in the *British Museum*. (viii, 675.)

[*Phot. British Museum*]

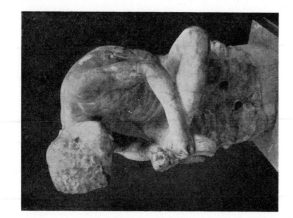

MALE FIGURES

[*a*] Head of a dying oriental—probably a Persian killed in a battle against Athenians. Copy, in marble of Asia Minor, from a bronze original of the dedication of Attalus I, third quarter of the third century B.C. From the *Palatine*; *Terme Museum, Rome.* (viii, 679.)

[*Phot. Anderson*]

[*b*] A Gaul stabbing himself to avoid capture, after killing his wife: the 'Ludovisi Gaul.' Copy, in marble of Asia Minor, from a bronze group forming part of the dedication of Attalus I at Pergamum, third quarter of the third century B.C. *Terme Museum, Rome.* The most serious restoration is the right arm of the man, the hand of which should be held with the thumb upward, so lowering the elbow. (viii, 679.)

[*Phot. Brogi*]

[a] DYING PERSIAN

[b] THE LUDOVISI GAUL

[a] MARSYAS tied to a tree to be flayed. Copy of an original of the first Pergamene School. From *Tarsus*; in *Constantinople.*

[*Phot. Sebah and Joaillier*]

[b] Scythian slave sharpening his knife before flaying Marsyas. Copy of an original of the first Pergamene school. *Uffizi, Florence.* The statue has suffered from patching and repolishing. (viii, 680.)

[b]

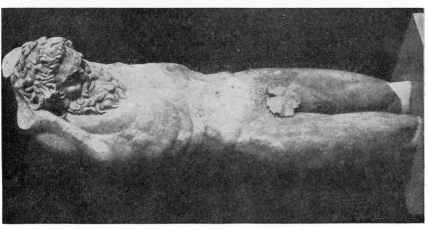

[a]

THE PUNISHMENT OF MARSYAS

[a] A fighting Gaul, from Delos; *National Museum, Athens.* An original of the end of the third century B.C. (viii, 681.)

[*Phot. Alinari*]

[b] A dead barbarian. Copy in marble from a bronze original set up on the Acropolis at Athens at the end of the third century B.C. by Attalus I. *Palace of the Doges, Venice.* (viii, 681.)

[*Phot. Giraudon*]

[c] MENELAUS carrying the body of PATROCLUS. Copy from an original of the late third century B.C. *Loggia de' Lanzi, Florence.* The head, arms, and upper part of the body of Menelaus, and the arms of Patroclus, as well as other parts, are modern. (viii, 682.)

[*Phot. Seemann, Leipzig*]

[a]

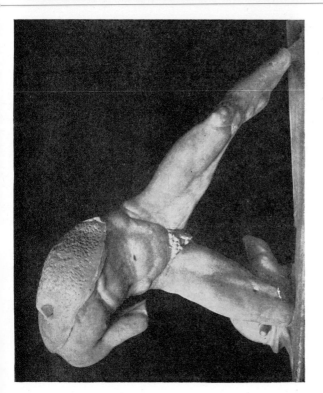

[b]

GAULS

[c]

MENELAUS

[*a*], [*c*] Young satyr fighting a snake-legged giant. From *Rome*; *Palazzo dei Conservatori*. Copy of a Pergamene original of the late third century B.C. (viii, 683.)

[Stuart Jones, *Conservatori Catal.* Pl. 28]

[*b*] Head of a young satyr repulsed by a nymph. From *Tivoli*; in the *British Museum*. Copy of an original of the early second century B.C. (viii, 683.)

[*d*] Head of an hermaphrodite escaping from an old satyr. From the neighbourhood of *Rome*; *Ince Blundell Hall, Lancashire*. Copy of an original of the early second century B.C. (viii, 683.)

[*e*] Head of the goddess NIGHT from the Great Altar of *Pergamum*; *Berlin*. From a cast. First half of second century B.C. (viii, 687.)

[*Phots. Prof. B. Ashmole*]

[a]

[b]

[c]

SATYRS

[d]

HERMAPHRODITE

[e]

'NIGHT'

[*a*] Bronze statuette of a satyr, from *Pompeii*; in the *Naples Museum*. Copy from an original of the late third century B.C. (viii, 682.)

[*Phot. Anderson*]

[*b*] Satyr turning to look at his tail. From *Rome*; *Terme Museum*. Copy from a bronze original of the late third century B.C. Parts of the legs are modern: the head is a cast from another replica. (viii, 677.)

[*Phot. Anderson*]

[*c*] Statue of POLYHYMNIA, the muse of lyric poetry. Copy from an original of the late third century B.C. (See also p. 122 [*c*].) Photograph from a cast combining a body in Berlin with a head in Dresden. (viii, 677.)

[Rodenwaldt, *Die Kunst der Antike*, p. 452]

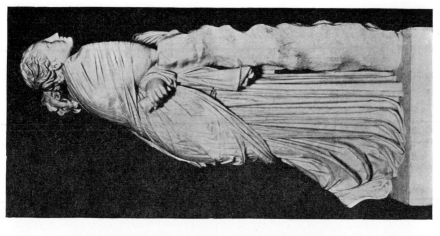

[b] SATYR

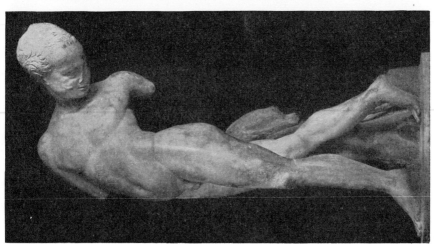

[c] POLYHYMNIA

[a] SATYR

[a] APHRODITE at the bath. From *Vienne*; in the *Louvre*. Roman copy from an original by Doedalsas of Bithynia, about 200 B.C. (viii, 684.)

[*Phot. Alinari*]

[b] An old woman with an empty wine-jar. Copy in marble from a bronze original by Myron of Thebes set up at Smyrna about 200 B.C. From *Italy*; in *Munich*; *Glyptothek*. The nose, right arm, left shoulder and breast, left foot and other patches are modern. (viii, 685.)

[*Phot. Munich Glyptothek*]

[c] Boy struggling with a goose. Copy in marble from a bronze original by Boëthus of Chalcedon, early second century B.C. From *Rome*; in *Munich*; *Glyptothek*. Some small patches on the child's face, and the head of the goose, are modern. Photograph from a cast. (viii, 684.)

144

[c] BOY AND GOOSE

[b] OLD WOMAN

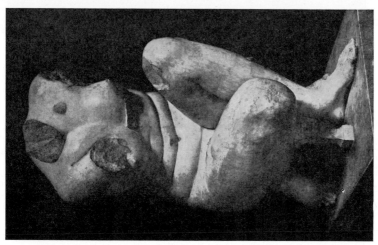

[a] APHRODITE

[a], [b] EROS sleeping. From *Rome*; *Palazzo dei Conservatori*. Copy from an original perhaps by Polycles of Athens, about 200 B.C. (viii, 684.)

[*Phots.* [a] *Prof. B. Ashmole*, [b] *Faraglia*]

[c], [d] Hermaphrodite sleeping. From *Rome*; *Terme Museum*. Copy from a bronze, perhaps by Polycles of Athens, about 200 B.C. (viii, 684.)

[*Phot. Brogi*]

[c]

[b]

[a]

[d]

SLEEPING FIGURES

ATHENA, crowned by Victory, tears Alcyoneus from the earth to destroy him. Ge rises to beg mercy for her sons. From the frieze of the Great Altar of *Pergamum*; in *Berlin*. Early second century B.C. (See p. 188 [*a*].) (viii, 686.)

[*Phot. Giraudon*, from a cast]

148

PART OF THE MAIN FRIEZE OF THE GREAT ALTAR OF PERGAMUM

[a] The legend of Telephus: the building of the boat for Auge. From the internal frieze of the Great Altar at *Pergamum;* in *Berlin.* Second quarter of the second century B.C. (viii, 687.)

[*Phot. Berlin Museum*]

[b] Worshippers approaching a god and goddess. Said to have come from *Corinth*; in *Munich*; *Glyptothek.* Athenian work of the third century B.C. (viii, 688.)

[*Phot. Munich Glyptothek*]

[a]

[b]

RELIEFS

[a], [b] Head of CHIRON the centaur, part of a group showing the musical education of Achilles. From the *Esquiline, Rome*; *Palazzo dei Conservatori*. Most of the nose is modern. Copy from an original of the first half of the second century B.C. (viii, 685.)

[*Phots.* [*a*] *Prof. B. Ashmole*, [*b*] *Alinari*]

[c] PAN teaching OLYMPUS or DAPHNIS to play the pipe; *Naples Museum*. Copy of the second century A.D. from an original of the first half of the second century B.C. The hands, and other patches, are modern. (viii, 685.)

[*Phot. Alinari*]

[a]

[b]

CHIRON

[c] PAN AND OLYMPUS

[a] Head of a woman, from *Pergamum*; in *Berlin*. Second Pergamene
School. (viii, 687.)

[*Phot. Berlin Museum*]

[b] Head of the statue of APHRODITE from *Melos*; in the *Louvre*.
(See p. 156 [c].) (viii, 691.)

[c] Colossal head of a goddess, by Damophon of Messene; in the
Capitoline Museum, Rome. Mid second century B.C. (viii, 690.)

[*Phot. Alinari*]

[d] Head of ATHENA by Eubulides of Athens; *National Museum,
Athens*. Second half of second century B.C. (viii, 692.)

[*Phot. English Photographic Co.*]

[a] [b]

[c] [d]

FEMALE HEADS

[a] Statue from *Pergamum*; in *Berlin*. Second Pergamene School, first half of second century B.C. (viii, 687.)

[*Pergamon, Plates, VII*, Pl. XIV]

[b] APHRODITE from *Capua*; in *Naples*. Roman copy in marble after a bronze original of the later fourth century B.C.

(*Note:* Against the view stated in the text (viii, 691) that this is a copy of the statue of Aphrodite on the Acropolis of Corinth, see O. Broneer in *Univ. of California Publications in Archaeology*, I, no. 2, pp. 65 *sqq.*)

[c] APHRODITE from *Melos*; in the *Louvre*. By ...andros, of Antioch on the Maeander, mid second century B.C. (Cf. p. 154 [b].) (viii, 691.)

[a]

[b]

FIGURE FROM PERGAMUM

APHRODITE FROM CAPUA

[c] APHRODITE FROM MELOS

[a] Warrior, by Agasias of Ephesus, end of the second century B.C. From *Anzio*; in the *Louvre*. (viii, 691.)

[*Phot. University of Berlin*, from a cast]

[b] Boxer resting. Bronze statue signed on the left glove by Apollonius son of Nestor, an Athenian, first century B.C. From the *Tiber*; in the *Terme Museum*. The rock is modern. (viii, 693.)

[*Phot. Alinari*]

[b] BOXER

[a] WARRIOR

[*a*] Satyr and nymphs. Archaistic relief, first century A.D. In *Rome, Palazzo dei Conservatori*. (viii, 692.)

[*Phot. Alinari*]

[*b*] Relief on one side of a four-sided marble basis or altar from *Capri*; in the *British Museum*. Early first century A.D. (viii, 692.)

[*Phot. British Museum*]

[*c*] Boy, by Stephanus, pupil of Pasiteles; from *Rome*, in the *Villa Albani*. End of the first century B.C. The right arm, half of the left forearm with the hand, and other parts are modern. (viii, 693.)

[*d*] Group, perhaps Electra recognizing Orestes; by Menelaus, pupil of Stephanus, in the *Terme Museum, Rome*. First half of the first century A.D. (viii, 694.)

[d]   GROUP, BY MENELAUS

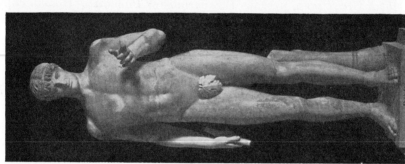

[c]   BOY, BY STEPHANUS

[a]

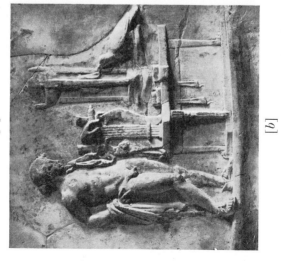

[b]   RELIEFS

[a] EPICURUS. Roman copy in marble from an original of the first half of the third century B.C. In the *Capitoline Museum, Rome*.

[*Phot. Oxford University Press*]

[b] A Greek poet, perhaps Epicharmus or Philemon. Roman copy in bronze from an original of the second century B.C. From *Herculaneum*; in *Naples*.

[*Phot. Anderson*]

[c], [d] CN. POMPEIUS MAGNUS. Third quarter of first century B.C. *Glyptotek Ny Carlsberg, Copenhagen*. (viii, 694.)

[*Phot. Ny Carlsberg Glyptotek*]

[a] EPICURUS

[b] A POET

[c]

[d]

[c], [d] CN. POMPEIUS MAGNUS

11-2

[a] Head of *Alexander the Great*, diademed and with the ram's horn of Ammon in his hair, from a coin of Lysimachus. 323–281 B.C.

[b] *Demetrius Poliorcetes*, diademed and with a bull's horn in his hair. 306–283 B.C.

[c] *Antiochus I*, diademed. 293–261 B.C.

[d] *Philetaerus* (284–263 B.C.), wreathed and diademed on a coin of *Eumenes II* of *Pergamum*. 197–159 B.C.

[e] *Berenice II*, wife of *Ptolemy Euergetes*, a gold octodrachm minted in *Ephesus*. The queen with diademed and veiled head. 258–222 B.C.

[f] *Antiochus III the Great*. 223–187 B.C.

[g] *Mithridates II*, King of *Pontus*. c. 255–220 B.C.

[h] *Euthydemus I*, King of *Bactria*. c. 222–187 B.C.

[i] *Euthydemus II*, King of *Bactria*, probably grandson of the last.

[j] *Antimachus I*, King of *Bactria*. Second century B.C.

[k] *Orophernes*, pretender to the throne of *Cappadocia*, a coin minted at *Priene*. 158–157 B.C.

[l] *Mithridates VI, the Great, King of Pontus*. 120–63 B.C.

[m] *Cleopatra VII*, 51–30 B.C.

All, except [e] gold, and [m] bronze, are silver tetradrachms, and all are slightly enlarged. The coins are in the *British Museum*. (viii,694.)

PORTRAITS ON COINS

ACHILLES, hidden among the daughters of Lycomedes, is discovered by Odysseus and Diomed. Copy of the first century A.D., from a painting of the third century B.C. From *Pompeii*; in *Naples*. (viii, 695.)

[*Phot. F. Bruckmann A.G., Munich*]

ACHILLES IN SCYROS

Wall painting of the first century B.C. after an original of the late third century B.C. from *Boscoreale, near Pompeii,* in the *Metropolitan Museum, New York.* [*a*] A Macedonian king and a sibyl (?). [*b*] A king and his queen (?). (viii, 696.)

[Barnabei, *Villa di P. Fannio Sinistore,* Pls. VI, VIII]

[a]

[b]

PAINTINGS FROM BOSCOREALE

HERACLES in bondage to OMPHALE in Lydia. Copy, of the first century B.C. or A.D., from a picture by an artist of Asia Minor of the third century B.C. From *Pompeii*; in *Naples*. (viii, 696.)

[*Phot. Sommer*]

HERACLES AND OMPHALE

HERACLES finds his son TELEPHUS in Arcadia. Copy, of the first century A.D., from a Pergamene painting of the second century B.C. From *Herculaneum*; in *Naples*. (viii, 697.)

HERACLES FINDING TELEPHUS

The initiation of a bride in Dionysiac ritual; after a painting of the second century B.C. *Villa Item, Pompeii.* (viii, 697.)

[*Phot. Alinari*]

PAINTING IN THE VILLA ITEM

[a] MEDEA contemplating the murder of her children. A copy of the first century A.D., probably after Timomachus of Byzantium, early first century B.C. From *Herculaneum*; in *Naples*. (viii, 698).

[*Phot. Alinari*]

[b] ORESTES and PYLADES before the temple of Artemis in Tauris. A copy, of the first century A.D., probably after Timomachus. From *Pompeii*; in *Naples*. (viii, 699.)

[*Phot. Sommer*]

[a]

[b]

COPIES OF PAINTINGS BY TIMOMACHUS

[a] Visit to a wise woman. Mosaic by Dioscurides of Samos after a picture of the second century B.C. From *Pompeii*; in *Naples*. (viii, 699.)

[*Phot. Alinari*]

[b] Still life. Graeco-Roman painting of the first century B.C. From *Pompeii*; in *Naples*. (viii, 700.)

[*Phot. F. Bruckmann A.G., Munich*]

[b]

STILL LIFE

[a]

MOSAIC BY DIOSCURIDES

Landscapes from the Odyssey, found on the *Esquiline*; in the *Vatican*. [*a*] The Laestrygones destroying the ships of Odysseus. [*b*] Circe's island. From a Graeco-Roman frieze of the first century B.C. (viii, 700.)

[*Phot. F. Bruckmann A.G., Munich*]

[a] [b]

LANDSCAPES FROM THE ODYSSEY

[a] Magnesian entablature. In *Berlin*. (viii, 701.)
[*Magnesia*, Blatt V]

[b] 'Hall of the Bulls.' In *Delos*. Detail and section. (viii, 702.)
[*Bulletin de Correspondance Hellénique*, VIII, 1884]

[c] *Miletus*; elevation of the Bouleuterion, restored. (viii, 703.)
[*Milet*, I, 2, Pl. VI]

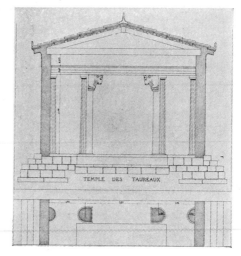

[a] MAGNESIA   [b] DELOS

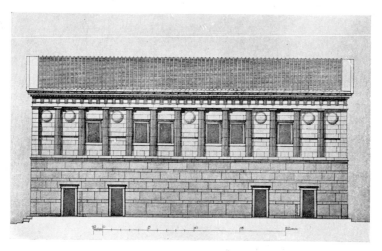

[c] MILETUS

Perspective view of the Acropolis of *Pergamum,* actual state. (viii, 705.)

[Collignon, *Pergame,* Pl. III]

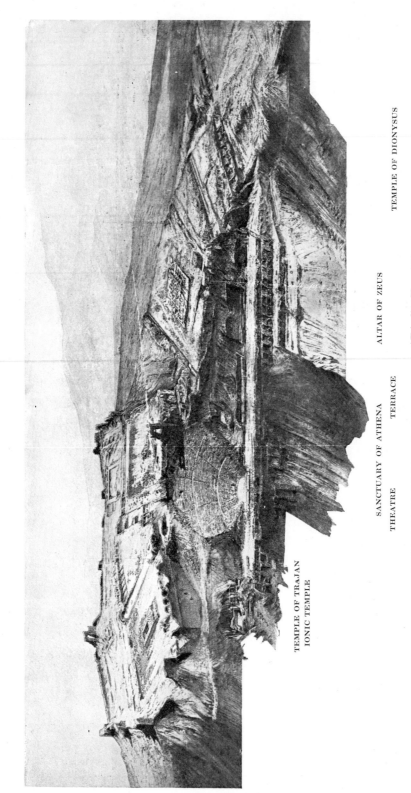

TEMPLE OF TRAJAN
IONIC TEMPLE

SANCTUARY OF ATHENA   ALTAR OF ZEUS

THEATRE   TERRACE

TEMPLE OF DIONYSUS

THE ACROPOLIS OF PERGAMUM (*Bird's-Eye View*)

Restored plan of *Pergamum*. (viii, 705.)

[Collignon, *Pergame*, Pl. XI]

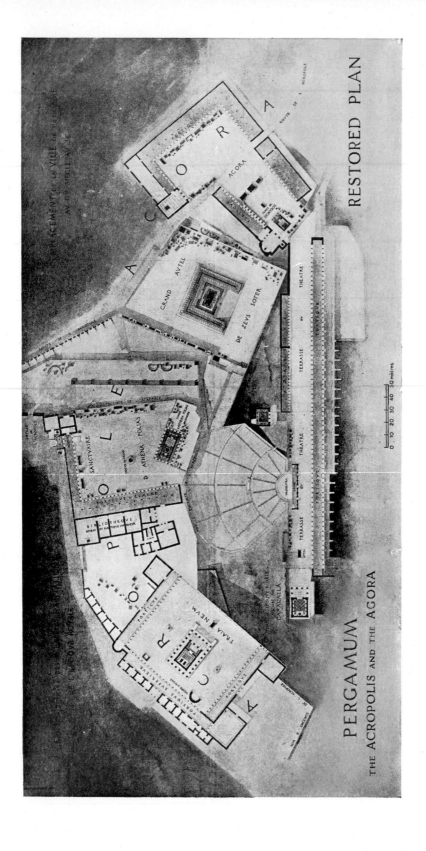

RESTORED PLAN

PERGAMUM
THE ACROPOLIS AND THE AGORA

[*a*] Restoration of the Great Altar of *Pergamum*. (See p. 148 above.) In *Berlin*. (viii, 686, 705.)

[*Pergamon, Vol. of Plates III*, Pl. XIV]

[*b*], [*c*] The *horologion* of Andronicus Cyrrhestes, the so-called 'Tower of the Winds,' in *Athens*. Elevation and plan. (viii, 702.)

[Stewart and Revett, *Antiquities of Attica*, I, ch. 3, Pls. II, III]

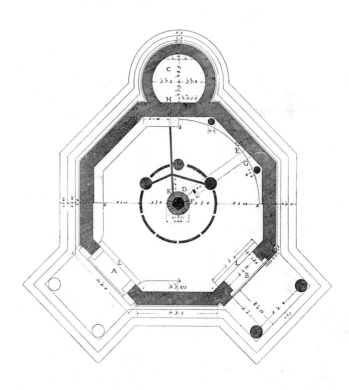

Clm 14823: Alcuinus, Grammatica.

Regensburg, St.Emmeram (Bayern), 2.Hälfte des 11.Jh.,
68 Bl.

Lit.: R.Bergmann 615.

Glossen: 5 ahd. Interlinearglossen von einer Hand der
2.Hälfte des 11.Jh.

Text: J.-P.Migne, PL 101,849ff.

f.21v   lien, milz - 864A

         rien, sniero - 864A

         suber [Migne: **tuber**], saph - 864B

f.25r   varix, warzi - 866B

         puls, prio - 866C

◪

Clm 18189: Hrabanus Maurus, In IV libros Regum.
Tegernsee (), 2.Viertel des 11.Jh., 249 Bl.

Lit.: R.Bergmann 639.
Christine Eder, Die Schule des Klosters Tegernsee im frü-
hen Mittelalter im Spiegel der Tegernseer Handschriften
(München,1972).

Glossen: Je 1 ahd. Interlinear- und Marginalglosse von einer Hand des 2.Viertel des 11.Jh.

Text: J.-P.Migne, PL 109,11ff.

f.73r   fusum, .i.spinnila - 79B

f.130r   (lateris), site [Lemma am Rand wiederholt] -
         144D

[a] PERGAMUM

[b] THE HOROLOGION

[a] A lamp-lighter, cloaked and hooded, carrying a lantern in his right and a ladder in his left hand. Lamp-lighters in the temples of Serapis are mentioned in the papyri. From *Alexandria*; in the *Bibliothèque Nationale, Paris.*

[b] A pedagogue carrying the bag of knucklebones for his charge.

[c] A gentleman wearing a *chlamys*, perhaps a young Greek delivering his first public address. The cloak is, however, rather long for a *chlamys* and may be intended for a toga, in which case a Roman would be represented.

[d] A boy in slave-garb, perhaps a herald, or 'Town-Crier.'

[b]–[d] In the *Louvre*. (viii, 656.)

190

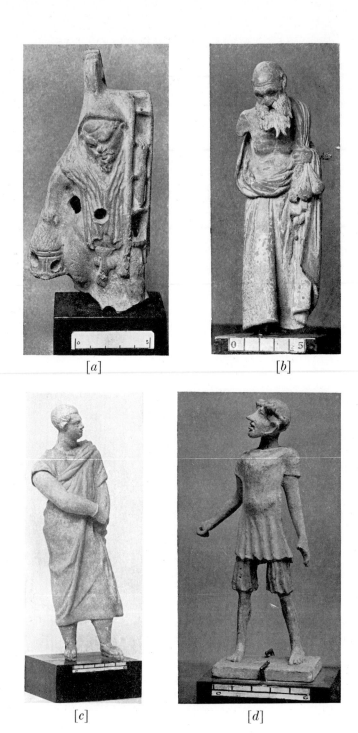

[a] [b]

[c] [d]

TERRACOTTA FIGURINES

[a] An old actor.
[b] A fisherman.
[c] A nurse and child.
[d] A school-girl.
All in the *Louvre*. (viii, 656.)

[a]   [b]

[c]   [d]

TERRACOTTA FIGURINES

[*a*], [*b*] Terracotta masks from *Carthage,* perhaps apotropaic; but, though caricatures, probably representing typical Carthaginian features.

[*Catal. du Musée Alaoui.* Pls. 72, 1; 74, 5]

[a]

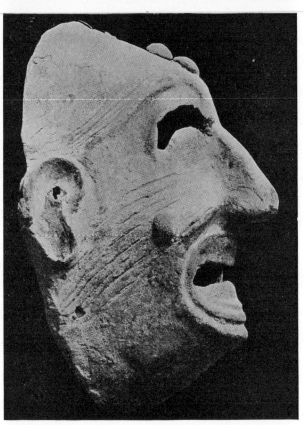

[b]

MASKS FROM CARTHAGE

[*a*] Large votive stele from *Carthage* of Greek style; the architectural decoration, as well as the figure representing Tanit (or Kore), is in the Greek manner. The animal in the pediment is, however, Carthaginian in style.

[*Corpus Inscriptionum Semit.* I, Pl. 41]

[*b*] Terracotta figure of Tanit, the great Punic goddess, found at *Carthage*. While head-dress and fan suggest Egyptian influence, the figure seems purely Carthaginian. Third century B.c. *Bardo Museum, Tunis.*

[*Catal. du Musée Alaoui*, Pl. 76, 1]

[a]   [b]

REPRESENTATIONS OF TANIT

Graeco-oriental figure in painted marble from *Carthage*. This figure forms the lid of a sarcophagus and represents a priestess of Tanit in ceremonial Egyptian garb with wings folded over the skirt. She holds the implements of sacrifice. The Greek element predominates. Fourth to third century B.C. In the *Musée St Louis, Carthage*.

[M. Rostovtzeff, *A History of the Ancient World*, II, Pl. XIV, 2]

A PRIESTESS OF TANIT